The Art and Science of Teaching and Learning

In the **World Library of Educationalists**, international experts themselves compile career-long collections of what they judge to be their finest pieces – extracts from books, key articles, salient research findings, major theoretical and practical contributions – so the world can read them in a single manageable volume. Readers will be able to follow themes and strands of the topic and see how their work contributes to the development of the field.

E. C. (Ted) Wragg has spent the last 30 years researching, thinking and writing about some of the key and enduring issues in education. He has directed numerous research projects and contributed over 40 books and 1,000 articles to the field and is regularly asked to commentate on educational issues for the media. He is an unusual academic, not only a prolific researcher and lecturer, but someone who teaches regularly in both primary and secondary schools.

In *The Art and Science of Teaching and Learning*, Ted Wragg brings together 18 of his key writings in one place, including chapters from his best-selling books, articles from leading journals, and some of his most amusing and important articles from his writing for the *Times Educational Supplement*, the *New Statesman* and *The Guardian*.

Starting with a specially written Introduction, which gives an overview of his career and contextualises his selection, the chapters are divided into five parts:

- classroom teaching and learning
- training new and experienced teachers
- curriculum in action
- educational policy and its implementation
- communicating with professional and lay people.

Through this book, readers can follow the themes and strands that Ted Wragg has written about for over three decades and clearly see his important contribution to the field of education.

E. C. Wragg is Emeritus Professor of Education at the University of Exeter.

Contributors to the series include: Richard Aldrich, Stephen J. Ball, John Elliott, Elliot W. Eisner, Howard Gardner, John K. Gilbert, Ivor F. Goodson, David Labaree, John White, E. C. Wragg.

World Library of Educationalists series

The Art and Science of Teaching and Learning

The selected works of Ted Wragg

E. C. Wragg

Routledge
Taylor & Francis Group

LONDON AND NEW YORK

First published 2005
by Routledge
2 Park Square, Milton Park, Abingdon, Oxon OX14 4RN

Simultaneously published in the USA and Canada
by Routledge
270 Madison Ave, New York, NY 10016

Routledge is an imprint of the Taylor & Francis Group

Typeset in Sabon by
Newgen Imaging Systems (P) Ltd, Chennai, India
Printed and bound in Great Britain by
MPG Books Ltd, Bodmin

British Library Cataloguing in Publication Data
A catalogue record for this book is available
from the British Library

Library of Congress Cataloging in Publication Data
A catalog record for this book has been requested

ISBN 0–415–35221–5 (hbk)
ISBN 0–415–35222–3 (pbk)

CONTENTS

ACKNOWLEDGEMENTS

The following chapters have been reproduced with the kind permission of the Taylor & Francis Group

'Class Management during Teaching Practice', by Wragg E. C. and Dooley P. A., in E. C. Wragg (ed.), *Classroom Teaching Skills*, Routledge, 1984, pp. 21–46.

'Explaining and Explanations', in E. C. Wragg (ed.), *Primary Teaching Skills*, Routledge, 1993, pp. 111–36.

'Implications and Consequences', in *Failing Teachers?* by Wragg E. C., Haynes G. S., Wragg C. M. and Chamberlin R. P., Routledge, 2000, pp. 207–30.

'Knowing the Subject Matter', in *Explaining in the Secondary School*, by Wragg E. C. and Brown G., RoutledgeFalmer, 2001, pp. 43–52.

'Life in the Future', in E. C. Wragg, *The Cubic Curriculum*, Routledge, 1997, pp. 8–22.

'Paying for Performance', in *Performance Pay for Teachers*, by Wragg E. C., Haynes G. S., Wragg C. M. and Chamberlin R. P., RoutledgeFalmer, 2004, pp. 171–83.

'Pupil Appraisals of Teaching', by E. C. Wragg and E. K. Wood, in E. C. Wragg (ed.), *Classroom Teaching Skills*, Routledge, 1984, pp. 79–96.

'Pupil Case Studies', in *Improving Literacy in the Primary School*, by Wragg E. C., Wragg C. M., Haynes G. S. and Chamberlin R. P., Routledge, 1998, pp. 250–7.

'Systematic Studies of Class Management', in E. C. Wragg (ed.), *Primary Teaching Skills*, Routledge, 1993, pp. 58–87.

'Teachers' First Encounters with their Classes', by Wragg E. C. and Wood E. K., in E. C. Wragg (ed.), *Classroom Teaching Skills*, Routledge, 1984, pp. 47–78.

'Teaching Skills', in E. C. Wragg (ed.), *Classroom Teaching Skills*, Routledge, 1984, pp. 1–20.

'The National Survey', in *Improving Literacy in the Primary School*, by Wragg E. C., Wragg C. M., Haynes G. S. and Chamberlin R. P., Routledge, 1998, pp. 35–65.

'Theory Good, Practice Bad' (Taylor & Francis Arena, Discussion Forum, 2003).

The following articles are reprinted with the kind permission of the respective publications

'A Five-day Week in the Lions' Den' (originally published in *Times Higher Education Supplement*, 28.5.1993).

'Descartes Thinks but Clarke Disney' (originally published in *Times Educational Supplement*, 7.2.1992).

'Digging Holes in Maths Tests' (originally published in *Times Educational Supplement*, 18.2.2000).

'Don's Diary' (originally published in *Times Higher Education Supplement*, 29.9.1978).

'Funny Things Happen on the Way to the Classroom' (originally published in *The Guardian*, 2.1.1979).

'Oh Boy' (originally published in *Times Educational Supplement*, 16.5.1997).

'On the Warpath with Spiffy' (originally published in *Times Educational Supplement*, 19.2.1999).

'Sir Keith: Epilogue' (originally published in *Times Educational Supplement*, 30.5.1986).

'Superteach and the Dinosaurs' (originally published in *The Guardian*, 16.1.1979).

'Take Tony Zoffis' Bullets Away' (originally published in *Times Educational Supplement*, 22.9.2000).

'Tell Sid: Beware of Flobbabytes' (originally published in *Times Educational Supplement*, 17.3.2000).

'The Farce of the Flashlight Brigade' (originally published in *Times Educational Supplement*, 4.11.1988).

'Who Put the Ass in Assessment?' (originally published in *Times Educational Supplement*, 16.2.1990).

' "Why Don't Your Teachers Riot?" ' (originally published in *New Statesman*, 2.10.2000).

'Why Ron Left the Wendy House for the Toilet' (originally published in *Times Educational Supplement*, 11.6.2004).

The following chapters have been reprinted with the kind permission of the respective publishers

'A Study of Student Teachers in the Classroom', in G. Chanan (ed.), *Towards a Science of Teaching*, NFER Publishing Company Limited, 1973, pp. 85–127.

'Education in the Market Place', E. C. Wragg, originally published as a pamphlet by the National Union of Teachers, 1988.

'Some Historical Exemplars', in E. C. Wragg (ed.), *Teaching Teaching*, David & Charles, 1974, pp. 15–43.

'State-approved Knowledge? Ten Steps Down the Slippery Slope', in M. J. Golby (ed.), *The Core Curriculum, Perspectives* 2, University of Exeter, 1980, pp. 11–20.

I should like to record my sincere thanks to the many research fellows and assistants with whom I have been privileged to work. They include Trevor Kerry, Pauline Dooley, Kay Wood, Caroline Wragg, Barbara Jansen, Felicity Wikeley, Gill Haynes, Sarah Crowhurst and Rosemary Chamberlin.

INTRODUCTION

Becoming addicted

There is something addictive about research. Its very routines are spellbinding: the search for an idea, planning a programme of enquiry, analysing the results, telling your fellows, hoping they will be as excited as you are, but knowing they will merely humour you by listening. Research seizes the imagination because it is a fundamental human drive that has gripped people from the beginnings of life. No one knows how the first cave-dwellers discovered and learned to use fire. Perhaps they were empiricists like Comenius, trial and error researchers who explored and savoured life at first hand, using their senses, sometimes even losing their life as a result of experimentation. There were no Nobel prizes for the first *Homo sapiens* to die from eating poisonous plants, but subsequent generations are eternally grateful. A few must have been rationalists, like Erasmus, making *a priori* judgements and then enquiring systematically to see whether or not they appeared to have substance.

I always knew that I would eventually want to join this timeless tradition and do research, once I had abandoned childhood ambitions to be a train driver or a professional musician. As a 16-year-old boy at school I studied poetry as part of the English course. One day I argued in class that it was difficult for naïve city youngsters of our age to develop a true appreciation of the verse we were required to read for our examinations, since it had been written by adults who were describing their more elderly experience. What we did, therefore, was merely learn the views and interpretations of authorities, like teachers and literary critics, for we had little equipment of our own. We could easily be fooled.

Arguments and counter-arguments were thrown across the room, until I made the bold assertion that even I, as an immature 16 year old, could write a poem the rest of the class would believe was a classic, although it would be nonsense. Later that day I produced two versions of a poem called 'Nothing is so beautiful as Spring', purportedly by Gerard Manley Hopkins, a writer we had studied, whose poems I loved, though there were few other poets in this category at the time. Only one, I told my fellows, was genuine, the other I had made up in a few minutes.

All but one classmate chose poem B, some saying it was 'obvious', as poem A was poorly constructed. The odd student out chose poem A, believing that it was a trick and I had selected a particularly bad poem by Hopkins, while writing a half decent one myself. 'OK, fair enough', I replied, 'it *is* poem B, but can you honestly say that it is a good poem?' Many picked out phrases like 'When wheely weeds thrust skywards' as a classic Hopkins line, just as we had been briefed.

The truth was, I had made up both versions. Only the first line of each 'Nothing is so beautiful as Spring' had come from a genuine Hopkins poem. The rest was invented nonsense.

There was no real resentment from my fellows at this young prig making a point. In the steel city of Sheffield, in the north of England, people pride themselves on their honesty, and 16 year olds are no exception. You want to do a bit of embryonic research? Fine. Twelve years later, when I was a university lecturer, I tried the same experiment on a group of postgraduates in English Literature. The results were almost identical, except that the graduates gave more sophisticated reasons why poem B was the genuine Hopkins. The one exception, on this occasion, argued that poem A was the real thing, but must be an early example of the writer's work.

If my appetite for hypothesis-generating and testing was whetted at school, it was as an undergraduate studying modern languages that the drive to discover developed further. In my final year I wrote a dissertation about the early mediaeval love poets of Germany and Austria. Hours spent in the library scouring obscure journals for equally obscure articles was useful training for all the reviewing of research literature I would carry out later.

How did these early troubadours evolve? Was Der von Kürenberg really a woman? Where did Dietmar von Aist come from? Might they both have lived in a part of Upper Austria, near Linz, that I had visited? What would their music have sounded like, for only the text survived? It was an early lesson that research can produce as many questions as answers. The eventual offer of a research scholarship was seductive and I might have stayed on at university to write a PhD on the 'particles' in German, short words that are inserted into sentences for various purposes, had a worldly-wise tutor not queried my choice of such a tedious topic. 'What do you really want to find out?', he asked. 'Something about what people do, and why', I replied. 'Well go and teach first then', was his response.

As a teacher I was inspired by one of my colleagues, Keith Swanwick, later to be Professor of Music Education at London University Institute of Education. He was head of music at the school where I was teaching and managed to write a Masters thesis at Leicester University, alongside all his other commitments. As part of his research we carried out an experiment with his classes, not unlike the one I had done as a 16 year old. Keith went into each group and put on a record of a piece of music, telling them that it was being played by one of the greatest orchestras in the world, which was true. I followed him and played exactly the same record again, but this time told the class it was being performed by a very competent amateur group, the Wigan Society of Music Lovers. We also varied the order in which we appeared.

The pupils then had to rate their appreciation of these two supposedly different versions of the same piece of music on a number of seven-point semantic differential, polar opposite scales. The results showed yet again, as they had in my own naïve childhood experiment, how easily pupils' own judgement could be overridden. Irrespective of the order of our appearance the classes esteemed the 'professional' version much more highly than the 'amateur' one. Thirty years later I met a former pupil from one of the classes who said he still recalled this event vividly.

The excitement of such experimentation was so gripping that I decided to stop doing *ad hoc* research into the effects of authority on children's attitudes and study teaching more systematically for a Masters degree. This involved observing student teachers in the classroom and relating what they did to their attitudes, anxieties and aspirations. Later my PhD was based on an analysis of the patterns of classroom interaction in nearly 600 lessons given by over a hundred student teachers, much more interesting than the German particles. As a result I became fascinated by the intricate processes of teaching and learning in school, and classroom observation has been my major research interest and tool of enquiry ever since.

Phases and focus

Setting out

Starting off as an educational researcher in Britain during the late 1960s and early 1970s was a relatively lonely business, for there were few opportunities and not many university courses in research methodology. Like most others at that time I was an almost entirely self-taught part-timer, having to winkle out time for research in between teaching and extra-curricular duties. Ignorance about quantitative methods required extensive and avid reading. Several of the books were indigestible, miserable examples of texts written to please the writer's reference group, not inform the student. Some of the classics, by contrast, like Guilford's *Statistics for Education and Psychology* and Gage's *Handbook of Research on Teaching*, were invaluable.

When I left teaching and was appointed to a lectureship at Exeter University the interview for the post made little reference to research, save for a passing mention of my Masters degree findings towards the end. The main focus was on training modern languages teachers, anything else appeared optional, though welcome, and I was always encouraged. It was at Exeter that I first met fellow spirits, especially David Evans and Tony Edwards, a psychologist and sociologist respectively, from whom I learned a great deal. Another psychologist, Paul Kline, was able to answer most of my questions about factor analysis, until I reached the point where I was able to do it by hand, albeit with an explanatory textbook never far from my elbow. It meant I could progress to teaching myself other multivariate strategies, such as cluster analysis, canonical correlations and multivariate analysis of variance, though these seemed powerful tools to apply to classroom observation data that could not always be precise, and sometimes might be downright fragile. They clearly had to be used sparingly and with due caution.

Early in my university career we had a visiting American professor for a year from Cornell University. Dick Ripple was like a breath of fresh air, coming as he did from a culture where educational research was much more deeply established. His own research was into the teaching of creativity and being able to take part in his project gave me an insight into a different kind of enquiry. The findings were fascinating, because it was one of the few experiments in educational research where, contrary to expectations, the control group outperformed the experimental group.

Class A was to spend half an hour each week for a term completing a set of fifteen booklets that would supposedly make them more creative. Class B, meanwhile, carefully matched for prior ability, would have 'ordinary' lessons. What confounded everything was that the teacher who supervised Class A was one of the profession's dreariest downbeats, a dour man who kept telling the pupils that they looked bored as they filled in their purportedly teacher-proof programmed booklets. Class B was given to a teacher who had recently completed a course on the expressive arts and so gleefully seized this golden opportunity to try out a few ideas. Dick Ripple was dismayed when this supposed 'control' group handsomely outperformed the experimental group on a post-test of creative thinking, but I learned important lessons about research design and intended or unintended teacher effects.

Another important influence at the same time in the late 1960s was being able to carry out research with Patrick McGeeney. He was a co-worker of Michael Young, founder of the Consumer Association, the Open University and one of the greatest social entrepreneurs of the twentieth century. McGeeney came to Exeter University to research the effects of home background on school achievement. The purpose of the project was to identify places, all over England, where interesting work was being done to involve parents more in their school's activities, and evaluate the effects.

My contribution to the programme, fitted in between university teaching commitments and my own classroom observation research, was to interview over a hundred parents in their own homes. It was in stark contrast to life in classrooms. Asking questions of such a wide variety of people in their natural social habitat opened my mind. I had been born in an inner city slum, so it was no surprise to witness poor housing conditions, but seeing some of the families in the dire conditions under which their children had to live and learn was a searing experience.

Some homes were happy and carefree, others were benighted and ravaged. One house had been smashed to pieces by a drunken father the day before I visited. Another home was a cellar, water running down the walls, where a single mother lived, whose careworn features and demeanour made her look like her 8-year-old boy's grandmother. The lad had to go to bed at five o'clock in winter, as he could not invite friends to the one-roomed hovel, nor go out to play. How could anyone who had not seen this dank cellar *really* know what the child's life was like? What would a teacher say next morning if he had not done his homework? Researchers are supposed to try and remain objective about events, but I was deeply moved by these experiences. I still become enraged when pious people pronounce that poverty does not matter in education, usually from a vantage point located at a very safe distance away from it.

The McGeeney and Young project was a life-changing experience for me. Although I would later write books for parents and school governors, they have never been a major research focus. What I did learn was how to interview, construct and apply a schedule, and then analyse the results. Moreover parents have often been interviewed, albeit as a minor, rather than major element of my classroom research projects. In the 1990s, during a large study of literacy teaching in primary schools, we would discover that three-quarters of mothers and a half of fathers read books with their 5–7-year-old children, while a half of mothers and a quarter of fathers read with their 7–11 year olds. Vivid images of the insides of over a hundred homes from twenty-plus years earlier were still burned indelibly on my memory. Most of all I had learned that the qualitative side of research was vital if we were to understand what lay beneath events, and I have used a mixture of quantitative and qualitative methods ever since.

Although creativity and home/school research were valuable adjuncts, my mainstream PhD research in the early 1970s was classroom observation. Dick Ripple had pointed me in the direction of American research by investigators like Ned Flanders and Ed Amidon. Flanders was especially helpful, sending me the manuscript of his not-yet-published book *Analyzing Teaching Behavior*. It was a godsend, as British classroom researchers were few in number at the time. They included Neville Bennett, Sara Delamont, David Hamilton, Rob Walker, Clem Adelman, Roy Nash, Ed Stones, and we met informally once a year, a self-help group supporting each other.

Years later I visited Ned Flanders at his home in Oakland, after the American Educational Research Association annual meeting had taken place in San Francisco. After dinner, when I sat down at his splendid piano and played some Puccini, he suddenly produced a cello and spontaneously joined in. Flanders taught me another of life's valuable lessons: how important it is to support the next generation of researchers, something I have tried to do since. During its low points research may seem a lonely and frustrating business, and duets can be helpful from time to time.

At this time I applied for and got my first external research grant, from the Social Science Research Council. The sum of £1,250, quite substantial at the time, enabled me to recruit five part-time research assistants to observe, between us, nearly 600 lessons given by student teachers. Collecting Flanders-type interaction data, whereby classroom events are given a code every three seconds, can produce massive numbers of digits to be analysed. I assembled over a third of a million of them and the resulting dataset was too large for the university computer, so it had to be sent away to the Atlas machine at London University. Today I would run it on my laptop in seconds.

Moving on

After seven years at Exeter I was reluctant to leave, but a professorship at Nottingham University, with special responsibility for the initial teacher education programmes and the opportunity to carry out classroom observation research, was too good to miss. For five years in the 1970s I was able to work alongside experienced researchers like Eric Lunzer, an expert on Piaget and much else, Jim Egglestone and George Brown, fellow classroom researchers, and Mick Youngman, who played the computer like a maestro. It was a hugely enlightening privilege. The team of academics was so strong that we were able to publish a whole series of booklets on different aspects of research methodology, the *Rediguides*, almost by whistling down the corridor and signing up whoever emerged.

Egglestone's research, with Maurice Galton, into different styles of science teaching, was ground-breaking. It was similar to my own studies at Exeter and to Neville Bennett's research into primary teachers' preferred styles, except that Bennett assembled his typology from questionnaire responses, while Egglestone and I used live-classroom observation data. What appealed about this kind of enquiry was the close fit between research and professional practice. Among many other possibilities it offered the means to collect information about what teachers actually did in their classrooms and feed it back to them.

It was at Nottingham that I obtained my first very large external grant, for a four-year research and development project, from the Department of Education and Science, the *Teacher Education Project*. Working in collaboration with Clive Sutton, an experienced science education specialist at Leicester University, we carried out an extensive programme of research into such topics as classroom management, questioning, explaining, the use of group work, teaching high and low ability pupils in mixed-ability classes, and the language of classroom interactions. This was followed by the production of self-instructional texts for student and experienced teachers, showing how they could use our research findings to study and work on their own professional practice.

The main focus of the *Teacher Education Project* had been on secondary classrooms. At the end of the 1970s, when I returned to Exeter University as Director of what was then the second largest school of education in the country, I was keen to extend this kind of research and development work to primary schools. A large grant from the Leverhulme Trust for the four-year *Primary Teacher Education Project* in the 1980s enabled me not only to study similar topics in primary classrooms, but also to work with Neville Bennett, who moved to Exeter, as did later a string of high quality researchers with a major focus on classroom teaching and learning, like Charles Desforges and Martin Hughes.

As I carried out more classroom research the focus of what I did widened. Studying teachers' practices soon involves an investigator in such matters as curriculum and educational policy. I have been fortunate never to have a period without a major research grant. Having access to external funding has brought major benefits, such as being able to work with the many talented contract research fellows listed in the acknowledgements section of this book. Between us we have been able to investigate such central topics as the teaching of literacy, teacher appraisal, competence and its rarely studied obverse 'incompetence', as well as the teaching of different subjects and age groups.

I have always carried on teaching in primary and secondary schools as a high priority, whatever the counter-pressures and distractions. This offers the opportunity to see classroom phenomena both as a researcher and a practitioner. It can be a bizarre and sometimes confusing experience, one day sitting in a lesson analysing someone's strategies of explanation or questioning, the next day standing before a class trying out my own, but it is a conflict worth living with. Everything in my professional life, therefore, presses me in the direction of research into teaching and learning, and for me there is no more gripping topic.

Although such classroom transactions have been an enduring mainstream interest, as time went on I became more and more fascinated by the dense, and sometimes unpenetrated penumbra that surrounds them. Inevitably this focussed my research on to matters like the training of student and experienced teachers; how curriculum is really implemented on a daily basis, as opposed to distant notions of what is supposed or believed to take place; and the endlessly fascinating topic of what happens when intentions of policy makers filter down to the reality of classroom life.

This sometimes involved communicating with lay and professional people, not just fellow investigators, as I have never wanted to write solely for the research community. Teachers are often deeply interested in accounts of research into their art and craft, but many prefer to hear about findings at a conference, or read about them in a professional journal or newspaper, rather than scour the books and journals, some of them elusive, in which the original reports appear. Not many academics write regularly in newspapers, or broadcast on radio and television, but contributing to sources which teachers, school governors, parents, members of the community might readily access has always been important for me, so I include in this collection a selection of such pieces.

Main areas of focus

This book is divided into four parts, covering some of the fields in which I have worked, and a fifth which contains newspaper articles aimed at practitioners and lay people. The distinction is sometimes slightly arbitrary, since classroom observation research can elide easily into teacher education, curriculum study, or policy implementation, so the dividing lines are not always crisp. The five areas are:

Part 1   Classroom teaching and learning
Part 2   Training new and experienced teachers
Part 3   Curriculum in action
Part 4   Educational policy and its implementation
Part 5   Communicating with professional and lay people

Each of these five sections has its own introduction in the book, and each of the chapters that appear in them has a short note indicating the context. In order to avoid overlap, or indeed so as not to bore the reader into a premature grave, some of the prose of the originals has been edited, but most of the text has been left in the form in which it was written at the time; despite the temptation to benefit from hindsight, I have not actually altered history.

One final point: the widely used star system has been employed in many of the quantitative sections of the book, to indicate the level of statistical significance:

$***$ Significant at or beyond the .001 level of probability (i.e. one in a thousand probability of occurring by chance).
$**$ Significant at or beyond the .01 level (one in 100).
$*$ Significant at or beyond the .05 level (one in 20).
n.s.   Not significant.

PART 1

CLASSROOM TEACHING AND LEARNING

Analysing classroom transactions and processes is the thread that runs through almost all the research that I do. In this section there are extracts from some of the books reporting the major research projects I have directed. Usually these have been three- or four-year programmes, often involving a mixture of large-scale questionnaire surveys, interviews and case studies of individual schools, teachers and children. I like the multi-layered 'big picture' approach, in which practices in a large number of schools are elicited and then the lifeblood is supplied to this large skeleton through intimate case studies. The survey provides an overall context, the case study furnishes the fine detail that brings it to life.

Sitting in classrooms is endlessly fascinating and lessons which might, in other circumstances, be excruciatingly tedious, can be utterly absorbing, if the research focus is on the teacher's classroom management strategies, or apparent lack of them, or on the behaviour of individual children. Managing a class, asking questions, explaining concepts, are fundamental teaching skills, and there is no shortage of events to study. Virtually, every research project I have undertaken has had a classroom observation element.

The five chapters in this part come from empirical studies in three of my biggest projects. Among them they involved the analysis of some 2,000 lessons observed in primary and secondary schools over a twenty-year period. Chapter 1 describes a study of the very first encounters between teachers and their pupils, a much understudied field, yet an important one. Chapter 2 addresses another neglected area: pupils' views of teaching, the findings of which are amazingly consistent over many years and age groups. Chapters 3 and 4 deal with the vitally important area of how primary, secondary and student teachers manage their classes. Chapter 5 was originally a long article, written in a 1973 book entitled *Towards a Science of Teaching*, describing what 104 teacher trainees did in nearly 600 lessons during which they were observed.

I had to smile from time to time as I re-read them all. My early work was much more quantitative than my later research, as I moved to a much more mixed mode of investigation. And did we really put data on punched cards in the 1970s? We did indeed. The results of the earliest statistical calculations (Chapter 5) thundered out on huge, fat wads of computer paper. The later ones were done on my own computer or laptop, using statistical packages that would have given our 1970s' university mainframe computer a nervous breakdown.

CHAPTER 1

FIRST ENCOUNTERS

Originally published as 'Teachers' First Encounters with their Classes', by Wragg E. C. and Wood E. K., in E. C. Wragg (ed.), *Classroom Teaching Skills*, Routledge, 1984, pp. 47–78

Teachers have to meet new classes every September, student teachers usually encounter them part way through the year, supply teachers may master a fresh environment almost every day. Yet, these first meetings have rarely been studied. This investigation of how experienced and student teachers handle classes when they first meet was part of the Teacher Education Project, Chapter 3 of my 1984 book *Classroom Teaching Skills*.

Student teachers usually begin their school experience or teaching practice part way through the school year. By the time they arrive routines, have been established which, for better or worse, will persist through the school year.

A chemistry graduate once arrived at his teaching practice school in January. Before commencing his own teaching he watched a third-year class's regular chemistry teacher take a double period of practical work. After a brief exposition delivered, whilst seated on the front bench, one or two shared jokes and asides, the experienced chemistry teacher signalled the start of the practical phase with, 'Right 3C, you know what to do, so get the gear out and make a start.' The class dispersed briskly to hidden cupboards and far recesses for various pieces of equipment, and an hour of earnest and purposeful experimental work ensued.

In the following week the chemistry graduate took the class himself, and began by lolling on the front bench in imitation of the apparently effortless and casual manner he had witnessed only seven days earlier. After a few minutes of introduction, he delivered an almost identical instruction to the one given by the experienced man the week before, 'Right 3C, get the gear out and do the experiment.' Within seconds pupils were elbowing their fellows out of the way, wrestling each other for bunsen burners, slamming cupboard doors. He spent most of the practical phase calling for less noise and reprimanding the many pupils who misbehaved.

This true story illustrates the problems faced by student teachers. What they have not seen is experienced teachers' first encounters with their classes in early September at the beginning of the school year, when rules and relationships are established. There are few studies available of teachers during their first phase of the year. Indeed a common response to a request to be allowed to watch lessons in early September, is for the teacher to say, 'Would you mind coming in a fortnight when things have settled down?'

The research reported in this chapter involved observing and analysing the first lessons of a sample of experienced teachers at the beginning of the school year from the very first minute of the first lesson in early September, and comparing these with the lessons given by a sample of third-year BEd students at the start of their final teaching practice in October, and then with the first lessons given by a sample of PGCE students on their block practice in January. Over 100 lessons were observed with each of the three groups, and this chapter describes the 313 lessons and the interviews with the teachers concerned before, during and after the observation period.

First encounters with a class

A number of social psychologists have looked at first encounters between human beings in a variety of social settings. Goffman (1971) has described the process of impression management which commences at first meetings and continues through subsequent encounters:

> The individual's initial projection commits him to what he is proposing to be and requires him to drop all pretences of being other things. As the interaction among the participants progresses, additions and modifications in this informational state will of course occur, but it is essential that these later developments be related without contradiction to, and even built up from the initial positions taken by the several participants.
>
> (pp. 21–2)

Argyle (1967) has described the rapidity with which people reach conclusions about those they meet, the difference in sensitivity of acute observers, like Sherlock Holmes, and mental patients whose perceptions appear distorted, and the growth of relationships in the early period of acquaintance.

> A will categorize B in terms of social class, race, age, intelligence or whatever dimensions of people are most important to him, and this will activate the appropriate set of social techniques on the part of A. It is found that people vary widely in what they look for first in others.
>
> (p. 46)

It is not merely the individual personalities which are important when people meet. The social setting is also a powerful influence on events: whether one person meets another as a colleague, employer, supplicant; whether someone holds a certain rank or status, wears a uniform; whether the encounter is in private or in public, is between two people or several, takes place informally on the street, in a home, or formally at a gathering, in an institution or work-place.

When teachers meet a new class of pupils, a variety of social, environmental and institutional factors are at work in addition to the effects of the several individual personalities involved. Teachers, whatever their individual style, are known to be legally *in loco parentis*. They are inescapably part of a national, local and professional culture, even if they personally reject a number of aspects of it.

When teachers have been in a school for some time, their reputation will precede them, and pupil folklore will have told their new classes a great deal about what to expect. Experienced teachers who have moved to another school frequently express surprise during their first few weeks about the difficulty of establishing their identity in a new location after their previous school in which so much could be taken for granted. Supply teachers in particular have to become adept at managing first encounters in new and varying locations, because they have so many of them.

It is not too surprising, therefore, that there has been relatively little research into these intimate first moments of contact between teacher and pupils. The success or failure of a whole year may rest on the impressions created, the ethos, rules and relationships established during the first two or three weeks in September, and that is one reason why many teachers see it as a private matter rather than something to be observed and analysed.

Evertson and Anderson (1978) studied 27 teachers of third-grade classes in eight American elementary schools for the first three weeks of the school year, followed by occasional visits later in the school year. They used a mixture of interviews and observations of lessons, concentrating largely on pupils' engagement in their task. Those teachers who secured highest pupil involvement as measured by their schedule showed more evidence of having thought in advance about rules and procedures, gave more time to clarifying rules and procedures, and introduced their pupils gradually to independent work. This kind of study is of considerable interest, but is sometimes criticised for being self-fulfilling, that is, by setting a premium on task involvement, finding that formal and carefully structured teaching is 'effective'.

Eltis (1978) in an Australian study, concentrated on the extent to which impressions formed in early lessons influenced subsequent events. He found that both experienced and student teachers' perceptions of pupils were influenced by speech, appearance, voice and written work. Pupils' accents were thought to be particularly influential on teachers' early and subsequent judgements. He also found that both trainee and experienced teachers were reluctant to discuss pupils' progress and attributes during this early phase.

Eisenhart (1977) concentrated on teachers' methods of establishing control in her 2-year study of fifth- and sixth-grade classes in a city in Southern USA. Most teachers assigned seats to pupils rather than let them choose, and several developed their own distinct style of control from the beginning. One teacher capitalised on the impending arrival of autumn by writing each pupil's name on a leaf which was pinned to a large picture of a tree. Children were exhorted to keep their leaf from falling, and miscreants found their personal leaf removed from sight.

Soar (1973) followed the progress of a cohort of children in 289 kindergarten, first- and second-grade classes for three years. In a small-scale study of twenty teachers who were especially high or low in class control, he found that teachers with a high degree of control had started by permitting little pupil freedom and then increasing it, and teachers with a low degree of control had begun with high pupil freedom which they then attempted to decrease.

Some investigators have concentrated on the establishment of classroom rules. Buckley (1977), in an ethnographic study of one classroom, identified 32 rules, of which 22 had been spoken of in some form by the teacher within the first six days of the school year. Of these 32 rules, some 15 came from outside the classroom, mainly from the principal. A number of rules emerged after the initial period, such as when a pupil in the third week played in a certain courtyard during break and was told by the teacher on duty that this was not allowed, even though no formal announcement had ever been made. Some rules were established indirectly and by euphemism. For example, the teacher, rather than stating that cheating was not permitted, proclaimed that some pupils 'had big eyes'. Duke (1978) analysed discipline matters raised at staff meetings in an American High School, and found considerable inconsistency in the establishment and enforcement of rules by different teachers.

Kelley (1950) looked at the effect of first impressions of teachers on college students. He distributed to the class, information about their 'new' teacher which was identical except that half the group had the phrase 'a very warm person' and the other half 'rather a cold person' in one sentence. When members of the class were asked to give their first impressions of the teacher, those given the 'warm' message consistently rated him higher on characteristics such as sociability, modesty, informality, humour and popularity, even though they had been exposed to precisely the same lesson.

There is not, therefore, a well-documented literature on first encounters based on observation from the beginning of the school year. On the other hand, there is a great deal of information about established classrooms from which one might speculate about first encounters. Woods (1979) has described the process of securing and maintaining dominance, which in some classrooms can be a harsh procedure, especially in traditional PE lessons where the more aggressive teachers strip the personality of their pupils as they coerce them through the changing room and into the gym, bark commands and finally drive them through the showers.

Several investigators, into aspects of teacher or pupil expectancy and the way people typify each other, have also identified factors which can be of concern during initial meetings. King (1978) observed infant teachers in three schools, and described how they typified children mainly from their own perceptions in the classroom rather than from written reports of other teachers, and how their typification changed as the school year proceeded. Nash (1973) used personal construct theory to study, what constructs eight junior school teachers had assembled about the children they taught. He found that teachers based their perception of the children they taught largely in terms of personality and behaviour rather than ability. Hargreaves (1977) identified three models of teacher typification from the literature, an ideal-matching model whereby pupils are set against some imaginary paragon, a characteristic model which is like an identikit, and a dynamic interactionist model, favoured by symbolic interactionists, which tries to reflect the effects of context and the changes in perception which occur over time as a result of events.

The preparatory phase

We began our research into first encounters with a series of interviews with 20 experienced and 40 trainee teachers taking either a BEd or a PGCE course. Three schools had agreed to co-operate in the sensitive matter of allowing us to watch experienced or student teachers from the first moments of their lessons with new classes, two of them were comprehensive high schools for 12–16 year olds in a city, the third was an 11 to 18 comprehensive in a town. All were used regularly for both BEd and PGCE teaching practice. They were regarded as good schools of their kind, and were thought by tutors to offer a fair challenge to students on teaching practice rather than a particularly easy or especially difficult assignment.

The intention during this preliminary stage was to try to interview teachers in July who might agree to be observed in September, and similarly to interview second-year BEd students who had already completed a phase of half or whole day per week school experience followed by a six-week block practice, and who would be starting their ten-week final block practice the following October. The one-year PGCE students were interviewed during the first term of their course, when they too had a half or whole day a week in school, prior to their one-term block practice the following January.

The final sample of 60 was not a random one therefore, though there were 31 female and 29 male teachers, and 20 experienced, 19 BEd and 21 PGCE students. None of those approached refused to be interviewed. A semi-structured interview schedule was drawn up and piloted, and the interviews were all conducted in a confidential setting. Interviews with student teachers took nearly an hour on average, and those with experienced teachers approximately one and a half hours, though some were considerably longer. The interviews were not tape-recorded, the interviewer noting down replies as they were given. A complete account of the research described in this chapter can be found in Wood (1983).

In each interview, respondents were asked to think of a class of mixed-ability 12–13 year olds that they would be meeting for the first time. Everyone in the sample were asked a series of questions about how they would enter the room, what sort of topic they might begin with, what rules they might establish and how they would set about this, what kind of relationship they would like to see develop, what they would intend to be doing one day, one hour and one minute before their first lesson.

In addition, they were shown four photographs: one of a girl staring at the teacher in a hostile way and refusing to move to another seat, another of five pupils splashing water at each other during a laboratory class, a third of a pupil launching a paper aeroplane across the room, and a fourth of a teacher reading to a class with several pupils showing signs of inattention. They were asked to say how they would respond, and this use of pictures turned out to be a most fruitful projective device for eliciting thoughts on class management. Experienced teachers only were asked questions about whether they behaved differently at the beginning of the year, and to comment on how their early behaviour compared with what happened later in the year. All the interview transcripts were then analysed by two readers selecting what they judged to be the main features of answers from the three groups under the six headings given below.

Information prior to meeting a class

There was a marked difference between experienced teachers and trainees about the information they would need prior to meeting a class. The experienced teachers almost all stressed that, other than essential medical information about deafness, epilepsy or the like, they preferred to find out for themselves rather than take on the prejudices of others. Several said they might look up pupils' records later in the year. This experienced art teacher's reply was typical of most replies:

> I don't deliberately read anything that might be about their characters and background which might prejudice my judgement. Later on reading about them [the pupils] might throw light on some of my experiences with them.

Some teachers described how they had learned this the hard way and reflected back on their first year, like this experienced English teacher:

> I like to meet them without any preconceived ideas. I like to teach them first and then look up information about them after. Otherwise I think that they tend to live up to their reputations. I wasn't like that to begin with. Once I wanted to know all about them before I met them.

An experienced maths teacher described how she had been given information in her first year that turned out to be incorrect. She was told that one of her classes was an especially bright group:

> I assumed that this was a correct statement of their abilities and I taught at top speed. They weren't that good and I had to lower my sights with them. You've got to do the assessing yourself.

There were only one or two exceptions to this general tone. An experienced French teacher said he wanted to know who were the 'bad eggs' so that he could think about where to seat them, and one drama teacher was quite precise about his need to be able to observe a future class beforehand if possible to assess the likely atmosphere:

> I'd like to see whether there are any noticeable problems, like isolation or over-exhibitionism... I'd like to see how far they can concentrate and how far they are inhibited with movement. This finding-out process is very important, especially if they have previously been taught by untrained drama teachers.

Student teachers, in sharp contrast, are extremely anxious about their relative lack of knowledge about children generally, and the classes they will take in particular. Almost all expressed their needs quite differently from the experienced teachers, and most were predictably anxious about potential discipline problems. There were only 4 out of 40 students who, like the experienced teachers, wanted to know little in advance. The great majority echoed this PGCE geography student:

> I'd like to know if they are a disruptive class. If they do mess about a lot, I expect that the experienced teachers will know why and I'll be able to avoid it when it does occur.

The PGCE students also showed special concern over individual needs, typified by this science graduate: 'I'd ask the last teacher to talk to me about every individual pupil for a few minutes. I'd be more interested in the individual than his capability in the subject.'

The BEd students, presumably because of their experience of their previous block practice, made much more reference to needing information about materials, resources and facilities. They also wished to know about school organisation, standards of work, punishment, discipline and the predominant system of routines and established signals used by the staff.

Thoughts on first lessons

When asked to reflect on the day before, an hour before, during the walk down the corridor and upon first entry to a new class, there were again predictable differences between experienced and novice teachers. The experienced teachers were able to describe events with considerable precision and certainty. For them, these first lessons were part of a taken-for-granted set of routines during which they established varying degrees of dominance by restricting pupils' movement, taking up a central position, clearly being 'in charge', and making use of their eyes, a feature mentioned by several:

> I'd make a point of not turning my back on them or taking my eyes off them.
> I would say that eyes are the greatest controlling factor.
>
> (French teacher, male)

> The amount of looking you do is important.
>
> (science teacher, male)

> I keep alert. It's very tiring, but I keep an eye on them all the time. I can keep
> this attention by staring a bit rudely for the first two or three weeks.
>
> (French teacher, female)

There was a larger-than-life quality as teachers spoke of how they exaggerated
themselves, established rules by being more pernickety than normal, defined
territory:

> I walk up and down the gangways. I don't hide behind the furniture. If they
> ask to leave the room I try to discourage them by umm ing and ah ing. I take
> their names and the time they left the classroom. I don't allow queuing. I don't
> allow standing by the teacher's desk. They only come out when I tell them to.
> You [the teacher] give the directions. They don't touch windows or blinds.
>
> (French teacher, male)

It was very much a personal matter, what an English teacher called 'my rules,
for my room, for my area'. Almost all the teachers stressed that they would stand
by the door and see the class into the room at the beginning of the first lesson and
supervise their exit at the end.

By contrast, the students were much more jelly-like in their apprehension and
uncertainty. Far from using their eyes to establish presence, they were self-
conscious about being looked at themselves. They spoke of thudding hearts and
excitement, especially the PGCE students:

> I think I'd just be a mass of nerves. I don't really know how I'll react in a class
> situation, but...deep breath, plunge straight in.
>
> (history PGCE, female)

> I'd briefly look over my notes, limber up my mind, feeling of 'help!' brush hair
> back, compose features, steady the nerves.
>
> (German PGCE, male)

> I'll be a bit apprehensive, what they'll be like. Will they be noisy? Will I be able
> to control them? Will they give me a hard time? I'll wonder if they'll compare
> me with their usual teacher. I wonder how they'll measure me up. I'll wonder
> how they'll react as I go through the door. Will they all be making a great
> noise whooping around, or will they be sitting down waiting?
>
> (geography PGCE, male)

BEd students tended to show more uncertainty about subject matter and whether
they were masters of it than PGCE students who, so soon after graduation, claimed
a degree of confidence in their subject knowledge.

First-lesson content

Both experienced teachers and BEd students described how they would outline work for the term. Postgraduates, surprisingly perhaps in view of their strong subject concern, hardly mentioned explaining their overall plan.

The most striking contrast between experienced and novice teachers was that for the former first-lesson content was almost irrelevant. They perceived this opening encounter largely in terms of management rituals: 'The lesson would be concentrating on establishing standards. The work wouldn't be the most important thing. It would be secondary. I would be setting up expectations of behaviour' (geography teacher, female).

Even with those teachers who had more firm intentions to make a start on their subject, there was a need to establish some predominant image, as in the lesson of this male science teacher:

> Right at the start of the lesson there must be something for them to do: games, workcards, anything, because they rarely arrive at the same time. I try to create an atmosphere in which they start science as soon as they come in through the door.

The work itself would be simple and unexacting, 'nothing too earth-shattering' in the words of one teacher, simply a means of keeping children busy whilst teachers gained some perception, both of individual pupils and the likely chemistry of the class mix.

Student teachers gave a great deal of thought to lesson content and little to managerial aspects. About half were desperate to make an impact with 'something interesting', 'a game', 'something dramatic like a fountain', 'quite exciting', 'interesting and active', 'a magic poetry machine that would make them look forward to the next time'. They spoke of their eagerness to sell themselves, to get introductions over quickly by writing their name on the board, and then give a performance that would sell themselves and their subject for the rest of term.

The other half were much more cautious, would adopt a lower profile, choose a topic that was 'safe' not risky, conservative rather than radical. One PGCE geography student described his approach to Australian grasslands:

> I'll introduce it and talk about it for a while, quite a conventional type of lesson, not flashy because it might go wrong and the kids will remember, quite a safe lesson, a good conventional approach. I'd leave the flashy things to later on when I knew them better.

The BEd students, more aware from their previous practice of the possibility of topic and tone being determined in some cases by the supervising teacher, and also, in some cases, having tried without success the spectacular opener, were more cautious than PGCE students. One remarked ruefully that she wished 'someone had said use something very set like cards, a textbook or worksheets, so that they know where they are going'.

Mood and image

The presentation of self in the first lesson was described graphically by all the experienced teachers in the sample. All stressed the projection of some larger-than-life image, though the nature of that image differed from teacher to teacher. The importance of what, for most respondents, was described in terms analogous to an opening-night theatre performance, was summed up by an experienced English teacher when she said: 'I think the first lesson is vitally important. If you don't make your mark in the first lesson in the way you want to, you will never make it again.'

The varying kinds of image, which teachers sought to project are shown by the responses of people from different subject areas. A drama teacher, even more prone than most, perhaps, to an opening theatrical style, described how he quite consciously generated a sense of mystery about himself:

> The first impression I try to give is of tight purposeful nervous energy. The children learn to expect this. I try to create a feeling that something's going to happen, even if I don't know what I'm going to do ... It's important to be hard in the first lesson. By 'hard' I mean a body thing, creating a shroud of mystery. I don't allow the kids to pierce it thoroughly until later.

In their reflections on the type of image they sought to project, several teachers described an element of self-caricature, even a deliberate cultivation of the crackpot in some cases:

> I'm well known for being mad. I do daft things, but they cannot do as they like.
> (English teacher, male)

> They consider me weird ... Everyone at school thinks of me as being a bit eccentric, a mad scientist. I play on this.
> (science teacher, male)

For experienced teachers, the first lesson with a new class is a time when they are acutely conscious of the need to reinforce and indeed exaggerate whatever they see as the predominant features of their reputation in the schools. In some cases, this reputation was thought to be fearsome:

> I have a reputation before they arrive here. They come in fear and trembling because they think I am severe ... It's important to put on a bit of a front at the beginning.
> (French teacher, male)

> I'm very stern and very hard. I am consciously being a little harder than I am.
> (PE teacher, male)

The reactions of the student teachers on mood and change in first lessons were different from each other. The BEd students' responses were much closer to those of experienced teachers, with emphasis on performance, the establishment of dominance, and even the exaggeration of eccentricity and 'character': 'I'd keep control in my hands by constantly stopping them' (BEd drama, female).

> Next time I'm going to be just as rough and aggressive as I was last time, scare the hell out of them at the beginning, it'll be alright afterwards. I shall say, 'I'm the new teacher. If you treat me fairly, I'll treat you fairly.'
> (BEd PE, male)

> I'd say, 'I'm going to be teaching you for the next x weeks. I've got a very
> funny name so we're all going to have a good laugh'...I'd ham this up com-
> pletely...'Everyone get ready to laugh'. The kids ask what it is. I say, 'You
> don't look ready to laugh.'
>
> (BEd drama, female)

By contrast, the PGCE students were quite different. Their emphasis was on
being friendly and approachable. They identified much more with the pupils, saw
themselves as reluctant to be socialised into the 'hard teacher' stereotype, regarded
their class as a collection of thirty individuals, and spoke much more in terms of
negotiation, 'appealing to common sense', not seeing them 'as a class to be lectured
at', reluctant to alienate by coming on too strong or setting too much homework.
Most had given little precise thought to the matter beyond recognising in general
terms what they guessed might be appropriate:

> Ideally I'd like a fairly intimate relationship with the class, but I realise that
> requires drawing a line between intimacy and cheek, a fine balance I'd like to
> achieve. I don't know how. I haven't given it a lot of thought. It's important.
> I need to think about it.
>
> (PGCE English, male)

Establishing rules

There were two major differences between experienced and novice teachers about
the establishment of rules. The first was that experienced teachers were quite clear
about which rules were important and how they would secure compliance. The
second difference lay in the nature of the classroom rules by which each group
would seek to live.

The most common rule mentioned by all groups was, 'no talking when the
teacher is talking', in public sessions rather than during private conversations with
individual children. Everyone mentioned this in interview, though subsequently
when teachers and students were observed there was considerable variation in the
extent to which the rule materialised.

Apart from this universal rule, there was a very noticeable distinction in the
tone of rules mentioned by teachers and students. Experienced teachers frequently
cited rules that governed territory (entering and leaving the room, who could move
where and when), respect for property, work ethic (having the 'right' attitude to
learning, homework, etc.) and safety. Teachers' responses made frequent use of
words with a strong moral component, like 'right', 'proper', 'correct', 'suitable',
a dimension that was rarely present in the interviews with students.

It was a moral tone that was set by the teacher, but most spoke of transferring
responsibility to the pupil, in the class of the science teacher below through a little
handing-over ritual. 'They understand the course cost...All books are numbered
and I check them. I say I hope they've got lots of pocket money for bills if they
damage things' (business studies teacher, female).

> I give out exercise books and textbooks calling them out to fetch their books so
> as to identify them further, and also to stress that *I* have given them the book
> and it is *their* responsibility...for homework after the first lesson I tell them to
> cover books and look after them. I reinforce that the books are in *their* care.
>
> (science teacher, male)

This greater moral certainty which distinguished so clearly between experienced and trainee teachers came out very clearly when interviewees responded to the four photographs of classroom scenes described earlier. Most experienced teachers took an immediate stance on each issue, and declared immediately who was right or wrong and what the teacher would do:

> She has got to be made to do it [move to another seat] because of the audience. If she has the 'why?' look, I'd not give her a reason, I'd become very authoritarian.
>
> (English teacher, male)

> I'd go over to the group and say ... 'the rules say you shouldn't do this.'
>
> (science teacher, male)

> Shout at them, particularly if I'm talking. It would be something short and sweet like, 'shut up!' You need a mental sledgehammer.
>
> (science teacher, male)

Student teachers on the other hand usually spoke of treating the incident lightly, often identifying with the pupils and recalling times when they had behaved in a similar way: 'I'd treat it fairly lightly – "Oh yes, very funny, ha ha. Can we get on with some work now." Then they'd realise that it's a bit stupid' (BEd drama, female).

Some teachers were extremely precise about their classroom rules, and one maths teacher listed ten rules immediately he was asked, without any hesitation. He was one of 7 out of the 20 in the sample who said he announced his rules in the first lesson. Other teachers 'discussed' the rules, though no one claimed the pupils had any right to change them. 'Discussion' was really an alternative and more memorable way of communicating what were principally determined by the school authorities or the teacher, as one science specialist explained: 'I know what the rules are, but we establish them through discussion. I believe that they remember them better if they have helped formulate them.'

Almost all teachers said they made use of case law. Whether they announced or discussed rules, they would assume that pupils were likely to make an inference from the way the teacher behaved in particular instances. It was common to hear statements like 'you have to make an example of someone early on' (maths teacher) or 'I stop the song if they aren't joining in' (music teacher).

There was a sharp contrast between experienced teachers and students on the question of rules, especially, though not exclusively, in the case of PGCE students, many of whom were reluctant to speculate and felt that an intuitive approach was better:

> I'd make up rules as appropriate when I see them doing something wrong. It's difficult to see what this would be.
>
> (PGCE geography, female)

> I'd bring the rules out gradually and naturally. 'I'd offer explanations because I think it is simpler to understand.
>
> (PGCE history, female)

> I'd establish the rules as the problem arises.
>
> (BEd English, female)

Most students were anxious not to hazard personal relationships by giving prominence to rules of behaviour: 'The Art Room should have a happy atmosphere, and if you start telling them they mustn't do this and they mustn't do that, it ruins the atmosphere' (PGCE art, female).

Personal relationships

Almost everyone in the sample, teacher or student, declared in interview that personal relationships were important. It is a concept in teaching which is, of course, hard to be against. Experienced teachers showed more awareness of contact outside the classroom than did trainees.

> A lot of understanding occurs outside the classroom, walking down the corridor...I play the clarinet. I have just started to learn. I play with the fourth year and am not very good...I put myself in a learning situation, and they can see that I also make silly errors.
>
> (English teacher, male)

> I try to go on school hikes and camps. I get the kids away from the classroom. I always take my own kids along so that they [the pupils] see me in a different context.
>
> (science teacher, male)

Student teachers spoke mainly of relationships within the classroom and were again aware of the, to them, thin line between friendliness and over familiarity. This geography PGCE student's fear of loss of control was echoed by many: 'I'm in favour of developing personal relationships as long as I don't get down to the "friend" level. I don't want to get too familiar, otherwise they will take advantage of me.'

Experienced teachers wanted to talk more of the longer term style of personal relationships with their class. It was almost as if, what they had said about establishing dominance was in conflict with their subsequent aspirations. We shall return to all these matters in the following section, which describes the observation study of 313 lessons.

The observation study of first encounters

The main study in this research was of 313 lessons given by 41 of the 60 teachers and students in the three schools described earlier, except for one BEd PE student who was observed in a fourth school, another 12 to 16 High School. The sample was not a random one. Not all the people interviewed could be observed, and constraints included whether they taught the principal target age range of 11–13 year olds and the extent to which their teaching timetable allowed observers to watch their lessons at appropriate times. All sixty people interviewed had agreed to being observed should the need arise, and no one subsequently refused.

Where choice permitted, we tried to include in the sample, teachers with varied views as well as different subjects and preferred teaching strategies. All observations were conducted by the two present writers and three observers who were trained on videotapes and in classrooms until a high level of agreement was obtained between all five. It was the view of all observers that the sample of students eventually observed was a fairly typical cross-section of trainee teachers. The experienced teachers were generally, though not exclusively, fairly competent, and it is not so easy to say how typical they were of teachers at large. Lest it be thought that only the confident, extrovert and successful agree to be observed, it should be said that some of the experienced teachers had discipline problems, as did a number of the students.

The 313 lessons observed were distributed as follows:

13 experienced teachers (7 male, 6 female)	103 lessons
13 BEd students (5 male, 8 female)	106 lessons
15 PGCE students (10 male, 5 female)	104 lessons
Total: 41 teachers (22 male, 19 female)	313 lessons

As intended, we were able to observe most lessons, that is 96 per cent, with the 11–13 age range, and there was the following distribution over subjects, with the number of lessons observed in brackets: English (65), humanities (60), science (52), languages (45), arts (31), physical education (26) and maths and business studies (34).

The data from interviews, our own and others' previous studies, were used to construct and pilot an observation schedule which consisted of a mixture of quantitative and qualitative items. It was in five sections. The first section recorded preliminary data about the teacher, class and subject of the lesson. The second section was about the entry and beginning of the lesson, how the teacher secured attention, opening words, voice, posture, movement, use of eyes, facial expression, response and behaviour of pupils, and how the task was set up. Section three was a 20-second pupil-by-pupil involvement and deviancy 'sweep'. The fourth section contained a set of five-point scales on the teacher's style during the lesson, with the observer, rating warmth, confidence, the extent to which the lesson seemed businesslike, stimulating, the teacher's use of eye contact, mobility and formality/informality. In addition, there was space for freehand accounts of establishment and maintenance of rules, personal relationships and the behaviour during transitions from one activity to another, all of which had been regarded as significant classroom matters in our earlier enquiry. Finally, the observer was asked to record one critical event during each lesson according to the same format as had been used in our earlier studies. There was also a space for a freehand lesson account, and for the observer to record any other field notes about matters judged to be of significance, and any comments from interviews with teachers after their lessons.

The five observers discussed and piloted the schedule, and observer-agreement tests were conducted. On all observer-agreement measures, there was over 80 per cent agreement between observers, and in final tests based on videotapes of lessons all five-point scale ratings were within one point of each other.

To check whether there was agreement between what teachers said in interview and what they actually did in practice in their first lessons, one of the research team went through all the interview schedules and drew up a list of explicit intentions such as 'I'll introduce myself and write my name on the blackboard' or 'I'll deal with infringements straightaway'. At the end of the research all the observation schedules and reports were read through and the list of intentions was checked. There was exceptionally high accord, of over 80 per cent in quantity, between the experienced teachers' stated intentions and actual practice. Only one teacher out of thirteen actually fell below this. He fulfilled less than half of his expressed intentions. Student teachers were much closer to this figure of a half, and in one or two cases there was little congruence between what was predicted and what ensued, especially amongst PGCE students.

On average, each teacher was observed for the first eight lessons with the same class, but because of timetable clashes it was not always possible to see all of these first lessons in sequence. In the event, the maximum number of lessons seen was twelve in the case of one teacher, and the minimum four in the case of one BEd student. Everyone else was watched for between six and ten lessons. Over 80 per cent of classes seen were of mixed ability, 10 per cent were of high ability and 7 per cent of average or low ability.

The quantitative data were transferred to punched cards, and the ethnographic data were analysed by two members of the research team. In the cases where ethnographic data were translated into coded form, or when lists were drawn up, systematic checks of agreement were taken and there was over 90 per cent agreement in the assigning of qualitative data to codes or headings.

Lesson openings

It soon became apparent that serving teachers have several advantages, in addition to their previous professional experience, which are not available to students. The most striking of these is that they meet their class right at the beginning of the school year, before any class identity has been established, and can therefore be influential in shaping it. All three schools which we observed in September made a massive communal effort at the start of the year with special assemblies, heads and senior teachers visiting all new classes, statements and re-statements about rules of conduct, dress, conventions, aspirations, expectations ('we're expecting great things from you', 'now that you've come to the senior school...') a buzz of excitement and busy chatter, a high degree of institutional control, an assertion of who was who and what was expected to transpire. Student teachers, arriving anonymously during the year, enjoyed none of this collective stamp of businesslike authority and had to join an enterprise which, for better or worse, had been functioning without them for some time.

Recording of actual opening words in lessons was not always possible as these were sometimes uttered in the corridor or were not audible. Analysis of the opening words in the 181 lessons where it was possible to note them showed that half of the first statements were directive, the most common words being 'settle down', 'be quiet', 'come in', 'sit down', 'stand up', 'do...' or 'don't...'. The next most common opening statements were the immediate introduction of the subject itself, ('Today we are going to look at matrices' etc.) which occurred in 13 per cent of lessons, and 'Is everyone here?' which happened on 10 per cent of occasions. About 7 per cent of lessons began with some form of criticism like, 'You don't call this lined up, do you?, LINE UP!'

Experienced teachers and BEd students, almost all, introduced themselves in their first lesson, whilst a number of PGCE students, who had said in interview they would, tended to pass over without any introduction. Experienced teachers had usually made an effort to be present before the pupils arrived as they had said during interviews, and this occurred on 71 per cent of occasions compared to 61 per cent for all students.

There were some interesting variations in the methods teachers employed to secure attention. The use of voice was easily the most common, this being noted as a predominant feature in about half the lessons observed. Some teachers, however, preferred to make use of posture (hands on hips, leaning against blackboard, arms folded), facial expression (smile, scowl), scanned the class rapidly with their eyes, or simply waited expressionless until the level of noise fell, each of these being commented on by observers in about one-fifth to one-quarter of lesson openings.

Experienced teachers and BEd students showed similar lesson beginnings. PGCE students on the other hand appeared self-conscious, often averted their eyes, made little use of commanding posture or gesture, and relied almost exclusively on voice. Observers' accounts of the lesson openings of experienced teachers echoed what the latter had said in interview: performances enacted centre stage, elaborate mannerisms, confident articulation, not much ambiguity at this point about who was in charge. The school staff were, in their different ways, writing the agenda for the whole year during the first few minutes of lesson one. The management and projection of image were striking features of almost every experienced teacher's first lesson.

By way of stark contrast, the image on arrival part way through the school year of one modern-language graduate, who was by no means a 'weak' teacher by the end of his teaching practice, was described by the observer as 'injured caring':

> The teacher spoke with a soft voice which he didn't raise at all. Phrases like 'pay attention' are said apologetically... A hurt note sometimes crept into his voice. He mostly remained standing, and walked up and down behind the desk at the front of the room. When he walked round the room he did not appear to convey any impression that his walking was to much purpose. He made few gestures and could almost be described as overlookable.

Teachers' manner during first lessons

There were some quite notable differences in manner of the three groups as revealed by the summary of rating scales in Table 1.1. The five-point scales were based largely on what were regarded as important characteristics in our own earlier studies, but were also influenced by the work of Ryans (1960) and others. Table 1.1. shows the means of the three groups, and in each case the higher the score the more positively the members of the group were rated on what characteristic or behaviour. The range of possible mean scores, therefore, is from 1, if all were given the lowest rating, to 5 if everyone were accorded the highest possible point on the scale. We have not given analysis of variance or gap-test values, preferring, because of the sample size, to consider the raw data to see similarities and differences. Rank order is given in parentheses.

With between 13 and 15 people in each group one interprets differences with some caution, but it is notable that the experienced teachers tend to display

Table 1.1 Mean scores and rank order of three groups on 8 five-point scales

Characteristic/behaviour	Experienced	BEd	PGCE
Warm and friendly	3.67(1)	3.36(2)	3.14(3)
Confident	4.44(1)	3.68(2)	3.54(3)
Businesslike	4.26(1)	3.62(2)	3.59(3)
Stimulating	3.52(1)	3.10(3)	3.14(2)
Mobile	3.52(2)	3.62(1)	3.11(3)
Formal manner	3.04(3)	3.05(2)	3.11(1)
Eye sweep across the class	4.00(1)	3.56(2)	3.42(3)
Eye contact with individuals	3.68(1)	3.28(3)	3.45(2)

distinctly more of most of these characteristics than do trainees, especially confidence, as one might expect. They are also rated more businesslike, stimulating, warm and friendly, and make greater use of their eyes than students. PGCE students seem to show less mobility than the other two groups, and are less likely to use their eyes to scan the whole class, though their eye contact with individual pupils is not very different.

Despite their greater identification with pupils during interview, PGCE students were not seen as more informal in their manner. The apprehension several expressed in interview that children might take advantage if they were too relaxed, seems to have ensured that they were on average fractionally more formal than either BEd students or experienced teachers. Consequently, they were also seen as a little more aloof than the other two groups on the warm-and-friendly scale. This slight tightness might explain why they were also less mobile, tended to teach from a fixed central point, and were less likely to move around the class monitoring pupils' work.

Establishing classroom rules

Two members of the research team analysed all lesson observation data and assigned references to classroom rules, however these were established, to one of eleven categories. It took a long time and a great deal of discussion before we agreed about the number of categories of rule that there appeared to be, and different analysts might have produced other formulations. Table 1.2 shows the number of lessons out of a total of 131 in which some aspect of the establishment of a classroom rule occurred, either because it was explicitly stated, or if an infraction was punished or commented on, or if the teacher communicated in some form, by action or response, that the rule applied.

The raw frequency count of rule mention does not, of course, reveal much about the effectiveness or appropriateness of the rules themselves. Some experienced teachers established a rule such as that forbidding pupils' casual chatter when the teacher is talking during phases of public exposition, by stating it quite explicitly in the first few seconds of their first lesson, punishing the first infraction moments later, and then fine-tuning the rule on perhaps one further occasion early in their second lesson. After three public references the rule was laid down and understood. In the lesson of one teacher in particular and some students, the same rule was stated frequently but rarely observed.

Table 1.2 Frequency of occurrence, out of 313 lessons, of 11 classroom rules

Rule	No. of lessons
1 No talking when teacher is talking (public situation)	131
2 No disruptive noises	125
3 Rules for entering, leaving and moving in classrooms	109
4 No interference with the work of others	99
5 Work must be completed in a specified way	84
6 Pupils must raise hand to answer, not shout out	55
7 Pupils must make a positive effort in their work	49
8 Pupils must not challenge the authority of the teacher	47
9 Respect should be shown for property and equipment	38
10 Rules to do with safety	26
11 Pupils must ask if they do not understand	8

Table 1.3 Percentage of occasions when rule mention occurred

Rule	Experienced	BEd	PGCE
1 No talking when teacher talking	25	31	44
2 No disruptive noises	19	39	42
3 Entering, leaving, moving	43	31	26
4 No interference with others	28	26	46
5 Work completed in specified way	56	17	27
6 Pupils must raise hand	18	38	44

There were several differences between experienced teachers and novices. Observation confirmed what people had said in interview: experienced teachers made most of the exhortations to respect property, show a positive attitude to work and complete it in a specified way. One might infer that since these rules have been established by the class's regular teacher in September it is less likely that students will need to remind pupils later in the year, but observers' lesson accounts show this is not the case and that students appear less willing or able to enforce such rules. Most of the examples of rule statements about disruptive noises, the need to raise one's hand before answering and talking when the teacher is talking, occurred in students' lessons because some beginners were not successful in making the rule apply. Table 1.3 shows how the six most common rules were distributed across the three groups. Thus, of the 131 lessons when rule 1 occurred, 25 per cent were in the lessons of experienced teachers, 31 per cent in those of BEds and 44 per cent in PGCE students' lessons.

Analysis of critical events recorded by observers shows the differences in style, degree of success and reasons for rules existing. If one takes the most common rule 'No talking when I'm talking', for most teachers, students and pupils this is a commonsense basic rule of discourse: that if one person is attempting to communicate something of interest or value, distractions prevent those who wish to listen from hearing and learning. For some on the other hand, there is a wider social aspect, not merely to do with discourse, but with general respect and concern for others. One or two teachers and students saw the rule more as the embodiment of their personal authority, and reacted much more aggressively to infractions, as the following extract from the observation of the second lesson of an experienced teacher reveals:

> The teacher was talking to the whole class when two boys, one of whom was in the class for the first time, began to chatter. The teacher swung round rapidly, pointed and glared at the offending lad and barked out in a very loud and frightening voice, 'Did I ask you to talk?' He paused for two seconds in the ensuing silence and stared. 'Well don't then.' The boys stopped talking, and the observer noted that the rest of the class appeared shocked. There had been a considerable change in the teacher's voice strength and tempo.

The use of voice and rapid movement into threatening social proximity to establish a rule were not unique to experienced teachers. Early in the lessons of a BEd science student, she explained that she would not tolerate talk whilst she was explaining something:

> One of the girls in the class began to talk as she was saying this. The teacher paused, noted the pupil talking, swung round, put her hands on the desk and

stared into the face of the offending girl. 'I will not tolerate (pause) talking at the same time'. The teacher's speed of movement and shortening of social distance had a frightening quality about it. The girl looked flushed and there was complete silence.

In the lessons of the less confident students, however, there are several accounts of the teacher repeatedly saying 'Sh... quiet please' with little appreciable difference in volume.

The territorial aspect mentioned in interviews was noted frequently in the descriptions of rules about movement, several of which related to the teacher's concept of territory, a phenomenon observed more rarely in the lessons of student teachers. Experienced practitioners spoke frequently of '*my* room', '*my* class', '*my* lab', emphasising the personal pronoun. They defined time as well as space, 'You go when *I* tell you to', 'The bell indicates only that the lesson *may* be ending'. Student teachers suffer from appearing later in the year when someone else has staked out the territory. Conscious that they are on another's ground, they frequently have to ask the pupils about the regular class teacher's rules, 'Does Mr Smith allow you to...?' It underlines to the class the alien and subordinate status of the student on teaching practice.

Establishing relationships

The need expressed by many teachers to establish some set of rules of procedure, however benign, might appear to cut across their equally keen aspiration for amicable relationships with their classes. After all, most of the rules described earlier were usually expressed in prohibitive form: no talking, no calling out, no shirking, no disrespect for people and property. With so much limitation and restriction and with most of the decisions taken by the teacher, it does seem at first glance, that many classrooms are totally unlike A. S. Neill's Summerhill, where pupils and teachers shared equal voting rights on such matters as rules, but rather like Geoffrey Bantock's (1965) assertion that a superior–subordinate relationship is inescapable.

> The teacher, however much he may attempt to disguise the fact, must, if only because he is not appointed or dismissed by pupils, represent an authority. He must do so, also because he is inescapably 'other' than the children... Power is an inescapable element in adult life, to which we all at some time or other have to come to terms; and I deprecate a great deal of the current insincerity which strives to hide the true situation.

Furthermore, as will be shown later, children seem to prefer teachers who are 'in charge'. Yet a number of both inexperienced and practised teachers managed to establish positive and harmonious relationships despite their professed need to exercise authority. They employed a wide variety of ways to achieve this.

Praise and encouragement

Quantified as a percentage of all classroom events, the use of praise occupies relatively little of a class's day, an average figure of around 2 per cent being commonly reported in the literature (Amidon and Flanders, 1963; Wragg, 1972). Teachers who practise systematic behaviour-modification techniques may make more extensive use of praise as a form of reinforcement, whilst those with an aversion to behaviourism may deliberately eschew praise so as not to condition and control behaviour so deliberately. Teachers using the Humanities Curriculum Projects materials developed by Lawrence Stenhouse in the 1960s were actively discouraged from saying 'good' or 'well done', on the grounds that this was not consistent with the role of 'neutral chairman'.

Lavish praise, encouragement and reassurance were significant features of the early lessons of some experienced teachers and BEd students, somewhat less so in those of PGCE students.

Aware that pupils feel apprehensive amid the pressure of their adolescent peers when faced with a new teacher, one BEd English student skilfully used praise to rescue a girl from public ridicule:

> The pupils had been making lists of the characteristics of the animals in *Animal Farm*. The teacher selects one person to read out her list. Amidst giggling the girl complies. The pupil appeared embarrassed at having to stand up. When she had finished reading the teacher said, 'Well done, that was very good.' She smiled encouragement at the pupil who smiled back and sat down

Attention to individual pupils

Experienced teachers and students tried to make opportunities to go around the class talking to individuals, as if conscious of the somewhat stentorian style of their early addresses to the whole class. The PGCE students in particular preferred individual contact. One English graduate spent almost the whole of his first two lessons walking around and talking to pupils, reading their work carefully, engaging individuals in eye contact and speaking with a soft voice. He frequently crouched alongside pupils to bring his height down to their level.

Experienced teachers were more capable of splitting their attention between the individual they were with and the rest of the class, not afraid to break off and comment on something happening elsewhere in the room, whereas some student teachers became so engrossed in their private exchanges with pupils, that they sometimes lost their overall perception of what was happening in other parts of the room.

Apologies

When teachers behave in a dominant way during first encounters they sometimes make errors, accuse the wrong pupil or shout at someone who did not understand. Some teachers and students were confident and compassionate enough to apologise for their errors, and on the relatively infrequent occasions that this occurred it made a considerable impact on pupils who, according to studies which will be mentioned later, appreciate fairness. One of the most striking examples of this came in an early lesson of a BEd drama student when she noticed for the first time a boy standing by the door of the drama studio:

> The teacher looks stern and demands in an angry voice: 'Why are you late?' Everyone is quiet. The teacher is looking aggressive. The child goes red and says nothing. A couple of the class tell the teacher that the boy has been there all the time. 'Have you?' asks the teacher. 'I thought you'd just slid in. My humble apologies for embarrassing you.' The teacher hugs him in a mock show of concern and then pats him on the head. The boy grins and the class laugh.

Explanations of classroom events

Despite what both teachers and students had said in interview, there were surprisingly few explanations of what teachers did and why. Occasionally a rule was justified rather than explained. When explanations were actually offered they seemed to be appreciated by the class. In one science lesson, pupils were given the county's rules of safety in the laboratory and asked to write under each one why they thought the rule was necessary. The rules were then discussed. Some of the other teachers simply gave out the rules with little or no comment.

It was equally appreciated when teachers occasionally addressed an explanation to a particular pupil who was confused but, in these early lessons, too shy to ask for help. One BEd student asked his class if anyone needed the task explaining again.

> One girl said, 'Yes, me.'

> 'Don't you understand what I want?' 'Oh yes. I understand what you want, but I don't see why.'

> The teacher stood by her and explained fully and carefully that it was an exercise in relationships and shapes, one with another. He had noticed that people were making mistakes, did not know what to emphasise, were not looking carefully. The pupil listened attentively and, apparently quite satisfied, went on carefully with her work.

Offers of help with work

Rather than merely explain, some teachers responded to pupils' occasional uncertainties at novelty by making positive offers of help and then working alongside the pupil. This was most marked in the lessons of PGCE students and experienced teachers. An extract from the lesson of an experienced business studies teacher shows how she was quick to help a girl who had arrived late.

> 'Ah, come in', said the teacher, 'you haven't missed much. I've done your folder for you.' She smiled at the pupil. 'Find yourself one of the seats. I'll help you get out your typewriter. We won't make her go through the embarrassment of trying to get it out herself. There.' The teacher got the typewriter out for her and returned to the front.

Children's names and target pupils

With only a few exceptions, experienced teachers learned pupils' names more quickly and deliberately than students. One experienced maths teacher had learned every name of the class observed by the end of the first week. He made his learning of names a public matter, and included an individual response with each name, promising to penalise himself when he made an error, as in this incident when he was handing back their very first test paper:

> What's your name? Robert – good boy Robert. Good girl – what's your name? – Andrea. Good girl. Well done Annabel. What a lovely name – when I have a little girl I'm going to call her Annabel. Good boy Freddie, excellent, excellent. Jean... It's not Jean is it? ... It's Jill, sorry, prize later for my getting your name wrong.

In some cases, name-learning was not so much related to making positive social relationship as to social control, in that it was easier to reprimand if the teacher could put a name to someone. Student teachers were more likely to address the whole class, 'Quiet everybody', 'Pay attention 3C', whereas some experienced teachers deliberately chose a target pupil. It was as if certain children were being sterotyped immediately as exemplars of a whole genus of pupils whose names were as yet unknown.

One of the most striking examples of this occurred in a science lesson with an experienced teacher. Billy became stereotyped as the bad boy in his first lesson. In each ensuing lesson the teacher used him as a target pupil. On one occasion he told the class not to collect equipment until instructed. Some seconds later, about ten pupils began to move towards the equipment cupboards. His response was swift. 'Billy, I did say wait until I told you to move.' During the interview after the lesson, he explained that the reason he had reprimanded Billy was because he was not very bright, his IQ was 'off the IQ scale' and he had to be watched. In other lessons Billy became a different kind of target. In another teacher's class he received frequent and fulsome praise from the teacher, who explained afterwards that she thought he was like a number of pupils who needed encouragement. Later in the year, all his teachers were surprised to discover that Billy had become the mouse-breeding champion of a large part of the country.

Humour

One could write at great length about the use of humour, which is already well documented by several writers including Woods (1979). Humour may be destructive if it is sarcastic or deprecating, just as it may relieve tension if it is positive and warm. PGCE students made much less use of humour than experienced teachers. Male teachers in particular seemed to disregard the familiar tip not to smile until Christmas by engaging in banter and cheerful insults soon after the first lesson or two had passed.

An experienced science teacher, who had conducted a formal and quite stern opening lesson, began his second laboratory session by tempering the first image with a skilful mixture of humour, self-deprecation and a reminder that he too was human and had a family:

> I've got a son your age, and so when my wife and I were invited out to dinner the other night we tossed up to see who would stay at home babysitting, and of course I lost. I decided to watch 'Match of the Day' with my boy and the commentator began to use some very funny language – 'a square ball', 'the referee blew up', 'he left his foot behind' (laughter). Well, we have some special language that we use in science that you will need to learn.

In general, humour occurred most easily and naturally in the lessons of the experienced male teachers in the sample; one or two teachers and a number of students made little or no use of it, and there were only occasional examples of humour that was destructive or deprecating of individual pupils. The most striking aspects of humour were first, that it occurred so soon, frequently in the second lesson, despite a general impression in folklore that teachers prefer to suppress laughter and amusement for some considerable time, and second, that it seemed to be used to mitigate the more stern and austere initial impression conveyed during opening encounters in the very first lesson.

Most, though not all, of the examples given in this section on relationships have been of a positive kind, and certainly a predominant feature of the lessons of almost all students and teachers was the effort they made, despite their frequently expressed need to establish a fairly dominating presence, to bring about a class-room climate in which the conditions for learning were supportive. Sadly, some teachers and students, but only a minority, established negative relationships. Confrontation occurred from the beginning, and whereas similar incidents would have been less explosive in neighbouring classrooms, in the case of three teachers in particular, one experienced, one PGCE and one BEd student, the foundations for a sour relationship were firmly laid from the very first lesson. We shall return to this matter and to one of these three teachers later when we consider the pupil's view of first encounters.

Pupil involvement and deviancy

Using the same procedures for calculating the rough-and-ready measure of deviancy and involvement described earlier, whereby a series of 'sweeps' of the class were made with every pupil being observed in turn for twenty seconds, giving a deviancy, and involvement-level score ranging from 0 to 100, we made a number of quantified comparisons of the three groups. We again recommend caution in interpreting these data, which raise interesting questions and hypotheses but which are inevitably frail because of the difficulty of quantifying such complex matters as misbehaviour and pupils' involvement in their task. Although analysis of variance and Tukey gap tests showed that differences between groups cited below were statistically significant, we do not quote these as they might give a false sense of precision.

Table 1.4 shows the involvement-level scores for the first eight lessons, and there is a noticeable difference between the average involvement level of 90 mea-sured in the lessons of experienced teachers and that of 81 and 80 in the case of BEd and PGCE students.

Table 1.5 shows the levels of deviancy noted during the same first eight lessons, and again teachers' lessons show less occurrence of misbehaviour than those of either student group.

The differences between scores for experienced teachers and trainees cannot be explained solely in terms of individual competence. For reasons given earlier the massive collective effort by all teachers early in September, and the fact that many

Table 1.4 Pupil involvement-level scores during the first eight lessons

Lesson	Experienced teachers	BEd students	PGCE students
1	91	86	86
2	91	78	82
3	94	84	86
4	86	80	81
5	91	80	84
6	94	75	73
7	91	84	73
8	84	78	75
Average	90	81	80

Table 1.5 Pupil deviancy scores during the first eight lessons

Lesson	Experienced teachers	BEd students	PGCE students
1	0.4	8.3	2.8
2	0.9	9.4	3.4
3	0.3	7.7	2.2
4	2.8	9.0	4.5
5	0.6	9.6	4.7
6	0.2	9.1	5.7
7	1.0	4.2	4.5
8	2.0	5.4	5.3
Average	1.0	7.8	4.1

younger pupils find themselves in new and strange surroundings, produce a sense of awe, uncertainty and expectation which has largely evaporated by the time students arrive later in the year. Deviancy scores as low as those obtained by experienced teachers mean, there was on average barely one pupil out of 30 mildly misbehaving during the period of observation. In the case of students, scores between 4 and 10 are obtained when about 3 to 6 pupils out of 30 misbehave.

The general climate even for students, therefore, is one of orderly involvement during the first few lessons, and it is only from the sixth lesson onwards that the level of pupil involvement begins to fall. It is not possible to make too many comparisons with the involvement level of about 60 and deviancy level of around 10 or 11 found with the sample of student teachers in another study in this project, because they were based on a whole term, included more lessons with older adolescents and were in large, Midlands comprehensive schools. It may be the case, however, that students on teaching practice enjoy a honeymoon period of about six lessons, though our analysis of observers' reports show that this was less in the few cases where the student's first lesson or two made a negative impression on the class.

Summary

This analysis of 313 lessons given by experienced teachers, BEd and PGCE students at the beginning of the school year and on teaching practice, shows the massive combined effort made by experienced teachers in September to establish a working climate for the whole school year, and the difficulties of students who arrive later when the territory has been staked out, rules and relationships have been developed and procedures established.

Experienced teachers seemed clear in their minds, before the year begins, how they would conduct themselves. What they described in interview was by and large fulfilled when they were observed in September. Most sought to establish some kind of dominant presence, usually though not always chose to make up their mind about children from their own experience rather than from a scrutiny of pupils' records, tempered any initial harshness with humour, and conveyed to their class that they were firmly in charge, using their eyes, movement and gesture to enhance what they were trying to do. There was a strong moral dimension to some of their classroom rules, and they strove to establish these substantially in the very first lessons.

Student teachers were less certain about their rules and aspirations, PGCE students in particular tending to identify closely with pupils and hoping that rules would become evident as the need arose. At the same time they were conscious of the difficulty they might encounter if they were too informal and were anxious about personal relationships with their classes.

Both student and experienced teachers were able, in most cases, to secure a high level of pupil involvement with little misbehaviour in their earliest lessons. Teachers were rated more businesslike, confident, warm and friendly than students, were usually more deliberate in their learning of children's names and male teachers in particular made use of humour from quite early in the year.

It would be wrong to infer, however, that the differences between groups described earlier persisted to the end of teaching practice. We did observe some lessons after the formal study of first encounters was over, but not on a scale or in a manner which would give a proper long-term account. Much of the early rawness and uncertainty of PGCE students, for example, tends to diminish during the term.

References

Amidon, E. J. and Flanders, N. A. (1963) *The Role of the Teacher in the Classroom*, Paul S. Amidon and Associates Inc., Minnesota.

Argyle, M. (1967) *The Psychology of Interpersonal Behaviour*, Penguin, Harmondsworth.

Bantock, G. H. (1965) *Freedom and Authority in Education*, Faber, London.

Buckley, N. K. (1977) *An Ethnographic Study of an Elementary School Teacher's Establishment and Maintenance of Group Norms*, PhD dissertation, University of Houston, TX.

Duke, D. L. (1978) 'How the Adults in Your Schools Can Cause Student Discipline Problems – and What To Do About It', *American School Board Journal*, 165, 6, 29–30, 46.

Eisenhart, M. (1977) 'Maintaining Control: Teacher Competence in the Classroom', Paper presented at the 76th Annual Meeting of the American Anthropological Association, Houston, TX, December.

Eltis, K. J. (1978) *The Ascription of Attitudes to Pupils by Teachers and Student Teachers*, PhD thesis, Macquarie University, Sydney.

Evertson, C. M. and Anderson, L. M. (1978) *Correlates of Effective Teaching*, University of Texas, Austin, TX.

Goffman, E. (1971) *The Presentation of Self in Everyday Life*, Penguin, Harmondsworth.

Hargreaves, D. H. (1977) 'The Process of Typification in the Classroom: Models and Methods', *British Journal of Educational Psychology*, 47, 274–84.

Kelley, H. H. (1950) 'The Warm-cold Variable in First Impressions of People', *Journal of Personality*, 18, 431–9.

King, R. A. (1978) *All Things Bright and Beautiful?* Wiley, Chichester.

Nash, R. (1973) *Classrooms Observed*, Routledge, London.

Ryans, D. G. (1960) *Characteristics of Teachers*, American Council on Education, Washington, DC.

Soar, R. S. (1973) *Follow-through Classroom Process Measurement and Pupil Growth*, Florida Educational Research and Development Council, Gainesville, FL.

Wood, E. K. (1983) *First Encounters between Teachers and their Classes*, PhD thesis, Exeter University.

Woods, P. (1979) *The Divided School*, Routledge, London.

Wragg, E. C. (1972) *An Analysis of the Verbal Classroom Interaction between Graduate Student Teachers and Children*, PhD thesis, Exeter University.

CHAPTER 2

PUPIL APPRAISALS OF TEACHING

E. C. Wragg and E. K. Wood, in E. C. Wragg (ed.), *Classroom Teaching Skills*, Routledge, 1984, pp. 79–96.

> Pupil perceptions of effective teaching are astonishingly consistent across age groups, and over time. This study of what children regard as skilled teaching was also part of the Teacher Education Project, Chapter 4 of my 1984 book *Classroom Teaching Skills*.

Whereas manufacturers of soap powder do not hesitate to solicit the views of the users of their product, relatively little educational research has employed pupil appraisals of teaching. The reasons are quite clear: some people believe that youthful consumers are not sufficiently mature to give a proper appraisal of quality or even utility; others are apprehensive about the effects on teacher–pupil relationships if pupils should be allowed to make a judgement about teaching, or even afraid that school discipline might suffer irrevocably if children are publicly permitted to flex their critical muscles.

Kurt Lewin (1943) claimed that children as young as 3 or 4 could be even more sensitive than adults to certain situations, yet a huge survey of 672 studies of teacher effectiveness by Domas and Tiedeman (1950) reported only 7 in which pupil ratings were used. In more recent times there has been some soliciting of pupils' views, but it is still the case that the production of many major new curriculum packages, the raising of the school-leaving age, mixed-ability teaching and comprehensive reorganisation were all undertaken with little, if any, soliciting of pupil opinion.

Perhaps this is understandable. Most children, have no experience of schools other than their own, have a restricted picture of what adult life or the next phase of schooling may hold for them, and often tend to favour the familiar. An educational system based entirely on pupil opinion would probably be ultraconservative.

On the other hand, although children of their own accord might never have designed a microelectronics program, there are many who are capable, from their reading and from watching television, of asking why such a subject is not on offer in their own particular school. Whilst few people would advocate basing teaching solely on pupil opinion, it is difficult to justify ignoring it completely, especially when such research as exists reports certain consistent findings.

It has commonly been found that pupils when given a list of teacher characteristics, rate competence in key professional skills most highly. In one of the earliest studies, Hollis (1935) analysed the rank order of seven statements about teacher behaviour accorded by over 8,000 pupils. Highest esteem was given to the teacher's ability to explain difficulties patiently, though the format of this particular enquiry does not allow one to infer whether it was the explanation or the patience that was valued.

Taylor (1962) co-ordinated a group of twenty-one teachers studying part-time for an advanced diploma. Among them, they analysed 1,379 essays written by primary and secondary school pupils on 'a good teacher' and 'a poor teacher', and constructed a checklist which was filled in by 897 children. About 40 per cent of their rankings were given to teaching skills and only about 25 per cent to personal qualities.

When Evans (1962) summarised research on pupils' views of teaching, she concluded that preferred personal characteristics included kindness, friendliness, patience, fairness and a sense of humour. They appeared to dislike sarcasm, favouritism, and domineering or excessive punishment.

In more recent times Meighan (1977) and Cohen and Manion (1981) have summarised enquiries into the pupil perspective. Research over the past ten years includes a well-known study by Nash (1976) in which he used a repertory-grid technique with a class of 12–13 year olds. The constructs which emerged concerned discipline, the ability to teach, explaining, degree of interest, fairness and friendliness.

Furlong (1976) studied a single class for two terms, and reported how some of the 15-year-old secondary modern girls in it appraised their teachers and behaved towards them. Even some of the aggressive so-called 'non-academic' members valued teaching skill, and were prepared to learn in the lessons of those able to arouse interest. Gannaway (1976), in a small-scale study of one school, proposed a sequential pupil model of teacher evaluation which began with the question 'can the teacher keep order?' If the answer was 'no' he would be rejected. The model progressed through a further series of yes/no questions such as 'can he have a laugh?' and 'does he understand pupils?' It is difficult to demonstrate that pupil judgements about teachers occur in precisely the order Gannaway formulates, but he mentions characteristics which consistently appear in the literature.

The present study

We decided to solicit pupils' views about teachers and teaching in one of the schools which we used during the study of first encounters in the same research project. It was decided to poll pupils' opinions through a questionnaire, and to interview a sample of children about some of the teachers we had observed.

The school was a six-form-entry city comprehensive high school for 12–16 year olds. It has a very mixed, well-established catchment area, partly drawing on a large, working-class estate, partly on a middleclass, privately owned residential area. The school is well regarded in the community and is one of the more popular choices amongst parents. The head and staff put a high value on both personal care and academic achievement.

A stratified random sample of 200 pupils was selected, 50 from each of the four year groups. Equal numbers of boys and girls were chosen, except in the second and fourth year where there were more girls than boys in the whole year group, so a 30/20 ratio was selected. As pupils come from 8 to 12 middle schools the new entrants are called second years. Details of the sample are given in Table 2.1.

Each pupil completed a 39-item questionnaire related to some of the areas of concern of the Teacher Education Project. The first three items were in forced-choice format and were to do with first encounters with teachers: how the teacher should introduce himself, how he should dress and how he should behave in his very first lesson.

Table 2.1 Stratified random sample of 200 pupils

Year	Boys	Girls	Total
2nd	20	30	50
3rd	25	25	50
4th	20	30	50
5th	25	25	50
Total	90	110	200

The next 32 items were all descriptive of teacher behaviour and were a modification of the pupil attitude instrument used by Flanders (1965) in his New Zealand study of teacher influence, pupil attitudes and achievement. They measured on a five-point, Likert-type scale aspects such as teacher enthusiasm, interest, use of praise, humour and teaching skills of various kinds. Items included such statements as 'This teacher would boss you about', 'This teacher would want you to help each other when working', 'This teacher would be enthusiastic in lessons', and 'This teacher would expect high standards'.

The remaining four items concerned grouping by ability, who should run schools, what size of group was liked for small-group work and preferred ways of learning (using the library, practical work, listening to teacher, work cards, reading a book).

Pupils were given the instruction 'Imagine that the best teacher in the world has been sent to your school (it might be a man or a woman). In all the following questions please answer with this teacher in mind. Please remember that your answers should be about the best teacher in the world.'

Pupils' views

The 200 questionnaire responses were analysed in a number of different ways. Means and standard deviations were calculated for all the five-point scale items as were product–moment correlations. Factor analysis is commonly used to reduce a large set of correlations and identify a smaller number of significant factors for better understanding of the relationships between sets of measures. A factor analysis was undertaken with rotation to simple structure according to the varimax criterion which maximizes zero and near-zero loadings. In addition, two-way analysis of variance was used to investigate sex and year-group differences.

The answers to the first three items on introductions, dress and style showed that 84 per cent expected the teacher to introduce himself with more than just his name, about half of these preferring details of his teaching and half personal details about interests and hobbies. On the matter of dress 48 per cent preferred casual dress, 33 per cent smart dress and 7 per cent very smart dress, with 12 per cent feeling that dress did not matter. From four different options about style in the very first lesson an overwhelming 75 per cent preferred 'understanding, friendly and firm' rather than the other combinations 'efficient, orderly and businesslike', 'friendly, sympathetic and understanding' or 'firm and serious but fair'.

The means of the 32 five-point scales are most interesting. Scores theoretically may range from 1 (everyone strongly agrees) to 5 (everyone strongly disagrees). The five items which attracted strongest agreement are shown in Table 2.2.

This confirms the findings of some of the enquiries cited above. As in the Hollis (1935) study the ability to explain is most highly valued. Statements in second, third and fifth place seem to stress good sympathetic personal relationships.

Table 2.2 Five statements showing strongest agreement

Item	Mean score
1 This teacher would explain things clearly	1.46
2 This teacher would call you by your first name	1.61
3 This teacher would help the slower ones catch up in a nice way	1.65
4 This teacher would help you learn a lot in every lesson	1.66
5 This teacher would be a good listener	1.86

Table 2.3 Five statements showing strongest disagreement

Item	Mean score
1 This teacher would hit you	4.37
2 This teacher would boss you about	4.28
3 This teacher would sometimes be too busy to talk to you	3.71
4 This teacher would let you mark your own tests	3.55
5 This teacher would do something else if that's what the class wants	3.52

At the other end of the spectrum the five statements attracting greatest disagreement shown in Table 2.3 are also illuminating.

What is noticeable here is the pupils' rejections of child-centredness in statements 4 and 5. One would expect the condemnation of physical aggression and an over-authoritarian approach in the two statements in first and second place, though Nash (1976), using the rep-grid technique, reports Scottish children's views which seemed more accepting of corporal punishment. Nevertheless, it always seems disappointing to the liberally minded when pupils appear not to wish to make decisions about their work and its assessment, seeing this as a central part of the teacher's professional job.

Analysis of variance of all the 32 five-point scales produced an astonishing lack of difference between sexes and between year groups. On some items the mean in each of the eight cells (four year groups and two sexes) was almost identical.

Some responses were, however, strikingly different. Older children claimed to be less hostile to being told off publicly, as the means in Table 2.4 show, where the year-group effect is significant at the 0.001 level.

On the question of response to pupils' wishes there was both a sex and a year-group difference, with girls more likely than boys to disagree that a good teacher would do something else if the class wanted (0.05 level) and fourth and fifth years significantly more hostile to this than second and third years (0.01 level) as Table 2.5 shows.

A varimax factor analysis of the 32 five-point scales produced six factors which between them accounted for 42 per cent of the variance. The strongest factor accounted for 14.5 per cent of the variance, and was characterised by interest and enthusiasm, loading on items such as 'This teacher would be interested in what you do outside of school as well as in it', 'This teacher would be enthusiastic in lessons' and 'This teacher would be a good listener'.

On the remaining items there was one very significant finding. When offered a choice between streaming, setting and mixed-ability classes, all of which were explained, 72 per cent opted for setting, 19 per cent for mixed-ability and 9 per cent

Table 2.4 Responses to item 12 'This teacher would tell you off in front of the rest of the class'

Year	Boys	Girls
2nd	4.09	3.45
3rd	3.72	3.60
4th	2.99	3.22
5th	2.92	3.00

Table 2.5 Responses to item 22 'This teacher would do something else if that's what the class wants'

Year	Boys	Girls
2nd	3.00	3.76
3rd	2.96	3.52
4th	3.44	3.53
5th	3.88	4.04

for streaming. Although the first two years were spent mainly in mixed-ability groups and the final two years were in sets, there was no significant difference between year groups: all heavily favoured setting.

The item on favoured small-group size produced a mean of about 4 with no significant differences between year groups. Girls, however, preferred larger groups (mean 4.22) than boys (mean 3.87) a difference significant at the 0.01 level.

When asked to evaluate on a five-point scale different ways of learning, the rank order was:

1   Practical work – 1.89
2   Listening to the teacher – 2.29
3   Reading a book or using the library – 2.36
4   Work cards – 2.91

The questionnaire data provided interesting information about pupils' views of teaching. There is a degree of congruence between the pupils' expressed preference for teachers who are understanding, friendly and firm, and both the teachers' views in interview and their behaviour in the lessons observed and described elsewhere in our research, which showed that they tended, on the whole, to establish a climate of businesslike firmness at the beginning of the school year, but with a tempering of warmth and humour.

On the other hand there are important points of difference and some warning signs. The pupils clearly dislike over-bossy and aggressive teachers, and it is the younger children, especially boys of 12 or 13, who are most hostile to being told off in public. Teachers who begin their year in an over-dominant manner with younger groups may not be able to redeem the situation subsequently.

Pupils' responses to the questionnaire items also explain some of the problems experienced by student teachers. PGCE students in particular identified with pupils, though they were well aware of the difficulties an over-familiar approach might cause. They frequently expressed a wish to accommodate pupils' wishes in their teaching, yet the children's rejection of items such as 'this teacher would let you mark your own tests' and 'this teacher would do something else if that's what the class wants' confirm that considerable negotiation and exploration will be necessary when teachers wish to share decision-making in their classrooms, skills that novice teachers may not possess at the beginning of their career.

Pupils' apparent need for compliance is sometimes difficult for those student teachers with discipline problems to understand. On the one hand, it would seem, they wish to be told what to do, on the other they are not willing, in the lessons of those with poor class control, to do as asked, a paradox which we could only partially explain. The pupils' overwhelming endorsement of setting, for example, caused little overt resentment of the school's policy of mixed-ability teaching in the first two years, probably because personal relationships between teachers and children were in general, sound.

Interviews with pupils

The final phase of enquiry in the class management studies was a series of interviews with groups of either two or three pupils, a total sample of 25, about teachers who had been observed during the first encounters study. There were 14 girls and 11 boys in the sample and each group was interviewed for about an hour. The interviewer was one of the present writers, and a semi-structured interview schedule was used. The interviews took place in the school, were informal in manner, and were not tape recorded, the interviewer noting down as accurately as possible what was said. There is a loss of exactitude in this procedure, but pupils are understandably anxious, and may be less than frank if their conversations about their teachers are recorded.

The pupil sample was not a randomly chosen one, but rather a group of second years who had been taught by a sample of the teachers we had observed the year after our fieldwork. No pupil approached refused to co-operate. The semi-structured interview schedule was in three parts. First of all the pupils were invited to recall their very first lesson with each teacher, then they were asked to talk generally about him or her, finally they were shown the same four pictures of classroom mis-behaviour used in teacher interviews, and asked how each teacher would react if such an incident occurred in his or her lesson. Pupils' reactions to two of the teach-ers are described, the first was successful in establishing harmonious relationships with his classes, the second was not. Most teachers in the sample in their different ways did secure positive relationships, and the unpopular Mr Baker was one of the very few students or teachers who aroused hostility from the beginning. Pseudonyms are used for both teachers and pupils in the descriptions given below. A fuller account of the interviews can be found in Wood (1983).

Mr Abel

Mr Abel is a science teacher in his mid-thirties. He was described by the observer who saw the first nine lessons with his mixed-ability, second-year class as 'relaxed and pleasant with a slightly disconcerting grin'. In interviews he had been extremely precise about what he would do in his first lesson, how he would see the children into the room, give out the books, write his name on the board and spend most of the first lesson on laboratory and classroom rules. When observed he had fulfilled everything he described to the letter. Sixteen statements were elicited for the purpose of verification from his interview, and he accomplished fourteen of them in the view of the analyst.

During their interviews all the pupils recalled with remarkable vividness what had taken place. Their account matched in every important respect features recorded by observers:

> We did the lab. rules. There were fifteen. They told us what to do and what not to do in the lab… We thought of rules like: Don't run in the lab, go in without a teacher, no eating or chewing, tie back long hair, don't suck or blow tubes.
>
> (Alison and Beryl)

> He gave us a sheet on lab rules and a blue sheet where we had to spot the mistakes. The rules were that you were not to eat in class; you don't put things near the edge of the table; you don't muck about with the burners; you report accidents; you don't let the chairs stick out; baggage must be under the table; do not run or fool in the lab; don't enter the lab without the teacher's permission; always ask if you're not sure.
>
> (Charles and David)

Mr Abel was keen on lesson and lab organisation, did not like pupils where he could not see them or those who sat with their back to him when he was explaining, and described in interview how he liked to surprise pupils. Science, he felt, was a mixture of excitement, unease and potential danger, and he had to keep pupils on their toes. Part way through the third lesson observed he had demonstrated how to use a fire extinguisher, and sprayed freezing-cold carbon dioxide at two boys who had turned their backs to him. They were temporarily shocked until Mr Abel made a joke of it. Usually Mr Abel's jokes were shared, but three of the girls took a different view as exemplified by the following statement from one of them:

> He likes to play tricks on people, especially the girls. He dropped a model of a bird-eating spider in front of me. I shrieked. He does this kind of thing mostly to the girls because he says they need toughening up. They're too soft.
>
> (Elizabeth)

Mr Abel recognised that his unpredictable style might be a little frightening occasionally, and had described in interview how he would diminish this effect with humour, support and mild flirtation. His view of himself was very close to that expressed later by his pupils:

> He looks like Bodie in 'The Professionals'. He's sexy. He's not too strict but he can be when you misbehave, like when you break more than two lab rules in any day or when you mess about with chemicals or break the test tubes. He asks those who break them to pay for them. He shouts then as well. Mr Abel's alright. He's not too strict and he's not too gentle.
>
> (Frances and Gail)

During interviews pupils were shown the picture of pupils splashing water in the lab to which their teachers had reacted during their own interview. Mr Abel had been prompt in his own response to this particular picture:

> He's turning the tap around. I think it calls for an unofficial thick ear. Shock situation, surprise. There are too many people around the bench. The picture is an organisational mess. The fact is that the situation should not have occurred. That boy has a pen in his mouth. He's in trouble.

The pupils, asked in interview to guess how Mr Abel might react to the situation in the same picture, were astonishingly close to his own reaction:

> Mr Abel would give a detention. You're not allowed to have bags on the table and that girl behind has. He would really shout. He would ask who started it first. That boy chewing his pencil, he'd get it. He'd tell the girl to tie her hair back. He'd say, 'You don't come in here to squirt water, back to work.' They'd have to clear up. Smashing things is wrong and Mr Abel worries about the cuts.
>
> (Hilary)

Mr Abel used his voice quite deliberately when misbehaviour occurred. 'I'm fortunate to have a deep voice. I can stop someone dead in their tracks by a quick sharp word', he had said in interview. An incident from the sixth lesson observed in his laboratory illustrated this. Early in the lesson he heard a test tube being dropped. 'Oi!' he shouted loudly in contrast to the low-key, benign voice that characterised most of his teaching, 'Did I say get your test tubes yet? Go back to your seats please. Go and stand where you are going to work. Right, one member from each group to fetch the test tubes.' It was the firmness in his voice and the insistence on his procedures being followed that led to compliance.

On another occasion in the eighth lesson observed he again used case law to illustrate his control and to define the limits within which pupils should operate. Two girls entered the classroom during the lesson. One had previously been given permission to go to the toilet. 'Where have you been?' Mr Abel asked in a loud and stern voice. 'To the loo', they replied. 'Where?' he persisted with by now the whole class watching. The girls repeated their answer. 'What both of you? You never go out of the room without permission.' Having established his point Mr Abel went over to the girls within a short time and talked in a very friendly manner with them about their experiment. It seemed a deliberate act on his part.

In interview Peter and Richard amongst others, reacting to the picture of pupils splashing water in the lab, described Mr Abel's loud voice. 'He'd shout at us to stop. "Oi you – stop it" (imitating Mr Abel's public voice). He'd probably give us a detention.' Alison recalled his friendly humour and ready response to pupils' work:

> We once made a mobile. Mine was very funny. It wasn't good. We both laughed at it. Richard he calls Noddy because he's always nodding his head when he is talking to you. We all think it's funny, so does Richard.

The girls seemed to know precisely how to handle Mr Abel, what to do, what not to try, and when to flirt back with him. Shown the picture of the girl who refused to move when asked by the teacher, two replied as follows:

> Mr Abel would shout and say 'Come on you've got to move' and she will because it's Mr Abel, because he's nice and a laugh. We wouldn't like to see him cross. He understands us and we want to keep it like that.
>
> (Iris)

> She'd say 'Oh sir, please can I stay here. Give us a chance.' He would probably let her. She would move if he really wanted her to though.
>
> (Alison and Beryl)

Analysis of the observation data for Mr Abel showed that he was rated extremely high by the observer on confidence, being businesslike, mobility and warmth. In his earliest lessons he also had a very high degree of eye contact with individual pupils. Pupil attention was high and misbehaviour almost non-existent. He knew how he wished to be perceived by his pupils, and they, in turn, apart from an occasional misunderstanding over one of his sudden surprises or jokes, reported a very similar impact to the one he intended.

Mr Abel demonstrated many of the characteristics used by other teachers in the sample to establish benign control: a brisk businesslike manner, high eye contact with individual pupils, quick reaction to the first signs of misdemeanour before it escalated, clearly defined rules about behaviour, devoting much of his first two or three lessons to these, a clear staking-out of the territory over which he had control. His ready humour, use of surprise, and interest in pupils' work, especially after they had been reprimanded, established very positive social relationships with his pupils who showed an incisive understanding of the processes which had been at work when interviewed two years later.

Many of these characteristic pieces of behaviour have been described by other researchers studying the establishment of teacher–pupil relationships. Stenhouse (1967) and Ball (1981) in his study of Beachside Comprehensive have described how children test the limits until the parameters of control are established. In Mr Abel's case any ambiguity was dispelled within the first three lessons, and pupils were clear both at the time and in retrospect what was permitted and what proscribed. Several writers, including Gannaway (1976), Woods (1976) and Willis (1976), have referred to humour and 'having a laugh'. In Mr Abel's case the purpose was not so much for 'being one of the lads' as described by Willis, but sometimes explained by Woods' proposal that a type of gallows humour can permit pupil and teachers an emotional escape from tension, and on other occasions offering a challenge to pupils to operate at a high level of arousal and attentiveness.

All the pupils interviewed were clear about Mr Abel: they knew where they stood, they respected and liked him, and they described his classes with affection. They were equally united in their view of Mr Baker, but this time for quite different reasons.

Mr Baker

Mr Baker was an older teacher whose reputation had preceded his first entry to his classes. Even pupils from the primary feeder schools knew about him and looked forward to their first encounter with a mixture of fear and excitement, as these pupils recalled in interview:

> Everyone warned us about him. We knew all about it before we got here. Our brothers and sister are in the fourth year and they told us what it would be like.
> (Janet and Kate)

> Nobody likes Mr Baker. We stood outside the library door and waited. I was excited to see him.
>
> (Hilary)

Mr Baker was observed teaching his first eight humanities lessons with a class of 13 year olds. His own view of first encounters had been very clearly expressed in interview. He stressed that he would be firm but consistent:

> I try to get over that you are God, the paternal figure. You need to get them screwed down a bit. It takes about two months to get them in order. When they arrive they stand outside the door. I would stand in the door and say 'Fill

up from the front of the class first.' Then they'd fill up the next row till it's all squared up. I look at the room and put their names on my plan. I might get them to sit in alphabetical order. Afterwards I put them in order of merit. It's a good idea to get people to sit according to their ability. I think mixed-ability teaching is inefficient. I would say, 'You call me Mr Baker or sir, and I'll call you by your christian name. I'm the boss and I give the orders.'

Whereas Mr Abel explained his classroom rules and even invited pupils to devise their own, on occasion, Mr Baker saw no room for pupils to express a view or have rules explained. Many of the analogies he used in interview were expressed in military language. He spoke of his 'forays' into the classroom, children's 'mutinies', and felt that sarcasm was one of his chief 'weapons' in the 'classroom war'. He was at odds with his colleagues, whom he thought soft and with poor standards. In terms of the distinction made by Woods (1979) between social control and situational control, where the former describes teachers' obligation to society to raise well-behaved citizens, and the latter is concerned with handling day-to-day problems which occur in a particular classroom, Mr Baker saw himself as responsible for social control, a front-line defender of standards not just in the school but in society at large. To achieve this he was prepared to provoke conflict:

> I believe in confrontation. It is an attempt to maintain standards. Most people just operate a policy of containment. To do this is just to cause problems for others. You have to remember that to clash with you is to clash with the school, the culture and ultimately with society. If they get away with it in school then they will end up as troublemakers in the unions and responsible for wildcat strikes.

His first few lessons were punctuated by lengthy monologues about pupils' behaviour saturated with statements about the importance of authority and obedience. Pupils tended to listen in silence and then resume their minor misdemeanours when he eventually ceased. In his fifth lesson a pupil was thought to be chewing and his ensuing monologue reveals the general tone of such addresses to the class.

> Are you eating? Well stop moving your jaws. Sit still. Some of you should be in strait-jackets. If you don't work then you'll have to copy out of the book. You are going to conform to my standards which are not in any way abnormal. In this life there are some people who want to work, there will be six million unemployed in the 1980s – none of you has convinced me that you are in any way employable. I'm in charge here. I can enforce it and I will. It's as simple as that (bangs fist on table). Sooner or later someone will get physically hurt. Don't push me too far. We're all human, boys and girls alike. You are my family. It's my legal right to punish you. Don't forget that.

The pupils' response to Mr Baker was almost universally negative. They all commented on his lack of humour and the unremitting tedium of his lessons. This confirmed the classroom data collected during observation where the ratings of the observer were the lowest of any person, teacher or student, on the stimulating-dull scale, lower than most on warmth, and, despite his apparently firm manner, lower than many teachers on pupil attention to the task and higher on pupil misbehaviour. He was rated high on confidence, but this reveals the frailty of rating scales in the appraisal of teaching. Analysis of critical events and transcripts of some of his exchanges with pupils seem to show that, underneath the rhetoric about himself being in sole charge, lurks a considerable anxiety about loss of control and lack of rapport for which he attributes blame to the pupils and the corruptness of his colleagues.

His lack of any rapport with the pupils was confirmed in all the interviews with them, as was the message he had given them about their likely unemployment:

> He gave out the books. He told us we were going to go through this book very fast. I didn't like it at first but you need to do well at school to get a good job so I got used to it later. Every day I was scared. He was firm and never laughed with us. He never forgot anything. I told my mum I wouldn't get used to him and I didn't. He didn't get better. He thinks he's soft on us!
>
> (Mary)

> He's too strict. He says he treats us like he was taught at school. He never does anything interesting. He makes the book a lot harder. He leaves the interesting pages out. He skips them and then goes back to the beginning again. He goes over and over the boring bits.
>
> (Stephen and Tom)

One or two pupils who were highly motivated were resigned rather than hostile to a certain degree of pain in their learning, were prepared to consider the possibility that effective teachers may not always be popular or good-humoured and vice versa. Even they, however, were easily dissuaded by their colleagues as the following conversation between William and Andy during their interview reveals:

William: He may be a good teacher, but pupils do not find his methods enjoyable. In fact they leave something to be desired. It all seems boring.
Andy: We learned it thoroughly though, didn't we? I mean we went over and over it much more than the other classes did.
William: Yes, but they all did much better than us in the test. It didn't do us much good, did it?

The interviewer recorded 'gloomy acceptance' of William's point by both Andy and Caroline, who were being interviewed together.

When the pupils looked at the pictures used in the interview there was again an astonishing concurrence between what Mr Baker had said and their own reactions. When considering the picture of a girl being asked to move by the teacher and refusing, Mr Baker's response was that it offered a confrontation he would relish:

> I have dragged another girl across five desks in this situation. I'd say, 'Go to the year head.' If she refused I'd dispatch another child to fetch the year head. You could push it to the point of confrontation.

All the pupils used the same kind of language to predict what would happen in Mr Baker's lessons if someone refused to move. There was no dissent from the view that his reaction would be quick and aggressive:

> He would shout. He'd go mad, out of this world. He'd drag her to the next place. He's too strict. He has no sense of humour.
>
> (Charles and David)

He'd kick up a stink. He'd kill her. He'd give her everything – in at break, dinnertime to do jobs. He'd have blown his top, grabbing her by the ear and picking her up.

(Graham)

Whereas Mr Abel had a picture of himself that was close to that of his pupils and field notes made by the observer of his lessons, Mr Baker's view of himself is not supported by others. Indeed, of his intentions stated in interview fewer than half were fulfilled in the view of the analyst who scrutinised lesson accounts. He saw himself as consistent, yet his reaction to pupils was erratic:

He told me that if I made a mistake to correct it underneath. So I did that. When he took our books in he forgot that he had said that and he did a line under it and shouted at me and told me that I should have done it on top. He changes his mind.

(Stephen)

He also said that he liked some laughter though not too much, but laughter was absent from his lessons and several said that if pupils smiled he told them to stop smiling. One expressed it much more strongly:

If anyone laughs or talks then they have to stand up for the rest of the lesson. He said, 'Smile and work well and you'll be alright.' I tell you if I saw Mr Baker smile then the next thing you would see would be a pink elephant.

(Graham)

It is beyond the scope of this short chapter to explain why Mr Baker behaves as he does. The simple explanation that he is out of touch with modern youth will not suffice. There are plenty of teachers whose own ideology is not that of their pupils who are nevertheless successful at working with them. Despite his insistence that he stood for the defence of high standards of work and behaviour he achieved success in neither. Although he aroused fear in some children his lessons actually became the war game in which he saw himself engaged. His seeking of confrontation, belittling of pupils and inconsistency provoke the very disobedience he seeks to avoid. Even apprehensive pupils described how they joined in the vengeful conspiracy to frustrate him:

I once threw something on to his desk. He wasn't sure who had thrown it. He didn't do anything. He just glared at me. I like getting him stewed up. I don't know why. It's fun, but sometimes he frightens me too.

(Alison)

These two brief descriptions of Mr Abel and Mr Baker do not permit many generalisations about how pupils perceive their teachers, or how other teachers establish relationships with their classes. What they do show is that pupils have a clear and consistent understanding of classroom events which often coincides with that of their fellows. They tended to give the same view of each teacher they discussed with very few dissenting voices. They also understood how teachers define or fail to define rules of behaviour, knew exactly how their teachers would respond, even in some cases using identical words and metaphors to those used by the teachers in their interviews.

They also understand how case law is used by teachers to establish limits, and are able to make inferences, not so much from the teacher's stated intentions, but rather from his or her interaction with individuals. Furthermore, this study confirms many of the findings of earlier enquiries. The pupils in the sample liked teachers who were firm but fair, consistent, stimulating, interested in individuals and had a sense of humour, and they disliked those few who showed the polar opposite of these characteristics. Although there have not been too many published studies of pupils' views of their teachers, the results of those available are remarkably consistent.

Thus, the first impression teachers make on their pupils when they encounter each other for the first time is crucial. Those who wish to make a firm start and establish control should recognise that, whilst pupils can see the need for and even expect such a beginning, if they are over-bossy, fail to temper their authority with humanity, they may never secure a positive working relationship with their class. Part of Mr Abel's success with his pupils was that he was quick to work alongside pupils after he had needed to reprimand them. For teachers who wish to involve pupils in sharing decision-making from the beginning, it is also clear that this is often contrary to their expectation and may even confuse and irritate them, so considerable thought must be given to explaining and winning support for this way of working.

References

Ball, S. (1981) *Beachside Comprehensive*, Cambridge University Press, Cambridge.
Cohen, L. and Manion, L. (1981) *Perspectives on Classrooms and Schools*, Holt, Rinehart & Winston, London.
Domas, S. J. and Tiedeman, D. V. (1950) 'Teacher Competence: an Annotated Bibliography', *Journal of Experimental Education*, 19, 101–218.
Evans, K. M. (1962) *Sociometry and Education*, Routledge, London.
Flanders, N. A. (1965) *Teacher Influence, Pupil Attitudes and Achievement*, US Office of Education, Research Monograph 12.
Furlong, V. (1976) 'Interaction Sets in the Classroom' in M. Stubbs and S. Delamont (eds), *Explorations in Classroom Observation*, Wiley, London.
Gannaway, H. (1976) 'Making Sense of School' in M. Stubbs and S. Delamont (eds), *Explorations in Classroom Observation*, Wiley, London.
Hollis, A. W. (1935) *The Personal Relationship in Teaching*, MA thesis, Birmingham University.
Lewin, K. (1943) 'Psychology and the Process of Group Living', *Journal of Social Psychology*, 17, 113–31.
Meighan, R. (1977) 'The Pupil as Client: the Learner's Experience of Schooling', *Educational Review*, 29, 123–35.
Nash, R. (1976) *Teacher Expectations and Pupil Learning*, Routledge, London.
Stenhouse, L. (ed.) (1967) *Discipline in Schools*, Pergamon, Oxford.
Taylor, P. H. (1962) 'Children's Evaluations of the Characteristics of the Good Teacher', *British Journal of Educational Psychology*, 32, 258–66.
Willis, P. (1976) 'The Class Significance of School Counter Culture', in M. Hammersley and P. Woods (eds), *The Process of Schooling*, Routledge and Open University Press, London.
Wood, F. K. (1983) *First Encounters between Teachers and their Classes*, PhD thesis, Exeter University.
Woods, P. (1976) 'Having a Laugh: an Antidote to Schooling', in M. Hammersley and P. Woods (eds), *The Process of Schooling*, Routledge and Open University Press, London.
—— (1979) *The Divided School*, Routledge, London.

CHAPTER 3

CLASS MANAGEMENT IN THE PRIMARY SCHOOL

Originally published as 'Systematic Studies of Class Management', in *Primary Teaching Skills*, Routledge, 1993, pp. 58–87

Skilful management of children, subject matter, time, space, resources and personal relationships, allow teachers' other abilities to come into play. How teachers manage their classes, therefore, was a central part of the Primary Teacher Education Project and this account comes from Chapter 4 of my 1993 book *Primary Teaching Skills*.

Managing the very first encounters with a new class is an important aspect of teaching, but sustaining and enhancing rules, relationships, application to the task in hand, preparation and planning must go on throughout the time that teachers and pupils are together. In order to monitor what happened in these more mature phases of the school year or term, once daily routines had been established, we decided to study the classrooms of a sample of experienced and novice teachers in different kinds of schools. Schools in ten local authorities were approached as being representative of a variety of large and small urban and rural schools. Thirty schools agreed to participate, and between one and nine teachers were observed in each school, giving a total of sixty teachers and students, of whom fifty-one were female and nine were male. Each was observed for four sessions, except for one teacher who was ill for several weeks and so was only observed for three sessions. The distribution of teachers and lessons is shown in Table 3.1. This chapter concentrates on the quantitative data from these observations. The qualitative data are also reported later in this chapter.

A mixture of observation methods was used, some structured and quantified, others semi-structured, yet others freehand. There were interviews with the teachers as well as observations of their 'lessons'. For this purpose a session, which usually lasted between half an hour and an hour, was termed a 'lesson', though it may have

Table 3.1 Number of teachers and lessons observed in present sample

Region	Teachers	Lessons
North-west	25	100
London East End	9	35
South-west	14	56
Student teachers in South-west	12	48
Total	60	239

consisted of more than a single type of activity. The observer used first of all a version of the Nottingham Class Management Observation Schedule (Wragg 1984). This is a category system in which the researcher ticks any of the seventy activities which occur in each observation period: what teachers do, what pupils do, what the outcome is, as well as the degree of deviance. This is done for five separate lesson segments lasting ninety seconds each, once the session has begun. Thus, 1,195 lesson segments were analysed from the 239 lessons observed. Most of the categories in the Nottingham Class Management Observation Schedule were used, but several were dropped, as primary classrooms are more complex to observe than secondary, so, for example, the three pupil movement categories of the original 'at wrong time', 'at wrong sped', 'to wrong place' were put together as 'inappropriate movement'. The principal focus in the schedule is on the teacher's handling of misbehaviour.

The definition of 'deviance' in classroom observation is not an easy matter. To some extent it is defined by the teacher. One teacher may permit free movement, another may forbid pupils to leave their seat without permission. However, observers do have to make a number of personal decisions about what constitutes deviant behaviour, for a teacher may ignore, albeit rarely, one pupil hitting another, and though this may appear to legitimise such behaviour in one classroom, it would not constitute acceptable behaviour in most. Observers took what were perceived as the teacher's rules of conduct as a starting point, but had to exercise judgement about misbehaviour that would have been perceived as deviant in most other classrooms. It is a judgement between the individual and the norm which is by no means perfect, but observers did reach a high degree of agreement about interpretations before the research began, and maintained it through the duration of the study, as described here.

The second part of the schedule involves a sweep of every pupil in the class. The observer studies each pupil in turn for 20 seconds and then makes two decisions about on-task behaviour and deviance. The on-task behaviour category involves a decision as to whether the child being observed spends roughly 0–6 seconds, 7–13 seconds or 14–20 seconds on the task in hand. 'Mild' deviance is defined as misbehaviour like noisy or illicit talk, distraction of others, or wrong movement, whereas 'more serious' deviance includes violence to another pupil or to the teacher, insulting behaviour to the teacher, or damage to property. An involvement and a deviance index are then calculated by the following formula:

$$\text{Involvement or deviance index} = \frac{\text{Factor A} \times 100}{\text{Number of pupils} \times 2}$$

In each case, factor A is calculated by weighting each of the three observation categories 0, 1 or 2 and multiplying by the number of pupils in each category. Thus if, out of 28 pupils, 2 were 'low' on task, 10 were 'medium' and 16 were 'high', then factor A would be $(2 \times 0) + (10 \times 1) + (16 \times 2) = 42$. Inserted into the involvement equation, this would give an index score of 75, that is, 42 divided by 56 (twice the number of pupils) times 100. The deviance index score is calculated in a similar manner. The possible range, therefore, is from 0 to 100, a score of 0 being obtained if all pupils were low on task and not deviant, and a maximum score of 100 achieved if all were on task and behaving in a more seriously deviant manner. This is inevitably a rough-and-ready estimate, as the categories could be weighted in different ways, or not weighted at all, but it was used consistently in each lesson, so despite its limitations it is of some interest.

Two trained observers carried out the observations and, in order to check the extent to which they agreed or disagreed with others, two inter-observer agreement measures were taken, before and after the fieldwork. A percentage agreement figure was used, that is, the percentage of times the two observers agreed with each other on all the categories for five lesson observation segments. Observations were done on videotapes, so that observers' ratings could be compared before and after the fieldwork. The use of percentages would be open to criticism if there were many unlikely categories like 'teacher flies through window' or events that never occurred, but the schedule consists of categories of behaviour all of which have been observed in classrooms. Agreement between observers was very high. Inter-observer agreement (comparing one observer with another) was 95.2 per cent before the fieldwork and 88.6 per cent after completion of all observation. Intra-observer agreement (the extent to which observers agree with themselves on two different ratings of the same videotaped lesson) was also very high, with observer A scoring 87.6 per cent, and observer B 88.1 per cent. The observation schedule does, therefore, seem to have been applied with a high degree of consistency.

Qualitative data were collected using two different approaches. The first involved the collection of 'critical events' that is, instances of classroom behaviour which the observer judged to be illustrative of some aspect of the teacher's class management, perhaps a rule being established, observed or broken, an aspect of interpersonal relationships or some other indicative event. The 'critical events' approach is based on the 'critical incidents' technique developed by Flanagan (1949). The observer wrote down what led up to the event, what happened and what the outcome was. After the lesson, teachers were interviewed and asked for their perception of what happened. The interviewer used neutral language like 'Can you tell me about ... ?' rather than loaded or leading questions, such as 'Why didn't you ... ?'

The second source of qualitative data was through the use of three photographs in the interviews with teachers. These were employed in other parts of the Leverhulme Primary Project to interview student teachers, class teachers, supply teachers and pupils. The first photograph showed two pupils pushing each other, second was of a class bursting into a room after break, and, the third showed a girl, who had been told off for scribbling on a pupils's book, standing at the front of the class and muttering, 'Old cow', under her breath. These photographs were selected from a larger sample of pictures which had been piloted as being illustrative of different types of deviance: a common piece of group misbehaviour (rushing into the room), a quarrel between a small group, with minor aggressive physical contact, and a more serious piece of misbehaviour involving damage to property and audible insult to the teacher. Teachers are asked how they would react were these events to happen in their own classroom.

We obtained, therefore, a considerable amount of data from the sixty teachers in the sample: structured lesson observations, critical events and interview statements.

Strategies observed

A wide range of lesson settings was covered for the whole sample. Most of the lesson segments, 58 per cent in all, covered mixed subject matter. Of the rest, 13 per cent were exclusively maths, 13 per cent English, 8 per cent humanities, 5 per cent science, and 1 per cent art, physical education and technology. None was exclusively music. The ages of classes ranged from 4 up to 12, with 18 per cent in reception or year 1 classes, 28 per cent in years 2 and 3, 28 per cent in years 4 and 5, and 26 per cent in years 6 and 7. In each lesson segment, the predominant type of activity was recorded, and Table 3.2 shows the breakdown according to whether the teacher was acting solo, for example, addressing the whole class, whether there was teacher–pupil interaction, if the pupils working with or without the teacher monitoring, or if there was a transition from one activity to another. In each case, the one predominant activity during the period of observation was noted.

The principal choice of working strategy by primary teachers in this sample, therefore, is for a two-thirds to one-third split between individual or group work and whole-class teaching. Of the larger category – that is, pupils working singly or in groups – almost all of it was being monitored by the teacher. In the case of whole-class teaching, about two-thirds involved teacher–pupil interaction and the remaining third usually the teacher addressing the class, often explaining the topic, telling a story or presenting information.

When we looked at misbehaviour, we found that very little of what was observed was serious, only 2 per cent deviant behaviour being coded in that category, the other 98 per cent being coded as 'mild'. What tended to happen was that in just over half the lesson segments analysed there was some minor misbehaviour. Coding was done quite strictly, so if, out of thirty pupils, one distracted another that would have been registered under the 'one pupil' category. Table 3.3 shows the number of pupils involved when misbehaviour was noted.

In about a fifth of cases, two to four pupils were involved, and in another fifth of cases it was five pupils or more. Very often this would be a single group: frequently, thought not always, boys sitting round the same table. The most common form of misbehaviour was noisy or illicit talk, which was noted in just under

Table 3.2 Predominant type of activity in each of 1,195 lesson segments observed for the whole sample

Activity	Percentage of occurrences
Teacher solo	9.7
Teacher–pupil interaction	20.6
Pupils working, teacher monitoring	63.4
Pupils working, teacher not monitoring	2.3
Transition with movement	1.5
Transition without movement	2.5
Total	100.0

Note: Whole sample = 48 teachers and 12 student teachers.

Table 3.3 Number of pupils involved in misbehaviour during lesson segments

Number of pupils involved	Percentage of occasions
No misbehaviour	44.6
One pupil	16.5
Two to four pupils	19.5
Five or more pupils	19.4
Total	100.0

Note: Whole sample = 48 teachers and 12 student teachers.

a third of lesson segments. Inappropriate movement, like leaving the seat without permission, when it should have been requested, or running, was the second most frequent form of misbehaviour, occurring in just over a quarter of lesson segments. Inappropriate use of materials – for example, twanging a ruler – occurred in 10 per cent of lesson segments. Defiance of the teacher, in fourth place, was observed in 8 per cent. Table 3.4 shows these and some minor categories of misbehaviour.

Almost always when misbehaviour did take place the teacher responded, usually before the deviance had escalated. Only in 9 per cent of cases was there no response. The most common responses were an order to cease or a reprimand, sometimes both, usually involving one or more pupils being named. Table 3.5

Table 3.4 Percentage of lesson segments in which various kinds of misbehaviour occurred

Types of misbehaviour	Percentage of occurrences
1 Noisy or illicit talk	32.9
2 Inappropriate movement	26.4
3 Inappropriate use of materials	10.3
4 Defiance of teacher	8.3
5 Taking something without permission	1.8
6 Physical aggression towards another pupil	1.4
7 Illicit copying	0.6
8 Damage to materials/equipment	0.3
9 Insult to teacher	0.3
10 Illicit eating or drinking	0.3
11 Refusal to move	0.1

Note: Total sample = 1,195 lesson segments.

Table 3.5 Teachers' responses to misbehaviour

Teachers' responses to misbehaviour		Percentage of occurrences
A1	To whole class	26
A2	To group	38
A3	To individuals	36
B1	Before escalation of misbehaviour	94
B2	After escalation of misbehaviour	6
C1	Order to cease	72
C2	Pupil named	68
C3	Reprimand	45
C4	Involve pupils in work	26
C5	Proximity (going over to pupil)	22
C6	Touch	16
C7	Facial expression	15
C8	Gesture	13
C9	Pause	7
C10	Pupil moved	5
C11	Praise/encouragement	4
C12	Humour	4
D1	Teacher response brief	78
D2	Teacher response sustained	22

Note: Total sample = 1,195 lesson segments.

Table 3.6 Outcomes of teachers' interactions, shown as a percentage of all responses

Outcome of teacher interaction	Percentage of occurrences
A1 Pupil(s) silent	90
A2 Pupil(s) accept(s) teacher's action	6
A3 Pupil(s) altercate(s) or protest(s)	4
B1 Misbehaviour ends	79
B2 Misbehaviour lessens	15
B3 Misbehaviour is sustained	5
B4 Misbehaviour increases	1
C1 Teacher calm	90
C2 Teacher agitated	8
C3 Teacher angry	2

Note: Total sample = 1,195 lesson segments.

shows the distribution of teachers' responses and the most common as well as some less frequently occurring categories. A1 to A3 figures show the targets of the response, B1 and B2 the times, C1 to C12 actual strategies, and D1 and D2 the length of the response.

Reprimanding the pupils who were misbehaving, often to re-involve them in their work, was a common strategy, as were other non-verbal forms of behaviour like gesture and facial expression. Touching was usually to steer pupils away, tap them on the shoulder or turn them round, not physical punishment, which was not observed once. Confiscation of objects, ridicule, detention and the involvement of other teachers, including the head, were all rare, occurring on 1 per cent or less of occasions. The involvement of another teacher was only seen seven times in the whole set of observations. The outcome of these interactions can be seen in Table 3.6, in which A1 to A3 give pupils' reactions, B1 to B4 reveal whether the misbehaviour increased, decreased, remained the same or not, and C1 to C3 show whether the teacher appeared calm, agitated or angry.

The summary of outcomes confirms the general orderliness. Mostly, teachers dealt calmly with the minor deviance which occurred, like noisy talk or unauthorised movement. In most cases, the immediate outcome was that misbehaviour ended or lessened, though other acts of minor deviance might recur later. Relatively few pupils challenged the teacher, only 4 per cent occurrences of altercating or protesting were observed. In about 7 per cent of lesson segments, the level of deviant behaviour was labelled 'high', which was interpreted as five or more witnessed acts of misbehaviour. The overall picture of primary classrooms observed in this particular study, therefore, is one of several minor irritations that affect harmonious working, rather than large insurrections or mayhem.

Classrooms in different contexts

Lessons were observed in a variety of contexts; some with older pupils, others with younger; some in city schools, others in more rural areas. It is worth considering what, if any, differences were found in these various circumstances, though it must be stressed that any descriptions in this chapter are of the present sample only. It would not be wise to generalise what is reported here to all classrooms in the regions or according to age groups. This is strictly a report of one study. All tables

Table 3.7 Percentages of different categories of teacher and pupil behaviour of experienced teachers in three regions

Category	North-west	South-west	London
Teacher solo	12	5	5
Teacher–pupil interaction	13	20	30
Pupils working, teachers monitoring	69	66	59
No misbehaviour	43	50	50
Noisy or illicit talk	29	25	36
Inappropriate movement	33	24	15
Inappropriate use of materials	9	9	10
Defiance of teacher	9	8	7
Order to cease	69	68	66
Pupil named	67	67	71
Reprimand	44	36	56
Involve pupils in work	29	44	10
Pupil(s) silent	94	84	85
Pupil(s) altercate(s) or protest(s)	2	3	12
Misbehaviour ends	86	78	84
Misbehaviour sustained	4	8	0
Teacher calm	89	94	93

Note: The study included experienced teachers only, students excluded.

and discussion in the remainder of this chapter refer to the sample of forty-eight experienced teachers only.

As shown in Table 3.1, there were 100 lessons observed in the North-west, 56 in the South-west and 35 in the East End of London. Table 3.7 shows the distribution obtained in each of those three locations on some of the major categories from the classroom observation schedule. The overall patterns in the three regions are more notable for their similarities than their differences. Categories of misbehaviour such as 'defiance of teacher' and 'inappropriate use of materials' occur on a virtually identical scale in each of the three locations. Teachers' strategies such as 'order to cease' and 'pupil moved' are also similar in distribution. The results have not been subjected to analysis of variance or any other statistical procedure for determining whether the differences between groups are statistically significant, as this would make them look more precise than they are. In the London schools there is a tendency for slightly more teacher–pupil interaction and a lower frequency of pupils working alone or in groups, with the teacher monitoring, than in the others. Noisy or illicit talk is slightly higher in London, but inappropriate movement is lower, the North-west showing highest incidence of this. South-west teachers were less likely to use reprimand and most likely to re-involve pupils in their work, a strategy more rarely used by the London teachers. London children were more likely to altercate or protest at the teacher's action than pupils in the other two places. However, it is worth repeating that these tentative findings refer only to the present sample and should not be generalised to whole regions, until significant numbers or other research projects report similar trends, and regional comparisons are very rare in classroom observation research.

Another aspect of context worth exploring in the similarities and differences in patterns across age groups. Table 3.8 shows the sample split into three different age groups, infant age, covering the reception class, and years 1 and 2, that is, children aged from 4 to 7; lower juniors, which consisted of years 3 and 4 with children aged

Table 3.8 Percentages of different categories of teacher and pupil behaviour with three age groups

Category	Age group		
	4–7	*7–9*	*9–12*
Teacher solo	7	9	14
Teacher–pupil interaction	22	22	18
Pupils working, teacher monitoring	65	65	61
No misbehaviour	46	32	54
Noisy or illicit talk	32	46	25
Inappropriate movement	27	36	18
Inappropriate use of materials	8	15	8
Defiance of teacher	6	12	5
Order to cease	70	76	69
Pupil named	62	69	61
Reprimand	43	51	39
Involve pupils in work	34	26	20
Proximity (going over to pupil)	23	23	19
Touch	30	13	7
Facial expression	13	19	11
Pupil(s) silent	95	90	85
Pupil(s) altercate(s) or protest(s)	4	5	4
Misbehaviour ends	87	69	85
Misbehaviour lessens	10	22	11
Misbehaviour sustained	2	9	4
Teacher calm	96	84	94

Note: The three age groups included reception class, year 1, year 2 (4–7 year olds); years 3 and 4 (7–9 year olds); years 5, 6 and 7 (9–12 year olds).

from 7 to 9; and upper juniors, which was classes 5, 6 and 7, children aged from 9 to 12, as there were some older middle-school groups in the sample. The three groups made up 28, 32 and 40 per cent of the sample respectively. Some very interesting trends and differences can be seen when different age groups are compared. The first striking feature is that there is more misbehaviour in the classes of younger junior pupils aged 7–9 than there is amongst infants or older primary pupils.

Whereas misbehaviour occurred in about half the lesson segments we analysed for infant and older juniors, in year 3 and 4 classes of younger juniors it was observed in about two-thirds. Consequently, Table 3.8 shows a noticeably higher incidence of noisy or illicit talk, inappropriate movement or use of materials, defiance of the teacher, as well as more reprimands, orders to cease and naming of pupils. Misbehaviour is less likely to end, though more likely to lessen, and also more likely to be sustained at the same level as before the teacher's intervention, and teachers are less calm. In order to check whether a degree of distortion may have occurred because of one or two especially badly behaved classes in a particular year group, we compared the separate profiles for 7–8 year olds and 8–9 year olds. They were virtually identical, noisy or illicit talk being 46 per cent for both year groups, no misbehaviour 32 per cent for both, defiance of the teacher 12 per cent for both, and reprimand being 51 and 49 per cent respectively.

Least misbehaviour was recorded with the oldest pupils and there were certain interesting trends across age groups. The most obvious difference in teachers' responses to misbehaviour is the sharply diminishing occurrence of touch from

30 to 15 to 7 in the three groups. Touch is not always a hostile act, like pushing someone into place or tapping them sharply on the shoulder. With younger children it was sometimes an affectionate hug or an arm around the shoulder. Touch and proximity were often observed together in infant classes. The teacher would go over to a misbehaving pupil and steer the pupil gently back to the task in hand, hence the higher incidence of the category 'involve pupils in work' with younger children. With older pupils there is much more of a touch taboo. Specific examples of these aspects are given in the section 'Managing children's behaviour and work' when the qualitative date are described.

Another feature we decided to investigate was whether there were differences between morning and afternoon activities. Some primary schools prefer a 'drills' and 'frills' approach, with more structured work or basic activities in core subjects like English and mathematics in the morning, and more project work and choosing in the afternoons. Others make no such distinctions. Inevitably we observed more morning lessons than afternoon sessions, about three-quarters of the observations being before lunch, as in all the schools we studied the morning half-day was longer, often much more so, than the afternoon period. We were also interested to see, as teachers sometimes said in interview that children were more tired in the afternoon and more likely to misbehave, whether this really was the case. Table 3.9 shows some morning and afternoon comparisons.

The profiles of morning and afternoon sessions are quite similar. There is slightly more teacher solo or teacher–pupil interaction in the afternoons and slightly less misbehaviour, though the incidence of noisy or illicit talk, inappropriate use of materials and defiance of teacher are all a little higher. Teachers tended to use more reprimands and were less likely to re-involve the pupils in their work, and misbehaviour was less likely to end after a teacher intervention, but these differences were all relatively small rather than dramatic. Nonetheless, the evidence here does corroborate, to a moderate degree, some teachers' belief that afternoon sessions contain more misbehaviour.

Table 3.9 Percentages of different categories of teacher and pupil behaviour in morning and afternoon sessions

Category	Morning	Afternoon
Teacher solo	9	12
Teacher–pupil interaction	19	27
Pupils working, teacher monitoring	66	53
No misbehaviour	46	39
Noisy or illicit talk	31	40
Inappropriate movement	26	27
Inappropriate use of materials	9	13
Defiance of teacher	7	12
Order to cease	71	76
Pupil named	67	69
Reprimand	42	55
Involve pupils in work	29	16
Pupil(s) silent	90	90
Pupil(s) altercate(s) or protest(s)	4	6
Misbehaviour ends	81	74
Misbehaviour sustained	5	5
Teacher calm	92	86

Table 3.10 Range of involvement and deviance scores obtained for total sample

Measure	Involvement score	Deviance score
Average of whole group	71	5
Lowest average for individual teacher (four lessons)	38	0
Lowest score for individual lesson	28	0
Highest average for individual teacher (four lessons)	92	20
Highest score for individual lesson	100	26

The evidence we obtained from the individual pupil studies, which allowed the calculation of task involvement and deviance levels, largely confirmed what has already been described in this chapter. Involvement and deviance index scores can, in theory, range from 0 to 100, but in practice the range is much smaller. During each observation period, every pupil in the class was observed in turn for twenty seconds. The average scores for the whole sample were 71 for involvement and 5 for deviance. What this means in practice is that if, during the lesson observed, there were thirty children in the class, average scores would be obtained for involvement and deviance as follows: the average involvement score of 71 would mean that about sixteen of the class would be engaged in the task in hand, whatever that might be – working individually, listening to the teacher, answering a question – but about three or four pupils, often in the same group, might be not working on their task, or be engaged in mild misbehaviour, most frequently talking to their neighbours instead of working, or moving round the room when they should have been at their place. The range of involvement and deviance scores is shown in Table 3.10. This reveals that individual lesson scores would range from as low as 0 up to 26 for deviance, and from 28 to 100 for involvement.

At the extremes, a score of 0 for deviance means no one misbehaved at all during the period of observation and 100 for involvement meant that every child observed was fully devoted to the task in hand. A score of 26 for deviance would be obtained in a class of thirty if sixteen pupils were misbehaving in a mildly deviant fashion and the other fourteen were behaving well, and an involvement score of 28 would result if, for example, five pupils were seen to be highly involved in the task, seven were medium involved, and the other eighteen were not involved in what they were supposed to be doing. Involvement and deviance scores alone are not, it must be stressed, measures of effective teaching and learning. After all, it would be possible to obtain a deviance score of 0 and an involvement score of 100 by terrorising children into copying out telephone directories. They are rough-and-ready estimates of attentiveness to the task and pupil behaviour. As will be shown in the section 'Managing children's behaviour and work', some teachers teach in very difficult inner-city schools with large classes of unruly pupils, and others are in smaller orderly communities. These figures may well be related to the quality of teaching, but they are not absolute measures of it. One would expect there to be a high inverse correlation between attentiveness and deviance, the more of the one the less of the other, and indeed the highly significant correlation obtained was -0.56***.

Teachers' decision-making

Teachers were asked in interview to say how they would react to the situations seen in the three photographs shown to them, as described earlier in this chapter.

The most common replies, in descending order of frequency of mention, are given below. Some teachers gave more than one response to a situation.

Picture A (two children seen pushing each other)

Introduction   'You're sitting with your back to this group when you hear a noise. You turn round and see two children messing about. You have told them off once that day for not getting on with their work. What if anything do you do?'

1   Separate the two children.
2   Find out what has happened (many of these also included movement, either by the teacher or the teacher calling the pupils over).
3   It would depend on the children/their expectations/children's response/school sanctions.
4   Look at the task the children are supposed to be doing and reassess it, check it or discuss it.
5   Tell them off/comment on the behaviour.
6   See it as time-wasting and so get them back to work.
7   Punish (this usually meant keeping the children in if they hadn't finished the work or because they had already been told off).
8   Threaten punishment or warn the children.

Other mentions   Shout or express emotion, send to the head, seat them next to the teacher, keep an eye on them, ask the class to reflect, throw them a glance/stare.

By far the most popular response, with almost two-thirds of teachers choosing this strategy, was to separate the children in some way. A number of these mentioned that this course of action would be taken because the children had already been warned:

> I'd separate them immediately, because if they'd already been warned, they'd had their opportunity to behave...I would just separate them, one at one end of the room and one at the other end of the room.

> If I'd already told them off once, I'd probably separate them straight away, either take one off the table...move them to the front of the class, whatever the system is. ...I might be tempted to say, 'Look, what's going on?' but if I'd already told them off once that day I don't think I'd question them, I'd just separate them...to stop the distraction.

Picture B (class rushing into the room after break)

Introduction   'This class has just been out for break. They come running back into the room, pushing each other, squealing and laughing. What, if anything, do you do?'

1   Send them outside and make them come in again.
2   Stop them as they come in.
3   Talk about their behaviour, which included pointing out the dangers of rushing into the room.
4   Seat the children.
5   It depends on the circumstances.
6   Tell off/pass comment on behaviour.

Other mentions   Get them to return to work, ignore it, keep them in, reassess the room's layout, shout at them.

The overwhelming response, given by nearly 80 per cent of respondents, was to send the children out. Many teachers gave reasons for their reaction, explaining that they wanted to calm pupils down or that they felt the class ought to know better:

> I would probably get them all to sit down in an area like this [pointing to one part of the classroom], an area where they can all sit down, and tell them that they are going to calm down and that break time is over, and if that isn't effective, I'd probably read a story to them to get them calmed down. ...

Others merely saw their action as punitive in a self-explanatory way:

> I'd make them all sit down and be quiet and then I'd say, 'Right! We're going back into the playground, and when I blow the whistle, line up at the door and walk in quietly.' And we'd just keep doing it over and over again, really, just wasting time, until they managed to come in quietly and sit down.

Picture C (girl scribbles on books and calls teacher 'old cow')

Introduction   'You have caught this girl scribbling on someone else's book. You have told her off in front of the class and you hear her mutter "old cow" under her breath. The children near by snigger. What, if anything, do you do?'

1   Speak to her on her own, now or later, to discuss her behaviour.
2   Show emotion – anger, sarcasm, upset, humour.
3   It would depend on the child.
4   Send to the head.
5   Involve the whole class in some way.
6   Punish the girl.
7   Ask her to repeat it.
8   Tell her off.
9   Ignore the behaviour.

Other mentions   Withdraw her, make a joke of it, be seen to deal with it, get her to rub out the scribbling.

About half the teachers gave the most common response, which was to avoid public confrontation by seeing the girl on her own:

> I would certainly take her somewhere and speak to her quietly. I wouldn't want to have a confrontation with her in front of the other children. I would deal with it (myself)...I would either take her aside, or take her to a quiet part of the classroom, where I could speak to her softly and sort it out from there.

About a quarter of respondents described how they would give some emotional reaction to signal to the girl and the class how they felt:

> I'd put her in a withdrawal situation. It would all depend on how I was feeling at the time. If I was level-headed and taking it very calmly...I'd say, 'You go over there and I'll talk to you later on. At the moment if I talk to you I'll get

too angry' and I'll explain to the others there may be reasons behind why she's doing this.... The group make themselves an audience and could send her up to be more of an actress than she need be...(I'd) talk about being more understanding (to the class).... I might know what the child's like...there's certainly a lot of investigative work can be done there.

Most teachers responded quickly and without hesitation to each of the pictures, and this confirmed not only the conclusions in the research literature on speed of decision-making, but also the findings of our own research, that teachers usually responded before the escalation of deviance. Teachers make thousands of decisions every week, often with only a second or so in which to sum up a vast amount of visual information, past histories, precedents, consequences, context factors and individual differences, so it is not surprising that most responded fairly quickly. Many of the popular strategies involved some degree of confrontation rather than evasion, though the exact opposite was the case in the third picture when personal insult to the teacher was involved.

The most common inclination in the first two pictures was to engage in a mild to medium confrontation of the situation, with immediate counter-measures: separate quarrelling pupils, send the class outside. In the case of the personal insult, it is a delaying strategy, a private conversation rather than a public harangue, possibly held later when the emotions on both sides have subsided. Occasionally, the suggestion was to ignore what had happened, but this was relatively rare. Telling off is the most common reaction predicated by pupils, but it is lower down the list in teachers' minds.

Another strategy proposed with the pictures, but not always observed so frequently in the classrooms of the teachers who advocated it, was that of reasoning and negotiation. Looking for explanations, asking children why they did something, was indeed a feature of some teachers' lessons, but the immediate pressure to respond to misbehaviour sometimes meant that such intentions evaporated in the heat of real classroom aggravation. On the other hand, the events in the photographs are a little more dramatic than the illicit chatter and movement which make up most classroom misbehaviour, so one cannot expect complete congruence. Many teachers did show, in their responses to these photographs, glimpses into their behaviour which mirrored their actual classroom practice. In a small number of cases there was a large gulf between armchair decision-making and the real thing.

Managing children's behaviour and work

It is 8.20 a.m. in the downtown area of a large Northern city. As the bleak morning light flickers across the broken tiles and the for years unpointed brickwork of the grim terraced houses round about, the first few pupils and teachers are arriving at school. In the playground lies a dead rat. How had it perished? There is speculation among pupils and staff. Perhaps someone had shot it with an air rifle, or maybe it had just finally breathed its last in the grimy environment in which it had spent its brief existence. It lay there, another symbol of decay and neglect in a crumbling inner city. Meanwhile the head greeted our project researcher with the news that this was a tough school in a tough area. There had been 13 break-ins in the last 13 months – even the few plants in front of the school had been dug up and removed. In a nearby school we visited, a pupil proudly told his teacher that his father had been on television. Pleased at this mark of recognition of an otherwise ignored sector of society, she enquired what programme he had appeared in. The answer was BBC national news. He had been shown throwing slates from the roof of a prison during a jail riot.

In a pretty town in another part of the country it is also 8.20 a.m. This is no wealthy commuter belt community, just a small market town in the south of England with a low crime rate and a more rural aspect. An abundance of green surrounds the local school, with small gardens, mainly well tended, a patch of grass and several trees. The children arriving are certainly not from rich families, quite the reverse, nor do they look sedated as they walk or jog into the playground, but the contrast with the city environment described earlier is a sharp one. The head greets our project researcher with a friendly welcome. She has a big problem today, she tells him, as the caretaker is away and he normally carries the heavy television equipment across to the temporary classroom in the playground. It seems a million miles away from the inner-city school charged with educating children in some of the most desperate circumstances found in our society.

Yet just as some classrooms fill out the stereotypes, others belie them. During the Leverhulme Primary Project we occasionally observed badly behaved classes in what looked to be idyllic surroundings and orderly classes in the most unpromising environments. As will be described later we sometimes saw two teachers in the same school, one with a high degree of task involvement and orderliness, the other with lower pupil application and more misbehaviour. Social conditions certainly do affect class management, but they are not the sole determinants of it. This section will give some further detail to flesh out the quantitative data described earlier.

Maintaining classroom rules

Classroom rules and conventions establish the framework within which learning takes place. Once the school year is under way many rules are so firmly established that they need no further reiteration. Others demand constant fine-tuning, especially those to do with noisy or illicit pupil talk, which was shown to be the most frequent form of deviant behaviour in the previous section. What constitutes 'noise' rather than normal conversation is a variable rather than a fixed concept. Some teachers' tolerance is quite high, whereas that of other teachers may be low. Young children in particular, partly because their voices are at a higher pitch, partly because they are not always fully socialised in whatever passes for 'acceptable' levels of excited conversation, were reminded frequently about the issue, sometimes with a dramatic display, as in the case of a reception class taught by an experienced teacher in a London school where we observed:

Teacher: (in a loud public voice, sounding shocked)
Stop! (The class falls quiet. Pause.) All the children in the home corner come out! (Children playing in the far corner of the classroom come forward sheepishly.) Why do you think I've asked you to come out?
Pupil: Because we're shouting.
Teacher: That's right. Now please go back and work quietly. (Children return to their corner and the noise level remains lower.)

In this particular instance the teacher chose a minor public shaming. She could have gone over to the children concerned and spoken directly to the small group involved, but she felt a rule was being broken that children were expected to know, as they revealed when they answered her question correctly. The minor public shaming was a demonstration and reaffirmation of the rule, and the likely consequences of breaking it, to others in the class. It illustrates a common sequence of events well understood by pupils: talk too loud = get told off in public. As a strategy it was in this instance, 'effective', if the chief criterion is whether it led to more tolerable levels of noise enabling others to work unimpaired, 'skilful' if the criteria are first of all exercising the vigilance necessary to pick up possible disruption before it escalates, and second to deal with it in a way that is understood and complied with by the pupils, and 'acceptable' if one takes as indicative of that term the pupils' apparent lack of resentment or hostility to the teacher's action.

Some rules have been made explicit, but children do not subsequently generalise them to every situation, so the teacher may then make the specific instance public. In a London class of 6–7 year olds there was a rule that equipment and materials must be put away. In one lesson a group of children had been painting and an apron had been left out:

Teacher: (calls back the children who had been working at the table concerned)
Who was wearing a red apron?
Pupils: (No reply.)
Teacher: (pause)
Will you put it back, please? (Child returns apron to storage space.) If you need an apron you need to get it yourself . . . and you need to put it back in the right place. I'm not going to do it for you. (Pause.) Now, off you go. (Children return to their tasks.)

This reaffirmation of a specific instance of a rule in a specific context occurred frequently with the second most common form of perceived misbehaviour in the present study, inappropriate movement, when pupils left their seat without permission, at the wrong time, to the wrong place, or in the wrong manner. In a class of 7–8 year olds in the North-west there was a rule that children wanting to solicit the teacher's attention were to raise their hand and wait. This rule causes difficulties for pupils, as they may wait for some time if the teacher is engrossed with one pupil, so three children walk over to where the teacher is standing:

Teacher: (making a show of counting them)
Now why are there one, two, three, people here? (One pupil returns to his seat and raises his hand. The teacher walks past the other two.) Peter's got his hand up, so I'm going over to him. (The other two sit down and raise their hands.) How many children are out of their seats? One, two . . . (Points and counts.)

The problem with this rule is that there is a price to pay for it. If children are not to leave their seat frequently to solicit the teacher's attention, then two conditions must obtain. First of all, the teacher must be perpetually vigilant, otherwise several children can sit, arms aloft, for inordinate lengths of time. Second, the teacher must establish a high degree of pupil independence which minimises the number of occasions when they will need to approach her. Many of the questions we observed asked by children standing in line to see the teacher, or sitting at their table waiting, were simple to answer, like how to spell a word when there were dictionaries in the room, or what to do next, when the answer was turn the page and carry on, or check your answers.

In a different classroom with 8–9 year olds in the North-west we observed an application of this rule which revealed the need for consistency. Some children put up their hands, others went over to the teacher. From time to time the teacher would attempt to delineate and reinforce the rule by sending someone away. On one occasion she said to a pupil, 'Go and sit down and put your hand up if you want help.' After thirty seconds she went over to him and answered his question. She then told another child not to interrupt her, but answered the questions of other pupils when they interrupted. One girl sat for over five minutes with her arm aloft and remained unnoticed until she called out, 'Miss', in frustration. The teacher then went over to her. It was easy to see what the rule was meant to be: put up your hand if you want help, and don't interrupt. It was much more difficult in practice, however, for children to see a pattern to breaches of the rule, because there did not seem to be one. The details of the rule were diffuse, ill-defined and unevenly reinforced. As a consequence, the lessons were full of instances of roaming pupils punctuated by sporadic and largely ineffectual reminders of what the rule was supposed to be.

Successful maintenance of classroom rules, irrespective of how they had originally been introduced or negotiated, appeared to require clarity of purpose, understanding and assent from the pupils, fair-minded and appropriate interpretation or adaptation in the relevant context, and consistent application and reinforcement. Absence of some or all of these conditions was often accompanied by a higher incidence of misbehaviour by pupils.

Maintaining interpersonal relationships

While some teachers continued to make use of some public displays of anger or to use minor shaming, rather than outright humiliation, to keep order, as Table 3.5 showed, about three-quarters of teachers' responses to misbehaviour were addressed to individuals or small groups rather than the whole class. Interactions with individual pupils can exert a powerful influence on the genesis and maintenance of personal relationships. Acts by the teacher which had positive or negative effects were noted by observers on numerous occasions. In most classrooms positive affect outweighed negative affect, but the obverse was also seen occasionally. Here are some instances, under several headings, of both positive and negative teacher behaviour which appeared to affect relationships and which was witnessed by researchers during the project:

1   Academic

    (a) Explaining patiently to a pupil who does not understand a new concept.
    (b) Making a sarcastic remark to someone who does not understand a new concept.

2   Managerial

    (a) Smiling at and thanking someone who has helped clear away.
    (b) Blaming someone for a mess, choosing wrong pupil.

3   Social

    (a) Talking to children as they enter the classroom about what they did at the weekend.
    (b) Belittling someone's hobby.

4   Expectation

    (a) Looking for positive qualities and achievements in children.
    (b) Having low expectations or always focusing on the negative side of pupils' work or behaviour.

5   Home/school

    (a) Talking positively with parents and members of pupils' communities.
    (b) Showing little or no interest in children's origins and values.

6   Individual

    (a) Taking a personal interest in a child as an individual.
    (b) Seeing the class as a group without individual identities.

There were many examples of teachers working in very difficult circumstances who made special efforts to raise the self-image of their pupils. One teacher of 5 year olds in a school in an exceptionally difficult area made numerous positive references to children. A child who arrives in tears and who has had no breakfast is first comforted and then taken to the reading corner. Shortly afterwards her tears have ceased and she is happily engaged in a piece of work. The teacher calls the class her 'smarties' ('Time for my smarties to go to assembly'), the combination of the name of a well-known sweet and the suggestion that the children are all 'smart' being well received by the class.

Some of the most striking examples of a predominantly positive climate of relationships were observed in the classroom which contained children who did not speak English as their first language. In establishing and maintaining interpersonal relationships most people rely heavily on spoken language, even though non-verbal cues and messages may play a part. Touch was noted much more frequently with younger children, especially when children cried or appeared upset, when the teacher would often put her arm round them. Stripped of language, however, the most obvious form of communication, many would find establishing good harmonious relationships very difficult. In the classrooms of all the London teachers we observed, in those of some of the North-west teachers, but very few of the South-west teachers, there were one or two, occasionally several, non-English-speakers. Most teachers made special efforts to establish positive relationships by involving pupils as well as themselves, as this event, noted in a London classroom, reveals.

There is a new pupil in the class of 11–12 year olds who has just moved to England and who speaks very little English. Often there are fellow speakers in the case of languages like Bengali and the teacher assigns a 'translator' from amongst the pupils, but on this occasion no one else in the class speaks his language. The class is studying Europe, and the teacher is writing the names of European countries on the blackboard. Pupils are suggesting names she can add. The new boy raises his hand and says 'France', following a whispered conversation with his neighbour, Michael. The teacher praises him fulsomely, 'Well done, Stefan, good boy.' In the interview following the lesson she explains how she has assigned Michael to help Stefan. She had discussed with the class how they could all help someone who did not speak English. Michael had sat beside Stefan and looked at the map with him, whispering to him the names of countries when he had indicated them.

Even well intended teachers, however, can fall short of their own aspirations amid the sustained distractions of classroom life, and risk arousing animosity by a piece of unfairness. A 6-year-old boy was seen in one classroom to tidy up voluntarily some pieces of equipment that had been left scattered across the floor. He had initiated this himself, even though he had not been using the pieces. The teacher went over to him and told him to leave them and go and do some printing instead. He did as he was asked, leaving 5 or 6 pieces still on the floor. About twenty-five minutes later the teacher came over to where he was printing, took him by the hand to where the remaining pieces still lay on the floor, told him it was untidy to have left them and he should now pick them up. Without protest or altercation he did so and then returned quietly to his printing. In over 90 per cent of cases where we saw a reprimand given to a pupil the target was judged to be fair by the observer, but in those cases where it was not, personal relationships could easily be soured. Unfairness is one of the events pupils resent most deeply.

Some teachers were so concerned about fairness in their relationships that they engaged in extended negotiation with pupils. Negotiated rules were relatively infrequent in our observations, as most were determined either explicitly by the teacher or implicitly by the pupils in terms of what they actually did. In the school in the North-west the extrinsic rewards and punishments system was built around house points and stars. Pupils doing well or badly could gain or lose points for their house team. One day the teacher gives Patricia house points for a piece of work:

Pupil 1: That's not fair, she shouldn't get that many points.
Teacher: All right. I'll give you one point Patricia. Are you all happy with that decision?
Pupil 2: No, it's still not fair.
Teacher: Well, can anybody suggest a way we can overcome the problem?
Pupil 3: Give everybody a point.
Pupil 4: No, that's silly. Don't give Patricia a point at all.
Pupil 5: Give her a star instead. It's worth a star but not house points.
Teacher: All those that agree with Mary's suggestion put up your hands. Right, that's virtually everybody. Are you happy with that decision, Patricia? (Patricia nods, smiles and seems to be pleased.)

Just as relationships between the teacher and pupils are regarded as important, so too are interpersonal relationships amongst the children themselves, for all are part of the same classroom culture. Whereas in the case of non-English-speaking Stefan, described earlier, the teacher had made special efforts to involve other pupils in his reception and accommodation within the class, there were examples when teachers appeared to be less effective at resolving problems between pupils.

In a class of 8–9 year olds, three girls were sitting together at the same table. Two of them, Alice and Rachel, would from time to time torment Caroline, the third girl, by refusing to give her a rubber, throwing things at her, preventing her from working. The teacher rarely intervened. Occasionally she would look at Alice's and Rachel's work, but not refer to their behaviour, except indirectly, by saying to Caroline, 'Just ignore them, Caroline, and get on with your work.' Her explanation of this strategy in interview was:

Alice and Rachel are just attention-seekers. Alice in particular is a very unsettled child. She does the same thing in the playground, picks an argument with somebody and runs up to whoever is on duty shouting about the offence being committed against her when in fact she's started it herself, or telling tales about somebody else doing something to somebody. It's a lot of attention-seeking behaviour.

To some extent, by ignoring what she rightly or wrongly judged to be attention-seeking, the teacher was following the tenets of behaviour modification, which decree that 'bad' behaviour should be ignored so that it is extinguished by not being reinforced. However, the corollary to not reinforcing behaviour of which the teacher disapproves is that approved behaviour should be reinforced. The teacher did not appear to find out further information about why Alice sought attention, and this event highlights the dilemma faced by many teachers. Since eliciting deeper-lying causes of antisocial behaviour is not only time-consuming but requires considerable expertise, it is sometimes the case that, during lessons at any rate, misbehaviour is accommodated, contained, treated or ignored, rather than its causes diagnosed.

Disruptive behaviour

The most common source of disruption of a pupil's work was interruption by another pupil or occasionally by the teacher, for reasons other than to monitor what was being done. Occasionally there were aggressive intrusions into the work of an individual, a small group or the whole class, often by a single pupil. In one classroom the same 5-year-old pupil was reprimanded three or four times each time registration was taken and his behaviour dominated the lessons. The teacher usually brought him to sit on the floor next to her during whole class sessions, and as he pulled objects out of the trolley that he wanted to use in the forthcoming activity she would gently take them from him and incorporate them into her explanation of what the children were to do. The demands of this 1 pupil consumed a great deal of her classroom time, and with 27 or 28 others it was often a matter of coping or containing strategies, rather than something which significantly altered his behaviour.

When more than one pupil disrupts, even more time can be consumed. An inexperienced student teacher was seen with a class of 7–8 year olds. Within one minute she asked for quiet seven times, stamped her foot, clapped her hands, named individual pupils, raised her voice, asked pupils to put their hands on their head, but none of these acts reduced the noise level. Once she had given out the maths worksheets, however, the noise diminished and most pupils worked assiduously at them, albeit with occasional conversations. When classes were engaged in work which seemed to them appropriate and worthwhile, such disruption as occurred tended to be caused by individual pupils or occasionally by a small group of 2 or 3 pupils.

As shown in the previous sections, most teachers took action before disruption escalated, often revealing a high degree of vigilance, and were able to split their attention between the child or group they were with and the rest of the class by employing the split glance, demonstrating what Jacob Kounin called 'with-itness'. Frequently, noticing potential disruption and nipping it in the bud took place almost instantaneously. One reception class was reading a book together when a child began to fiddle with the laces on a pair of shoes, distracting others. Within seconds of this beginning the teacher called out, 'Sally, what are you doing? If you play with your shoelaces you won't learn the words. Put your shoes away.' The child complied, but before starting to talk about the next page the teacher glanced up and said, in a firm but friendly manner, 'Now, are you listening, Sally?' There was no further interruption.

By contrast, in another class of 5 year olds four children were playing with scales and bricks. One child hit another, unseen by the teacher, then another boy hit one of the girls, who asked him to stop punching her. He hit her again, so she left the table to work elsewhere. The aggressive boy called out the teacher's name several times. Twice she came over to check his work, but never commented on his behaviour, even though he continued to be noisily aggressive towards others throughout the lesson. Disruption caused by distracting behaviour, chatter, minor teasing and attention-seeking were, in general, easily contained by most teachers. It was the individual aggressive child who caused greatest dismay, both to fellow pupils and to the teacher, and the demands made by such individuals on the teacher's time and energy during a lesson could be considerable.

Yet many of the teachers who encountered this more aggressive style of disruption did deploy strategies which appeared successful in resolving or even eliminating anti-social aggression. Some used extrinsic rewards, like points or stars when the pupil had behaved well. Others eschewed this more formal recognition and made use of extensive praise instead. There were examples of assigning responsibility for some logistical operation, like giving out books or collecting in work, but where these are perceived as privileges, there can be some resentment from other pupils if aggression is thought to have been rewarded and good social behaviour ignored.

Touch was rarely used with older children but it was a common feature with younger pupils, as reported earlier. For example, when a boy was said by others to have been kicking pupils, one teacher said, in a half joking, half serious manner, 'Would you like me to kick him?' and then seized him by the shoulders and pushed him towards a table. Other pupils laughed but the boy's face was expressionless. This is an interesting example of a strategy which was 'successful' in terminating the disruption, but about which opinion might be divided, given the possible apprehension of the boy concerned.

Another teacher, investigating why a 5-year-old girl was crying, found that a boy had hit her. There followed a conversation between the teacher and the two pupils concerned which ended with the teacher telling them to be friends and give each other 'a big hug'. This done, no further aggression was noted. The strategy of looking for the positive was sometimes exemplified by the teacher holding up the disruptive pupil's work for admiration by the rest when he had done especially well.

Classroom routines

The daily repeated rituals of classroom life, arrival, registration, 'circle time' or 'carpet time', where children sit with the teacher to discuss matters of concern, lesson endings, are in many classrooms the secure framework within which transactions take place. In some classrooms these were highly formalised: lined-up supervised entry, great formality over registration, regimented departure. More frequently they were simply regular occurrences which signalled important messages and established or maintained a particular classroom climate.

Teachers showed considerable variation in their use of time. In some classrooms there was little sense of urgency, assignments were open-ended, to be done in the pupil's own time, even if that was slowly paced. Others made the issue of time more public, using group alerting to tell pupils how long there was left or reminding individuals of when they would be expected to have finished. In one class where 'time' was actually the topic of study, two 7-year-old boys had not been working diligently, so the teacher went over to their table, put a clock on it and showed them how long they had to finish the task in hand. When one of the boys had finished, however, he reported to the teacher that the other boy had turned back the clock to give himself more time. The teacher smiled at him, seemed pleased that he had understood time well enough to realise how to create more of it, but then reset the clock and gave him a fresh target.

Within the major routines there were often minor ones. One teacher of 5 year olds whose lesson endings always seemed to pass smoothly would warn children to be ready to stop, and then, when she actually said, 'Stop working', all the pupils put their hands in the air and waved them. 'They're all supposed to waggle their arms in the air,' she explained in interview, 'so I can see they've actually stopped, because I only say "stop!" in order to say something to everybody.' She would then give the class ten seconds to sit on the carpet, which she counted out slowly, taking more than ten seconds so they would not rush, and then announced, 'Give yourself a clap', when all had complied. Many other teachers had established a formal exit at the end of the day, one insisting on a very precise and straight line before anyone was allowed to leave: 'I've asked you to line up and I can see (points finger as she counts) one, two, three, four, five, six, seven, eight not in line.' Major and minor routines were observed on a regular basis in virtually every classroom observed, other than those of a few student teachers.

More effective and less effective management

Taking as two criteria of effectiveness the extent to which pupils were involved in the task and the amount of misbehaviour, it was sometimes possible to see two teachers in the same or a similar environment, where one obtained high task involvement and low deviance, and the other the reverse. Although the class itself can sometimes be the main determinant of such differences, especially when one group contains more disruptive pupils than another, there were occasions when it was not major differences between two classes, but noticeable distinctions between the teaching styles of their teachers, that seemed to explain differences in behaviour. Mrs Abel and Miss Baker taught third-year juniors and second-year juniors respectively in the same school. There were serious social problems in the area, so it was not an easy assignment teaching in that particular school. Yet, as these short accounts reveal, the two teachers were quite different from each other in terms of relationships, amount and quality of work from pupils and classroom climate. Even having a whole-school policy for such matters as discipline cannot always eradicate individual differences in temperament and practice.

Mrs Abel

There is a sense of benign urgency about Mrs Abel's lessons, whether she is checking scores on a maths test and discussing children's 'silly' mistakes, or whether the class is engaged in individual and small group work. There is a rule that children waiting for help must get out their reading book, not sit doing nothing. Yet when she asks questions she says, 'Don't panic', to anyone not sure of an answer and makes extensive use of praise. She seems well prepared and sets tasks which hold and maintain pupils' attention. When there is incipient misbehaviour, she often defuses the situation with quick but pointed humour: 'Jason, it won't help if you're chopping her neck off with a ruler.'

From time to time she alerts the whole class to some matter of principle with specific reference to a particular event. On one occasion a girl has finished maths book No. 4 ahead of the rest. After checking her work she tells the whole class that this deserves a round of applause. In interview she explains that, when she took over the class, they were so far behind what she expected that she has put a high premium on successful achievement: 'We are so far behind in this class with maths...when I got them two were doing second-year work and the rest first-year work, and they were so far behind...so we've made this big thing about every time they finish a particular stage they get praise...they're really proud of themselves if they do it.' When she asked children to pat themselves on the back, some did it literally. Large-scale display of pupils' work around the classroom reinforced this public recognition of positive achievement.

Mrs Abel's high task involvement and low deviance scores (see below) seem to be the result of considerable thought about appropriate work for the class and individuals; extensive use of reinforcement, especially in the form of praise, some private, much public; completely consistent classroom rules, enforced in a benign but firm manner, so that calling out is not a problem and, when it threatens to be, children are reminded of the rule; and a considerable amount of good humour, both from herself and the children, which defuses potential trouble and cements positive interpersonal relationships. She also reminds pupils of the time available and regularly monitors their work, especially those with difficulties. When her pupils were interviewed, for the research on pupil perceptions, many named her as 'the best teacher in the world'.

Miss Baker

At the beginning of lessons Miss Baker quickly announces what pupils will do, but there is a long settling down period and children seem to move around the room, often on what seems to be a purposeless perambulation, before commencing work. Task involvement levels are comparatively low and deviance is higher than average (see below). This can be partly explained by two very noticeable elements. The first is that the rules of behaviour are not always clear or consistently applied, and this relates to the second factor, which is that relationships between pupils and teacher are more negative than in Mrs Abel's classroom.

Some of the instances of misbehaviour exemplify these differences. On one occasion a boy donned a baseball cap. 'Get that hat off. I'm not going to tell you again, young man', the teacher called across the room. He hurled his hat into the centre of the table. The teacher did not comment, though she clearly saw his response. Afterwards the teacher said she had ignored it because 'he was just being silly'. In another lesson, she asked children to put their hands up before speaking. Few did. She also requested them not to walk around the room, but several ignored her. She then shouted at six pupils not in their seats and told one to go out into the corridor. He stayed in the room and she made no comment.

In interview she says, 'They're wasting their time and they're wasting the other children's time. In the last few weeks what I've actually been doing is saying they can't get out of their seats without permission. They've got to put their hands up to tell me why they want to (move) and ask me if they can. It's really just a disruptive thing that I've got.' The intention was clear but the implementation was unsuccessful.

Alongside this inconsistency in rule enforcement is a harsher style of relationship. Praise is rarely used and Miss Baker is frequently critical of the same two target pupils, Darren and Lloyd, even when they are not misbehaving. On one occasion during a PE lesson she drags Lloyd across the hall floor by his legs, shouting at him to be quiet and sit still. Two children giggle. Later she sends him out of the room. He stands by the doorway. 'Remove yourself from that doorway.' He eventually moves. She sends Darren out. Then, when he is leaving the room, she calls him back. He leaves anyway. In interview she says of Lloyd, 'He tends to put on affection. He comes up and cuddles you, but it's all put on, trying to creep to you, attention-seeking...otherwise it's conflict with Darren all the time.'

Miss Baker's relatively low task involvement level and higher deviance rate seem to be related to two principal related factors: the inconsistent application of classroom rules – applying them harshly one moment, ignoring them the next – and negative interpersonal relationships, with few examples of good work being recognised. The only occasion she was seen to smile was once at the end of a school day when all but one group of children had been dismissed. Her answers to the questions posed in the photographs were also more diffuse than Mrs Abel's. For the third picture, where the girl has called the teacher 'old cow', she admitted that this had happened to her, but said she might ignore it, or try to defuse it by saying she did look like an old cow. Mrs Abel, by comparison, felt it was natural to react angrily, but that teachers' anger must be expressed in a proper manner.

During a school year children may spend a thousand or more hours in the company of their class teacher. The cumulative effect of patterns of high involvement and low deviance, or low involvement and high deviance, can be considerable. Mrs Abel's average task involvement score was 84, and her range was from 79 to 94. This means that, typically, out of thirty children, about twenty-three would be observed to be highly involved in their work, about four would be medium involved and two not involved. Given that children must sometimes wait, and that no one concentrates for sixty minutes in every hour, this is a high degree of application.

By contrast, Miss Baker's average task involvement score was 38, with a range of from 28 to 53. In practice this means, in a class of thirty, about seven pupils highly engaged in the task in hand, nine would be medium involved and fifteen would not be engaged, quite a different picture. Mrs Abel's average deviance score was 2, with a range of 0 to 4. This means that one pupil might be mildly misbehaving, say distracting a neighbour. Miss Baker's average deviance score was 20, with a range of from 10 to 26. This would involve say nineteen pupils not misbehaving, ten engaging in minor misbehaviour, and one behaving more badly, perhaps hitting another pupil.

So in one room in the school virtually everyone is working on the task in hand and behaving well; a few doors away, with pupils from a similar social background, about half are not involved in their work and a third are chattering or moving around the room when they should not be. Contemplating one such hour multiplied by 1,000 over a school year may help to explain some aspects of the differences in learning achievement by two classes in similar circumstances at the end of a school year.

CHAPTER 4

CLASS MANAGEMENT DURING TEACHING PRACTICE

Originally published as 'Class Management during Teaching Practice', by Wragg E. C. and Dooley P. A., in E. C. Wragg (ed.), *Classroom Teaching Skills*, Routledge, 1984, pp. 21–46

This study of student and experienced teachers, originally Chapter 2 of my 1984 book *Classroom Teaching Skills*, was another Teacher Education Project perspective on how experienced and student teachers handle their classes in secondary schools. It makes an interesting comparison with the previous chapter on primary teachers' class management strategies and experiences.

Ask student teachers before a block teaching practice to describe any source of apprehension, and they will before long talk about some aspect of class management, using terms like 'keep order', 'have class control' or 'maintain discipline'. Tibble (1959) questioned a sample of student teachers on a PGCE course and found that three-quarters were worried about class control, though after teaching practice only half felt their anxieties had been realised, albeit on a smaller scale than they had envisaged. Wragg (1967) in a study of ninety PGCE students identified the same kind of apprehension, and 'keeping order' was mentioned most frequently when students were asked to reveal anxieties they felt about their first few years of teaching.

Although class management is now a topic which increasingly attracts research interest, it is a contentious field with disagreement about what constitutes an effective classroom climate. Far more studies of classroom interaction have been conducted in recent times than was the case twenty years ago, but relatively little work has been published on class management which was based on direct observation of lessons, and there is almost nothing of this kind on student teachers.

The issues surrounding class management are complex, and Johnson and Brooks (1979) have produced a useful model (see Figure 4.1) which depicts the intricate nexus of relationships between the tasks which society obliges teachers to perform, such as planning and organising lessons, the many kinds of setting in which teaching and learning may take place, the values that teachers and learners may hold, and the tensions between people and amongst roles.

For student teachers on teaching practice, the picture is much more confused. In his classic text *The Theory of Social and Economic Organisation* (1964) Max Weber observed that power in any social relationship is reflected in the probability that one person will be in a position to carry out his own will despite resistance. The apprehension of student teachers before teaching practice is that they may not be able to fulfil their own intentions, and that they will encounter resistance beyond their ability to cope.

Speculation by certain politicians and in-press reports sometimes suggests that schools suffer from considerable disruption, and prominence is frequently given to

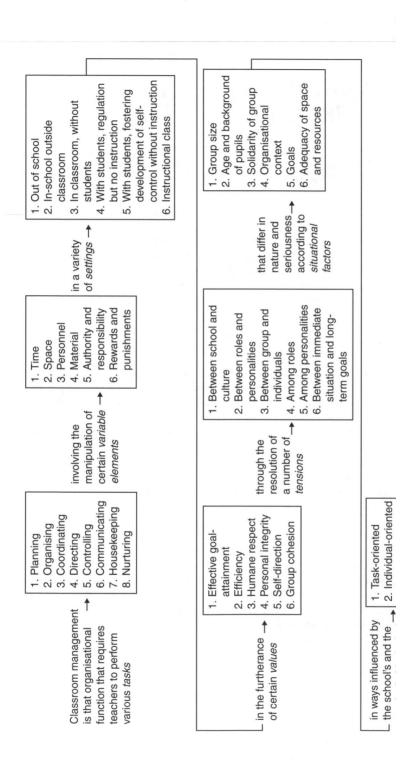

Figure 4.1 A conceptual model of classroom management.
Source: Johnson and Brooks (1979).

reports of riots or violent behaviour when they occur. Systematic enquiry, however, reveals a less alarming picture. The survey of 384 secondary schools by Her Majesty's Inspectorate (DES, 1979) showed that only 25 schools, mainly, though not exclusively, in inner-city areas and older housing estates, reported serious problems of indiscipline, violence between pupils or hostility to teachers.

That serious indiscipline in tough schools can reduce the teacher's ability to teach and the pupils' opportunities to learn was underlined in an American study by Deutsch (1960). He studied classroom procedures in an urban school where teachers spent up to 75 per cent of their time trying to maintain order, with a consequent reduction to as little as 25 per cent being left for actual teaching and learning.

In the absence of any clear picture based on direct observation of how student teachers manage their classes during teaching practice, it was decided early in the Teacher Education Project to study a sample of trainees throughout their long teaching practice, and this chapter describes a two-year enquiry into student teachers' class management which used a mixture of individual case study and quantitative analysis of classroom transactions.

Studies of class management

It is not possible to describe here more than a small amount of the research done in class management, but the field has been surveyed by several writers such as Dunkin and Biddle (1974) and Docking (1980). There is no shortage of 'how to handle classes' books for student teachers, often written by practitioners such as Francis (1975) and Marland (1975) or teacher trainers (Robertson, 1981). Some of the books and pamphlets on class management for teachers try to incorporate research findings, like *Maintaining Discipline in Classroom Instruction* (Gnagey, 1975) and the workbook *Class Management and Control*, which was field-tested as part of the Teacher Education Project by Wragg (1981).

Although a great deal of the research in the field has been undertaken in the last twenty years, American studies by Wickman (1928), who enquired into teachers' definitions of behaviour problems, and the so-called 'attention studies' of the 1920s and 1930s, when an observer sat at the front of the class scanning faces to assemble a simple measure of attentiveness (Jackson, 1968), show that interest in the topic is not entirely recent.

In Britain Highfield and Pinsent (1952) obtained estimates of what were perceived as pupil misdemeanours from a sample of 724 teachers. Restlessness and fidgeting, laziness and boisterous, noisy behaviour were seen as the most common forms of misconduct. During the last ten years several surveys, some by local authorities or teacher associations, addressed the problem of more serious misbehaviour. Lowenstein (1975) intended to show trends in 'violent and obstructive behaviour', but failed to do so because, he claimed, there was a lack of objectivity and accuracy on the part of teachers filling in report forms and describing incidents.

Lawrence *et al.* (1977), in a detailed study of a boys' school, found similar difficulty in eliciting objective responses about misbehaviour. Events were most likely to be reported by teachers if they followed several similar happenings, and the investigator found that teachers tended to report incidents which interfered with their teaching, rather than violent or aggressive behaviour.

Hilsum and Strong (1978), in their study of the working day of 201 secondary teachers in 72 Surrey schools, found teachers averaged less than $1\frac{1}{2}$ minutes of their day disciplining pupils, with a range of from 20 down to no instances per day, and an average of 9. They concluded, 'in the current climate of allegations of indiscipline in schools, one might have expected more instances of disciplining.' Teachers with less than five years' experience reprimanded pupils almost twice as frequently as their more experienced colleagues.

An interesting comparison with a parallel study of the primary teacher's day (Hilsum and Cane, 1971) which used similar methods of observation and analysis, shows that primary teachers were engaged on average in over four times as many disciplinary incidents each day. It is not clear from this type of study, however, to what degree teachers ignored misbehaviour, or how much 'indiscipline' has been subsumed under other categories in the observation schedule such as 'pupil organisation'.

A number of investigators, some through scrutiny of several teachers, others by in-depth case studies of individual classrooms or schools, have tried to map out the strategies which teachers use to control the behaviour of groups or individual pupils. One of the best-known and most influential series of research programmes was undertaken by Jacob Kounin and his associates from the late 1950s to the early 1970s. Kounin concentrated on, among other events, the teacher's reaction to pupil deviancy, and studied the clarity, firmness and roughness of what he called 'desists', that is teachers' attempts to terminate behaviour of which they disapproved.

In a study of forty-nine teachers of grades 1 and 2 Kounin (1970) observed each for one whole day, and concentrated in his analysis of videotapes and transcripts on the techniques of group management each employed. He coined a set of some-what off-beat terms to describe various kinds of teacher behaviour that seemed to be positively related to involvement of pupils in their work or to freedom from deviancy in the classroom. These involved the following:

Withitness   Having eyes in the back of your head and thus picking up misbehaviour early.
Overlapping   Being able to do more than one thing at once, for example deal with someone misbehaving whilst at the same time keeping the children you are with occupied.
Smoothness   Keeping children at work by *not*

(a) intruding suddenly when they are busy (thrusts);
(b) starting one activity and then leaving it abruptly to engage in another one (dangles);
(c) ending an activity and then coming back to it unexpectedly (flip-flops).

Overdwelling   Avoiding staying on an issue for longer than necessary.
Momentum   Freedom from slow-downs.

Kounin found strongest relationships between 'withitness', the ability to scan the class, and pupil involvement and lack of deviancy, with correlations of from 0.307 to 0.615, depending whether children were working individually at their desks or engaged in whole-class activity, when the correlations were higher.

In an earlier set of studies Kounin and Gump (1958), looking at twenty-six kindergarten teachers, identified the 'ripple effect', that is, the impact of something the teacher does on pupils other than the target child, for example when a teacher says 'Haven't you started yet, John?' and other pupils nearby begin work because they read the signal that the teacher expects pupils to have commenced work. The findings were not entirely conclusive, though a later study suggested that the ripple effect made most impact on the highly motivated pupils, and that liking or disliking the teacher also influenced the degree of effect. It should be remembered that most of the Kounin studies referred to earlier were of 5–8 year olds.

A number of significant case studies of class management have been reported. Amongst the most notable are those by Woods (1979), who described 'mortification techniques' used by some teachers which strip the personality of certain pupils, as well as forms of fraternisation and negotiation which are often employed when other approaches fail. Hargreaves *et al.* (1975) analysed the rules of behaviour operating in two secondary schools during five different phases of the lesson. Other investigators have catalogued various 'coping strategies' witnessed during observation, including Hargreaves (1975), Hargreaves (1978) and Stebbins (1981). These include not only those described by Woods (1979), but also the use of promises, and keeping pupils busy so there is little time for deviance.

Freiberg (1983), writing about the notion of consistency in classroom management, cites a number of models of class management, including those that focus on psychological roles, methods of communication, the behaviour of the individual, pupil responsibility or rule-based models. A comprehensive summary of these has been produced by Charles (1981). Several of the models, notably those based on Skinnerian behaviourist theory using behaviour-modification techniques, have a sizeable, and in some cases controversial research literature attached to them. Others, like Rogers' (1970) influential writing on interpersonal relationships, or the proposals of Glasser (1969) for what he calls 'reality therapy', that is the involvement of pupils in decisions about rules and procedures, have produced some empirical research, but it tends to be less positivistic in style.

The notion of time management

Brophy and Evertson (1976) in a correlational study of 7–9 year olds, found that Kounin's categories of *withitness*, *overlapping* and *smoothness* were not only related to good behaviour, but also to greater pupil learning. Their conclusion was that the amount of time the pupil was engaged in the task was 'the key to successful classroom management' (p. 54). The notion of 'time on the task' or 'academic engaged time' attracted considerable research interest, and the California Beginning Teacher Evaluation Study (Denham and Lieberman, 1980) devoted much of its enquiry to the nature and amount of time spent by pupils on the task in hand.

Gage (1978) summarised some of the studies into academic learning time, and concluded that time was in itself 'a psychologically empty quantitative concept' (p. 75). What was needed, he argued, was a more refined analysis of the notion of time. In the California Beginning Teacher Evaluation Study, such factors as allocated time and success rate were taken into account, but more value- and problem-laden concepts, such as the degree to which the tasks set were worthwhile, were not fully scrutinised.

The apportioning and management of time may be seen as a set of concentric circles (Figure 4.2 not to scale), the largest, circle A, would be 168 hours per week, that is the total time available during seven days and nights. Inscribed within it, the next circle, B, would be quite small by comparison, only some 24 hours, being roughly the amount of time spent in school averaged over the year. This ranks in scale with some studies of children watching television which have shown an average of 25 hours per week (DES, 1975).

Circle C would show the amount of time assigned to the area under scrutiny, for example number work in the primary school or physics in the fifth year of secondary school. This would vary from school to school. In a subject like French in the third year of a secondary school the range might be from 0 to 4 hours.

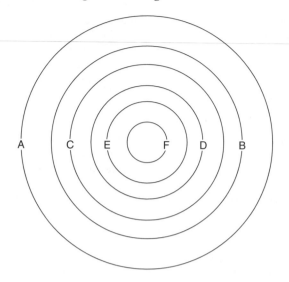

Circle A = all time
Circle C = time assigned to a subject
Circle E = time on a worthwhile task

Circle B = time spent in school
Circle D = time actually spent on the task
Circle F = with some degree of success

Figure 4.2 Time circles: a model of time management (not to scale).

So far none of the circles is a direct reflection of the class-management skill of the individual teacher, since allocations are fixed by local authorities, heads and senior teachers. The size of the smaller circles, however, are indeed affected by the individual teacher's skill. Circle D would be the amount of time pupils actually spend on the tasks in hand. If the school had assigned 3 hours to French, then teachers with ineffective class management or very adverse circumstances, like some of those in the study by Deutsch (1960) cited earlier, might find pupils engaged in learning French for less than an hour. Other classes might spend over 2 hours. Totals for individual pupils, rather than class means, will show an even wider spread.

Circle E brings in the domain of 'worthwhile' tasks. Engaged time in a certain classroom might be high, but the task set might involve the equivalent of copying out telephone directories, so the concept of what is worthwhile, a major philosophical issue discussed by, among others, Peters (1966), is important but highly subjective and contentious. It must, however, logically be a subset of engaged time. Again, it will be a function of the skill of the teacher to decide much time is spent on worthwhile activities.

Finally, the concept of success at the task must be incorporated. If children spend time learning erroneous forms of French, their experience is less profitable than it would have been if they had learned correct forms. Thus, the final circle F encompasses that portion of circle E which is done with some degree of success. One operational definition of skilful class management, therefore, would be the extent to which teachers are capable of maximising circle F for each child, that is the amount of time spent on something worthwhile with some degree of success. The model is certainly not the only way of conceptualising time management; one could add such important aspects as enjoyment, but we offer it as a way of depicting some of the factors frequently mentioned when the matter is discussed.

McNamara (1981) has criticised the emphasis on time management in some studies, arguing that taken too far it can become an end in itself. It can also become a recipe for over-directive teaching. In our present study described later in this chapter, time-on-the-task constitutes but a small element, because it is one of the few outcome measures that can be appraised in different student teachers' lessons which is arguably of some significance.

Class management on teaching practice

There have been few large-scale studies of students on teaching practice which were based on actual observation of lessons. The largest British study by Wragg (1972) documented 578 lessons given by 102 PGCE students during a ten-week practice, and showed that lessons at the end of term had a higher incidence of project-type activities, and that many students had fairly fixed patterns of teaching which hardly altered during their practice. This study was based on Flanders' (1970) categories of interaction, and paid only slight attention to class management.

Fink (1976), in an American study of twenty-five student teachers, used diaries, questionnaires and observations. She found that student teachers became more custodial towards their pupils as the teaching practice progressed. In a British study of discipline problems experienced by 100 PGCE students at Exeter University, Preece (1979) used self-inventories and tutor ratings. By means of a cross-lagged panel analysis he attempted to infer causal relationships between anxiety and disorder in lessons. He found that anxiety affected order for scientists but not for non-scientists, and that the general level of anxiety fell during the practice.

Dreyfus and Eggleston (1979) observed forty-four science specialists who were PGCE students at Nottingham University, and found that early in their practice they employed similar strategies to those of experienced teachers, but that their teaching tactics bore less resemblance to experienced teachers as the practice progressed.

The evolution of styles of class management, student teachers' responses to pupil misbehaviour, the extent to which pupils are engaged in their task during lessons on teaching practice, all these matters are inadequately documented. It was partly because of this lack of a proper account that we decided to examine the field more closely. The remainder of this chapter describes a study conducted at Nottingham University as part of the Teacher Education Project.

The pilot study

Our research into student teachers' class management was in two parts. The first stage consisted of 56 case studies of student teachers thought to be good or poor at handling classes. Subsequently, the main enquiry analysed 204 lessons given by 34 PGCE students at six Nottinghamshire comprehensive schools, three in a city and three in other parts of the county.

In the pilot phase a case-study instrument was piloted and then mailed to a number of co-operating tutors who supervised PGCE students on teaching practice. Each was invited to select one student thought to be effective and one regarded as ineffective in the management of classes. Copies of the case-study outline were also given to the teacher in the school who had most frequent contact with the student. The sample was in no sense random, therefore, and was purely an opportunity sample of tutors and teachers willing to co-operate. The principal purpose of this preliminary exercise was both to collect useful case material and to prepare the ground for the main study.

The case-study instrument consisted of a booklet which the observer completed in a particular lesson during the second half of a block practice. The observer had to describe important aspects of class management, and to record up to three 'critical events' during the lesson which seemed illustrative of the teacher's good or poor handling of the class. Pilot work had shown that free-hand recording by experienced teacher trainers, or teachers not familiar with case-study research, produced too many generalities, such as 'kept class busy' or 'had a firm grip'. The advantage of the critical-event approach, based on the 'critical incidents' technique developed by Flanagan (1949), was that it compelled observers to describe some of the actual happenings in the classroom on which they based their judgement about whether the student was an effective or ineffective class manager. The observer was also asked to interview students after the lesson to elicit their own perception of the events recorded.

The case studies, mainly of science, English, maths and language lessons in the early years of secondary schooling, produced a rich set of insights, and included some 150 critical events. Two pairs of analysts worked independently of each other on the completed case studies. The first pair analysed all the lesson accounts, the critical events and the notes on interviews with the student teachers in order to distil features which observers reported as being illustrative of good class management. The second pair looked for the obverse: characteristics felt to be related to poor management. Finally, a third pair of analysts considered the analyses of the first two pairs, and selected illustrative case material from the case studies. The account of this final analysis is reported by Partington and Hinchliffe (1979).

The briefing notes to observers tried to explain clearly what constituted a 'critical event', but there were minor differences of opinion amongst them, some seeing it as unexpected or novel, others as more routine. It is not possible to draw too firm a set of inferences from subjective case-study data collected by observers other than oneself, even when these are fully documented, as one can only speculate on the quality or accuracy of someone else's insight; nevertheless, some interesting if tentative conclusions can be described.

Effective managers were seen as those who were well prepared, anticipated difficulties, and reacted quickly to disruption rather than allowed it to escalate. Teachers and tutors often highlighted good management which was executed with verbal deftness. There were usually affective messages in addition, such as briskness in the following physics extract, and humour in the English one:

> *Physics*   The class asked, 'Why do we have to do this?' The student's response was that they had to do it because she was there and if they didn't pay attention they wouldn't learn anything. She was brisk, determined, earnest. The class sensed her purpose.

> *English*   The theme for the session was 'Equality'. During discussion the problem of individual differences arose and she contrasted herself with one of the girls in the group (height, eye colour, age etc.) 'I'm better looking than you,' said one girl. Teacher smiled. Defused with ease. Decided that this was not threatening and came back rapidly with, 'Wait till you're my age and the wrinkles start to show.' Smiles all round and the discussion continued.

Many of the critical events highlighted aspects of management noted in research studies of experienced teachers. Successful student teachers usually arrived at the classroom before the pupils, personally admitted them to the room, established a presence, were seen to be in charge, but in a subtle rather than shouting or overbearing manner. Conversely, unsuccessful managers attempted to begin lessons before attention had been secured, and were not able to deal with simultaneous distractions like late arrivals, especially as these often coincided with the transition from an expository stage to a phase of pupil activity. The contrast between different degrees of social control achieved during lesson beginnings is shown in the following three extracts from accounts of critical events.

A. The student began the lesson before many pupils were paying attention and most were milling about. She attempted to give detailed instructions about the first class activity, but repeatedly interspersed rebukes to individuals and shouted orders. The general effect was of obscurity and confusion about what, if anything, was wanted.

B. The teacher began by giving out classwork books and collecting homework books. Teacher...to one of the boys

'This book's very thin.'

'Yeah, 'tis, i'n't it.'

'Why!'

'I've bin drawing in it.'

''E's bin usin' it for toilet paper, sir'. (Uproar)

There then followed a general argument about missing books with much shouting out from the rest of the class. The lesson proper got underway about 15 minutes late.

C. The tone of the lesson was set before the pupils entered the room. The teacher met them at the door and supervised their entry into the room. The teacher further reinforced his position by insisting on quietness and calm before attempting to start the lesson. In consequence the teacher was able to ensure that the lesson proceeded according to plan.

The observers themselves are an important consideration. Not everyone admired the more firmly teacher-controlled start, nor did every observer deprecate the kind of minor chaos amid which some student teachers learn their craft.

The pilot study also showed how personal relationships improve or degenerate during teaching practice. Events which in one classroom would be innocuous become magnified in lessons where the basic relationship between teacher and pupil had become sour. Windows are opened and closed during student teachers' lessons without incident in most cases, but the following extract, from the account of a critical event, reveals the potential for disarray in the most harmless-looking circumstances when interpersonal relationships have become poor:

Girl at back asks if she can open the window but is ignored.

'Get on with it!'

'May I open the window, sir?'

Half noticing, the teacher says 'O.K!'

Thereupon Carol opens the window fully. Gale blows in.

'Shurrit, yer fool!' says boy who is receiving the full force down his neck.

'Yeah, shu' it' says teacher.

But the window appears to have jammed.

'Can't move it, sir!'

A catch had stuck on the sliding window. Carol wrestles with window. Friend wrestles with Carol. Everyone gathers round. Work is abandoned. A milling struggle.

'Sit down! Sit down will you!' shouts teacher, but in vain. Pandemonium whilst teacher tries brute force on the window. Much advice from boys.

'We'll have to leave it', says teacher. 'Now get back to yer places!' No sooner have all resumed their intermittent labours when Carol quietly slides the window closed!

In their analysis of critical events and observers' interpretations of and comment on them, Partington and Hinchliffe summarised their conclusions about the constituents of effective management in student teachers' classrooms under five headings:

(1) *The establishment of good personal relationships* – learning pupils' names, getting to know individual pupils well during and outside lessons, responding to pupils according to what was known about them personally, rather than according to some general stereotype, using humour constructively.
(2) *Effective preparation* – knowing and feeling confident with the material of the lesson, appropriate organisation of material in the light of methods being used and time available, anticipation of conceptual, linguistic or practical problems and the devising of appropriate tactics to deal with them when they occur.
(3) *Organisation of materials and pupils' work during lessons* – which included the ability to decide when and how to use whole-class groups and individual work, to be aware of movement around or outside the room, and to recognise and work effectively within the location in which learning took place, gym, laboratory, drama studio or classroom.
(4) *Specific pedagogic skills* – the development of skilful explaining and questioning, learning to read the myriads of cues about pupils' difficulties or moods and then making a suitable response.
(5) *Personal characteristics* – the qualities a student teacher needed for effective presentation of self. When certain students were observed failing to cope with their classes, whilst some of their fellow novices were more successful, it sometimes came down to aspects of personality, some of which may not be very amenable to modification.

The main study

In the light of this pilot work and after scrutiny of the literature we decided to conduct a systematic analysis of the class management of a sample of PGCE students during their long block practice. An observation instrument, the Nottingham Class Management Observation Schedule (reproduced in Galton, 1978) was developed, and the emphasis in it was on pupil deviance and teachers' responses.

The first step was to extract from the pilot case studies described earlier, from accounts of other observations of lessons of students undertaken during the pilot phase, from interviews with two classes of pupils seen individually or in pairs, and from the research literature, a set of over 200 statements related to the discrimination of effective and ineffective class management. Each piece of classroom behaviour was then noted on a separate card, as suggested by Berliner and Tikunoff (1976), using, wherever possible, the natural language employed by observers, respondents and people interviewed. Examples included the following:

Effective teacher	*Ineffective teacher*
82 Responds immediately when rule broken	Responds only when deviance is widespread or serious
85 Avoids threat/ultimatum	Threat/ultimatum frequent
92 Confrontation rare	Confrontation frequent
94 Sees pupils privately now or later	All investigations, etc. conducted in public

Similar and overlapping statements were eliminated, and the number was thereby reduced to 120. These were then put into groups and used to determine the final form of the schedule which fell into four major sections. Section 1 consisted of background information such as the name of the school, student teacher, class, subject, the predominant lesson activity and the degree of task involvement. Section 2 described the deviant act, whether it involved noise, interruptions, damage, movement, non-verbal factors and the degree of seriousness of the deviancy. Section 3 recorded the student teacher's response, including such verbal factors as orders to cease, reprimands, threats, statements of rule, humour, praise or encouragement, non-verbal elements like gesture, facial expression, proximity, that is moving towards pupils, punishments of various kinds, whether the response was to a named pupil, to a group, whether the target was correct or incorrect. Finally, Section 4 showed the pupils' response and whether deviancy lessened or increased.

In addition, there was a section in which individual pupils were studied one by one for 20 seconds in regular 'sweeps' of the class to make a judgement about the extent to which the pupil observed appeared to be (a) on- or off-task, and (b) engaging in mild, serious or no deviancy. These data were used to compute an on-task and deviancy index, which gave a rough-and-ready picture of the overall amount of on-task and deviant behaviour in the class during the periods of observation.

The final schedule was piloted in a school and on videotapes, and used by the two present writers and two other observers who were trained for several hours. There were extensive discussions about the categories in the schedule and, for the individual pupil 'sweeps', of what could be regarded as mild or serious deviancy and on- or off-task behaviour. A full account of all the procedures used can be found in Dooley (1982).

Three measures of observer agreement were taken, two were of inter-observer agreement, that is the degree of concurrence between all four observers before and after the research, and one of intra-observer agreement, that is the extent to which an observer agrees with himself recording data from the same videotape before and after the research. There is no single standard method of calculating observer agreement in classroom-observation research, though the matter has been discussed in most of the standard works on classroom interaction such as that by Medley and Mitzel (1963).

We decided to opt for a percentage agreement figure, though this would be open to criticism if a system contained many unlikely or infrequent categories, such as 'teacher flies through the window'. The present schedule does not have such bizarre categories. One further reservation about a percentage agreement measure is that it could hide consistent disagreement on one particular category. Close inspection of the trial data did not reveal any such inconsistency.

Agreement between observers was high. In the pre-test they range from 77 to 85 per cent, in the post-test from 80 to 86 per cent, and intra-observer agreement ranged from 78 to 90 per cent. Deviancy level measures showed an agreement of 82–92 per cent, and task involvement from 65 to 83 per cent. The appraisal of whether pupils are on- or off-task, therefore, is slightly less reliable than the other parts of the schedule, as one might expect. Although it is frequently self-evident whether pupils are engrossed in their work, there are several occasions when observers have to make a judgement on inadequate evidence, hence the slightly higher amount of disagreement on this aspect.

The arguments for and against the use of observation schedules have been well rehearsed (Delamont, 1976), but we decided that the instrument we had devised would provide a great deal of useful quantified descriptive and correlational information about student teachers' handling of their classes which was missing in the literature. A sample of 34 PGCE students in 6 comprehensive schools was selected. Though it was not, strictly speaking, a random sample, being rather all the students doing their teaching practice in six large comprehensives, it did not seem to be unduly biased. There were 17 science and 17 non-science students, and 20 of the sample were male and 14 female. The schools were the commonly used teaching practice schools in city and county, and were regarded as 'typical' of the spread of schools in the area, in the judgement of tutors.

Wherever possible, first, second or third-year classes were watched. Each student teacher was observed for six lessons during his or her one-term block teaching practice, which came in the second term of their one-year PGCE course, following a term in which they had spent a whole or half-day per week on school experience. Two lessons were observed in the first third of the term, two in the middle period and two in the final third. In each lesson, five successive 3-minute lesson segments were recorded on the schedule, followed by a sweep of every individual child for the deviancy and task-involvement measures, and free-hand notes were written. In summary, the study provided data from 1,020 segments in 204 lessons given by 34 student teachers in six schools.

Findings of the main study

Pupil deviancy

In the event the 204 lessons observed were distributed as shown in Table 4.1.

The type of teaching which occurred during the 1,020 lesson segments, normally observed during the first 20–25 minutes of any lesson, consisted mainly of pupils working and teacher monitoring, 38 per cent of the time, and public teacher–pupil interaction for 30 per cent.

Table 4.1 Distribution of 204 lessons observed

Year	Percentage
1st	32
2nd	37
3rd	24
4th	7

In 76 per cent of lesson segments some deviant act was recorded, and in 50 per cent of these cases five pupils or more were involved. Analysis of the kind of deviancy noted reveals a predominance of minor pieces of naughtiness. The most commonly recorded kinds of misbehaviour are shown in Table 4.2. In each case they are percentages of all 1,020 segments in which the particular piece of misbehaviour occurred.

All these categories, as in any observation schedule, require subjective judgement by the observer, and what is 'excessive' or 'inappropriate' for one person may not be so for another. However, student teachers themselves often reinforced the judgement of the observer, as will be seen in the following section, by saying 'there's too much noise' or 'don't bend the ruler like that'.

That most of the deviance reported was irritating rather than alarming, is shown by the high frequency of general noise, off-task gossip and minor jostling recorded, and the infrequency of damage, insult to teacher, or downright disobedience of a request or order. Physical aggression to other pupils was also rare, and there was no example of physical aggression to the teacher. The nearest to this occurred in only one confrontation: when a teacher asked a pupil to move to another seat, the pupil refused and the observer felt that physical violence by the pupil seemed likely until the teacher backed away. Unexpectedly, at this flashpoint the pupil did then move as requested.

Observers were also asked to make a subjective judgement about the degree of seriousness of misbehaviour which occurred. Their ratings in Table 4.3 revealed that approximately five out of six pieces of deviancy were regarded as mild.

Table 4.2 Most common forms of misbehaviour observed

Misbehaviour	Percentage
Excessively noisy talk	38
Non-verbal behaviour not appropriate to task	24
Irrelevant talk	23
Inappropriate use of materials/equipment	20
Illicit eating/drinking	12
Movement at the wrong time	11
Fidgeting	9
Provoking laughter (derision, not shared humour)	6
Teacher interrupted (excluding normal exchanges)	5
Physical aggression	2
Damage to materials/equipment	1.5
Disobeying teacher	1.5
Cheating	1.5
Pupil insulted	1.5
Teacher insulted	1

Table 4.3 Observers' ratings of mildness/seriousness of misbehaviour

Rating	Percentage
Mild	83
More serious	15
Very serious	2

The student teachers' responses

In 71 per cent of the lesson segments where deviancy occurred the teacher made some response. The kinds of reaction given in Table 4.4 are expressed as percentages of the 543 lesson segments in which a response to deviancy was noted.

Physical punishment was noted only on one occasion during the whole research. Punishment was threatened ten times more frequently than it was actually administered. Typically, therefore, the response was a statement to cease, a reprimand or a reminder of a rule, occasionally a threat, rarely an actual punishment. In those classes where there was a persistent buzz of noise 'stop talking', 'there's too much noise', 'pay attention John', 'if you don't work quietly you'll be kept in' became part of the landscape. In 84 per cent of segments the response was brief rather than sustained.

Several other characteristics of the student teachers' responses were coded. Observers were asked to judge the timing of responses in relation to the escalation of deviance. Table 4.5 shows that nearly three-quarters of reactions to misbehaviour occurred before it had escalated, leaving slightly over a quarter taking place afterwards.

This failure by some to nip misbehaviour in the bud produced class-control problems, whilst those who were prompt in recognising and responding to deviance had less difficulty.

Table 4.6 reveals that most responses were made to the whole class, followed by reactions to groups and individuals in roughly equal amounts.

Table 4.4 Student teachers' reactions to misbehaviour

Reaction	Percentage
Order to cease	61
Reprimand	25
Statement of rule	24
Proximity (moving towards pupils)	20
Involving pupils in their work	16
Threat	10
Facial expression	8
Dramatic pause	7
Gesture	5
Pupil moved	3
Humour	2
Touch	1
Ridicule	1
Punishment	1

Table 4.5 Timing of response to deviance

Teacher responds to escalation of deviance	Percentage
Before	73
After	27

Table 4.6 Target of teacher's response

Teacher's response to	Percentage
Whole class	44
Group of pupils	27
Individual	29

Table 4.7 Student teachers' manner

	Percentage
Calm	79
Agitated	16
Angry	5

In some 39 per cent of cases a pupil's name was used. Table 4.6 denotes the principal target of the teacher's response, so there were some cases when an individual pupil was named during a reaction aimed primarily at a group or the whole class.

It is sometimes speculated that student and experienced teachers accuse the 'wrong' pupils, that they, for example, turn round from the blackboard and name someone who was not actually guilty of misbehaviour. Observers recorded whether in their view the 'incorrect' culprit had been accused, and this happened on 9 occasions out of 1,020 lesson segments analysed, which at less than 1 per cent, seems lower than one might have predicted from a group of novice teachers.

The student teachers were generally calm in their manner, but in just over one-fifth of all the events studied they appeared angry or agitated as Table 4.7 shows, though this quantifies only the observer's view of external characteristics. Whether the anger was feigned, or whether external calm masked internal rage is not revealed.

Pupil responses and behaviour

Once some kind of misbehaviour had taken place and the teacher had made a response, observers were asked to record whether, in their view, the deviance escalated, stayed the same, reduced or ended. Table 4.8 shows that in just over half the cases deviance ended, and in nearly a third of cases it lessened. It was only rarely that it actually increased.

The most common result, on 80 per cent of occasions, was that pupils fell silent or appeared to accept the teacher's reaction. In 9 per cent of cases there was some kind of altercation between teacher and pupils.

The individual pupil data, that is the aggregated 20-second 'sweeps' of the class, were used to compute a deviancy and involvement index which ranged from 0 (no-one deviant or no-one involved in the task) to 100 (everyone engaged in serious deviancy or everyone highly involved in the task). The deviancy-index scores for all 204 lessons showed a mean of just over 10, which might typically represent, for example, six children engaging in what the observer regarded as mild misbehaviour out of a class of thirty. The overall involvement-index scores produced a mean of 60, which could, in a class of thirty, for example, consist of a distribution such

Table 4.8 Outcome after teacher
intervenes over deviance

Deviance	No. of cases
Ends	53
Lessens	30
Sustained	15
Escalates	2

Table 4.9 Mean deviancy and involvement-index scores
during early, mid- and late teaching practice

	Deviancy index	Involvement index
Early	10.5	57.5
Mid	11	60.5
Late	10.5	61

as twelve pupils highly involved, twelve medium involved, and six barely or not at all involved in their task.

Scores for individual student teachers showed quite a wide range, with deviancy spread from a low of 4 to a high of 37, and involvement from a low of 26 to a high of 81.

When deviancy and involvement scores were computed for three different phases of the teaching practice as shown in Table 4.9, there was little significant difference in the means other than a small increase in involvement, though some individual students showed more marked changes over the term.

Bivariate and multivariate analysis

Group comparisons

A number of further analyses of the data were undertaken using the PMMD program CATT (Youngman, 1976), including certain group comparisons where the sample size justified them. Comparisons of lessons given by male and female student teachers revealed few differences other than might have occurred by chance. Women teachers showed a slightly higher incidence of pupil interruption, talk provoking laughter and fidgeting, all significant at the 0.05 level on a 't' test for planned comparisons.

When the lessons of different year groups were compared using the same program with linear and non-linear trend tests, Scheffé's group atypicality test and the Tukey test for unequal-sized groups, some significant differences did emerge, full details of which are described by Dooley (1982). The most significant were a marked increase in deviancy of certain kinds with older age groups, especially talk irrelevant to the task, talk provoking laughter and physical aggression to other pupils.

The deviancy-index scores show an increase each year significant at the 0.01 level, but the involvement-index scores decline slightly, before moving sharply up at fourth-year level, one guesses because most classes at this stage are in public examination groups, though caution must be exercised because the fourth-year sample was much smaller than the rest (Table 4.10).

Table 4.10 Deviancy and involvement scores for
different year groups

Year	Deviancy index	Involvement index
1st	8.46	60.51
2nd	9.78	59.05
3rd	12.59	56.10
4th	12.86	73.57

Teachers' responses to older pupils also show some changes. As pupils grow older there is less use of reprimands, threats and statements of rule, though humour is used more frequently, and observers' notes confirm a more subtle, more adult response to older classes.

Correlational analysis

With so many variables in the schedule it would be easy to produce a huge product moment and biserial-correlation matrix and give prominence to any significant correlation, when one knows that by chance several values significant at the 0.05 and 0.01 level can be obtained with such a big matrix. Some correlations are of special interest, however, including the relationship between deviancy and involvement, and that between classroom behaviour and measures of teaching competence.

Predictably, the correlation between involvement and deviancy measures is a large inverse one (more involvement means less deviancy, and vice versa). The actual value was $r = -0.48$ which is significant beyond the 0.001 level, and would have occurred by chance, therefore, less than one in a thousand times. On the other hand, it is well short of perfect agreement, and this reveals that involvement in the task and mild deviancy can, and frequently do, coexist.

Other highly significant correlations of over 0.5 showed that pupils were more likely to be named during more serious misbehaviour ($r = 0.66$), and the more serious the deviancy the more likely the teacher was to make a response ($r = 0.91$). These findings accord with common sense, but the size of the correlation coefficient is of interest.

The supervising tutors of each student were asked to rate them for general competence as teachers, and also to record on a seven-point scale their appraisal of personal relationships with the class, task involvement, the degree of interest aroused, and the amount they thought the pupils were learning. Given the complexity of teaching practice and the difficulty of measuring accurately student teachers' performance, this was the nearest we could obtain to measures of teaching competence and pupil learning.

Surprisingly, there was only a low insignificant correlation between tutors' appraisal of task involvement and our carefully collected observation data ($r = 0.13$). This low agreement is not easy to explain. Tutors do not, of course, attempt specifically to analyse the involvement of every pupil in a systematic way as we did; they might indeed get a rude shock sometimes if they did. On the other hand, they do, albeit in an *ad hoc* way, make judgements about pupil involvement. Furthermore, observers and tutors never observe the same lessons. Perhaps this partially explains the lack of significant agreement; but some degree of mystery remains.

On the other hand, there was greater congruence between tutors' appraisal of the amount pupils were learning and several of our measures, notably task involvement ($r = 0.37^*$), and deviancy ($r = -0.46^{**}$).

Finally, the lessons were analysed according to the type of lesson activity in progress. Deviancy was highest during a transition from one activity to another, being noted in 61 per cent of the transitions when movement took place. This compares with 50 per cent during periods of teacher–pupil interaction. Involvement in the task was highest during teacher–pupil interaction at 89 per cent, compared with 79 per cent when the teacher was addressing the class.

Factor and cluster analyses were also performed of all 1,020 lesson segments. The factor analysis added little to what had already been learned from other analyses. A cluster analysis of several items on the schedule was performed using the PMMD CARM program (Youngman, 1976), and the six-cluster solution gave the clearest picture. Cluster analysis groups together those lesson segments which are most similar. The largest cluster consisting of 259 segments was characterised by noisy, disruptive behaviour with the teacher issuing orders to cease. Another large cluster (243 segments) represented orderly periods with no disruption at all. A third cluster of 192 segments shows examples of behaviour inappropriate to the task, and inappropriate use of materials which attracts little or no response from the teacher.

Summary

This analysis of 204 lessons given by 34 PGCE students shows that most acts of deviance occurring in their lessons are of a minor nature, typically the buzz of chatter punctuated by requests or commands to desist. Few students had serious discipline problems, and almost no examples of severe disruption were observed, though many lessons sank into minor chaos and showed prolonged mild deviance. Most teacher responses were brief, and misbehaviour subsequently ceased or lessened.

Deviance occurred most frequently during transitions or change of activity, especially when movement occurred, and with third- and fourth-year pupils. Students showed a different style when dealing with older pupils, and involvement in the task was highest for fourth-year classes, though the sample was small. Students whose classes showed low deviancy and high involvement were more likely to be given a high grade by supervising tutors for the amount they thought pupils were learning, but there was only a small agreement between tutors' ratings of task involvement and the observation data collected systematically by the research team.

Those tutors and teachers who conducted case studies in the pilot stage tended to rate personal relationships highly, and students who had prepared well, organised their lessons and materials effectively, and developed the skills of explaining, questioning and using their eyes to read pupils' difficulties and anticipate problems, were thought to be more effective than those who were not able to do these things. Certain personal characteristics were also rated very important, and in the case of students who had poor class control there was some doubt whether their ineffective personality was always amenable to change.

Although a great deal of information was obtained in this study, many questions remained unanswered. Amongst these was the intriguing question of how student teachers compared with experienced practitioners, and it was to this matter that we next turned our attention.

References

Berliner, D. C. and Tikunoff, W. J. (1976) 'The California Beginning Teacher Evaluation Study: Overview of the Ethnographic Study', *Journal of Teacher Education*, 27, 24–30.
Brophy, J. E. and Evertson, C. M. (1976) *Learning from Teaching: A Developmental Perspective*, Allyn & Bacon Inc., Boston, MA.
Charles, C. M. (1981) *Building Classroom Discipline from Models to Practice*, Longman, New York.
Delamont, S. (1976) *Interaction in the Classroom*, Methuen, London.
Denham, C. and Lieberman, A. (eds) (1980) *Time to Learn*, National Institute of Education, Washington, DC.
DES (1975) *A Language for Life* (The Bullock Report), HMSO, London.
——(1979) *Aspects of Secondary Education in England*, HMSO, London.
Deutsch, M. (1960) *Minority Group and Class Status*, Society for Applied Anthropology, Monograph no. 2.
Docking, J. W. (1980) *Control and Discipline in Schools*, Harper & Row, London.
Dooley, P. (1982) *Class Management and Control by Student Teachers*, MPhil. thesis, Nottingham University.
Dreyfus, A. and Eggleston, J. F. (1979) 'Classroom Transactions of Student Teachers of Science', *European Journal of Science Education*, 1, 3, 315–25.
Dunkin, M. J. and Biddle, B. J. (1974) *The Study of Teaching*, Holt, Rinehart & Winston, New York.
Fink, C. H. (1976) 'Social Studies Student Teachers – What Do They Really Learn?' Paper presented at the Annual Meeting of the National Council for the Social Studies, Washington, DC, November.
Flanagan, J. C. (1949) 'Critical Requirements: A New Approach to Employee Evaluation', *Personnel Psychology*, 2, 419–25.
Flanders, N. A. (1970) *Analysing Teaching Behavior*, Addison-Wesley, New York.
Francis, P. (1975) *Beyond Control?* Allen & Unwin, London.
Freiberg, H. J. (1983) 'Consistency: The Key to Classroom Management', *Journal of Education for Teaching*, 9, 1, 1–15.
Gage, N. L. (1978) *The Scientific Basis of the Art of Teaching*, Teachers College Press, New York.
Galton, M. J. (ed.) (1978) *British Mirrors: A Collection of Classroom Observation Systems*, University of Leicester.
Glasser, W. (1969) *Schools without Failure*, Harper & Row, New York.
Gnagey, W. J. (1975) *Maintaining Discipline in Classroom Instruction*, Macmillan, London.
Hargreaves, A. (1978) 'The Significance of Classroom Coping Strategies', in L. Barton and R. Meighan (eds), *Sociological Interpretations of Schooling and Classrooms: A Reappraisal*, Studies in Education, Nafferton, Driffield.
Hargreaves, D. H. (1975) *Interpersonal Relations and Education* (revised student edition), Routledge, London.
Hargreaves, D. H., Hester, S. K. and Mellor, F. J. (1975) *Deviance in Classrooms*, Routledge, London.
Highfield, M. E. and Pinsent, A. (1952) *A Survey of Rewards and Punishments in Schools*, National Foundation for Educational Research (NFER), Windsor.
Hilsum, S. and Cane, B. S. (1971) *The Teacher's Day*, NFER, Windsor.
Hilsum, S. and Strong, C. (1978) *The Secondary Teacher's Day*, NFER, Windsor.
Jackson, P. W. (1968) *Life in Classrooms*, Holt, Rinehart & Winston, New York.
Johnson, M. and Brooks, H. (1979) 'Conceptualizing Classroom Management', in D. L. Duke (ed.), *Classroom Management*, NSSE Yearbook 78, 2, University of Chicago Press, Chicago, IL.
Kounin, J. S. (1970) *Discipline and Group Management in Classrooms*, Holt, Rinehart & Winston, New York.
Kounin, J. S. and Gump, P. V. (1958) 'The Ripple Effect in Discipline', *Elementary School Journal*, 35, 158–62.
Lawrence, J., Steed, D. and Young, P. (1977) *Disruptive Behaviour in a Secondary School*, University of London, Goldsmiths College.
Lowenstein, L. G. (1975) *Violent and Disruptive Behaviour in Schools*, National Association of Schoolmasters, Hemel Hempstead, Herts.

McNamara, D. (1981) 'Attention, Time-on-task and Children's Learning: Research or Ideology?' *Journal of Education for Teaching*, 7, 284–97.

Marland, M. (1975) *The Craft of the Classroom*, Heinemann, London.

Medley, D. M. and Mitzel, H. E. (1963) 'Measuring Classroom Behavior by Systematic Observation', in N. L. Gage (ed.), *Handbook of Research on Teaching*, Rand, McNally, Chicago, IL.

Partington, J. A. and Hinchcliffe, G. (1979) 'Some Aspects of Classroom Management', *British Journal of Teacher Education*, 5, 3, 231–41.

Peters, R. S. (1966) *Ethics and Education*, Allen & Unwin, London.

Preece, P. F. W. (1979) 'Student Teacher Anxiety and Class Control Problems on Teaching Practice', *British Educational Research Journal*, 5, 1, 13–19.

Robertson, J. (1981) *Effective Classroom Control*, Hodder & Stoughton, London.

Rogers, C. R. (1970) *On Being a Person*, Houghton-Mifflin, Boston, MA.

Stebbins, R. A. (1981) 'Classroom Ethnography and the Definition of the Situation', in L. Barton and S. Walker (eds), *Schools, Teachers and Teaching*, The Falmer Press, Barcombe, Sussex.

Tibble, J. W. (1959) 'Problems in the Training of Teachers and Social Workers', *The Sociological Review*, Monograph no. 2.

Weber, M. (1964) *The Theory of Social and Economic Organization*, Free Press, New York.

Wickman, E. K. (1928) *Children's Behavior and Teachers' Attitudes*, The Commonwealth Fund, New York.

Woods, P. (1979) *The Divided School*, Routledge, London.

Wragg, E. C. (1967) *Attitudes, Anxieties and Aspirations of Graduate Student Teachers Following the Postgraduate Certificate of Education Course*, MEd thesis, Leicester University.

—— (1972) *An Analysis of the Verbal Classroom Interaction between Graduate Student Teachers and Children*, PhD thesis, Exeter University.

—— (1981) *Class Management and Control*, Macmillan, Basingstoke.

Youngman, M. B. (1976) *Programmed Methods for Multivariate Data* (version 5), University of Nottingham.

CHAPTER 5

A STUDY OF STUDENT TEACHERS IN THE CLASSROOM

G. Chanan (ed.), *Towards a Science of Teaching*, NFER Publishing Company Limited, 1973, pp. 85–127

This is an abbreviated version of the chapter I wrote in the book *Towards a Science of Teaching*, edited by Gabriel Chanan in 1973. It seems very quantitative to me now, describing research based on the observation of nearly 600 lessons given by over 100 secondary student teachers, but there was little on this scale at that time. Indeed, British classroom researchers worked largely in isolation during the 1970s. Later on, a few sizeable projects of this kind emerged, like the ORACLE study at Leicester University.

The research context

This inquiry, sponsored by the Social Science Research Council, was designed to provide more information about graduate student teachers, about their personalities, their behaviour in the classroom and about factors influencing success and failure.

[…]

Against a 1970s background of increasing student numbers, substantial criticism of teacher training procedures, and the absence of any major study of student teachers based on live classroom observation, it was decided that this inquiry should have four main objectives:

(a) to study the classroom behaviour of 100 graduate student teachers;
(b) to relate observed behaviour to measures of personality, values, creativity, intelligence and academic achievement, as well as ratings of effectiveness;
(c) to analyse classroom observation data by subject, sex of class, sex of teacher, type of school and stage of teaching practice at which observations were made;
(d) to explore certain training procedures designed to make the student teacher aware of classroom interaction, and to evaluate their effectiveness in enabling students to modify their behaviour.

[…]

Design of the research

Definition of terms and theoretical model

Throughout this account the terms *presage*, *process* and *product* variables will be used in the sense in which many American writers use the terms when writing about research in teaching. *Presage* variables are those which exist in the situation *before* manipulation, or at the beginning of the research, and would include scores such as IQ, attitude measures, personality test scores of either teachers or children or both. *Process* variables are those which are measured during the *actual teaching*, and include any indications of classroom behaviour, verbal or non-verbal, equipment used etc. *Product* variables are the *results* of what happens in classrooms and would involve gains or losses on achievement tests, attitude change shown by teachers or children, and ratings of effectiveness of teachers by pupils or supervisors.

The theoretical model on which the research is based assumes that there is a constant flow of influence across the three types of variable in both directions. *Presage variables* such as the teacher's personality or a child's IQ can influence the classroom *process*, sometimes significantly. Warm, accepting teachers may be more likely to listen to children talking, accept their ideas and feelings. Bright children may initiate a great deal more than duller children.... Both *presage* and *process variables* can influence the *products* of teaching, either separately or together. Bright children might learn despite the teacher or because of her. Physically attractive teachers might be rated more highly despite their classroom performance, or their attractiveness might enhance their rapport with children and hence their rating.

The influence is also to be detected in the reverse direction. The *product variables* will affect future *processes*. For example, teachers of children learning effectively may be reinforced to continue teaching along similar lines, and teachers suspecting unfavourable attitudes or learning developing may feel they must change their teaching. The influence can go back to the *presage variables*, in that on future occasions they will be different as a result of time and experience. A measure of children's values, for example, made before research began would be a *presage variable*. If classroom *processes* changed children's values then the extent and direction of change would be a *product variable*. On a future occasion, however, a second piece of research would record the new changed value structure as *presage variables*. A simplified theoretical model showing some of the variables in each category and highlighting the ones measured in the present research is given below.

The review of research showed that a number of questions about student teachers remained unanswered in the literature. At the graduate level, for example, where students were preparing to teach in secondary schools, what were the differences amongst teachers of different subjects? Were there differences in classroom behaviour between men and women, or between classes in single sex schools and mixed schools? Were there differences according to type of school – Secondary Modern, Grammar or Comprehensive? Did patterns change as teaching practice progressed? Were there different patterns in classes containing younger or older children?

In addition, because of the lack of descriptive material about the classrooms of student teachers there was obviously going to be no research describing the effect of presage variables on process variables. What influenced different patterns of classroom behaviour? Was it a student's personality, his values, his intelligence or academic achievement? Were 'creative' teachers very flexible and less 'creative' teachers very rigid in their approach?

Nor was there any evidence about possible links between process and product variables. The absence of live observation data left a number of questions in this area unanswered. What effect did various kinds of classroom behaviour by the teacher have on children's attitudes? What effect did it have on the ratings of effectiveness given to students by schools and supervisors? Did they tend to favour some types of classroom behaviour and not others? Were there any common characteristics in the observed behaviour of those students rated as 'good'? Similarly was there a recognisable pattern or series of patterns amongst student teachers rated as 'poor'?

Simplified theoretical model

Presage variables	Product variables	Product variables
Children	*Children*	*Children*
Physical attributes	Verbal interaction	Amount and nature of
Social and family	**with teacher	learning achieved
background	(**)with pupils	Attitude change
Experience in school	Non-verbal interaction	
Personality	with teacher	
Values	with pupils	
Cognitive skills – IQ,	with equipment, etc.	
creativity, etc.	movement	
*Attitudes	thought processes	
Teachers	*Teachers*	*Teachers*
Physical attributes	Verbal interaction	Amount and nature of
Social and family	**with class	children's learning
background	(**)with individuals	induced
Experience in school	Non-verbal interaction	*Amount and nature of
**Personality	with class	teacher's learning
**Values	with individuals	(including feedback
Cognitive skills – **IQ	with equipment	about own behaviour)
**Creativity	movement	**Ratings of competence
Attitudes	thought processes	
**Academic achievement		

Notes: **Indicates variables measured in the present research; (**)Sometimes recorded; *Pilot phase only.

Furthermore, there were no known 'norms' against which innovations in teacher training procedures could be matched. Colleges and departments of education seeking to change their training procedures have no published data about classroom behaviour with which to compare their own students. Consequently, the measures and procedures in the present research were chosen to provide information as partial answers to some of the general and specific questions outlined earlier.

Measuring the presage variables

A great deal of thought preceded the final choice of the twenty-eight presage variables and the procedures for attempting to measure them. The presage variables were intended here to serve two purposes. They were to be related to both the process variables and the product variables.

Consequently, what was needed was the maximum amount of useful information which could be collected from students as a group at the beginning of the session. For this and other reasons a number of approaches were rejected. A lengthy series of successive testing sessions was rejected because it would (a) postpone or interfere with the beginning of the course and (b) quite possibly lose the goodwill of a number of students who might come to resent being scrutinized and subjected to testing sessions so shortly after many of them are relieved to have finished with finals. Previous research suggested that students often begin their training year with a number of expectations. They hope, for example, that the year will be different from what they have experienced previously, and that they will broaden what they regard as a previously narrow education. Lengthy testing sessions might needlessly antagonize them.

[...]

It was decided to administer four carefully chosen tests on the first day of the Michaelmas Term to all students in the Department. The tests were (a) Cattell's 16PF test form C for variables 1 to 16, (b) The Allport, Vernon, Lindzey 'Study of Values' (Richardson's British form) for variables 17 to 22, (c) The Torrance tests of Creative Thinking (Verbal Test) for variables 23 to 26, (d) The Alice Heim AH5 Group test of high grade intelligence for variable 27. (Variable 28 was to be the student's class of degree taken from his record card.)

All of these tests have been used with teachers or trainee teachers. The Cattell 16PF test 'tests as much of the total personality as can be covered by questionnaire, according to the most up-to-date psychological research.' Its advantage is that it provides scores of 16 personality variables and can be completed in around 30 minutes. The 16 factors identified are the results of extensive factor analysis by the test author.

Measuring the process variables

What goes on in the classroom can be measured or described in a number of different ways. Live observation of lessons has the disadvantage of making it likely that the lesson may be altered in some way by the presence of an outside observer. Flanders (1970) reports an inquiry by Samph who studied the effects on teachers' behaviour in the presence of an observer in the classroom. By monitoring tapes of the lessons, Samph was able to see what the differences were when observers appeared. Using the Flanders system for analysing the observation data he found some tendency to become more oriented towards the children when an observer was present as shown by increases in the categories describing acceptance of children's ideas and questioning. This research was based on a small sample of only ten teachers, but it does provide tentative evidence that teachers are likely to make some changes in their behaviour when outsiders are present.

The advantages of a live observer are numerous. He can focus on particular aspects of lessons, his perceptions are first-hand, and he can record as he observes. The Flanders system used in this research requires one observer who concentrates on verbal behaviour: what is said by teachers and children. It divides talk into ten categories, seven for talk by the teacher, two for talk by the children, and a tenth category for non-talk such as silence, or for periods when nothing can be coded at all. The ten categories, with Flanders' own description of them, are given below.

[...]

On the negative side the Flanders system could be said to have ideological components in that it looks specifically for 'indirect' teacher talk (with which it would be easy to associate value terms such as 'progressive', 'child-centred', 'democratic') and 'direct' teaching (with its associations of 'authoritarianism', 'telling', 'learning-centred'). Flanders has always stressed, however, that he is not positing a single model of 'good' teaching or recommending teachers to follow any one type of behaviour. Nevertheless it would be wrong to deny that many of the research findings point in the direction of indirect teaching being associated with various measures of effectiveness as the review of research showed.

The Flanders system – the ten categories

Teacher talk		
Indirect influence	1	Accepts feeling: accepts and clarifies the feeling tone of the students in a non-threatening manner. Feelings may be positive or negative. Predicting and recalling feelings are included.
	2	Praises or encourages: praises or encourages student action or behaviour. Jokes that release tension, not at the expense of another individual, nodding head or saying 'uh huh?' or 'go on' are included.
	3	Accepts or uses ideas of student: clarifying, building, or developing ideas or suggestions by a student. As teacher brings more of his own ideas into play, shift to category five.
	4	Asks questions: asking a question about content or procedure with the intent that a student answer.
Direct influence	5	Lectures: giving facts or opinions about content or procedure; expressing his own ideas; asking rhetorical questions.
	6	Gives directions: directions, commands, or orders with which a student is expected to comply.
	7	Criticizes or justifies authority: statements intended to change student behaviour from non-acceptable to acceptable pattern; bawling someone out; stating why the teacher is doing what he is doing; extreme self-reference.
Student talk	8	Student talk-responses: talk by students in response to teacher. Teacher initiates the contact or solicits student statement.
	9	Student talk-initiation: talk by students, which they initiate. If 'calling on' student is only to indicate who may talk next, observer must decide whether student wanted to talk. If he did, use this category.
	10	Silence or confusion, pauses, short periods of silence, and periods of confusion in which communication cannot be understood by the observer.

On the negative side the Flanders system could be said to have ideological components in that it looks specifically for 'indirect' teacher talk (with which it would be easy to associate value terms such as 'progressive', 'child-centred', 'democratic') and 'direct' teaching (with its associations of 'authoritarianism', 'telling', 'learning-centred'). Flanders has always stressed, however, that he is not positing a single model of 'good' teaching or recommending teachers to follow any one type of behaviour. Nevertheless it would be wrong to deny that many of the research findings point in the direction of indirect teaching being associated with various measures of effectiveness as the review of research showed.

Another criticism one could make is that the system fails to subdivide important categories like two (praise), into 'cursory praises' and 'sincere praise', or category four (questions) into 'narrow questions', that is, those which require a short response, usually self-evident, and 'broad questions' which require a longer answer or offer a wider area of possible response. [...]

One can also point out that the Flanders system fails to identify the individual child responding, that it is difficult to use in informal settings, and presupposes that the teacher is going to give what some American writers call 'a recitation lesson'. It is heavily biased towards the cognitive side and has little on the affective side, though one must not forget category one and elements of two and three. Category 10 is also far too broad.

On the positive side the system has a great deal to recommend it as a research tool. The ten categories make for easy processing. Training observers, a problem discussed later, is, on the whole, straightforward. The information provided is comprehensive within the limitations mentioned earlier, and the ten categories are very much less cumbersome than the vast numbers of categories employed by some investigators, such as Adams and Biddle (1970) with 87 different categories. In addition it has extra uses as a feedback tool in that the data can easily be put in a comprehensible form for teacher trainees or experienced teachers, and it is less value-laden than some systems, despite the points made earlier. [...]

Given the reservations expressed earlier about the problems of direct observation of classroom phenomena, of the numerous observations system published in research journals the Flanders system seemed the most compact, providing the greatest amount of useful information which could be collected by trained observers without either putting too great a strain on them, or intruding too much in the lessons being observed.

Flanders (1970) describes a number of ratios which can be calculated from matrices assembled from raw data. In the present research, each student was observed for between four and six lessons, producing between 2,400 and 3,600 raw tallies. Several matrices can be summed and reduced to a base of 1,000, called a millage matrix, thus making the data comparable between one teacher and another. A total of 22 process variables were extracted from the students' millage matrices and a 23rd variable computed from the matrices on their first four lessons.

Measuring the product variables

In the foregoing review of research the difficulty of rating teacher effectiveness was discussed; it was decided in the present research to use three measures of competence. The first was the rating by the Head and supervising teachers in the teaching practice school. A team of four judges experienced in the assessment of student teachers read school reports independently and interpreted them as ratings of effectiveness on the commonly used A–E scale. Product moment correlations for inter-observer agreement were very high, ranging from +0.91 to +0.94. The four ratings were summed and the mean calculated.

The second measure of effectiveness was a rating by the supervising tutor, again using the A–E scale. Since both the tutor and the school ratings are subjective a third measure, the composite of the two scores, was used as a consensus of 'those competent to judge'.

The execution of the research

In the pilot study, observations were made during approximately 100 lessons given by thirty-one students. Computer programs were written for high speed processing of Flanders matrices on the Exeter University computer, and certain alterations made to the original plans. A new lesson observation sheet was designed, as were pocket timers to signal a three-second interval to the observer collecting interaction data.

For the main study in 1969/70 all 153 entrants to the Exeter University Department of Education were given the test battery on the first day of the Michaelmas Term. All the tests were scored according to procedures described in the test handbook. The two scorers of the Torrance tests showed correlations with each other of +0.99 for fluency, +0.87 for flexibility and +0.86 for originality.

Videotapes and sound tapes were prepared for training observers and for reliability checks. All materials were assembled and pocket timers were made and tested. Heads of schools received letters asking for co-operation should their school be in the sample of students being watched. No head refused; many showed considerable interest when observers later travelled around the schools.

Five observers were recruited and trained, using sound tapes, videotapes and live lessons. Inter-observer agreements were high. Flanders suggests that reliability coefficients should be given as comparisons with another trained observer when one is training new observers, the other trained observer usually being the investigator himself. On the final reliability check based on a 30-minute live lesson, the five observers obtained coefficients of 0.83, 0.84, 0.86, 0.86 and 0.90 with the present writer.

After two weeks out in schools all the observers met once more for a conference and further reliability check. Coefficients on this occasion based on a 20-minute sound tape of a lesson were 0.85, 0.86, 0.87, 0.89 and 0.89 with the present writer.

At the end of the whole project a final reliability check was made and on a 15-minute sound tape the five observers obtained coefficients of 0.85, 0.85, 0.87, 0.87 and 0.91 with the present writer. A check for *intra*-observer reliability was also made at the same time on a 15-minute sound tape which had been coded by the observers two months previously. Intra-observer reliability for all six people, including the present writer who had also been collecting data, was 0.86, 0.88, 0.88, 0.89, 0.91 and 0.92. Intra-observer reliability is the amount by which an observer agrees with his former coding of the same sound tape.

A sample of 104 students was chosen on the basis of geographical location and what each observer could be expected to cover in one term. Of the original sample of 104 one student left the course and so could not be observed, and one other student changed schools midway through the term and was also ill, so he was dropped too, giving a final sample of 102 students.

The 102 students consisted of 56 men and 46 women teaching in forty-one different schools in the South-west of England.

Once the observers had been trained to a high level of inter-observer reliability and the 102 students to be observed had been chosen, the next stage was to plan the observation schedules for each individual observer. Since the 23 process variables were eventually going to be calculated from the observation data, and since an analysis of all the data was going to be performed by age of children, type of school, stage of the teaching practice term and so on, it was important that each student should be observed for a 'representative' set of lessons.

[...]

Flanders suggests six lessons as constituting a usable sample, though many published researches have used two or even a single lesson, and few have in fact used as many as six. It was decided that the target would be six lessons, and that no student would be induced in the sample if he had been observed for less than four. Since all the data were eventually to be converted to millage matrices[1] for each student, the differences between students who had been watched for four, five or six lessons would be minimized. In practice this target was 94 per cent realized. Out of a maximum possible 612 lessons, 578 were actually observed. Seventy-eight students were watched for six lessons, 14 for five lessons and 10 for four lessons.

Another important point was that the lessons should be spaced. Observers were told to arrange the term in three periods, roughly equal to a beginning, middle and end period, and see that each student was visited in each of these periods. Similarly, observers were told to see each student with a spread of classes representing what he had on his timetable, so that lower school (first and second year), middle school (third, fourth year) and upper school (fifth, sixth year) lessons would be included. Obviously some students would not teach a fifth- or sixth-year class, and others might not teach a first or second year, but observers were to use their judgement. Visits were reported to the present writer weekly, and duplicated visiting schedules were maintained as a check in case any observer was not spreading visits evenly. This check was carried out carefully, but all observers covered the students very successfully.

The observers not only collected Flanders interaction data on each lesson; they also wrote an account of the lesson on the back of the data sheet shortly afterwards, usually the same day. This meant that there were also 578 detailed accounts of the lessons in addition to the interaction data. They also wrote a separate account of any lesson which seemed to need a special report for any reason, and a summary report of their experiences at the end of the whole project. These accounts of the lesson were necessary (a) to amplify the interaction data by giving a fuller picture of what happened in the lesson, and (b) to enable the present writer to give explanations in behavioural terms to certain patterns observed in different subjects, different schools etc.

After teaching practice was concluded, school and tutor reports were collected and a correlation of +0.648 between the two sets of scores was obtained.... Finally, the 578 lesson matrices were computed on the University computer and subjected to the data processing described below.

The results of the research

Analysis by group and stage of teaching practice

Matrix interpretation has been discussed by Flanders (1970). A simple flow chart can be drawn over a full matrix showing important transitions from cell to cell. Matrix interpretation plays an important part in interaction analysis research, and it should not be undertaken separately from some written accounts by observers of the lessons watched, otherwise the attempted analysis of flow in a lesson or group of lessons becomes too speculative.

In addition to the percentages of talk and teacher talk, ten other ratios are given with each matrix. All are described fully by Flanders (1970), but are summarized briefly here.

I/D ratio   A measure of teacher 'indirectness' which compares categories one, two, three and four with five, six and seven.

i/d ratio   Another measure of teacher 'indirectness' which Flanders claims is less dependent on content than the I/D ratio because it ignores categories four and five (question and lecture) and compares categories one, two and three with six and seven.

Teacher response ratio (TRR)   Like the remaining ratios, lies between 0 and 100. It measures the teacher's tendency to respond with praise or acceptance to children's answers.

Teacher question ratio (TQR)   Measures the teacher's tendency to use question rather than lecture in the more content-oriented parts of the lesson.

Pupil initiation ratio (PIR)   Shows how much of the children's talk was initiated by them rather than by the teacher.

Instantaneous teacher response ratio (TRR8/9)   Measures the teacher's tendency to integrate children's ideas into class discussion as soon as they have stopped talking.

Instantaneous teacher question ratio (TQR 8/9)   Similar to the ratio above in that it measures the teacher's tendency, immediately children have stopped talking, to ask a question rather than begin lecturing.

Content cross ratio (CCR)   A high score usually indicates greater concern with subject matter with the teacher playing a very active part.

Steady state ratio (SSR)   A high score indicates that talk tends to stay in the same category, whereas a low score is produced in lessons where there is rapid interchange between teacher and pupils.

Pupil steady state ratio (PSSR)   Measures the extent to which children sustain their contributions to classroom dialogue. Teachers who interrupt the flow of children's talk produce lower scores than those who do not.

The abbreviated forms, TRR, TQR, etc., are given below the matrices.

The whole group

[...]

Table 5.1 shows the millage matrix computed for all 578 lessons in the sample and represents a reduction from 337,617 raw tallies.

To summarize the data for the whole group it seems as if comparison with reported American data shows the British student teacher group as a whole to be less likely to accept ideas and feelings, but also less likely to give commands and use criticism. The British group was, on measures comparing the two sets of categories, more likely to make use of accepting or praising rather than commanding or criticizing than the experienced American teachers (TRR scores). There was a greater likelihood that the present group would use lecture rather than question in

Table 5.1 Matrix for all teachers (337,617 tallies from 578 lessons)

	1	2	3	4	5	6	7	8	9	10	Total	
1	0	0	0	0	0	0	0	0	0	0	1	Accepts feeling
2	0	1	3	3	3	1	0	1	2	2	17	Praise
3	0	1	4	8	9	1	0	1	2	3	30	Accepts ideas
4	0	0	0	13	4	1	1	43	2	14	79	Question
5	0	1	0	21	222	7	1	4	17	29	303	Lecture
6	0	0	0	2	4	13	1	5	2	11	39	Command
7	0	0	0	1	2	1	2	1	1	4	12	Criticism
8	0	8	17	12	12	4	2	36	3	6	99	Solicited children's talk
9	0	4	4	4	21	2	2	0	32	5	74	Unsolicited children's talk
10	0	1	0	16	26	9	3	8	12	270	346	Silence or non-codable

Notes: Talk = 65%; TRR = 48; TQR 8/9 = 32; Teacher talk = 73%; TQR = 21; CCR = 50; I/D = 0.36; PIR = 43; SSR = 59; i/d = 0.94; TRR 8/9 = 80; PSSR = 39.

the content-oriented parts of the lesson, but a wider range of practice in this area as measured by the Content Cross Ratio was noted from the student groups than amongst the American groups.

There was a substantially greater probability that children's talk would be initiated by the children themselves amongst the British student groups, who were also much more likely to respond to children's ideas and feelings with immediate praise or acceptance. The student group however was much less likely to respond to children with immediate supplementary questioning than the American group, and verbal activity was much more likely to stay in the same category with the student group.

The most striking differences seem to be in the much greater occurrence of pupil-initiated talk in the British students' lessons, and also the students' greater use of lecture compared with questions.

Analysis by sex of teacher

Table 5.2 gives the category totals for men teachers and women teachers.

A first analysis shows that men teachers make slightly greater use of praise and criticism and a substantially greater use of lecture, whereas women are more likely to ask questions and to accept ideas. It is however in the area of pupil talk that the most striking differences occur. In category eight (pupil talk in response to the teacher) women teachers register 121 tallies as opposed to 82 by the men teachers, but in category nine (spontaneous pupil talk) 69 tallies compared with 79 by the men.

Table 5.2 Category totals and ratios – men and women

	Men	Women
Category		
1 Accepts feeling	1	1
2 Praise	19	14
3 Accepts ideas	27	34
4 Question	70	89
5 Lecture	331	267
6 Command	38	40
7 Criticism	14	10
8 Solicited pupil talk	82	121
9 Unsolicited pupil talk	79	69
10 Silence, etc.	339	356
Ratios, etc.		
Talk	66%	64%
Teacher talk	76%	71%
I/D ratio	0.31	0.44
i/d ratio	0.89	0.99
TRR	47	50
TQR	18	25
PIR	49	36
TRR 8/9	79	80
TQR 8/9	32	32
CCR	51	49
SSR	63	56
PSSR	40	39

An interesting distribution is also to be seen in the cells of the matrices (not shown here) representing prolonged talk by the children, 8–8 and 9–9. Although the women teachers produce more sustained category eight talk, the men have more sustained spontaneous pupil talk in the 9–9 cell.

To test the significance of some of these differences t tests were applied to the individual scores of men and women students. Solicited pupil response ($t = 2.896$), I/D ratio ($t = 2.919$), TQR ($t = 3.232$), PIR ($t = 2.762$) and SSR ($t = 2.673$) were all significant at the 1 per cent level of confidence.

Analysis by age group of class

Analysis of lessons according to age group of class was also undertaken. Extraction of some of the category totals and ratios highlights certain interesting progressions.

	Lecture (5)	Criticism (7)	Silence (10)	CCR	Pupil talk (%)
1st year	232	16	385	43	32
2nd year	231	18	376	45	30
3rd year	307	16	342	50	25
4th year	306	9	351	52	26
5th year	341	5	338	58	23
6th year	436	1	249	63	23

Some of these trends appear remarkably clear. In use of lecture there is a noticeable and regular increase as the children get older, almost dividing the year groups exactly into lower school, middle school and upper school. This is reflected in the gradually increasing CCR which, according to Flanders, effectively measures the content-oriented parts of the lesson. The reverse of this trend is seen in the sixth year, the decline of category ten, as more and more time is devoted to open-class talk and less to project and workshop activities, and the marked and regular decrease of pupil talk from 32 per cent in the first year to 23 per cent in the sixth year.

The pattern of continuous working, continuous pupil talk both of a solicited and spontaneous kind, and continuous lecture, 10–10–5–5–4–8–8–2–9–9, is markedly present in the first two years. In the third and fourth years there is a sharp rise in lecture, especially continuous lecture (5–5 cell).

The fifth year, in most cases the 'O' level or CSE group, shows some differences which are worthy of closer examination. These lessons, whilst not unlike the third- and fourth-year lessons in certain respects, form a bridge between these and the sixth-year lessons. For example, whereas at first- and second-year level there were twice as many tallies in the 10–10 cell as in the 5–5 cell, and at third- and fourth-year level there was still a marked difference, at fifth-year level there is an almost exact balance (252 compared with 254 tallies). There is very little difference between the *category* total for silence and non-verbal activity when one compares third- and fifth-year lessons (342 compared with 338), but closer inspection of the full matrices shows clearer differences in distribution, especially in the 10–4 and 10–5 cells, and correspondingly in the 4–10, 5–10 cells. This suggests that whereas the silence or group working occurs more in blocks of time at third-year level, there is a greater incidence of short silences between questions and periods of lecture at fifth-year level. Also there is a higher frequency of questioning at fifth-year level than anywhere else with a concomitant higher loading in the 4–4 cell (continuous or repeated questioning) and the 4–10 cell as mentioned earlier. This suggests that at fifth-form level the student teachers asked more and longer questions, many of which, possibly because they were hard or thought-provoking, or because the students had greater difficulty eliciting responses from fifth-year classes, were followed by a short silence. There were fewer maintained answers (8–8 cells), but for the first time the sustained spontaneous talk (9–9 cell) exceeds the 8–8 cell.

The sixth-year lessons show a further sharp rise in lecture, and the 5–5 cell contains over twice as many tallies as the lower school matrices. Although the overall percentage of talk by the pupils is lowest of all year groups, it is interesting to note that the 50 tallies in the 9–9 cell, representing continuous spontaneous pupil talk, far exceed any other year group matrix, and PSSR is also higher than any other. Acceptance of ideas (category three) on the other hand is highest for any year group, and of special interest are the higher loadings in the 8–3 and 3–5 cells. This suggests a pattern of continuous information giving (5–5) spontaneous interruption (5–9–5), often prolonged as well as question and answer, and the acceptance of ideas rather than praise (8–3 rather than 8–2). Similarly, there is a greater incidence of acceptance of feeling (category one) than in any other year group.

Analysis by subject

Nine subjects: Maths, Physics, Chemistry, Biology, English, French, German, History and Geography, provided more than 15,000 tallies and are included under five headings, (a) Mathematics, (b) Sciences, (c) English, (d) Modern Languages, (e) History and Geography. (As these results are very lengthy and detailed, they are not included here.)

[...]

Analysis of individual students' scores

In addition to analysing the data by groups, certain comparisons have been made between the scores obtained by students for various of the presage, process and product variables.

Comparison of presage and process variables

For a sample of this size a product moment of $r = 0.194$ is significant at the 5 per cent level (*) and $r = 0.253$ is significant at the 1 per cent level (**). Table 5.3 shows correlations between presage and process variables found to be significant at the 1 per cent level of confidence. Since 1,431 separate intercorrelations have been calculated, a number of significant relationships are to be expected by chance.

The correlations between Cattell A (warmth) and certain kinds of accepting behaviour (ID ratio and TQR), and both Cattell I (sensitivity) and the Aesthetic value and high sustained pupil talk (PSSR, category eight and negative correlation with teacher talk) are especially interesting as they do appear to have a logical basis. Such links between measured personality traits and observed classroom behaviour are worthy of further study.

The Torrance test scores show a small number of interesting relationships. There are correlations between fluency scores and acceptance of ideas ($r = 0.271**$), use of question ($r = 214*$), and use of commands ($r = 0.223*$). Flexibility correlates with use of commands and solicited pupil talk ($r = 0.225*$ and $r = 0.228*$).

Table 5.3 Summary of correlations between presage variables and process variables found to be significant at the 1 per cent level

		Cat 3	Cat 4	Cat 6	Cat 8	Cat 10	% Teacher Talk	I/D	TQR	SSR	PSSR
1	Cattell A							0.272	0.313		
8	Cattell I				0.271		−0.370				0.317
12	Cattell O			0.267							
15	Cattell Q3						0.277				
16	Cattell Q4						−0.256				
18	Economic value						0.270				−0.337
19	Aesthetic value				0.304		−0.422				0.268
20	Social value		0.264						0.282		
23	Fluency	0.271									
28	Degree class						−0.392				−0.272

Originality correlates negatively with Teacher talk ($r = -0.196^*$), suggesting the original teacher is more willing to listen to children talking. [...]

Finally, the negative correlation between class of degree and category 10 ($r = -0.392^{**}$) either suggests that the more academic teachers talk more, which may be the case, or it may be an artifact due to the Arts/Science differences both in level of qualifications and classroom patterns. [...]

The relation of product variables to both presage and process variables

Variable 54 (composite of ratings of effectiveness by schools and tutors) was used to group the 102 students in the sample into three groups rated above average, average and below average. One way analysis of variance was used to test the significance of the differences in the scores obtained on the presage and process variables by the three groups. For the F ratio to be significant with groups of this size it must exceed 3.09 at the 5 per cent level and 4.81 at the 1 per cent level. Significant F ratios were obtained for presage variables 9 (Cattell L), 15 (Cattell Q3), 24 (Torrance Flexibility) and 28 (class of degree). For Cattell Q3 (self-control), the F ratio was 8.41**, and both the above average and below average groups had a higher mean score than the average group, that is, tended to show greater self-control. This might suggest that for student teachers to be self-controlled can be both good and bad. Start (1966) reported good teachers to be low on Q3, whereas Erickson (1954) found them high on the same variable.

On Cattell L, the above average teachers were highest (more trusting) and the below average lowest (more paranoid), giving an F ratio of 3.57*. This supports the finding of Start (1966) with experienced teachers.

On variable 24, Torrance flexibility score, the above average group scored higher than both the average and below average groups who had nearly identical mean scores, and the F ratio was 3.21*. Finally class of degree, usually known to the raters, was also significant with an F ratio of 5.23** with the above average group tending to have the best degrees and the below average group the poorest.

Although no significant F ratios were obtained between classroom behaviour measures and ratings of effectiveness, there were a number of significant correlation coefficients. Use of criticism (category seven) correlates negatively with Tutors' ratings ($r = 0.267$**) and composite rating ($r = -0.223$*) though not with schools' ratings ($r = -0.140$ n.s.). This suggests that tutors are less likely to favour those students who make greater use of criticism. For many student teachers, extensive use of criticism, especially in the later stages of teaching practice, often occurs in classes where the teacher has lost control and has to shout and threaten in order to restore some kind of order.

The second classroom variable to correlate with measures of effectiveness was solicited pupil talk (category eight). This correlated $r = 0.251$* with schools' ratings, $r = 0.201$* with tutors' ratings and $r = 0.250$* with composite ratings, suggesting that both supervising parties value high solicited talk. It is interesting to compare this with the very low correlation between ratings and category nine which are $r = 0.000$ n.s., $r = 0.010$ n.s. and $r = 0.005$ n.s. for schools, tutors and total respectively.

On the whole there is the expected low incidence of significant relationships between measures of effectiveness and presage and process variables.

[...]

Conclusions

Research design and procedures

As this was a first live study of a large number of student teachers, it was difficult to decide what should be controlled for in an area where the number of significant variables was high and complex. In practice, there was some control for stage of teaching practice and age group of class. Future studies could well concentrate on particular subject areas and type of school, as well as other priorities.

The test materials used in the present research were satisfactory but certain reservations must be expressed. The Cattell 16PF would have been better if the longer and more reliable forms A or B had been administered. The Torrance tests are not entirely satisfactory for reasons stated earlier. It is a matter of some urgency that valid and reliable creativity tests for intelligent adults are developed in this country. The AH5 produced little which proved to be related to other measures.

The Flanders system was shown to have a number of limitations. The main inadequacy of the Flanders system was shown to be in the laboratory/workshop situation. In practice, most teachers having private consultations with individual pupils could be heard by the observer, except when there was considerable noise, or when the teacher spoke very softly, and it must be assumed, because of the 'ripple effect' that these private interactions had some effect on classroom climate, since others could hear them. The low incidence of pupil talk in these lessons, however, could easily lead to the usually unjustified conclusion that children did not talk, because the Flanders system looks only at teacher–pupil interaction, and only codes pupil–pupil interactions when these occur in open-class discussion.

Category one, an infrequently appearing category, is retained by Flanders because he feels that acceptance of feeling is significant where it occurs. It would be worthwhile investigating a little more closely the effects of this category. It is the writer's experience both from personal observation and from training almost 100 observers in three years, that it is a category which is frequently missed. The reliability of observers for category one is low, yet overall inter-observer reliability using the Flanders system tends to be very high, when observers have been trained thoroughly. This is because, out of 500 tallies, one observer may record ten tallies in category one, another five and, a third none at all. These differences are minimized in the Scott formula calculations as they only amount to 1 or 2 per cent.

The present research did not support Flanders' claim that category three, accepting ideas, shows few differences according to subject matter. Subjects tended to polarize with Maths and Sciences low and some Arts subjects high. This may reflect differences in English and American teaching patterns as mentioned earlier.

The CCR needs closer analysis. It was shown in the present research to be correlated significantly with class of degree, suggesting that the better qualified students recorded more interactions in this area. It still needs to be validated more rigorously, however, and this might be done by two observers coding separately 'subject-oriented talk' and Flanders categories. This ought to show how meaningful the term 'content cross' really is. Student 39 for example, an English teacher who had long class discussions and recorded higher category one and nine totals than any other student, has a CCR of 34 which is one of the lowest, largely because of the heavily tallied 8–8 and 9–9 cells which are outside the content cross area. Yet few would have disputed that these extended class discussions were relevant to the task. For a student like this the term 'content cross' has little meaning.

Perhaps greater standardimation of lesson reports might have been advisable. It was thought best to leave this to the discretion of the observer who had been trained in what to look for and knew the kind of information needed. Nevertheless, there were differences in lesson reports. Some were long and detailed, others short and less detailed. This caused few problems in practice, but if more information were needed about classroom organization and its relationship to Flanders data, a more formal way of reporting the lesson would be essential.

A number of category systems already in use might be more suitable for certain studies of student teachers than the Flanders system.

[...]

Some theoretical considerations

Flexibility

Variable 51 in this research, the so-called Flexibility Factor is a measure of variety within the terms of the Flanders system. As a measure of variety of teaching pattern it merits closer scrutiny.

Two examples are given below in Table 5.4 of contrasting types of Mathematics teacher. Student teacher A chose a lecturing style in every one of the four lessons given in the table, as shown both by the lesson reports, and a range of 72 per cent to 89 per cent was recorded in category five (lecture). Because of this, the lecture category is always large and the other categories correspondingly small. The flexibility factor of Student A was 16, among the lowest recorded. Student B, another mathematician, had a varied lesson pattern in terms of the ten categories. In the first lesson she made extensive use of question and answer, and a similar pattern is seen in her fourth lesson, though with more lecture. Her second lesson was more of a workshop, after a lecture and question and answer introduction, but her third lesson consisted almost entirely of children working out problems from a duplicated sheet she had distributed. Her flexibility factor is 52, much higher than Student A, but not among the highest recorded in the sample.

[...]

Table 5.4   Comparison of the flexibility factors of two Mathematics students

Cat.	Lesson [Student A (FF = 16)]				Lesson [Student B (FF = 52)]			
	1st	2nd	3rd	4th	1st	2nd	3rd	4th
1	0	0	0	0	0	0	0	0
2	0	0	2	0	8	0	0	4
3	0	0	1	0	2	4	0	4
4	7	4	6	1	21	10	2	13
5	72	82	80	89	11	24	6	21
6	7	4	0	1	3	2	0	5
7	0	0	0	0	0	2	0	2
8	6	2	2	2	17	6	1	15
9	2	1	1	2	4	5	2	4
10	6	7	8	5	34	47	89	32
Total	100	100	100	100	100	100	100	100

English	64	Geography	38	Languages	32
Art	42	Chemistry	37	Biology	30
History	42	Maths	33	Physics	28

This underlines the subjective lesson reporting by the observers that English teachers tended to have varied lesson patterns, whereas Languages and Science tended to be more stereotyped.

Finally, one needs to consider whether the flexibility factors are low generally, that is, whether most students tend to use a limited range of strategies as measured by the Flanders system. This is difficult to decide because (a) there are no published norms, nor can there be unless conditions are made similar, and (b) in any case little research has been conducted in the area.

[...]

Teaching styles

The cluster analysis as well as flow chart analysis of subject matrices showed certain common strategies in use. Seven micro-paradigms can be constructed from chains of Flanders categories frequently observed.

1. *Continuous lecture* occasionally punctuated by silence gives a sequence of 5–5–5–5–10–5–5–5–5–10 which was frequently observed in Geography lessons and was a part of most lessons.

2. *Reinforced high-speed drill* consisted of a question–answer–praise sequence and was frequently noted in the foreign language parts of modern language lessons or when teachers were testing. The sequence of 4–8–2–4–8–2 is repeated.

3. *Programmed instruction* uses the sequence 5–5–4–8–3–2–5–5, showing the 'frame' of information followed by question, answer, acceptance, praise and further information. It was used extensively by some Geography and History teachers and was more common in the lower and middle school rather than in the upper school.

4. *Directive style* centred around the 6–6 cell and was common in Science lessons, especially Biology, certain types of Language lessons and with younger age-groups. The sequence was 6–6–10–10–6–8–10–10.

5. *Disorder* often manifested itself as strings of category ten representing chaos rather than silence and category seven. It was rare in girls' schools and the Upper Schools. Category nine occurred when children called out, giving a sequence such as 10–10–7–7–7–9–7–10–7.

6. *Pupil-oriented discussion* had its focus around the 9–9 cell and tended to be most common in English and History lessons and with the youngest and oldest age groups. It was commonly observed after half-term, possibly because students then felt able to act as non-directive chairmen. It rarely occurred in Science or Language lessons. The sequence was 9–9–9–9–1–9–9–9–3–9–9–5–9–9.

7. *Workshop* produced a heavily tallied 10–10 cell as children worked in pairs or small groups. The teacher tended to service the groups, going round asking questions. The Flanders system is not entirely adequate to describe this kind of activity. Science and Maths lessons regularly produced a sequence like 10–10–10–9–5–9–5–10–10–10–4–8–4–8–8–10–10.

[...]

Note

1 A millage matrix is used to enable rough comparisons to be made between large raw matrices. All tallies in the large matrices are reduced to a base of 1,000. The process is similar to that used for calculating percentages, except that a millage matrix has a base of 1,000, and a percentage has a base of 100.

References

Adams, R. S. and Biddle, B. J. (1970). *Realities of Teaching*, New York: Holt, Rinehart and Winston.

Erickson, H. E. (1954). 'A Factorial Study of Teaching Ability', *Journal of Experimental Education*, 23, 1–39.

Flanders, N. A. (1970). *Analyzing Classroom Behavior*, New York: Addison-Wesley.

Start, K. B. (1966). 'The Relationship of Teaching Ability to Measures of Personality', *British Journal of Educational Psychology*, 36, 158–65.

PART 2

TRAINING NEW AND EXPERIENCED TEACHERS

One logical sibling of classroom-observation research is studying the training of teachers. The relationship, however, is not a straightforward one. On the surface, teaching stands in apposition to medicine as an evidence- or research-based profession: find out what 'works' and then get all teachers/doctors to do it. The reality is, sadly, not so neat. Events and 'treatments' do not always impact as predictably on human minds as they might on human bodies. Fifty milligram 'doses' cannot be as precisely administered in classrooms as they are in a hospital. Some researchers have even tried to script teachers' questions. Unfortunately they cannot script the answers. Moreover, children are not sick creatures to be cured of their illnesses.

If the same amount of cash and researcher time had been applied to the study of teachers' and learners' strategies as has been devoted to gene mapping, we might be a little closer to a true science of teaching. Even if there were vastly more banks of knowledge available, however, about the effects of every conceivable pedagogical move on every known type of learner, it would still be inadvisable to try and prescribe to teachers exactly what they should do in the face of every single eventuality.

The massively different *contexts* in which teaching and learning take place mean that teachers usually have to decide for themselves, and within a second or two, what action they should take. It is what Nate Gage (1975) called, in the title of his book, *The Scientific Basis of the Art of Teaching*. That is why the 'development' phase of my own research has been conceived more in terms of helping novice as well as experienced teachers to look closely at events and phenomena, rather than telling them what to do: activities such as analysing classroom interactions, videoing teachers at work, studying pupils, evaluating the curriculum, or devising one's own.

I have not written a great deal of historical text, but Chapter 6 is one I particularly enjoyed writing for the first book I ever published, *Teaching Teaching*, in 1974. I spent a whole summer in the library researching it and found the topic absolutely fascinating. Chapter 7 is a short extract from *Classroom Teaching Skills*, written ten years later, trying to define the elusive notion of 'skill' in teaching. More illustrative of my work in this field are Chapters 8 and 9, showing how research and development can combine and complement each other. Chapter 8 describes what I think is one of the most interesting pieces of research I have ever carried out, analysing the art of explaining in the primary school, from a 1993 book *Primary Teaching Skills*. Chapter 9, from a 2001 series on topics like explaining, questioning, class management and others, translates research into practice, by showing secondary teachers how to analyse and improve their own explanations.

Children consistently rate explaining as the professional skill they value most, a research finding I highlighted in Chapter 2, so although I have done exactly the same type of 'research into practice' exercise with topics like 'class management' and 'questioning', I have always regarded my work on 'explaining' as the most significant, both in terms of educational research and teacher development. It is an area I want to develop further, as it is potentially highly fruitful and under-explored.

CHAPTER 6

TEACHER EDUCATION
A historical perspective

Originally published as 'Some Historical Exemplars', in *Teaching Teaching*, David & Charles, 1974, pp. 15–43

My first book was called *Teaching Teaching*, published in 1974. It grew out of my research into classrooms and teacher training and I was keen to start it with a chapter describing the evolution of teacher education. This chapter gives an account of teacher training from classical times right up to the twentieth century and researching it was probably one of my most enjoyable experiences. The exercise taught me a lot and what I learned has been very useful ever since.

Factors influencing the course of teacher education and training

The history of teacher education runs closely parallel to the history of schools and indeed to that of the society concerned. In modern Communist China the prepara-tion of teachers, with emphasis on service to the people, factory experience for the student teacher and the thoughts of Chairman Mao Tse-tung as its inspiration, bears but slight resemblance to the senseless chanting of the Chinese classics to which generations of trainees had been subjected. Similarly, the issues facing those whose task it is to prepare teachers in contemporary Britain or the United States, where, for the first time, prospects of teacher surplus are in view, are quite different from those which Bell and Lancaster encountered in early nineteenth-century Britain, or Horace Mann in Massachusetts in 1840, when qualified teachers were scarce and the demand for popular education was beginning to grow.

There are several factors which can determine the content and pattern of teacher education programmes. The sheer size of a country can produce proportionate diffi-culties, as in China in 1956, for example, when the Ministry of Education estimated that over 1 million new teachers would be needed in the following seven years. The problem of size is sometimes compounded by the after-effects of war, so that in the late 1940s the USSR had to face rebuilding its institutions without the aid of its 20 million dead of World War II. In Japan also one in four houses had been destroyed and some cities in both Japan and Germany were almost completely obliterated.

Some postwar priorities are clear, such as the need for denazification of German teacher training in the period from 1945 onwards. Occasionally wars produce a welcome bonus, though the price paid has usually been a heavy one. In both the United States and Britain emergency training programmes after both world wars, despite the need for expediency, relative brevity of courses and many large classes, produced new ideas and procedures which persisted long after the courses had ceased to exist. In addition, the arrival of large numbers of mature recruits, often with a high level of skill and experience, tended to alter, substantially in certain cases, the nature of the training institution.

Social conditions of the time have proved powerful determinants in the pattern of teacher preparation. Bell and Lancaster at the beginning of the nineteenth century saw the need to provide teachers for vast numbers of boys and girls of working-class families who spent most of their days labouring in mills and factories or on the land. The requirement of Sir Robert Peel's 1802 Factory Act that they should receive instruction in the three Rs and religion on Sundays was often ignored by the factory and mill owners. The situation was made worse by the dire poverty of the children and the almost total lack of any educational tradition in the families. In this context the monitorial system, which used older children to teach the younger ones, was a brilliant, if in retrospect obvious, solution. The brief mechanical nature of the monitors' training was almost inevitable, since extended and more leisurely education would have seemed a cruel luxury, enjoyed by a minority at the expense of the suffering mass. The privileged few who were able to enjoy a lengthy and broad education at that time tended, with some notable exceptions, to make little contribution to the education and welfare of the working-class population.

Religious organisations have frequently used their autonomy and experience to establish sectarian centres of teacher education or to influence existing institutions and patterns of training. This was notable in countries such as Ireland, India, Germany and the United States, where different religions competed for devotees and needed to some extent to spread into teaching in order to reach people at an early age. It was not solely, however, to compete or to maintain a position of strength that led to the foundation of religiously based training institutions. The tradition of preparing others to teach is often rooted in the very beginnings of a religious movement, and Christ's own recruitment and preparation of disciples has parallels in the history of other great religious and political movements. Mao Tse-tung's early experiences at the strongly humanist First Teachers' Training School at Changsha, and later as a primary school teacher and headmaster, were important to the development of his political thought, and subsequently led him to recruit and inspire others who would teach his political ideas to the nation.

In Europe the Jesuits, especially in the period 1450–1850, introduced a systematisation of teacher training which was almost without precedent. Books such as the *Ratio Studiorum*, produced in 1586 and revised in 1599, were blueprints which described teaching techniques in detail and were followed almost to the letter. In Tsarist Russia under Peter the Great, in the late seventeenth and early eighteenth centuries, all available teachers were priests, and most of them had been trained at theological seminaries. When Catherine II established a pedagogical seminary at St Petersburg to reduce the teacher shortage, she was largely dependent on the bishops' willingness to release candidates from the theological seminaries. Since they were understandably reluctant to surrender their best students, they responded by sending some of their more lazy and drunken students.

The teacher-priest, nevertheless, tended to be a formidable figure, a man of great breadth and authority. Dean Church describes the role he might play in a rural parish in England:

> When communication was so difficult and infrequent, he filled a place in the country life of England that no one else could fill. He was often the patriarch of his pupils, its ruler, its doctor, its lawyer, its magistrate, as well as its teacher, before whom vice trembled and rebellion dared not show itself.[1]

In Britain, the Church was the first body to establish a system of licences for its teachers in the Middle Ages, when it also formed teaching orders. The Church of England in the nineteenth century was instrumental in creating two of the very first training colleges – St Luke's College, Exeter, and the College of St Mark and St John in London. Before this, the fact that Joseph Lancaster was a Quaker significantly influenced the pattern of training received by his monitors.

The religious orders have at various times and in many countries played an important part in the education and training of teachers, but at the same time a vigorous secular tradition has developed, reaching its height at the present day. Universities have figured prominently in these developments, although they tended to have religious connections in the earlier part of their history. In most countries a university degree has entitled its holder to teach, usually at secondary level, but graduates have entered elementary schools, too. No further training was deemed necessary, as is still the case with university teaching itself in the greater part of the world.

One of the most interesting aspects of the secular tradition in teacher education is the style of influence developed by its exponents. With a religious order many of the possible channels of communication and control are already established. There are devotees, buildings, a tradition, a hierarchy, administrative expertise and considerable authority in the community. Pioneers in the secular field have often begun with none of these.

In some cases those who have influenced the course and content of teacher education have been practitioners like Pestalozzi and Froebel, running schools or working with children, and using methods which attracted international attention and led to frequent visits from abroad as well as invitations to assist in the training of new or experienced teachers. Some of the so-called 'great educators', such as Montessori and Dewey, became very active in the training of teachers, whereas others, like A. S. Neill, positively resisted attempts to institutionalise their 'methods' or lure them into moving out of their schools and into teacher training.

Most of the best known and most influential figures had considerable personal dynamism and charisma. Froebel, for example, was very excited after a visit to Yverdon to see Pestalozzi. They fired others with enthusiasm by their example. David Stow, whose Glasgow Normal Seminary was, in 1837, years ahead of its time in terms of sophistication and methodological variety and subtlety, was inundated with visitors, most of whom were very impressed by what they saw, especially when they compared it with the relative sterility of Bell's monitorial training scheme. Fuller[2] describes a tour made by stagecoach in 1840 by the first Principal of St Luke's College, Exeter, and a member of the Exeter Diocesan Board. A contemporary account of their tour and report shows how a visit of this kind can be influential in affecting the content and nature of a training course: 'They were of the opinion that some of the improvements suggested by Mr Stow and others in the practice of teaching may, with propriety, be engrafted on Dr Bell's system, but recommended that the introduction of these should be made with caution.'[3]

A significant factor in the in-service training of teachers has always been the head of the school, especially in the smaller units of the elementary sector. To a large extent the British 'primary school revolution' was pressed through vigorously, often in the face of severe counter-pressures from parents, teachers or authorities, by this hardy and intrepid band of pioneers, many of whom would work in the classrooms with their teachers until the changes were effected.

Seaborne reports a retired primary school teacher recalling vividly the details of her teaching in 1910:

> My headmistress was very foreseeing. She was one of the first people to help us to realise that we should stop teaching children in the mass and to see that they were little individuals. We started to teach 'free arithmetic'; we bought rolls of paper and measured them with the children and we began to go to the shops for boxes. We cut pictures out from advertisements and the rooms began to look brighter. The headmistress fought a battle with the HMIs (His Majesty's Inspectors) and local people, and we did no set arithmetic in the infants' department. No doubt the most important mark we made was in the beginning to get children to live with numbers, and enjoy them.[4]

These then are some of the factors which have helped shape the history of teacher education and training: social and political pressures, wars, religious organisations, the great educators, and the zeal of individual practitioners in schools and training institutions.

It is clearly outside the scope of this chapter to give detailed histories of all civilised and primitive societies' attempts to prepare their teachers, but there follows a consideration of a number of the many interesting models reported in the literature.

Primitive communities

Accounts by anthropologists of twentieth-century primitive communities in New Guinea, Borneo, South America or Africa, or by historians depicting the early stages of industrialised societies like Britain and the United States, abound with descriptions of teaching. It is quite clear that a great deal of teaching takes place in tribes and families. What is missing in most cases, however, is formal training for those who do the teaching. To know something or to possess a skill is to be in a position to teach it to others.

Since there is often common agreement within the tribe about what children need to learn, such as the basic skills of hunting, cooking, making materials and weapons, and perhaps certain tribal dances and rituals, much of the teaching is informal. Indeed in some tribes care of children is a task given to trusted tribe members quite early in their lives. Okafor-Omali describes the practice in Nigeria:

> Nweke was only four months old when his mother entrusted him completely to the care of a baby-nurse. Baby-nurses were generally children of about eight to ten years. It was their duty to take care of the child and keep him playing while the mother was busy in the compound or at the farm or market. ...
>
> This work was usually done by members of the child's family or extended family, or by a close relation of the mother with good personal qualifications. It was a matter of pride for children to have such an assignment and they were happy to be relieved, to some extent, from domestic work.[5]

Subsequently all children tend to be the responsibility of their mothers for the early part of their lives, after which boys become attached to their fathers and girls to other women in the tribe as well as their own mother.

Where parents or close relatives do not have a high level of performance in a skill thought to be important for the children, there is often a competent and respected member of the tribe who is willing or even expected to teach it. He is 'untrained' and 'unqualified' in any formal sense, yet, because of the intimacy of the society in which he lives, common acknowledgement of his skill and ability to teach it are clearly sufficient. Were he manifestly unskilled or unable to teach children, he would be unlikely to attract pupils, especially where some token payment is made.

Smith gives what is probably a fairly accurate, if slightly idealised, version of the primitive system at its best:

> In the earlier order of things the father educated his son by a varied life out of doors, by growing food and breeding cattle, and the boy acquired his skill at an early age. His object lessons were got from the smithy, the weaver's shed, the mill, and the carpenter's shop, and his imagination was fired by the stories and legends which belonged to the familiar woods and streams and the neighbouring castle and manor.[6]

At its worst the primitive system produced teachers who were charlatans; they extorted money from their more simple and trusting fellows, and were cruel, perhaps even expected to be cruel, to the children in their care, and education and training based on nothing but each individual's perception of how children learn produced steretyped and ineffective teaching.

In certain respects, the primitive model has persisted well into modern times. The self-appointed local teacher, often barely ahead of his pupils in the skills he was teaching, was widely known in Britain in the mid-nineteenth century, as advertisements in shop windows, such as the following from Wellcombe in Devon in 1851, reveal:

> Roger Giles, Surgin, Parish Clark and Skulemaster, Groser, and Hundertaker, Respectably informs ladys and gentlemen that he drors teef without wateing a minit, applies laches every hour, blisters on the lowest terms, and vizieks for a penny a peace. He sells Godfather's Kordales, kuts korns, bunyons, doktors hosses, clip donkies, wance a munth, and undertakes to luke arter every bodies nayles by the ear. Joes-harps, penny wissels, brass kannelsticks, fryinpans, and other moozikal Hinstrumints hat grately reydooced figers. Young ladys and genelmen larnes their grammur and langeudge, in the purtiest manner, also grate care is taken off their morrels and spellin. Also zarm-zinging, tayching the base vial, and all other zarts of vancy work, squadrils, pokers, weazils, and all country dances tort at home and abroad at perfekshun. Perfumery and Znuff, in all its branches. As times is cruel bad, I begs to tell ey that i his just beginned to sell all sorts of stashonery ware, cox, hens, vouls, pigs, and all other kinds of poultry...P.S. I tayches gography, rithmetic, cowsticks, jimnastiks, and other chynees tricks.[7]

Despite his Renaissance Man self-image, poor Roger Giles was obviously down on his luck, but he deserves some credit for both persistence and divergent thinking.

Classical models

Although features of the primitive system of self-elected or communally approved teachers without formal qualifications and training, whose pupils used them as their models, have survived into modern times, in the so-called 'classical' periods of Greece and Rome, and earlier still in China and India, teachers received more systematic preparation for their profession.

The nature of professional training has been contingent upon, first, what was deemed to be important for children to learn in a particular society, and second, upon the philosophy of the person entrusted with the task of preparing the teachers. Broudy has drawn attention to three elements in the first of these:

> In every age the school has been expected to provide, first of all *linguistic skills*, the basic tool of learning in any well-developed culture. It is most surprising, therefore, that much of the history of pedagogy hovers about the ways and means of teaching language – for the most part, Latin and Greek as foreign languages. Next in the order of expectation was *a stock of knowledge* – whatever knowledge was in vogue: what the poets said, or what the astronomers, astrologers, theologians, physicists, and alchemists certified as truth. Finally, it was expected that instruction would build into the pupil *habits* of using his acquired skill and knowledge in the forum or in the courts of law and kings, as teachers and prelates, princes and ambassadors, doctors, clergymen, lawyers, scientists, and statesmen, or, in later centuries, as tradesmen, workers, and citizens.[8]

In ancient India, knowledge of the sacred texts was held to be of great importance. The teacher had to be very familiar with the content and meaning of the scriptures. Essentials of his training to teach others were self-knowledge and humility. To achieve all these objectives he was attached to the household of his own teacher or guru for quite a lengthy period of time. His task was to serve the guru in however menial a way, to acquire from him wisdom, a way of living and ultimately the supreme goal of knowledge of Brahman, the Absolute.

The Bible contains similar teacher-priest models both in the Old Testament and the New, where Christ's preparation of his own disciples illustrates this pattern of training. They, too, had to share his way of life and learn from his insights before being sent out to teach others.

Holmes highlights the special importance of the teacher of teachers at this time: 'If, however, the teacher is one of a professional group charged with special tasks, what should be his training? An ancient tradition places great stress on the need for close personal contact with a practising teacher and on the desirability of learning through long and supervised experience.'[9]

Confucius, himself a successful teacher at the age of 20, resigned his post as Chief Justice in China in the fifth century BC to wander around with his disciples. They, too, lived and worked with him before being released to go their own way as teachers. In the Chinese tradition, his views on teaching were also set down in written form to be studied by future disciples. His philosophy of teaching, as set down in the *Analects*, is full of shrewd observation, much of which would not be out of place in modern texts:

> I shall not teach until the pupils desire to know something, and I do not help unless the pupils really need my help. If out of the four corners of a subject I have dealt thoroughly with one corner and the pupils cannot then find out the other three for themselves, then I do not explain any more.
>
> (*Analects* VII, 8)[10]

The authoritative book on teaching methods is found at various stages of history in ancient China. It is at the heart of any new developments during the various dynasties, and familiarity with it was a prerequisite for the trainee teacher. Richardson describes the stereotyped teaching to which it could lead:

> It is explained in the classic Book of Rites (Li Chi) how the training is to be accomplished: the moral by word of mouth and the practical or technical by imitation and emulation of the teacher. The teacher reads out the principles and the pupils repeat them after him, echoing every intonation and stress, and this is continued until the pupils are word-perfect. The teacher performs the action in the ceremony or dance or musical or military exercise and the pupils slavishly follow his every movement, and this is repeated until the pupils are action perfect.[11]

The Chinese pattern of the teacher as the paragon ideal, the model on which learners were to base their development, has survived to the present day, as has the chanting of the mentor's wisdom. The *Sab Zi Jing* (*Three Character Classic*), written in 960 AD, was still being taught by peasants to their sons as late as the 1950s. Once the classic had been long extant, the children understood little of what they were repeating, but teachers were not being trained to question the mindlessness of the activity, so it survived. Wu Yun-duo describes the hostility which might greet any deviation from the pattern: 'The master never explained anything, and when I asked a question, he simply stared me into silence.'[12]

In contrast to the Chinese experience, trainee teachers in classical Greece and Rome were often exposed to a variety of patterns, some of which could be quite disturbing in their lack of an authoritarian lead. The early stages of teaching in Athens merely exposed children to good examples from parents and other respected members of the community. Subsequently, they would meet teachers who would develop whatever skills were thought to be important at the time. Isocrates, for example, developed the model of the rhetoric teacher. To hold his own a young man of democratic Athens would need to be able to argue a point of view or stand up in public and make a speech. His teachers, therefore, would need to be skilled rhetoricians themselves, and much of the teaching, though it tended at its worst to become systematised imitation, was designed to make pupils verbally alert. Protagoras was so well esteemed as a teacher of oratory and skill in argument that he was able to charge 10,000 drachmas from parents who wished their sons to be turned into successful men of affairs in three or four years.

For Socrates the final stage of education was liberation, the very element missing from much of classical Chinese teaching. The pupil was liberated when his questioning led him to reject habit and prejudice:

> No-one can teach, if by teaching we mean the transmission of knowledge, in any mechanical fashion from one person to another. The most that can be done is that one person who is more knowledgeable than another can, by asking a series of questions, stimulate the other to think, and so cause him to learn for himself.[13]

None of the well-known Greek and Roman teachers was solely a teacher of teachers. Of course, many of their pupils did themselves become teachers, and sitting at the feet of a distinguished man was at least a considerable boost to prestige even if not a prerequisite.

The Sophists, like Protagoras, Prodicus of Ceos and Giorgias of Leontini, subjected known examples of good writing to systematic analysis, and this led to the creation of what were virtually teaching handbooks by later figures such as Dionysius of Thrace, who laid down a sequence of steps to be followed when giving a lecture on a literary work (166 BC):

1   Give the selected passages an exact reading with respect to pronunciation, punctuation, and rhetorical expression.
2   Explain the figures of speech.
3   Explain the historical and mythological references.
4   Comment on the choice of words and their etymology.
5   Point out the grammatical forms employed.
6   Estimate the literary merit of the selection.[14]

In Rome, Cicero and Quintilian analysed teaching methodology in considerable detail, and their analysis of, for example, delivering a lecture on a topic, or asking children to write sentences which copied the style of the writer being studied, were extremely influential.

The teacher-orator model is seen in Christian times later on. St Augustine, who educated Christian teachers, emphasised that knowledge of the scripture was not sufficient. Trainees had to be trained in the skills of oral expression, so that they could both communicate meaning to their pupils and, if necessary, defend their faith against the educated non-believer in public.

In later times when classical ideals were revived, Cicero's techniques were still held in esteem. The twelfth-century scholar Peter Abelard, who also taught teachers, made extensive use of discussion and debate in his own teaching. Eventually skill in argument was judged and became a prerequisite for early teaching licences. Students at medieval universities who could demonstrate their skill might be accepted as members of a teachers' guild. At the University of Paris, in the thirteenth century, students were trained in the skills of lecturing and were then asked to dispute a thesis with a master before a board of examiners. If successful, they would be granted the chancellor's licence to teach. At Bologna University, a candidate for a bachelor's degree had to have given a course of lectures to other students in order to get his degree. The poorer performers had to bribe their fellows to get an audience.

Alongside the trained rhetoric teacher in classical Rome was a strong father-teacher image. Horace, in his *Satires*, describes his father as 'always present, an incorruptible overseer, at all my studies'.[15] As in earlier societies, a boy might later be handed over to a personal tutor at about the age of 16. This man would usually have experience and good reputation, and often be held in much greater esteem than the Greek or Roman elementary schoolmaster, who was not highly regarded. Lucian classed elementary schoolmasters with sellers of kippers in terms of poverty, and they had a reputation for administering cruel corporal punishment. The personal tutor would initiate the boy into public life. Cicero himself was attached to Quintus Mucius Scaevola, a distinguished lawyer.

The features of teacher training in classical societies which distinguish it from primitive cultures are that some of the methodology was written in books for students to learn; that attachment to a distinguished scholar, orator, philosopher or religious leader was sufficient to qualify a person to teach what he had learned, provided he had also absorbed the required way of life; that teaching methods were being systematically analysed and some attention was being given to how children learned; and that in certain cases both teaching and preparation for teaching were becoming stereotyped and unrelated to the needs of the students. Seneca, in his *Epistles*, voices a common lament: 'Non vitae sed scholae discimus' ('We learn not for life but for school').[16]

Teacher training in industrialised societies

The advent of large-scale industralisation in many European countries in the late eighteenth and early nineteenth centuries produced a concomitant increase in the size of cities. In addition, pressure was being applied for compulsory education for children, and the lack of sufficient 'qualified' teachers was clearly an obstacle to progress.

Consequently, much of the experience in all countries at the early stages of their industrial evolution centres around expediency. The pressing need was to produce as many respectable candidates for teaching as possible, rapidly cement the more gaping holes in their own education, and process them through a brief teaching methods programme whose emphasis was on survival skills. It was merely one further exercise in mass production to match the methods seen to be effective in the factories.

There were few other models on which to base training programmes. The primitive and classical patterns described above were known, of course, but they tended to presuppose small numbers of highly motivated and often privileged pupils. Occasionally one country, such as Prussia, would be ahead in some respect, but its experience might not be of value to others at a more rudimentary stage. Rich describes the situation in the early days of the training colleges:

> England was far behind her Continental neighbours in the establishment of training colleges, and her earliest efforts were almost uninfluenced by what was taking place abroad. The result was that whilst on the Continent they were busy instructing their teachers, rather than showing them how to teach, in England the main emphasis was laid on the actual methods of instructions.[17]

Much of the teacher training before the Industrial Revolution had in any case been done by the Church or the universities. The universities had concentrated to a large extent on subject matter, and, with very few exceptions, had ignored preparation in teaching methods. Some of the teaching orders, notably the Jesuits, had analysed teaching strategies in considerable detail, but their special emphasis on character training, while influential, was not central to the needs of an illiterate mass. Nevertheless the Jesuit style of teacher training was one of the most highly organised and documented. Each pupil was to be matched with another member of the class whose task it was to expose his mistakes. Competition was emphasised, small teams of two or three pupils being matched against others during the year. Teachers were urged to make extensive use of praise, to refrain from sarcasm, not to have favourites, not to speak to pupils outside class, and to review the week's material every Saturday. Books like the *Ratio Studiorum* (1586) detailed teaching methods with considerable thoroughness and attention to detail:

> If an oration or poem is being explained, first its meaning must be explained, if it is obscure, and the various interpretations considered. Second, the whole method of the workmanship, whether invention, disposition, or delivery is to be considered, also how aptly the author ingratiates himself, how appropriately

he speaks, or from what topics he takes his material for persuading, for ornament, or for moving his audience; how many precepts he unites in one and the same place, by what method he includes with the figures of thought the means of instilling belief, and again the figures of thought which he weaves into the figures of words. Third, some passages similar in subject matter and expression are to be adduced and other orators or poets who have used the same precept for the sake of proving or narrating something similar are to be cited. Fourth, let the facts be confirmed by statements of authorities, if opportunity offers. Fifth, let statements from history, from mythology, and from all erudition be sought which illustrate the passage. At last, let the words be considered carefully, and their fitness, their elegance, their number, and their rhythm noted. However, let these things be considered, not that the master may always discuss everything, but that from them he may select those which are most fitting.[18]

While of great importance to the teaching orders, such wisdom clearly had little relevance to the preparation of boy monitors for teaching illiterate pupils who had found themselves, sometimes reluctantly, and usually with no family tradition of schooling, in the monitorial schools of the early nineteenth century.

Bell and Lancaster

At the beginning of the nineteenth century in Britain there were already a number of 'schools' in existence. Many working-class children in towns would only attend a Sunday school, such as the one founded by John Wesley in 1737, where the emphasis was on Biblical knowledge and reading. In the villages children from rural backgrounds might attend one of the numerous dame schools run by a wide variety of usually elderly ladies who charged a small fee in return for giving elementary instruction in reading and numbers. The dames were almost inevitably untrained, and on their death or retirement the schools might disappear altogether, or else the 'franchise' might be passed on to a trusted neighbour.

The Society for Promoting Christian Knowledge (SPCK) ran a number of charity schools from the end of the seventeenth century. A notable feature of these schools was that they used pupil–teachers, and furthermore that they attempted to train them in an elementary way by sending them to watch experienced teachers at work (to London schools, if necessary) or by attaching them to an older colleague in a local school for supervised practice.

Alongside these were the schools for older children, the private or common day schools. The men who ran these had no formal training and were often poorly educated themselves. They often had formidable reputations for drunkenness and cruelty to the children in their care. It was partly out of revulsion for these wretches, described by Joseph Lancaster as 'too often the refuse of superior schools, and of society at large', that he and Andrew Bell set up the monitorial system.

Dr Andrew Bell had been an army captain in Madras, where he had encouraged older children to stay on at school to teach the beginners. In 1797 he published a pamphlet describing the methods he had used, and in 1798 and 1799 applied his system to schools in Aldgate and Kendal. Meanwhile, in 1798, Joseph Lancaster, a 20-year-old Quaker, started the Borough Road School. It was not unusual at that time for very young people to have charge of schools containing as many as 400 children. To Bell's chagrin, Lancaster, on reading the pamphlet, began to apply a great deal of energy to improving and augmenting the Madras method, and the succeeding long arguments about who invented the monitorial system became even more bitter when Lancaster gained the approval of George III and international recognition.

'What Lancaster did was to apply the method on such a scale and to organise it in so complete a fashion that the problem of numbers in a school seemed to be solved, and the question of cost abolished.'[19] Lancaster in his 1810 book *The British System of Education* explained his training system in detail. The school was divided into eight classes as follows:

Class 1   ABC
Class 2   Words of syllables of 2 letters
Class 3   Words of syllables of 3 letters
Class 4   Words of syllables of 4 letters
Class 5   Words of syllables of 5 letters
Class 6   Reading or spelling lessons of 2 syllables and New Testament
Class 7   Bible study
Class 8   A selection of the best readers from Class 7

The teacher would choose the best pupils in the school to act as monitors, as Lancaster argued that any pupil who could read could teach others to read. Some of the material the monitors had to teach, however, was so baffling in its complexity that few of them understood it themselves. Reading Sheet number 14 for the seventh class of the Northampton Lancasterian School contains passages such as: 'If thy brother be waxen poor, and fallen in decay with thee; then thou shalt relieve him; yea, though he be a stranger or a sojourner; take thou no usury of him, or increase.'[20]

By 1820 about 200,000 children were being taught in over 1,500 Bell or Lancaster monitorial schools. Lancaster was urging the general public 'to consider no person practically qualified to teach (on the "British" plan) who have not a certificate from J. Lancaster of their having been under his care.'[21]

Both Bell and Lancaster aimed at austerity and efficiency. Training was limited (Bell claimed he only needed 24 hours), and the monitors spent most of their time actually teaching, and often learning the material themselves in the process. Even such strategies as classroom commands were to be given in stereotyped form. Despite this, Lancaster personally regarded his monitors as a family, and he spent a great deal of his spare time with them. He also gave them a rather primitive 'theory' course which consisted of a series of lectures on the 'passions'. Bell scorned this approach: 'It is by attending the school, seeing what is going on there, and taking a share in the office of tuition, that teachers are to be formed, and not by lectures and abstract instruction.'[22]

His preparation for the monitors was essentially practical:

> The course of training was largely a matter of 'learning by doing'. However, it began with a study of books that explained the system, 'manuals of method' in the narrowest sense of the term. When some mastery of the work had been manifested the pupil was placed either as 'teacher' (ie monitor) or assistant in a class, starting at the bottom of the 'sand class', and working up through the school in a period of six or eight weeks.[23]

Such was the success of the method, especially in Lancaster's case, that its principles were widely adopted by other countries all over the world where similar problems were being faced. Lancaster visited Montreal in 1822, and in addition to Royal approval had the support of a number of prominent politicians. There were even moves to get the system adopted nationally: 'The principles upon which he (Lancaster) proceeds at the Free School in the Borough are upon examination, so obviously founded in utility and economy, that they must prevail, and will finally, I have no doubt, furnish a mode of instruction, not only for this country, but for all the nations advanced in any degree of civilisation.'[24]

There was not, however, total satisfaction with the system. A number of those who on the whole supported Lancaster were aware of some of the shortcomings, and one can detect here the modern beginnings of the as yet uncompleted debate about what teachers need to learn. A subcommittee of the British Society, the society which grew out of the Royal Lancasterian School Society, examined the training methods and decided there were some serious defects. It suggested that student teachers' education should be improved in three areas: they should have 'firstly, a knowledge of English grammar sufficient to qualify them to speak and write their own language with correctness and propriety; secondly, the improvement of their handwriting; thirdly, geography and history, and in addition, when time and other circumstances will admit...other useful branches of knowledge.'[25]

Many years later the Cross Commission of 1888 pinpointed the flaws in the monitorial system with devastating accuracy:

> They were not even to use a book. Teaching by books was prohibited, at least in the beginning. All they could do was faithfully to transmit the letter of the lesson they had received, for how should they have seized its spirit? Consequently all they were called upon to do was to apply exactly the mechanical processes in which they had been drilled.
> These children under this mechanical discipline often mistook and confounded the formulas they were called upon to apply. The only remedy for this was to drive into them by constant repetition the daily course of instruction.[26]

Despite these valid criticisms, it should be remembered that, given the state of education existing at the time in Britain and other countries which used the monitorial method, many more children received a basic schooling than might have been the case without the boy monitors.

David Stow and the Glasgow Normal Seminary

The founding of the Glasgow Normal Seminary in 1837 was like a breath of fresh air. It placed Scotland well ahead of the rest of Britain in teacher training methods, and several of Stow's former pupils took important positions in schools and teacher training institutions all over the world. In addition, it began a tradition whereby innovations in teacher training spread to schools, with the training institutions providing a valuable source of inspiration.

In 1837 the Glasgow Educational Society opened a unique complex of buildings. There were four 'model' schools graded for various age groups and achievement levels and a so-called 'Normal Seminary'. Rich explains the use of the term 'normal' which was applied extensively to teacher training institutions all over Europe and North America:

> the use of the term 'normal' in connection with teachers' training is significant of an 'idol' of the training college – the idea that there exists some norm or type in teaching, and the nearer the teacher comes to that norm the better will

his teaching be. It is this conception that explains the popularity of the model school, which was looked upon as the concrete embodiment of the norm so far as the school as an institution was concerned, whilst the teaching of the master of method was to be regarded as the norm in the technique of class teaching.[27]

Altogether there were sixteen classrooms, playgrounds, a library, a museum, and rooms for 1,000 children and 100 students. Tutors taught 'model' lessons and four students in succession gave 15-minute lessons which were observed by half the trainees sitting and observing while the other half were teaching classes elsewhere. Occasionally the student would be required to teach a public criticism lesson, when the observers' benches would be filled with fellow students, the rector of the Seminary, the heads of the model schools, experienced teachers and often Stow himself. Gallery lessons were always followed by criticism sessions, when the other students or experienced teachers passed their judgements on what they had seen.

The playgrounds of the model schools contained an elaborate assembly of outdoor apparatus. There were poles with ropes attached and circular swings. Part of Stow's philosophy demanded that children should be allowed to let off steam, and student teachers had to join in the activities in the playground as well as insert brief spells of physical jerks into their classroom teaching. After the repressive style of teaching of the traditionally cruel Scottish 'dominie', the sheer humanity of Stow's students was a welcome change. Cruickshank describes the real superiority of the method compared with the Bell and Lancaster system. 'The spirit of Stow's work and the method he employed demanded of the trainees, insight, understanding and a degree of sensitivity associated with maturity.'[28]

The thoroughness of Stow's preparation was remarkable. Although his recruits were usually better educated than the boy monitors had been, he was not satisfied with their level of achievement and set about improving it. They had to learn to be school masters and mistresses in the fullest sense of the terms. They constructed timetables, kept registers and school accounts, and learned to read and carry out government regulations. In addition, they had to apply Stow's unique philosophy of teaching, partly based on common sense, partly on whim, but always stressing deep concern for the children in their care. Stow himself described these novelties:

> First, the addition of direct moral training, in conjunction with the branches usually taught, including the requisite platform and apparatus, with the method of using them – second, a mode of intellectual communication, termed, 'Picturing out in words', conducted by a combination of questions and ellipses, analogy, and familiar illustrations – the use of simple terms by the teacher, within the range of the pupil's acquirements – and answers, chiefly simultaneous, but occasionally individual, by which the pupils are normally trained to observe, perceive, reflect, and judge, and thus to draw the lesson for themselves, and to express it to the trainer in such terms as they fully understand – being made to perceive as vividly by the mental eye as they would real objects by the bodily eye.[29]

Much of what Stow advocated would receive general approval even today: the adventure playgrounds are still popular, student teachers are encouraged not to remain aloof but to join in activities with children. Indeed the 15-minute criticism lesson is not unlike microteaching without playback facilities or the re-teach cycle. Some of the psychology, though crudely expressed by Stow, is still relevant today if rephrased in the light of what is currently known about children's thinking. Consequently it is not surprising that elements of the Glasgow Normal Seminary were incorporated in their early stages of development in colleges such as Homerton, Westminster and St Luke's, Exeter, and that the best of the Glasgow trainees were eagerly sought all over the world in preference to Bell and Lancaster's robots.

The early training colleges

Jeffreys has described the embarrassing shortage of good teachers in a number of countries in the first half of the nineteenth century:

> The remarkable thing in the modern history of education is that it took so long for the various countries to realise the importance of teacher-training – to realise, in fact, that schools cannot be better than their teachers. Throughout the first half of the nineteenth century in England the attempts to establish a general system of elementary education were continually hampered by the hopeless inadequacy of the teachers.[30]

Prussia was in a better position than most other European countries, having had normal schools since the early eighteenth century at Halle (1704), Berlin (1748) and Münster (1759) among others. By the middle of the nineteenth century there were 156 well-established normal schools in Germany. Visitors were impressed by the strong esprit de corps among the students and by the high level of their academic work compared with other countries.

In France the *école normale* was founded in 1808 to train teachers for the *lycée*. The emphasis in these institutions was on practical matters, and trainees learned to draw up certificates of birth, death and marriage, as well as to prune trees. By the middle of the nineteenth century the *écoles normales* had become centres of liberation and political agitation. Only the national shortage of teachers protected them from firm government action.[31]

In the United States the Lancasterian method had been used since as early as 1806, and ideas were constantly being brought in from Europe by immigrants and travelling teachers or administrators. The tradition of communities establishing their own schools and training and recruiting teachers for them was already a developing one. By 1837, for example, there were 2,000 schools in various parts of Massachusetts, but few were open for more than twenty weeks of the year, and large numbers of children attended for less than half that time. Horace Mann,[32] the humane and far-seeing Secretary to the State Board of Education, was greatly impressed by the Prussian normal schools, and they were one important source of influence on the Lexington Normal School founded in 1839. Mann was also familiar with the home-produced model seminary for teachers established by Samuel Hall in Vermont in 1823, so he had at least two major sources of inspiration. The founding of the Lexington Normal School was an important development in teacher training in the United States. Not unusually, this was due once again to a particularly energetic and imaginative principal, Cyrus Peirce, who himself taught as many as 10 different subjects in one term, 17 in a year, supervised a model school of 30 pupils, acted as demonstration teacher, developed his own teaching ideas and materials, fulfilled the duties of janitor, and still found time to give the student teachers courses on the science and art of teaching the various subjects.[33]

Mann's efforts did not cease here, despite considerable hostility from the Governor of Massachusetts. He went on to found other normal schools, increasing the amount of time student teachers would spend there (it could be as little as a month initially), and set up a number of impressively elaborate in-service workshops where up to 100 teachers might attend refresher courses, further their education, or watch demonstrations of the latest teaching techniques.

In England, a similar pattern began to emerge. The models available to Kay-Shuttleworth when he founded the Battersea College in 1840 were the monitorial system and what he had seen in the European normal schools when he had visited them on his travels. Initially 13 year olds were to be taken for a 7-year apprenticeship. They were to study English, Art, Music and practical subjects such as land-surveying and accountancy. They were given lectures on the theory of teaching similar to what Kay-Shuttleworth had seen in the 'Paedagogik' lectures in Prussian and Swiss normal schools. They had nature walks, as did the Swiss trainees. Later, in 1846, the pupil–teacher system was made a national scheme, and promising 13 year olds were apprenticed to school managers until they were 18 and able to go to training colleges proper.

Kay-Shuttleworth himself described the course he gave on the theory and art of teaching:

> They have treated of the general objects of education, and means of obtaining them. The peculiar aims of elementary education; the structure of school-houses in various parts of Europe; the internal arrangement of the desks, forms, and school apparatus, in reference to different methods of instruction; and the varieties of those methods observed in different countries. The theory of the discipline of schools . . . To these subjects have succeeded lectures in the great leading disputations in the methods of communicating knowledge.[34]

The certification system was borrowed from Holland, and teachers could take a one, two or three-year course with corresponding gains in salary. Most of the early colleges established their own 'practising school', and students were required to spend time doing supervised teaching practice under the supervision of the 'normal master', who was often the only qualified teacher in the school. Rule X of the St Luke's College 1855 Prospectus states:

> Every student is expected, whenever he may be required, to become a teacher in the Practising School, under the direction of the Normal Master. His success will mainly depend upon the zeal and efficiency which he displays in this department.[35]

The 'normal master' not only taught at the school but went into the college to lecture. Fuller describes a report on the work of such a teacher. 'Mr Barrett gave a "useful and sensible lecture on the construction of timetables" as well as a lesson on Plato at the Practising School which was "a good specimen of teaching where the lads were very dull." '[36]

The student teachers spent three weeks at a time with the normal master in groups of four. They were able to teach three or four lessons a week which were criticised by the normal master, watch him teach, and occasionally run the whole school for a day. The normal master at the St Luke's Practising School in 1849 had to rate the students formally for such qualities as 'energy as a teacher', 'skill in keeping a class attentive and active', and 'whether the instruction as to matter and manner is addressed to the understanding of the children'.[37]

Despite the obvious progress since the monitorial system, there was still no wide-spread satisfaction with the training and education of teachers. Teaching methods were criticised. Taylor describes the comments of Her Majesty's Inspector Moseley:

> In his report on the training School at Battersea, Moseley was not enthusiastic about the oral method that Kay-Shuttleworth had encouraged. If it made teachers, it did not make students, giving neither the habit of self-instruction, nor the taste for it.[38]

There was concern about the effectiveness of the by now widely used gallery criticism lesson:

> The Revd. F. Temple...commented upon the limitation of the popular 'gallery' lesson, so called because this was the part of the hall used by one student, who gave a lesson of 15 minutes which was criticised by the other students. There was a tendency to stimulate the other students rather than convey information to the children. 'The business of the schoolmaster is not so much to teach as to make children learn.'[39]

Nor was there agreement about what student teachers should learn. Some of the colleges tried to be severely practical. The St Luke's College 1857 examination papers on school management contained questions such as:

1   To what subjects would you apply Collective Instruction? What are the disadvantages of this method?
5   Draw up a form for a 'Summary of Attendance and Payments' for a school, and fill it up for one quarter.[40]

Other colleges had a syllabus which was less useful to schools. Taylor points out that a number of principals of colleges in the middle of the nineteenth century were Oxbridge clerics with little awareness of the social background of children in elementary schools.[41]

The Principal of the College of St Mark and St John in the 1840s, Derwent Coleridge, 'admitted to taking his models, not from the pedagogical seminaries of Switzerland and Germany that Kay-Shuttleworth so much admired, but from the "older educational institutions of (this) country, originally intended, even those of the higher class, with their noble courts, solemn chapels, and serious cloisters, for clerks to the full as humble as those I had to train." '[42]

The Newcastle Commission in 1861 expressed a number of reservations, and was especially critical of the poor practical training and the superficial nature of much of what was covered. The Commission's members pressed for better trained adults and were critical of pupil-teachers who showed 'great meagreness of knowledge, crudeness, and mechanical methods of study, arising largely from neglect of their training by their head teachers'.[43]

So the criticisms were of two kinds. There were those who claimed that pupil–teachers especially, and also newly qualified teachers, were badly prepared for teaching and sparsely educated in any general sense, and others who derided the arrogance of the over-educated teacher:

> He and some one hundred and forty schoolmasters had been lately turned at the same time in the same factory, on the same principles, like so many pianoforte legs...He knew all about the water sheds of all the world

(whatever they are) and all the histories of all the peoples and all the names of all the rivers and the mountains, and all the productions, manners, and customs of all the countries, and all their boundaries and bearings on the two and thirty points of the compass. Ah, rather overdone, M'Choakum child. If he had only learnt a little less, how infinitely better he might have taught much more?[44]

A hundred years of popular education

It would be difficult to do other than briefly mention a small number of the developments in teacher education and training in the 100 years during which most industrialised societies have had compulsory schooling for all children. There are a number of features, however, common to several countries.

First of all there has been a colossal increase in numbers. Many English colleges of education doubled or trebled in size within relatively short periods of time at various stages in their history, followed by perhaps decades of stability. In the year 1958, for example, 18,000 students began training as teachers, whereas by 1968 the number had increased to 46,500.

Second, training has tended to lengthen rather than contract. Except for emergency schemes operating after major wars or other civil disasters, few countries now consider less than three years of post-secondary school as adequate, many demand four or five years, and in countries with open-ended degree courses, such as Germany, it is possible for a secondary teacher to take seven years or longer over his courses, most of which time is consumed by subject work.

A third factor is the influence of the 'great thinkers'. These were people who might not necessarily train teachers themselves, though some did, but whose thoughts and writings reached the teacher trainer and were interpreted by him to the student in training. In addition to the best known such as Pestalozzi stressing the importance of immediacy, the object lesson, simultaneous instruction of the whole class; Froebel emphasising play, motor forms of activity and aesthetic expression; Dewey, whose activity programme radically broke away from the common recitation lesson formula; psychologists and writers on psychology such as Thorndike; Watson and the later behaviourists like Skinner; Max Wertheimer and the Gestalt school; Freud and his followers Melanie Klein and Susan Isaacs; and T. P. Nunn, whose book *Education, Its Data and First Principles* ran to twenty reprints between 1920 and 1945, there were sociologists, anthropologists, ethologists, and shrewd observers of children in classrooms with a persuasive style of writing like A. S. Neill and more recently John Holt. In fact the college lecturer is overwhelmed at the present time by the plethora of material being produced; and his task of filtering and interpreting, formerly straightforward, has become extremely difficult. The days of the 'normal school' or 'normal master' are past. Vast numbers of teaching models are proclaimed, and there is little common agreement about what constitutes effective teaching.

Rugg has described the beginnings of this change as manifested in the United States:

> For twenty years – nearly thirty – there was no split in thought and feeling in Teachers' College or in most of the other teacher-education institutions of the country. The reason is clear – the professors all thought alike. There was no real minority. Not until the 1920s did one appear and then it was tiny.[45]

Despite the changes described above, some writers argue that the basic pattern has remained the same. Dent states his criticism of the colleges over-harshly.

> What they (the colleges) did not do, even in this period of extensive and inten-sive change, was to alter the basic pattern of teacher education. Despite all the modernisation and liberalisation that have occurred over the past century and a half, the 1814 pattern has persisted. Nearly everyone says it must be changed. One hopes the change will be for the better.[46]

It is indeed true that one can point to earlier models and then find training insti-tutions which still have them. For example, there are the 1907 Committee of Seventeen recommendations for the training of secondary school teachers in the United States:

> II   That definite study be given to each of the following subjects, either in separate courses or in such combinations as convenience or necessity demands:
>
> (a) History of Education:
>   1   History of general education.
>   2   History of secondary education.
> (b) Educational Psychology with emphasis in adolescence.
> (c) The principles of education, including the study of educational aims, values and processes. Courses in general method are included under this heading.
> (d) Special methods in the secondary school subjects that the students expect to teach.
> (e) Organisation and management of schools and school systems.
> (f) School hygiene.
>
> III   That opportunity for observation and practice teaching with secondary pupils be given.[47]

[...]

There have certainly been cyclical elements in the history of teacher training. Methods die and are rediscovered in modified form by an exultant future generation. The gallery lesson survives but may be televised or viewed through a one-way screen. The normal master may be a teacher tutor or cooperating teacher in the United States. The monitorial system might be termed 'team teaching' or 'study practice'. The model schools remain in the extensively used campus schools in the United States, though in Britain the trend has been to use almost all available schools. But modern versions have the advantage of a considerable reservoir of earlier models on which to draw, and it is an over-simplification to pretend they have no new elements.

Notes

1 Church, Dean. *The Oxford Movement.* Quoted in G. Ogren, *Trends in English Teacher Training from 1800* (Stockholm, 1953), 10.
2 Fuller, F. *The Founding of St Luke's College Exeter (1839–1864)* (Exeter, 1966), 42.
3 National Society Report (May 1840). Quoted by Fuller, op. cit., 46.
4 Seaborne, M. *A Visual History of Modern Britain – Education* (London: Studio Vista, 1966), 70.
5 Okafor-Omali, D. *A Nigerian Villager in Two Worlds* (London: Faber and Faber, 1965), 51.

6 Smith, F. *A History of English Elementary Education 1760–1902* (London: University of London Press, 1931), 37.
7 Baring-Gould, S. *The Vicar of Morgenstow*. Quoted by Fuller, op. cit., 15–16.
8 Broudy, H. S. 'Historic Exemplars of Teaching Method', in N. L. Gage (ed.), *Handbook of Research on Teaching* (Chicago, 1963), 3–4.
9 Holmes, B. 'Teacher Education in a Changing World', in G. Z. F. Bereday and J. A. Lauwerys (eds), *The Education and Training of Teachers* (London: Evans Brothers, 1963), 5.
10 Richardson, T. A. 'The Classical Chinese Teacher', in Bereday and Lauwerys (eds), op. cit., 30.
11 Ibid., 27.
12 Price, R. F. *Education in Communist China* (London: Routledge and Kegan Paul, 1970), 222.
13 Howie, G. 'The Teacher in Classical Greece and Rome', in Bereday and Lauwerys (eds), op. cit., 43.
14 Broudy, op. cit., 6.
15 Horace, *Satires* i, 6, 81–82. Quoted in Howie, op. cit., 51.
16 Seneca, *Epistles* 106, 12. Quoted in Howie, op. cit., 56.
17 Rich, R. W. *The Training of Teachers in England and Wales during the Nineteenth Century* (Cambridge, 1933), 22.
18 Fitzpatrick, E. A. *St Ignatius and the Ratio Studiorum* (New York, 1933), 212–13. Quoted in Broudy, op. cit., 22–3.
19 Smith, op. cit., 71.
20 Seaborne, op. cit., plate 110.
21 Dent, H. C. 'An Historical Perspective', in S. Hewett (ed.), *The Training of Teachers* (London: University of London Press, 1971), 12.
22 Southey, R. and Southey, C. C. *Life of Rev. Andrew Bell* (1844). Quoted in Rich, op. cit., 4.
23 Rich, op. cit., 11.
24 1807, Parliamentary debates. Quoted in Ogren, op. cit., 25.
25 Binns, H. B. *A Century of Education* (London: British and Foreign School Society, 1908), 79.
26 Cross Commission, 1888. Quoted in Ogren, op. cit., 28–9.
27 Rich, op. cit., 78.
28 Cruickshank, M. 'David Stow, Scottish Pioneer of Teacher Training in Britain', *British Journal of Educational Studies*, XIV, 2, 205.
29 Stow, D. *The Training System, Moral Training School and Normal Seminary or College* (Glasgow, 1836), 26.
30 Jeffreys, M. V. C. *Revolution in Teacher-Training* (London: Pitman, 1961), 3.
31 Thabault, R. 'The Professional Training of Teachers in France', in Bereday and Lauwerys (eds), op. cit., 244–55.
32 Messerli, J. C. 'Horace Mann and Teacher Education', in Bereday and Lauwerys (eds), op. cit., 70–84.
33 Elsbree, W. S. 'Teacher Education in the United States', in Bereday and Lauwerys (eds), op. cit., 177–91.
34 Ogren, op. cit., 132–3.
35 Fuller, op. cit., 160.
36 Ibid., 182.
37 Annual Report of the Exeter Diocesan Board of Education (1849), 6.
38 Taylor, W. *Society and the Education of Teachers* (London: Faber and Faber, 1969), 97.
39 Fuller, op. cit., 178.
40 Ibid., 177.
41 Taylor, op. cit., 95.
42 Ibid., 95.
43 Newcastle Commission (1861), 270.
44 Dickens, Charles. *Hard Times* (1854). Quoted in A. Tropp. *The School Teachers* (London: Heinemann, 1957), 24.
45 Rugg, H. *The Teacher of Teachers* (New York, 1952), 37.
46 Dent, op. cit., 22.
47 National Education Association. *Addresses and Proceedings* (1907), 537.

CHAPTER 7

WHAT IS A TEACHING SKILL?

Originally published as 'Teaching Skills', in E. C. Wragg (ed.), *Classroom Teaching Skills*, Routledge, 1984, pp. 1–20

The word 'skill' is used freely in conversations about teaching, but defining more precisely what it might mean, or researching how it might manifest itself in practice, is not as easy as casual conversation about it on a 'taken for granted' basis. This is a much abbreviated extract from Chapter 1 of my 1984 book *Classroom Teaching Skills*.

[...]

Identifying and defining teaching skills

There is less dissent about what constitutes effective teaching in discussion between people outside the profession than there is in the research and evaluation literature. Good teachers, it is commonly held, are keen and enthusiastic, well-organised, firm but fair, stimulating, know their stuff and are interested in the welfare of their pupils. Few would attempt to defend the converse: that good teachers are unenthusiastic, boring, unfair, ignorant and do not care about their pupils.

Once the scrutiny of teaching is translated into the more precise terms demanded by the tenets of rigorous systematic enquiry, the easy agreement of casual conversation evaporates. The books and articles on effective teaching are numerous, and Barr (1961) summarising a massive amount of American research, concluded, 'Some teachers were preferred by administrators, some were liked by the pupils, and some taught in classes where there were substantial pupil gains, and generally speaking these were not the same teachers.' Biddle and Ellena (1964), reporting the Kansas City role studies, found that there was not even clear agreement amongst teachers, parents and administrators about the role teachers should play.

More recently, even the attempts to see consensus in the research literature have been criticised. For example, Gage (1978), summarising research studies which had attempted to relate teaching style to children's learning, concluded that in the early years of schooling certain kinds of teacher behaviour did show some consistent relationship to children learning reading and arithmetic. From this he derived a set of prescriptive 'Teacher should' statements, like 'Teachers should call on a child by name before asking the question', 'Teachers should keep to a minimum such activities as giving directions and organizing the class for instruction', or 'During reading-group instruction, teachers should give a maximal amount of brief feedback and provide fast-paced activities of the "drill" type'.

Critics of such prescriptions argue that much of the American research is based on short-term memory tests, that formal didactic styles of teaching appear to be more successful, and could too easily be perpetuated as the best form of teaching. Longer term objectives which teachers might have are less frequently measured, so that the music teacher who hopes that children will have a lifelong interest in music is less likely to be investigated than the one who merely wants children to recall sonata form or define a triad in a short memory test.

There was once an interesting experiment at the University of Michigan which illustrates neatly the dilemma of trying to elicit what forms of teaching are most effective. Guetzkow *et al.* (1954) divided first-year students on a general psychology course into three groups. The first group was given a formal lecture course with regular tests, the second and third groups were based on tutorials and discussions. At the end of the course, the lecture group not only outperformed the tutorial discussion groups on the final examination, but was also more favourably rated by the students. So far this represents a victory for lecturing and testing on two commonly used criteria: test performance and student appraisal.

The investigators discovered, however, that the students in the discussion groups scored significantly higher than the lecture groups on a measure of interest in psychology, the subject being studied. They hypothesised that though the lecture group students gave a favourable rating of the teaching they had received, this may have been because they had less anxiety about grades for the course through their weekly feedback from test scores. It was decided to monitor the subsequent progress of all the groups. Three years later not one student in the lecture group had opted to study the subject further, but 14 members of the two discussion and tutorial groups had chosen to major in psychology. Thus, on short-term criteria the lecture method was superior, but taking a longer perspective the discussion method appeared to motivate students more powerfully, and ultimately some must have learned a great deal more.

Defining teaching skill in such a way that all would agree, therefore, is not a simple matter. If we were to say that teaching skills are the strategies teachers use to enable children to learn, then most people would want to rule out intimidation, humiliation, the use of corporal punishment or other forms of teacher behaviour of which they personally happen to disapprove. It is perhaps easier when seeking a definition of teaching skill to describe some of the characteristics of skilful teaching which might win some degree of consensus, though not universal agreement.

The first might be that the behaviour concerned *facilitates pupils' learning of something worthwhile*, such as facts, skills, values, concepts, how to live harmoniously with one's fellows, attitudes or some other outcome thought to be desirable. A second quality could be that it is *acknowledged to be a skill by those competent to judge*, and this might include teachers, teacher trainers, inspectors, advisers and learners themselves. Pupils can be shrewd in their appraisal of the teacher's craft, and that the ability to explain is often highly rated by them.

For it to be a recognised part of a teacher's professional competence the skill should also be *capable of being repeated*, not perhaps in exactly the same form, but as a fairly frequent rather than a single chance occurrence. A chimpanzee might randomly produce an attractive colourful shape once in a while given a brush and some paint, but an artist would produce a skilfully conceived painting on a more regular basis. Teachers who possess professional skills, therefore, should be capable of manifesting these consistently, not on a hit-or-miss basis.

One frequently cited observation on skills is that of the philosopher Gilbert Ryle (1949) who distinguished, in his book *The Concept of Mind*, between being able to state a factual proposition and perform a skilful operation. The difference between knowing *that* and knowing *how* is the difference between inert knowledge and intelligent action. Unfortunately, some competent teachers are not especially articulate about their skill, and it would be a mistake to assume that it is a prerequisite for skill only to be recognised as such if the person manifesting it is capable of explaining and analysing it in textbook language. The intelligence of an action may perfectly well be explained by another, and the behaviour is not necessarily unintelligent or shallow if its perpetrator is tongue-tied about it.

One problem encountered in defining teaching skills is that though in some contexts the term 'skill' has good connotations, attracts adulation, is a gift of the few, the result of years of practice or the mark of an expert, in other circumstances it is looked down upon, regarded as mechanical, the sign of a rude technician rather than an artist. We tend, for instance, to admire a surgeon's skill or that of a tennis player. Both may have had the same years of dedicated practice, but the intellectual nature of the knowledge and understanding required by the surgeon is vastly more exacting than that required by a sportsman.

Where the imagination is involved, even more fine distinctions exist. A sculptor would probably be disappointed to read a report that describes his latest masterpiece as a piece of skill. He would expect eulogies to contain words like 'artistic' and 'creative'. For those who liken teachers more to expressive artists than to surgeons, the very term 'skill' may be seen as belittling, reducing creative endeavour to mechanical crudity. It is difficult to dry-clean the term of these emotional associations with other kinds of human enterprise.

This uncertainty about the proper standing of the notion of skill when applied to teaching is partly explained by the varied nature of the teacher's job. Pressing the right button on a tape recorder, or writing legibly on the blackboard require but modest competence, and are things most people could learn with only a little practice. Responding to a disruptive adolescent, or knowing how to explain a difficult concept to children of different ages and abilities by choosing the right language, appropriate examples and analogies, and reading the many cues which signal understanding or bewilderment, require years of practice as well as considerable intelligence and insight. Although the term 'interpersonal skills' is now quite widespread, there is still some reluctance to classify human relationships in this way.

When children learn something there is often a magical quality about the excitement of discovery, the warmth of regard between teacher and taught, or the novelty to the learner of what is taking place, and the romanticism seems to be destroyed if teaching is seen as too deliberate, calculated, manipulated or over-analysed. Hence the debate about learning to teach and whether the act of teaching should be seen as a whole or whether it is at all capable of being separated into discrete if interrelated skills. My own view is that the extreme optimism of the supporters of the so-called Performance or Competency-based Teacher Education programmes fashionable in the United States during the 1970s was misplaced.

It was assumed that teaching would be broken down into hundreds and indeed thousands of particles, that trainees could learn each of these, and that they could be certificated on the basis of their proven ability to manifest whatever set of competencies had been prescribed. Lists of approved competencies were produced, such as the 1,276 compiled by Dodl (1973) under the heading *The Florida Catalog of Teacher Competencies,* and hierarchies were assembled with the skills required given a level. Thus, an operation by the teacher like 'form reading groups and give a good rationale for the grouping' was seen as being at a lower level than 'implement managerial procedures for efficient group operation'. There was an arbitrary quality to some of these hierarchies, and competency-based teacher education was criticised by writers such as Heath and Nielson (1974) for not being founded on any sound empirical evidence.

[...] Teaching and studying minute facets of behaviour like 'smiling' can soon become comical and divorced from overall reality, and at the other extreme constant denial that there is anything other than some global notion of 'teaching' which is sacrosanct, ethereal and must not be subjected to scrutiny, simply produces paralysis. Areas such as class management, mixed-ability teaching, questioning and explaining, seem, according to the tenets described earlier, to represent activities which required skill, intelligence and sensitivity from teachers. They are not so vague as to defy any analysis, nor so minute and piddling as to be silly. They are aspects of teaching thought by experienced professionals to be important both for experienced and trainee teachers.

[...]

References

Barr, A. S. (1961) 'Wisconsin Studies of the Measurement and Prediction of Teacher Effectiveness', *Journal of Experimental Education*, 30, 5–156.

Biddle, B. J. and Ellena, W. J. (eds) (1964) *Contemporary Research on Teacher Effectiveness*, Holt, Rinehart & Winston, New York.

Dodl, N. R. (1973) *The Florida Catalog of Teacher Competencies*, Talahassee, Florida Department of Education.

Gage, N. L. (1978) *The Scientific Basis of the Art of Teaching*, Teachers College Press, New York.

Guetzkow, H., Kelly, E. L. and McKeachie, W. J. (1954) 'An Experimental Comparison of Recitation, Discussion and Tutorial Methods in College Teaching', *Journal of Educational Psychology*, 45, 193–209.

Heath, R. W. and Nielson, M. A. (1974) 'The Research Basis for Performance-based Teacher Education', *Review of Educational Research*, 44, 4, 463–84.

Ryle, G. (1949) *The Concept of Mind*, Hutchinson, London.

EXPLAINING AND EXPLANATIONS

Originally published as 'Explaining and Explanations', in E. C. Wragg (ed.), *Primary Teaching Skills*, Routledge, 1993, pp. 111–36

The ability to explain clearly is highly esteemed by children. Although I had written previously about moving towards a science of teaching, I have never believed that one yet exists, certainly not in a form that would allow someone to prescribe precisely what a teacher should do. This study, Chapter 8 from my 1993 book *Primary Teaching Skills*, analyses how primary teachers explain topics like 'Insects' to their classes and I have always felt proud of it as something that at least attempted to tackle a topic often thought to be intractable: what is involved in clear explanations.

Explaining is not only a professional skill which is highly esteemed by children. It is an aspect of communication which lies at the centre of human discourse in many fields: parents explain things to their children; radio and television presenters explain what lies behind news stories to listeners and viewers; pilots explain the cause of delay to air travellers. In the case of doctors and patients there can be, as in teaching, reciprocal explanations: the patient first explains symptoms to the doctor, and the doctor then explains causes and treatments to the patient. Explaining is not, however, a uni-dimensional activity, and the words 'explain' and 'explanation' are used in many different ways. For the purposes of this research we took as an operational definition the statement: 'explaining is giving understanding to another'. This interpretation allows the notion to embrace strategies other than imparting information directly, as it can include, for example, asking questions which encourage pupils to reach their own conclusions, engaging in practical work or giving a demonstration.

Explanations can help some to understand a concept like 'density' or 'prejudice', and the notion may be new to the learner, or already partly familiar. They can also illuminate cause and effect, for example, that rain is produced by the cooling of air. There are many other possibilities, such as the explanation of procedures, including both those within the subject domain, like how to convert a fraction to a decimal, and those to do with the management of the lesson, such as ways of ensuring that no one has an accident in a gymnastics lesson. There can be explanations of purposes and objectives, when a teacher explains why children are going to embark on a study of their own village, or what they will have learned at the conclusion of some activity; of relationships between people, events or the different parts of something, like why bees and flies are insects but spiders are not, or what religious festivals like Christmas and Easter have in common; of the processes involved in the working of a piece of machinery or the behaviour of

Table 8.1 Three typologies of explaining

After Hyman (1974)	After Smith and Meux (1970)	After Brown (1978)
Type I Generalisation – specific instance		
Empirical The effects of pressure on the volume of gas	*Empirical-subsumptive* Seasonal changes on mammals	*Reason-giving, answering the question 'Why?'* Why does the volume of a gas decrease as pressure increases? Why do certain mammals hibernate in winter?
Probabilistic Relation between lung cancer and smoking	*Judgmental* Causes of higher crime rate in urban areas	Why do heavy smokers have a greater risk of contracting cancer? Why is there more crime in inner-city areas?
Non-empirical A verb agrees with its subject	*Normative* The proper use of knives and forks	Why do we say, 'He runs,' but 'They run'? Why do we hold a fork in the left hand?
Type II Functional		
Purpose The motives behind Lord Jim's actions	*Teleological* Birds of prey as efficient hunters	*Interpretive, answering the question 'What?'* What led Lord Jim to become the strange character he was? What uses do talons and curved beaks serve in birds of prey?
Function Unions and their members	*Consequence* Inflation and our money	What can unions do in an industrial dispute? What are the effects of a high inflation rate on the currency?
Type III Serial		
Sequential Making a sponge cake	*Sequential* Constructing a perpendicular to a given line	*Descriptive, answering the question 'How?'* How do you make a light sponge? How can a perpendicular be constructed using compass and ruler?
Genetic Differences between cats and dogs	*Mechanical* The operation of a car engine	As animals, how do cats differ from dogs? How does the internal combustion engine work?
Chronological Events leading to the war in Vietnam	*Procedural* Conducting a formal meeting	How did colonial history lead to the Vietnamese war? How does the chairman lead a meeting?

people or animals. Explanations often answer real or imaginary questions based on common interrogatives like Who? What? How? Why? Where? When?

Numerous investigations have sought to assemble a typology of explanations, and Brown and Armstrong (1984) have summarised work by Swift (1961), Bellack *et al.* (1966), Ennis (1969), Smith and Meux (1970) and Brown (1978). They produced a chart (Table 8.1) which compares three views of the process of explaining. Research into explanations in the classroom has been summarised by Crowhurst (1988). Such research is sparse compared with enquiry into other teaching strategies. Smith and Meux analysed transcripts of eighty five lessons given by seventeen teachers in five high schools. They split the lessons into a series of 'episodes' and found that describing, designating and explaining were the three operations that occurred most frequently. Tisher (1970) used the classification scheme developed by Smith and Meux to analyse the relationship between teachers' strategies in nine science classes and children's understanding in science. Explaining ranked as the fourth most frequently used strategy after designating, describing and stating.

Brown and Armstrong (1984) used their own system for analysing discourse to elicit which features distinguished the lessons of twelve student teachers explaining biological topics to children. They used independent ratings of videotapes of the lessons and pupil learning as measured by post-tests to identify the more 'effective' explanations. These were shown on analysis to be characterised by more 'keys', that is, central principles or generalisations which help to unlock understanding. The more successful explanations also had more framing statements which showed the beginnings and endings of sub-topics, more focusing statements emphasising the key points, and used the rule–example–rule structure – for example, an insect has, among other characteristics, six legs (rule), a fly is an insect (example), so insects have six legs (rule) – which had also been identified by Gage *et al.* (1972) as effective. However, the rule–example–rule pattern seemed to work best in interpretive explanations, when technical terms were being explored. In reason-giving and descriptive explanations, when processes were being explored, the example–rule–example model seemed to be effective.

The matter of cognitive level is also relevant to research into explaining. The level of thinking involved in classroom teaching and learning has been discussed by Bloom (1956), whose taxonomy of educational objectives in the cognitive domain has frequently been used or modified. Bloom formulated a hierarchical view of learning at six levels, starting with knowledge and then going on to comprehension, application, analysis, synthesis and finally evaluation. The assumption was that one needed the lower levels in order to achieve the higher levels: you need to have knowledge in order to comprehend, and you must comprehend in order to be able to analyse, synthesise or evaluate. Taba (1966) devised a similar set of thought levels in her work at San Francisco State College helping teachers move children up to higher levels of thought, though there is no conclusive research evidence that operating at higher levels is inevitably associated with 'better learning'.

The present study of teachers' explanations

It was decided to study teachers explaining new subject matter to primary pupils in two major domains of the school curriculum, science and English, as this would enable us to investigate the field in two distinctive and contrasting subject areas.

Preliminary informal observations in the classrooms of five teachers in three different schools were made, and lessons whose subject matter ranged from mathematics to country dancing were studied. Examples of explaining episodes were collected. There were also extensive interviews with the teachers concerned. The pilot study involved asking teachers to explain a variety of topics such as 'the water cycle', 'erosion', the difference between 'their' and 'there' and mathematical concepts such as 'parallel' and 'perpendicular' to small groups of children of different ability.

The pilot study confirmed that explaining took place regularly in lessons, that teachers appeared to use a variety of strategies, that explaining to individual pupils caused some management problems, like children waiting with hand in the air, or standing in a queue if the teacher was explaining at her desk, and that it would be worthwhile studying explanations to children of different levels of ability. The pilot also revealed that several explanatory episodes were related to misbehaviour and class management, like 'why we need to wipe our feet when we come in on a wet day'; that it was not too difficult to test more able children and those of average ability, but that testing low-ability children, particularly in younger age groups, caused great difficulty, as written forms of assessment were often not appropriate and oral forms were extremely time-consuming. Indeed, teachers in the pilot commented on the difficulty of explaining basic concepts to lower-ability pupils generally, about the time taken and the disappointment when little seemed to be understood.

Following the pilot it was decided to concentrate on two topics, one in English, one in science; to study in particular high- and medium-ability pupils, as lower-ability pupils would really need a separate study; to give a post-test of learning; to limit the time available for the 'explanation' to ten minutes, as this had been shown to be the sort of time teachers devoted to public discussion of a new topic and to give teachers a completely free hand in the strategies they used. It was also decided to confine the study to 8- and 9-year-old pupils, on the grounds that they were old enough to be able to write and were in the middle years of primary education, and to have four children in each group, as these could be monitored effectively and four was a size of group to which teachers had often been seen explaining something.

Thus the research was part experimental and part naturalistic. It was experimental, in the sense that the researchers controlled the amount of time available for the exploration (up to ten minutes maximum), the amount of time the children had to complete the post-test (up to fifteen minutes maximum), the two topics in English and science, the ability levels of the children and the number of children in each group (four). Furthermore, there was a control group of children who took the post-test but had not been given the teacher's explanation first, as we wanted to see what differences having an explanation appeared to make. The research was also, in part, naturalistic, in that the children were from the teacher's regular class, the explaining took place in a location near the normal class with which children were familiar, say the library, or another classroom, and teachers had a completely free hand in deciding how they explained the topics.

A total of 32 teachers from sixteen schools in both urban and rural areas took part in the research. The sample was virtually random, as only two schools approached did not wish to take part. Every teacher gave four explanations, two to groups of 4 children each consisting of 2 boys and 2 girls (1) of above average ability (IQ range 110 to 120) and (2) 4 children of average ability (IQ range 95 to 105). The control group consisted of four children of average ability, so that their

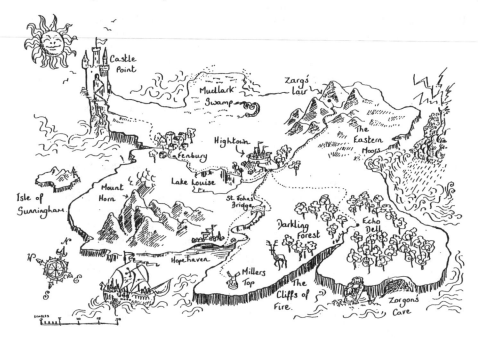

Figure 8.1 The Island of Zarg.

test scores could be compared with the experimental average-ability group. It would not always have been possible to have a control group of above-average ability, owing to small numbers in some classes. Two topics were selected: first, a factual scientific topic, 'Insects', and teachers were told that children should, at the end of the explanation, be able to identify insects and know the parts of an insect; second, there was an explanation of an imaginary island (Figure 8.1) called the 'Island of Zarg', which was to be followed by children writing a story entitled 'My Adventure on the Island of Zarg'. The design was thus a very balanced one and the order of teaching was randomised, so that the topic and the ability range were not always taught in the same order by different teachers, otherwise artefacts might have been produced that were relevant to the order in which groups were taught. A summary of the design is given here.

No. of schools: sixteen.
No. of teachers: thirty two (sixteen of 8 year olds, sixteen of 9 year olds).
No. of topics: two, 'Insects' and 'Island of Zarg'.
No. of pupils:
Experimental groups: 128 above-average, 128 average ability.
Control groups: 128 average ability.
Total: 384 pupils.
Total number of explanations: four for each teacher (two on 'insects', two on 'Zarg'), 128 in all.

Order of teaching groups and topics randomised.

The research instruments

A great deal of data was generated in the study and several forms of analysis for both process and product data were used (Crowhurst, 1988). In the case of the process data, that is, the actual analysis of the classroom explanation, all the explanations were observed live by one of the research team, and an observation schedule, Teacher Explanation Observation Schedule (TEXOS), was developed, which was first piloted in schools and then used in the main study. The TEXOS schedule was a category and sign system derived from observations made at the pilot stage and from ideas in other observation instruments such as those used by Galton (1978) and Brown and Armstrong (1984). All explanations were recorded on sound cassette for further analysis and corroboration.

The first section summarised background information about the teacher and the class. The second part was a coding system for tallying the nature of questions, pupil responses, teacher responses, linguistic moves such as using analogies, examples, or giving or eliciting summaries and pauses, social moves such as humour, praise or chiding, and visual aids. Five two-minute lesson segments were coded, with the observer recording whether or not each form of behaviour took place in a two minute segment. There was also an 'opportunity to learn' section, in separate form for 'Insects' and 'Zarg', in which the observer noted whether such matters as number of legs, number of wings, spiders not being insects and features of the Island of Zarg were mentioned during the explanation by pupil or teacher.

The third section made use of a critical events technique; one event was recorded which seemed to the observer to be related to an important aspect of that particular explanation, followed by an interview with the teacher about it, during which the teacher was also asked about the teaching approach used and, after the final observation, whether any conscious distinction had been made between the explanation to the above-average and average groups of children. There were also seven bipolar opposite rating scales of teacher characteristics which included warm/aloof, dull/stimulating and items which rated eye contact and fluency. Inter-observer (between two people) and intra-observer (each observer with self, before and after research) agreement coefficients were calculated from observations of videotapes. These were high and correlations of 0.779 to 0.934 were obtained for intra-observer agreement and of 0.674 to 0.723 for inter-observer agreement. The higher levels of agreement were, in each case, on the Insects topic, which seemed easier to code than the more discursive Island of Zarg explanations.

The product data were of two kinds. First of all there was a test of insect recognition, which involved pictures of several real insects and other creatures, like arachnids and crustaceans. There were also questions about insects and an invitation to describe them freehand. Second, for the Island of Zarg, children had to write a free composition entitled, 'My Adventure on the Island of Zarg'. The insects questions were scored according to a scheme devised during the pilot study, giving a maximum score of thirty points. The correlation between two independent markers was a very high 0.941.

The creative writing piece scoring system was influenced by the work of Wilkinson *et al.* (1980) and Bennett *et al.* (1984). It consisted of a series of five-point scales covering imaginativeness, mention of island features, coherence, sentence complexity and story length. Correlations between independent markers were 0.778 (island features mentioned), 0.784 (sentence complexity), 0.789 (coherence), 0.791 (imaginativeness), 0.841 (overall impression) and 0.920 (length).

Research findings

Lesson observation

Analysis of the strategies used by teachers revealed a fascinating range of tactics, with short questions, short responses and teacher repetition of pupils' replies lying at the heart of many explanations. Table 8.2 shows the most frequently occurring features of all explanations recorded using TEXOS. In each case, the range is from a minimum of 0 if the behaviour had not occurred at all, to an absolute maximum of 5 if it had occurred in every single one of the five lesson segments observed in each explanation. The pattern confirms that questioning is a frequently used strategy which leads to shorter or longer pupil answers. Table 8.3 shows, by contrast, the ten least frequently recorded categories.

The common pattern of teacher question, short answer, teacher repeats, teacher probes was observed in both science and English explanations. For example:

Insects

Teacher: What sort of things does an insect have on its head?
Pupil: Big round eyes.
Teacher: Big round eyes, yes – and why do you think an insect needs big round eyes?

Table 8.2 Ten most frequently occurring categories for all explanations ($n = 128$)

TEXOS *category*	*Frequency (max. = 5)*
1 Short pupil responses	4.4
2 Teacher repeats pupil answer	3.8
3 Teacher open question	3.7
4 Spontaneous pupil response	3.7
5 Teacher probes	3.4
6 Teacher closed question	2.9
7 Long pupil response	2.9
8 Teacher pauses	2.6
9 Teacher rephrases	2.6
10 Teacher summarises	2.5

Note: max. = maximum.

Table 8.3 Ten least frequently occurring categories for all explanations ($n = 128$)

TEXOS *category*	*Frequency (max. = 5)*
1 Teacher rejects pupil response	0.2
2 Use of analogy	0.4
3 No pupil response	0.5
4 Teacher elicits summary from pupils	0.7
5 Teacher chides	0.8
6 Teacher explains links	0.9
7 Teacher elicits example from pupils	1.1
8 Teacher corrects pupil	1.4
9 Teacher gives example	1.4
10 Teacher gives verbal cue	1.4

Note: max. = maximum.

Island of Zarg

Teacher: What is a Zarg?
Pupil: He's a big, black, furry monster.
Teacher: A big, black, furry monster. And what sort of monster is he? Is he friendly? Or fierce, perhaps?

The results of the analysis of the processes of explaining show that teachers tended to control the interaction quite carefully, making many of the significant moves themselves, like summing up, questioning, repeating answers and probing. At the same time, there was considerable interaction, and rarely was there no response from pupils, even though their answers were likely to be short. Relatively little use was made of analogies and examples. Analogies occurred mainly in the insect explanations, when referring to the exo-skeleton as being like a suit of armour, or when talking about the eye:

> The surface of the eye looks like lots of marbles packed together in a plastic bag.
> It looks like lots of TV screens put together side by side.

The patterns of interaction were further analysed to see what predominant moves occurred. The most highly significant product–moment correlations between the more frequently occurring categories of the TEXOS data are given in Table 8.4. All are significant at beyond the 0.001 level of probability, that is, they would have occurred by chance less than once in a thousand times. There were high correlations between some of the less frequently occurring categories, but these have been omitted as there can often be spurious correlations between infrequently occurring pieces of behaviour. This analysis confirms the predominant question-and-answer pattern of interaction, with a variety of questions, some occurring in sequences, followed by short rather than long responses from the pupil (though spontaneous contributions from pupils were more likely to be long, rather than short).

Table 8.4 Highest correlations between most frequently occurring process variables

TEXOS *features correlated*	*Correlation*
1 Long pupil responses and spontaneous pupil responses	+0.65
2 Teacher repeats pupil responses and short responses	+0.62
3 Teacher probes and sequenced questions	+0.60
4 Teacher probes and open questions	+0.56
5 Sequenced questions and teacher repeats pupil responses	+0.56
6 Open questions and short pupil responses	+0.53
7 Teacher corrects and short pupil responses	+0.50
8 Sequenced questions and short pupil responses	+0.50
9 Open questions and teacher repeats responses	+0.49
10 Closed questions and teacher repeats responses	+0.44
11 Sequenced questions and closed questions	+0.43
12 Closed questions and short pupil responses	+0.43

Note: All correlations are significant beyond the 0.001 level.

The following exchange was typical of this common pattern:

Teacher: Is a woodlouse an insect?
Pupil 1:   Yes.
Teacher: Does it look like an insect?
Pupil 1:   Sort of.
Teacher: What about its three body parts? Can you find the head, thorax and abdomen?
Pupil 1:   I can't find the thorax and abdomen.
Pupil 2:   It looks like it's got lots of little body parts.
Teacher: Ah! How many legs has it got?
Pupil 2:   More than six.
Teacher: More than six, and lots of body parts. Is it an insect?
Pupil 1:   It can't be.

Comparisons between science and English lessons

It was hypothesised that science and English lessons would be different in explanatory styles adopted by the teacher, but this might not have been the case. Analysis showed that there were notable differences, however. Tables 8.2, 8.3 and 8.4 above show the mean category scores for both topics combined, but when we compared the type of explaining categories used by teachers for the two topics separately, some quite spectacular differences emerged. In order to investigate what differences there were between explanations in the two topic areas of Insects and the Island of Zarg, as well as between explanations to older (9-year-old) and younger (8-year-old) pupils, and to above-average and average pupils, we used analysis of variance. The F ratios for these comparisons are shown in the following tables. The higher the F ratio, the more significant the difference between the groups.

One of the most spectacular differences was in the category 'Teacher engages pupils' imagination'. Although it was not unknown in the Insects topic, for example, when a teacher occasionally asked children to imagine what it must be like to be an insect, the science topic was usually dealt with in a much more factual manner. Almost all the examples of engagement of the imagination, therefore, occurred in the English lessons on the 'Island of Zarg' map. The F ratio was a massive 531.4, the most significant of any obtained, well beyond the 0.001 level of significance.

Most highly significant differences of this kind, however, occurred in the opposite direction. Table 8.5 shows the greatest differences where there was a much higher incidence in the category of behaviour concerned in the Insects lesson. 'Use of visual aids' figures prominently, because teachers rarely used additional visual aids in the 'Zarg' lesson, as the map of the island was provided, though a few did occasionally amplify the map with additional visual aids. All the categories in Table 8.5 occurred more frequently in the Insects lessons at a degree of statistical significance beyond the 0.001 level.

The two differences where the incidence was higher in the English lessons on the Island of Zarg are worthy of comment. Table 8.6 shows the hugely significant difference in the category 'teacher engages pupil imagination', but also the higher occurrence of verbal cues, where the teacher 'nudged' the pupils along with a helpful word. Though the F ratio is much lower, it too is significant at beyond the 0.001 level.

Table 8.5 Most significant differences between Insects and Zarg explanations

TEXOS category	F ratio
1 Teacher gives example	239.9
2 Teacher elicits example	158.6
3 Teacher gives summary	85.1
4 Teacher elicits summary	64.0
5 Eye contact	34.8
6 Closed questions	16.9
7 Teacher praises	15.3
8 Organisation	13.4
9 Clarity	12.5
10 Teacher explains links	7.3

Note: In each case higher frequency of occurrence being in the Insect lessons, all differences significant beyond the 0.001 level.

Table 8.6 Most significant differences between Insects and Zarg lesson

TEXOS category	F ratio
1 Teacher engages imagination	531.4
2 Verbal cue	7.5

Note: Both significant beyond the 0.001 level.

These quantitative data confirm other observations made earlier. The format of many explanations of insects was essentially that of programmed learning, with a short 'frame' of information, a closed question, a short answer, a reinforcement (usually praise) or repetition, and sometimes a summary from the teacher. There was also much more eye contact, organisation and conceptual clarity on the rating scales. The English lessons, by contrast, were more discursive, with a challenge to the imagination being central, and longer answers also featuring.

Some of these and other more qualitative aspects of explaining the two topics can be illustrated from transcripts of lessons. The programmed learning format is implemented in the following rapid-fire exchange. The children were looking at a centipede:

Teacher: What makes this different from insects? What did we say an insect has?
Pupil 1: Six legs.
Teacher: Right, how many legs has that one got?
Pupil 2: Forty-two, I've counted.
Teacher: So, is it an insect?
Pupil 3: Well, I think it looks like one.
Teacher: Have a look. Is its body arranged like that? (Shows pupils diagram of an insect body.)
Pupil 2: Not at all.
Teacher: So is it an insect?
Pupil 4: No. But spiders have eight legs, so they're insects.

Teacher: Are they?
Pupil 4:   I think so.
Teacher: Well, are we going to say spiders are insects and spiders have six legs?
Pupil 4:   No, silly me. I always thought they were, though.

Despite the apparently neat programmed learning format, there is still some conceptual confusion. Pupil 1 has confirmed the prerequisite that insects should have six legs, but in the eyes of pupils 3 and 4 it is still a matter of intuitive 'feel' rather than criteria or 'must have' characteristics. Having what looks to be a tightly controlled 'information–question–pupil answer–teacher response' pattern does not of itself ensure clear structure or universal understanding.

Another teacher used a similar clipped rapid-fire dialogue approach, but in a different manner, this time to probe and challenge, starting with a 'not' analogy (a camel not being an insect):

Teacher: A camel is not an insect. Why?
Pupil 1:   It hasn't got antennae.
Teacher: A snail has got antennae.
Pupil 2:   Insects have wings.
Teacher: So do nightingales.
Pupil 1:   Insects collect pollen.
Teacher: So do humming birds.

This challenging, slightly adversarial style raises interesting possibilities about teachers' reflections on teaching. Such is the speed of the exchange that there can be little time for reflection. Intelligent action by teachers may be based on deep and surface structures, the deep ones, laid down by reflection and experience over a period of time, determining the surface structures which are also influenced by rapidly processed context clues.

The features of high-scoring lessons will be discussed in the following paragraphs, but here is an example of a teacher whose pupils performed particularly well on post-tests who used the same programmed short frame approach in her summary when she was revising the main points children would need to remember:

Teacher: So, then, let's go back to my little friend here (pointing to a model of an insect she has made and used earlier). Who's going to tell me the names of the parts?
Pupil 1:   Head.
Teacher: Head, yes.
Pupil 2:   Thorax and abdomen.
Teacher: Well done. What are these?
Pupil 3:   Feelers.
Teacher: And what are they for?
Pupil 3:   'Tasting' the air.
Teacher: Yes, tasting the air, that's a good description.

In the case of the lessons on the Island of Zarg there were numerous examples of attempts to invoke the imagination. Some responses were elicited through open but focused questions, such as:

If there was something terribly dangerous on this island, where do you think would be a good place to hide?

Let's say that ship down there is a pirate ship. Imagine you are on that ship, arriving in Hopehaven. What's going to happen to you when you land?

Tell me where the best place on this island would be for me to have my holiday?

What does the name 'Darkling Forest' conjure up in your minds?

Verbal cues were more frequent in the Zarg explanations because teachers tended to give clues about what pupils might do just before they began writing. It should be pointed out, incidentally, that the two differing patterns described above were predominant tendencies, not exclusive patterns. Imagination was sometimes evoked in Insect explanations:

What must it be like to be an insect?

Do you know that butterflies can taste with their feet? (Laughter.) Yes, when they land on things they can taste them using their feet. Wouldn't it be funny if we could taste with our feet?

Age and ability of pupils

The issue of matching tasks to pupils has been investigated by a number of researchers (Bennett *et al.*, 1984). The task is, however, but one part of the matching process, for the other important element must be teaching strategies. One might expect that, just as there were significant differences between the strategies used for the factual Insects topic and the discursive Island of Zarg creative writing assignment, so too there might be differences in patterns of teaching average and above-average pupils and 8 and 9 year olds.

Analysis of variance was again used to elicit whether significant differences did occur between the TEXOS categories obtained for the various groups. In the case of age of pupils the most striking finding is that not one single element of the observation schedule reached even the 5 per cent level of significance. Given that there are more than twenty categories in the schedule, at least one difference at the 5 per cent, 1 in 20, level would have been expected to occur by chance, but no such differences emerged. Furthermore, the teachers of 8 year olds were not the same people as the teachers of 9 year olds, another reason why some significant differences might have occurred, yet none did. Perhaps the slight difference in the ages of pupils, only one year, may account for this similarity of approach. Had the study involved a wider age difference, say, 7 year olds and 11 year olds, the differences might have been more marked. The lack of contrast found in the quantitative reports was analysed. No differences of any note emerged here either. The inescapable conclusion, on the matter of the age of pupils, in this study, therefore, is that a small difference in age, like one year, appears not to be associated with different strategic approaches.

Whereas the non-significance of pupil age as a factor was not too surprising, the findings on pupil ability level were perhaps more noteworthy. Analysis of variance on the process data from the explanation given to average ability and those given to above-average ability showed astonishingly little difference, even though, in this case, it was the *same* teachers who were involved in both cases. Table 8.7 shows that only four elements of classroom process showed any significant difference at all. In each case all the differences were in the direction of more of the behaviour concerned occurring in the classes of the average-ability group, and only one was highly significant at the 0.001 level, the other three being significant at the 0.05 level.

Table 8.7 Four process measures found to be most
significant in the comparison between
explanations to average and above-average
pupils, in each case more occurring in the
lesson with average-ability pupils

TEXOS category	F ratio
1 Teacher corrects	7.7***
2 Teacher rephrases	6.4*
3 Teacher explains links	4.5*
4 Teacher gives summary	4.5*

Notes: ***Significant at <0.001 level; *Significant at <0.05
level.

Analysis of both interviews with teachers and lesson observation field notes confirmed that the differences in process were slight, confined mainly to the consequences of incorrect or partially correct responses in the Insects lesson, when teachers corrected, rephrased, explained links and gave summaries. Most teachers, however, confirmed in interview, when asked specifically, after the explanation had been given to both groups, 'Were you conscious of any differences in the way you explained to high- and average-ability children?' that they had not consciously sought to vary their approach.

Only 2 teachers outlined different strategies for the two ability groups for the Insects topic and only 6 for the Island of Zarg. Only 1 teacher said he used different strategies on *both* topics. One style changer was the teacher whose pupils obtained the highest scores of any in the sample on the test following the Insects explanation. He was a biology graduate teaching in a small village school in a not especially privileged area, where the ability of the children in the two groups was no different from that of children observed in other schools. He explained how he had deliberately made the explanation to the average-ability group 'more concrete'. Whereas, with the more able pupils, he had discussed the characteristics of insects and then looked at specific examples, with the average-ability pupils he began with a 'not analogy', an approach favoured by other teachers, which involves inviting pupils to compare an insect with a non-insect, like an elephant, a cow or, in this case, a bird.

Teacher:	Is a bird an insect?
Pupil 1:	No, that's silly.
Teacher:	Why?
Pupil 1:	Well, it's too small. A bird's bigger.
Teacher:	So all insects are small, then, and all birds are big?
Pupil 2:	No, you can have little birds...and big insects.
Pupil 3:	It's got the wrong number of legs.
Teacher:	Why, how many does an insect have?
Pupil 3:	Six.
Pupil 1:	No it doesn't. It's eight. A spider's got eight legs.
Pupil 3:	A spider's not an insect.
Teacher:	Well, let's clear that one up first.

The children went on to consider each part of the insect and then looked at actual insects. The matter of strategies used by teachers in higher- and lower-scoring explanations is discussed below, but the most important issue here is that so few teachers did consciously opt for a change of approach. Even those that did sometimes found that circumstances brought about the change rather than pre-planning. For example, one teacher who had obtained several responses from the above-average group about the castle on the Island of Zarg found little response when he asked the same questions to the average-ability group.

Teacher: Who do you think lived in that castle?
Pupils: (No response.)
Teacher: No ideas at all?
Pupils: (No response.)
Teacher: James, what about you?
Pupil 1: (No response.)
Teacher: Anybody? Well, I think perhaps it could be some important dignitary, either a king or a queen.

He then continued with an extended monologue, but in interview said that this was as a result of the poor response of the pupils, not through pre-planning. This finding that so few teachers opted for different styles of approach with pupils of different abilities could be explained by two factors. One is that the explanations were undertaken back to back, with the second group coming in about an hour after the first group, though the order of topic and ability group was randomised, so that some teachers explained first to higher-ability pupils, others first to average pupils, and similarly with the order of the two topics. Given the slight artificiality of covering the same topic on the same day with two different groups, perhaps this imposed constraints which might not apply in a more naturalistic setting. Second, it might be argued that the difference between the two groups was relatively small – mean IQ 100 in the average group, mean IQ 115 in the above-average group – and that, had two groups of mean IQ 85 and 115, or 80 and 120, been compared, the differences might have been spectacular. Nonetheless, it is worthy of note.

Styles of explaining

One further analysis was undertaken on the classroom observation process data. In order to reduce a large set of data (640 lesson segments) to something more parsimonious and easier to interpret, as well as to corroborate or refute other forms of analysis, a principal components factor analysis and non-hierarchical cluster analysis were performed. A principal components factor analysis puts together those measures which correlate most highly and produces a smaller set of factors. Three factors were obtained which had latent roots above 1.0, with latent roots of 5.3, 4.5 and 2.1 respectively. These accounted for 20.3, 17.3 and 8.3 per cent of the variance.

Factor 1 (20.3 per cent of variance): a programmed learning factor   This factor loaded most heavily on all categories of questions, open, closed and sequenced, and on short pupil responses, teacher corrects, repeats, rephrases, praises and teacher summary. It was confirmation of the question–answer–reinforcement pattern described earlier, reminiscent of programmed learning principles.

Factor 2 (17.3 per cent of the variance): a topic dissemination factor   The second factor had both positive and negative loadings. The factor loaded *positively* on visual aids, teacher and pupil giving examples, summaries from teacher and pupils, and explaining links, and *negatively* on open questions, long pupil responses, teacher probes and rephrases, and engaging pupils' imagination. It reflects the essential differences between the more highly structured Insects explanation and the more discursive Island of Zarg lesson.

Factor 3 (8.3 per cent of the variance): a pupil response factor   The third factor also showed both negative and positive loading, and pupil responses figured in both. The factor loaded *positively* on no pupil response, pauses, sequenced teacher questions and probes, and *negatively* on long and spontaneous pupil responses. It confirms that a higher frequency of teacher behaviour, like sequencing questions and probing, was associated with a lower frequency of long and spontaneous responses from pupils. It does not mean that there is a *causal* link, however. As was shown above, teachers sometimes resort to reserve strategies as a result of poor pupil response, so it cannot be said that sequencing questions and probing *cause* a zero pupil response or low occurrence of longer, spontaneous pupil contributions, merely that the two go together. It could equally be argued that low pupil response might be a cause of the teacher using sequences of questions and probes, not the result of it.

The non-hierarchical cluster analysis took the whole explanation as the unit of analysis, so all 128 explanations were used to assemble a taxonomy of teaching styles. Whereas factor analysis puts together the various *measures* to form a smaller number of factors, cluster analysis puts together individual profiles of explanations to form a smaller set of groups or clusters. The procedure begins with 128 clusters and ends with one, when all have been combined. The 4, 5 and 6 cluster solutions were inspected, and the 4 cluster solutions displayed the clearest, least diffuse model. The clusters, from now on called 'styles', were as follows:

Style 1 (containing thirty-nine explanations)   This style involved a higher incidence of pupil responses, especially long and spontaneous ones, more open questions, much more engaging of the imagination, more teacher rephrasing and much less use of visual aids. The emphasis is on pupil contributions to discussion. Not surprisingly the 39 explanations in this style contained 35 from the Island of Zarg creative writing lessons and only 4 from the Insects lesson.

Style 2 (containing sixty explanations)   The style here was as described earlier in the description of the Insects topic, for all sixty were about insects, with greatest emphasis on teachers giving and eliciting examples and summaries. It was the more tightly structured factual topic approach with far lower engaging of the imagination.

Style 3 (containing twelve explanations)   All of these were Island of Zarg lessons and most of the differences between this style and the rest are because of much lower occurrence of short pupil responses, summaries and praise and because the teacher repeats, asks closed question and makes personal references.

Style 4 (containing seventeen explanations)   These were also exclusively Island of Zarg lessons, and the distinguishing characteristics were both in a positive and in a negative direction, with much higher occurrence of engagement of the imagination and verbal cues, but much lower use of visual aids, sequenced questions, giving and eliciting examples and praise.

In general these multivariate analyses, like factor and cluster analysis, gave a similar picture to that described in the list, and certainly confirmed the significance of the relationship between type of topic and strategies adopted.

Pupil achievement and learning

At the conclusion of each explanation, tests of insect identification, knowledge of insect characteristics and ability to explain insects to others were given, as described earlier, and after each Island of Zarg lesson pupils were asked to write a story entitled 'My Adventure on the Island of Zarg'. The post-tests were scored by two independent markers whose scoring correlated highly, as was described earlier in this chapter.

There were three aspects of these outcome measures that were of particular interest. The first was the effectiveness of having had a teacher explanation at all. That would be resolved by inspecting the scores of the 64 children in the sixteen average ability 9-year-old groups to whom the teachers had explained, and the 64 in the sixteen control groups of similar ability from the same classes, who had received no explanations. The scorers did not know which pupils were in which groups. In order to test the significance of any difference in scores a null hypothesis was adopted, that is, it was assumed that teaching would make no difference and the scores of the experimental and control group would be the same. A two-tailed *t* test of all outcome measures was then undertaken.

The second element of interest was whether having an 'opportunity to learn' made any difference. For example, if a teacher does not mention or elicit the fact that insects have six legs, then there has been no 'opportunity to learn' it, in that lesson at any rate. Pre-tests were not used, as the research design was quite complex and time-consuming, and adding extensive pre-testing might have alienated children and teachers, so conclusions are based on post-test assumptions only and must have some reservations attached to them.

The third area of interest was what distinguished high-scoring and low-scoring lessons. This is as near as one usually gets to measures of 'effectiveness' in research on teaching, but, given that the tests are short-term measures of learning, or may reflect prior knowledge and experience, again a caveat must be applied. The epithet 'effective' would have to be used purely within the limitations and constraints of this particular piece of research.

Did 'teaching' make a difference?

Table 8.8 shows the results of the *t* tests on the scores obtained by the experimental and control groups of average-ability children. Although in general the experimental groups outperformed the control groups, this was not always the case. Some teachers had merely 'toured' the Island of Zarg in their explanations. This produced 'listing' responses which did not score high on the 'imaginativeness' dimension:

> I started at Mount Horn and then I went to the castle and fell in the swamp and met Zarg outside his lair and he sent me to visit Zorgon in his cave. After that I went to Miller's Top, Fenbury, Hopehaven and sailed home.

On the other hand there were pupils in the control group clearly capable of writing imaginative stories with nothing more than the map of the island, as this extract from a high-scoring story shows:

> Deeper and deeper we plunged into the cave. CRUMP! We hit the bottom. In the distance we heard a strange rumble as if someone was snoring very loud...

Table 8.8 Mean scores of experimental and control groups of average-ability pupils on tests about insects and creative writing (sub-scores and total scores)

Test	Experimental	Control	t value
Insects	22.9	15.8	4.69***
Creative writing			
Length	2.8	2.0	2.5*
Sentence structure	2.6	1.9	0.56 (n.s.)
Coherence	2.9	2.2	2.6*
Features	2.9	2.4	1.4 (n.s.)
Imaginativeness	3.3	2.2	2.8*
Overall impression	2.9	2.1	1.8 (n.s.)
Total score	17.8	12.7	2.4*

Notes: ***Significant at <0.001 level; *Significant at <0.05 level; n.s. = not significant.

In general, however, the experimental groups did better than the control groups on each of the sub-measures of creative writing, though not all the differences reached statistical significance.

The scores in Table 8.8 show that having received an explanation was associated with higher achievement on every single measure in the whole set of post-tests and that in the tests of knowledge about insects the superiority of the experimental over the control groups was significant at beyond the 0.001 level. There was no statistical significance in the differences on sub-scores of creative writing, like sentence structure, mention of the island's features and overall impression, but in sentence length, coherence, imaginativeness and total score the differences in favour of the taught groups were significant at the 0.05 level. Having had an explanation did, therefore, seem to make a significant impact on pupils' learning and achievement in several important respects.

Opportunity to learn

The analysis above shows that having some sort of explanation appears, in general, to be better than not, but we wanted to see whether specific mention of certain aspects of insects' characteristics did appear to be related to their ability to recognise them accurately. The creative writing exercise was not scrutinised in the same way, as it would have been difficult to relate specific and discrete pieces of process data to such outcome measures as 'imaginativeness'. It was easier to inspect the analyses of the Insects explanations to elicit whether, for example, the teacher had mentioned that spiders were not insects, and whether this was related to pupils answering that question correctly.

A correlation analysis was undertaken, therefore, relating frequency of factually correct mentions of feelers, thorax, abdomen, number of legs, number of wings, and spiders not being insects, to number of pupils in the groups correctly identifying each of these in the post-test. Analysis of observation data showed that over 90 per cent of teachers made at least one mention of feelers, thorax, abdomen and number of legs during one of their explanations, whereas the figures for number of wings and spiders were 78.4 per cent and 64 per cent respectively. Table 8.9 shows the correlations obtained for all sixty-four lessons to 256, 8- and 9-year-old pupils receiving Insect explanations.

Table 8.9 Correlations between frequency of mention of insect features and number of pupils correctly answering relevant item on post-test

Feature mentioned	Correlation with test item
Feelers	0.29**
Thorax	0.46***
Abdomen	0.46***
Number of legs	0.05 (n.s.)
Number of wings	0.04 (n.s.)
Spiders not insects	0.38***

Notes: ***Significant at <0.001 level; **Significant at <0.01 level; n.s. = not significant.

These results must be interpreted with caution. For example, if teachers feel that most children already know that insects have six legs, they may mention this feature less frequently than, say, 'thorax' or 'abdomen', which are likely to be new to 8 and 9 year olds. Also since correlations are of frequency of mention, not intensity or context, these quantitative measures do not distinguish on qualitative grounds, and are thus relatively crude, needing to be set alongside other kinds of information, like that in the section on high- and low-scoring lessons below. Within these limitations it is of some interest to note that the correlations between frequency of mention of thorax, abdomen and spiders not being insects were significant beyond the 0.001 level.

High- and low-scoring lessons

A qualitative analysis was performed on the lessons of the teachers whose pupils obtained the highest and lowest post-test scores on both topics. The following cases show the flavour of some of these high-scoring lessons:

Mrs Archer (high-scoring insect explanation)

The explanation began with Mrs Archer producing two large display cases full of insects.

Teacher: Do you know what these are?
Pupil 1: Bees and wasps.
Teacher: Yes, that's right and what are these?
Pupil 2: Bluebottles
Teacher: Yes, bluebottles, greenbottles. They're all flies.... What about this beautiful creature?
Pupil 3: He's a dragonfly.

At this stage one of the pupils wanted to talk about frogs, which also live by ponds. The teacher listened and then skilfully redirected and refocused.

One of the most notable features of her explanation was her use of voice intonation and emphasis, and pauses. At the end of the first phase of the explanation, she recapped with some vigour:

All of these creatures (pointing to the display cases) are all so different, *but* (emphasis) (pause) they do have *one* (emphasis) thing in common (pause). They *all* (emphasis) belong to the family called (pause) insects (pause) – insects.

The main body of the explanation was devoted to covering each of the features of the insect body. When talking about the insect's feelers she used an analogy:

> The feelers are rather like radio aerials, they pick up all sorts of messages in the air around the insect.

Much of the explanation involved question-and-answer and reference to the insect display cases, but she also had a model of an insect she had made herself, and this featured frequently in the exchanges.

A high degree of learning in Mrs Archer's explanations appeared to be related to clear structure and explanation of key points through question-and-answer, skilful use of different types of visual aid, both simplified home-made insect shapes and cases of actual insects, refocusing discussion when it strayed off the point, eliciting a summary from pupils in which the main characteristics of insects were again illuminated and effective modulation of voice with emphasis and pausing for effect.

Mr Barlow (low-scoring insects explanation)

By contrast with Mrs Archer, the explanations in Mr Barlow's lessons lacked clarity from the beginning. What is more, they were also factually incorrect and confusing from the very outset.

Teacher: I'm going to give you the little word 'insect'. Immediately in your mind there's a picture of something, I expect. There is in mine. What sort of picture have you got, Cassandra?
Pupil 1:   A spider.
Teacher: OK, you think of a spider. You keep the spider there. Peter, what about you?
Pupil 2:   (No response.)
Teacher: When I say 'insect' what do you immediately think of – an insect?
Pupil 3:   A ladybird.
Teacher: Yes, that's right.
Pupil 4:   A worm.
Teacher: Yes – anything else?
Pupil 3:   A snail.
Teacher: How do insects move around, Peter?
Pupil 2:   Legs.
Teacher: How many legs has an insect got?
Pupil 2:   Six.
Teacher: Yes, six; but do insects get around any other way?
Pupil 2:   Some insects fly.
Teacher: Yes, some insects use wings. Can you think of an insect that flies?
Pupil 2:   An eagle.
Teacher: An eagle? Is that an insect? No, it's a bird. A bird is definitely not an insect.

The factual inaccuracies and lack of conceptual clarity, with shape, movement and example confused and blurred, were compounded at the end of the lesson when Mr Barlow summed up for the pupils what had supposedly been learned.

Teacher: So we've thought about a whole set of different insects today: snails, centipedes, ladybirds, caterpillars and wood lice, and we've also found a lot of ways in which these insects move about – crawling, walking, sliding, swimming, flying and hopping.

The low degree of learning during Mr Barlow's explanation appears to be related to a lack of distinct key points which would have given conceptual clarity, and factual inaccuracy. He establishes that insects have six legs, but never returns to the spider mentioned by Cassandra, nor explains why such creatures as worms, centipedes or snails are allowed into the genus when they do not have six legs. It was not surprising, therefore, that the concept 'insect' in the children's minds wrongly included gastropods, arachnids and other unlikely members. The pupils' test responses showed that their concept of an insect was anything smallish that crawls, swims, flies or hops around and is not a bird.

Mrs Charles (high-scoring Island of Zarg explanation)

In the interview following this lesson Mrs Charles modestly said, 'I reckon they could have managed quite well without me.' Yet this explanation was located in Style 4 in the cluster analysis, emphasising the stimulation of pupils' imagination and verbal cues. She concentrated in her exposition on encouraging children to use their imagination about the features of the island and on extending or exploring their vocabulary, as this exchange shows:

Teacher: Can you see anything that attracts you about the island? Anywhere you'd like to visit, David?
Pupil 1: Castle Point.
Teacher Why would you like to go there?
Pupil 1: It's exciting.
Teacher: Yes, it's exciting. Have you found anywhere you'd like to go, Emma?
Pupil 2: I think...
Teacher: No, it's Emma's turn. I'd like to hear what Emma has to say.
Pupil 3: Eastern Moors. There's a creature...it's...it's...
Teacher: There's something up there that Emma's found. What has she found coming out of the sea?
Pupil 4: A monster.
Teacher: Yes, it could be. What's coming out of his hand?
Pupil 2: Lightning.
Teacher: What else has he got coming out of him?
Pupil 2: Rain.
Teacher: Rain and thunder, so it's almost as if he's in control of the...?
Pupil 2: Weather.
Teacher: The weather, yes, I think so... What would be a good word to describe Darkling Forest?
Pupil 2: Spooky and creepy.
Teacher: Better than 'spooky and creepy'?
Pupil 1: Strange and weird.
Teacher: Yes, strange and weird. How about a word beginning with two e's? Do you know it?
Pupil 1: Eerie.
Teacher: Yes. What does 'eerie' mean?
Pupil 1: Scary.

What the transcript does not show is the high degree of pleasure, signalled through voice, intonation and facial expression, at the pupils' responses. The exchanges were fairly rapid, the responses brief; however, the management was benignly but tightly controlled. The level of excitement was high, like the pace. This enthusiasm, pace, regular involvement of pupils, albeit with short replies and discriminating response to their answers, which were not automatically accepted, may all be related to the quality of the children's written work, which was scored very highly by the markers. If these explanations were snapshots of what had happened over a longer period of time, it would appear that the effect of these strategies may well be cumulative. Children do not become skilful writers overnight, or after one such lesson. In interview Mrs Charles stressed the importance of the initial stimulus: 'They need a starting point. Once they have that, their story can take them anywhere.'

Miss Dogger (low-scoring Island of Zarg explanation)

It soon became clear in Miss Dogger's lesson that the story the pupils were to write was one she would provide, not one that they would invent. The transcript shows that her explanation was a mixture of 'Guess my story' and 'Here's what you're going to do'. This was evident from her opening:

Teacher: In a minute I'm going to ask you to write a story. Do you think your story is going to be about modern days or olden days?
Pupil 1: About olden days 'cos there's a castle on the island.
Teacher: Oh, well, you see lots of castles around today. No, there was one thing I thought gave it away. Can't you see it?
Pupil 2: The windmill.
Teacher: No.
Pupil 3: The ship.
Teacher: Yes, that's right – the ship.

She gave more information about the ship, and then the first and only spontaneous response came from a pupil:

Pupil 2: Hey, there's a monster there.
Teacher: Yes, I don't think he's a monster though, I think he's supposed to be some sort of rain god. Look – there's rain coming from his hands.

No further spontaneous responses occurred, and the children listened patiently as she elaborated more detail of what was essentially her own story that they were to attempt to reproduce:

Teacher: You're on that ship, and it's called *Gull*. You're sailing over to the island, when there's a storm and you're washed overboard. You get washed up here at Mudlark Swamp. Now, the inhabitants of Hightown are unfriendly, but up in the hills you'll see a cave – Zarg's lair. Now, Zarg is a fearsome creature, a bit frightening, but he's friendly.

The approach was a contrast to that of Mrs Charles, who often sought precise vocabulary but was open minded about story lines. The children's low scores in Miss Dogger's group seem to be related to restrictions on their imagination imposed by this more prescriptive approach and the lack of enthusiasm and drive which was a feature of the lesson of Mrs Charles.

Summary of features of high-scoring explanations

The main points that emerged when two separate analysts went through the explanation tapes and transcripts are a little different for the two topics. The highest-scoring Insects explanations were, in general, clearly structured, with the 'keys' or central ideas made distinct and linked to one another in a logical sequence and shape, often with a teacher or pupil review at the end of the section or the whole explanation, and the teacher's subject knowledge was factually correct. Language choices were sensible, neither too banal nor at too high a level of abstraction, an appropriate register being employed. Voice was clear and well modulated, with effective movement, facial expression and animation, and there was fluency and pace. Good visual aids to learning were employed and the occasional illuminating example or analogy was given or, more likely, elicited. There was an overall simplicity of structure which gave clarity. Indeed, one high-scoring teacher, who began with a simple line drawn on the blackboard, said in interview, 'You just need the very basics in an explanation like this, other pictures would have confused the children.' Another, who started by establishing why insects were a distinct group, stated in interview, 'I thought it would be a good way to go from the general to the particular. I wanted the children to be sure that "insects" is the name of a group of animals early on.'

In the creative writing lessons on the Island of Zarg, some of the above applied, but personal characteristics like enthusiasm and voice being used to create or evoke an atmosphere of mystery or curiosity figure prominently. Questions and statements that provoked thought and stimulated the imagination were notable ('A thick fog comes down,' said one teacher), but both prescriptive and exploratory approaches could be successful. The effectiveness of this single lesson was probably a reflection of the cumulative effect of strategies which led to skilful writing being employed over a period of time.

Other features of high-scoring lessons were the occasional use of humour which was relevant to the topic, as opposed to gratuitous humour. The use of the 'advance organiser' (Ausubel *et al.*, 1978) sometimes occurred, when the teacher employed what broadcasters call a 'tease' at the beginning of their explanation, to give shape or to arouse curiosity:

Teacher: If I told you in, say, a bucket of earth there were hundreds of them. They're in the air, they're even in ponds and rivers. There are millions of them in a tree. They live all over the world, except at the North and South Poles. There are over a million different types of them. There are 200,000 different types in this country alone. Some of them can fly, some can swim, some make holes in the ground, and some make holes in wood. What do you think I would be talking about?

As is often the case, however, despite some communalities, high-scoring explanations were also different from each other, with their own unique qualities. The general conclusions above are not universal prescriptions, but rather interesting illuminations from one intensive study.

References

Ausubel, D. P., Novak, J. D. and Hanesian, H. (1978) *Educational Psychology: A Cognitive View*, Holt, Rinehart & Winston, New York.

Bellack, A. A., Hyman, R. T., Smith, F. L. and Kliebard, H. M. (1966) *The Language of the Classroom*, Teachers College Press, New York.

Bennett, S. N., Desforges, C. W., Cockburn, A. and Wilkinson, B. (1984) *The Quality of Pupil Learning Experiences*, Erlbaum, London.

Bloom, B. S. (ed.) (1956) *Taxonomy of Educational Objectives: Cognitive Domain*, David McKay, New York.

Brown, G. A. (1978) *Lecturing and Explaining*, Methuen, London.

Brown, G. A. and Armstrong, S. (1984) 'Explaining and Explanations', in E. C. Wragg (ed.), *Classroom Teaching Skills*, Routledge, London.

Crowhurst, S. J. (1988) *Explaining in the Primary School*, PhD thesis, Exeter University.

Ennis, R. H. (1969) *Logic in Teaching*, Prentice-Hall, Englewood Cliffs, NJ.

Gage, N. L., Belgard, M., Rosenshine, B., Unruh, W. R., Dell, D., Hiller, J. H., Carrol, J. B. and Glaser, R. (1972) Chapter 9 of I, in Westbury and A. Bellack (eds), *Research into Classroom Processes*, Teachers College Press, New York.

Galton, M. J. (ed) (1978) *British Mirrors: a Collection of Classroom Observation Systems*, University of Leicester, Leicester.

Hyman, R. T. (1974) *Teaching: Vantage Points for Study*, Lippincott Press, New York.

Smith, B. O. and Meux, M. (1970) *A Study of the Logic of Teaching*, Urbana, University of Illinois Press, IL.

Swift, L. F. (1961) 'Explanation', in B. O. Smith and R. H. Ennis (eds) *Language and Concepts in Education, 179-94*, Rand McNally, Chicago, IL.

Taba, H. (1966) *Teaching Strategies and Cognitive Functioning in Elementary School Children*, USOE Cooperative Research Project No.1574, San Francisco State College, San Francisco, CA.

Tisher, R. P. (1970) 'The Nature of Verbal Discourse in Classrooms and Association between Verbal Discourse and Pupil Understanding in Science', in W. J. Campbell (ed.), *Scholars in Context*, Wiley, Sydney.

Wilkinson, A., Barnsley, G., Hanna, P. and Swan, M. (1980) *Assessing Language Development*, Oxford University Press, Oxford.

CHAPTER 9

████████

EXPLAINING IN THE SECONDARY SCHOOL

Originally published as 'Knowing the Subject Matter', in *Explaining in the Secondary School*, by Wragg E. C. and Brown G., RoutledgeFalmer, 2001, pp. 43–52

Research reports are one thing, action by teachers quite another, often several light years away from each other. Unit 4 from the 2001 book *Explaining in the Secondary School* shows how teachers can use research findings, perspectives and procedures, not as something to copy, but as a means of taking charge of their own competence by improving their own ability to explain clearly.

Throughout the world knowledge is being produced at a phenomenal rate in every conceivable subject. Teachers are the bearers of social genes in our fast-moving society, able to transmit knowledge, skills, values and culture to future generations. In order to carry out this task successfully, particularly when passing on a concept or an idea, their own knowledge of the relevant subject matter must be accurate and correct. There is no point in being a brilliant exponent of the art of explaining and then filling children's heads with incorrect information and dreary ideas, or equipping them with low-level skills when he/she and his/her pupils are capable of achieving something better.

Mastering subject matter

The professional expertise of people who have become masters of different kinds of subject matter can consist of many elements. Mastery involves more than the mere mechanical acquisition of certain factual information, though having a formidable body of knowledge is a central requisite. Those who have mastered a particular subject or profession will usually have acquired:

- a significant body of knowledge;
- an understanding of the major and many minor concepts central to the subjects;
- an understanding of the structure of the subject and a desire to learn more about it.

Take a subject like music as an example. Professional musicians will have a considerable grasp of, usually, a wide range of musical knowledge, from simple concepts of notation up to an intimate knowledge of numerous symphonies, concertos, operas, songs and other types of music. They will have the skill to play certain instruments at a very high standard of proficiency, or to sing, to compose, to conduct, to score and to improvise. They will also usually have a lifelong interest in music that leads them to broaden and extend their repertoire, improve their playing or singing, or create new compositions, throughout their career. There is even some evidence to suggest that, in the case of those musicians who use their fingers, for example, the parts of their brain that control fingering will develop greater capacity and that this may be related to the amount of practice they have done (Howe, 1999).

The subject demands on secondary teachers are now formidable, no matter what subject they teach. Modern linguists are expected to be right up to date with contemporary spoken and written language, able to cover non-fiction as well as traditional fiction. Science specialists are expected to know about both physical and biological sciences, earth science, technology, meteorology and astronomy. Since their classes may have watched television programmes on any conceivable scientific topic, from polymers to genetic modification, they may also be asked questions about topics about which they know less than their better-informed pupils.

Even very young children would have seen spectacular films about their environment. I was once teaching a class of 6 and 7 year olds. The topic was 'The World Around Us' and pupils were invited to ask questions about their own immediate environment. In the first thirty seconds this group of children of modest ability asked, 'Why are cars made of metal?', 'Why does smoke come out of the back of a motor bike?', 'Why does it snow?' and 'Why does a wagtail wag its tail?' It was nothing that a couple of lifetimes in the nearest multimedia library could not have solved, but most of us are as competent to handle the more searching questions asked by children as to perform a piece of triple bypass surgery.

Knowledge of subject matter and strategies for explaining are often closely connected. If you have a good grasp of the content (i.e. *what* is to be taught), it puts you in a better position to determine appropriate strategies (i.e. *how* to explain the topic), though mastery of subject matter does not actually guarantee clear exposition. Some knowledgeable people, paralysed by the complexity of what they know, are not able to communicate and empathise with those in possession of less knowledge. Not every Nobel prize-winner would be able to instruct a group of 13 year olds, though some are brilliant explainers of their knowledge.

Different topics involve different kinds of subject matter. In order to explain to a class how to use a microelectronics kit, why certain materials are better than others when designing and constructing something, the causes and course of the Civil War, how to calculate the volume of a three-dimensional shape, or what erosion is, teachers need to possess, or have access to, considerable bodies of the relevant subject matter. Explaining the quality of writing in a book, the finer points of citizenship in the twenty-first century, how people deal with moral dilemmas, the impact of a poem on the emotions, painting, piece of music, or the spirit in which team games should be played, involves a mixture of factual content, judgements about values, the intelligence of feeling and a degree of imagination.

Explanations, where part of the 'subject matter' requires use of the imagination, pose an interesting problem. If the teacher prescribes too much in advance, then both children's and teachers' imagination could be inhibited. Yet a certain amount of explaining and exploring must take place.

Activity 1

The following exercise is worth doing even if you are not a teacher of English, citizenship, or personal, social and health education. It is an interesting idea to use during tutor group time, for example, and gives insights into aspects of children's learning that might not always be apparent during lessons in your main subjects.

1 Plan a lesson for a group of pupils in which you will explore ideas with them on a topic of general interest prior to their doing a piece of writing. For example, the topic could be: why do girls often do better than boys at school? Work out what information/resources they may need (e.g. information about test scores at the age of 11 for boys and girls, nationally and within the school; gender, social and cultural issues).

2 Explore the topic interactively with the class and then ask them to write their own account of the issue. Make a tape- or video-recording of the lesson, if possible.

3 Read and mark the class's written work and discuss it with them.

4 Consider the following questions:

(a) *What was the nature and structure of your lesson?*
How did you introduce the topic?
What seemed to be the main ideas or keys: statistical evidence, like test results; pupils' feelings and beliefs about gender differences; creating a sense of enquiry about the nature of different subjects, the functioning of the human brain and whether boys' brains worked differently from girls' brains; exploration of prejudices and comparison with such 'facts' as exist; excitement; exploiting curiosity; considering the future of employment? How did these evolve? Were they linked?

(b) *What strategies did you employ?*
What did you *tell* the class?
What sort of *questions* did you ask?
What additional *aids* did you use – tables? pictures? anecdotes or stories?
Did you use any other approaches, like drama or role play?

(c) *What did members of the class do?*
Were they active or passive?
How did they respond to the main ideas and keys?
What did they initiate themselves?
How did their contributions and ideas affect the development of the lesson?

(d) *What was the written work like?*
Did it appear to have been influenced by the activities that preceded it? If so, in what way? If not, why not?
Was the written response what you expected?
What particularly pleased you? What disappointed you?
What did the pupils say to you about the activity and their own writing?
Did they seem to have found it an interesting and absorbing assignment?

    (e)   *How did you assess their writing?*
         What features of the writing did you particularly value? Factual accuracy? Argument? Use of evidence?
         What did you do about spelling, punctuation, grammatical or syntactical errors?
         What sort of explaining did you do when you handed the work back?

5   In the light of your experience of teaching the lesson, of listening to and viewing it on tape, and, if you had the opportunity, of discussing it with the class, and with an observer if that was possible, of reading the pupils' writing, and reflecting on the whole exercise, how would you improve what you did? See if you can do a similar activity with the group and then compare the two. Was your second effort more effective?

Explaining concepts

Learning subject matter often involves mastering a set of concepts. These can be of several kinds. Some of the salient concepts can be said to be the 'keys' which, when linked, lead to understanding. Like pieces in a jigsaw puzzle, if you put them together in the right way you may have a picture of the whole thing. Some concepts are tiny and precise, others are large and diffuse, open to different interpretations. The concept 'happiness', for example, may have quite different features in the eyes of an Inuit Eskimo, a child, a millionaire and a Trappist monk, but what is in common is that their individual versions of it give them pleasure or satisfaction.

   There are four essential features that need to be considered when explaining concepts. These are:

1   *Label or name*   The actual word(s) used to name the concept – 'crops', 'reptile', 'electricity', 'harmony', 'colour', 'monarchy', 'ambition'.
2   *Attributes*   These are of two kinds:

    (a)   *must have* – features which are essential parts of the concept, indeed, that are criteria for its definition, such as 'wings' (bird), 'having a grandchild' (grandparents), 'eagerness to succeed' (ambition);
    (b)   *may have* – features which occur in certain cases, but are not prerequisites, such as 'brown coloured' birds (applies to sparrows and thrushes, but not to every bird), 'retired' grandparents (many are still working), 'seeking wealth' in ambitious people (some may seek power and scorn wealth).

3   *Examples*   These are also of two kinds:

    (a)   *illustrative examples* – actual cases which meet the criteria, such as 'robin' (bird), 'Mr and Mrs Scroggins' (grandparents), 'seeking out influential people to further one's career' (ambition);
    (b)   *not-examples* – cases which do not meet the criteria, but then, by comparison, illustrate what the real criteria for inclusion in the concept actually are, such as 'dragon-fly' (flies, but is not a bird), 'Mr and Mrs Bloggs' (elderly, but not grandparents), 'obtaining promotion' (often the result of ambition, but could also happen to the unambitious).

4   *Rules*   The full definition listing the 'must have' attributes and their relationship to each other.

If we were to map out the familiar concept 'Insects' according to this scheme, it would look like this:

Subject area   Science (*subdivisions* – biology – zoology)
Name   Insect
Attributes   (i) *must have* – six legs, head, thorax, abdomen, two antennae, wings;
                 (ii) *may have* – a woodland habitat, a black or brown body, stripes, a beautiful appearance, a liking for fruit, a smooth shell, hairy legs.
Examples   (i) *illustrative examples* – house-fly, beetle, butterfly, wasp, ladybird;
                 (ii) *not-examples* – spider (arachnid), scorpion (arachnid), snail (gastropod), woodlouse (isopod land crustacean).
Rules   Insects have six legs, a head, thorax and abdomen, two antennae and two or four wings.

Another valuable use of 'not-examples' is to clarify what the true attributes of the concept are. By comparing a honeycomb, a chessboard or a crossword puzzle where the shapes do 'tessellate' – that is, fit together in a regular pattern – with what happens when you try to press differently sized circles or most star shapes together, where they will not meet all round, the concept of 'tessellation' becomes clearer.

Looking at the 'not-examples' and 'may have' attributes can also help avoid stereotyping, as well as aid the development of more rigorous thinking in children. Stereotyping is often wrong and crude, but its origins lie in it being, on occasion, a biological lifesaver. If we stay well away from all snakes, simply because some are poisonous, then this will help us avoid being bitten by those that are venomous. Stereotyping is the acquisition of a fixed mental attitude to something on the basis of one or more characteristics.

Unfortunately it is also an oversimplification that is sometimes, indeed can often be, incorrect, even though it is related to accommodating the environment in order to survive. In childhood, for example, most of us are at some time stung by a bee or a wasp. We then stereotype all black-and-yellow striped insects as likely to sting and therefore to be avoided, yet many are completely harmless and enjoy, as a result of their colouring, some immunity from predators. If a teacher were explaining the concept 'Ruritanian', then the only definition of it may be 'those born in, or naturalised as residents of, Ruritania'. But if children have met or read about a Ruritanian who is lazy, violent or dishonest, they may generalise this 'may have' attribute to all Ruritanians and wrongly stereotype them.

Activity 2

1   Choose two key concepts which you are likely to need to explain to a class, a group or an individual. Select one which is fairly specific and definable, like 'mammal', 'island', or 'the Romans', and one which is more diffuse and difficult to pin down, such as 'progress', 'a good building', or 'great music/art'.

2   Map out each of the two according to the scheme suggested earlier with attributes, examples and rules.

3   Explain the concept to a group of pupils, or even to an individual. See what strategies and teaching aids you need to make the concept

clear – a video of a current affairs programme or part of a debate in Parliament? A drawing or photograph of an island or a map? Pictures of various buildings? A tape of different kinds of music or a collection of different styles of painting, so the group can discuss what constitutes 'great' music or art?

4   Evaluate to what extent your 'map' of the concept helped in the exposition of it.

Written explanations

Teachers are not the sole sources of information available to pupils. In addition to pictures, videos, tapes, various forms of interactive technology, television and radio, there is a wide variety of print material – books, worksheets, pamphlets, newspapers, magazines and the printed word parts of pictures or diagrams. Many of the acts of explaining in which teachers find themselves engaged are related to printed text – a worksheet, perhaps – which has been compiled by the teacher, or a textbook published commercially.

Much of what has been learned about explanations in textbooks is of relevance to what is covered in this book. Explanations of critical subject matter and key concepts can be clouded, both in textbooks and classroom teaching, by such factors as lack of clarity, inappropriate language, poor links between ideas, or inaccuracy. In some cases it may be the presence of only one or two technical words or phrases which make a text difficult, and teachers might have to explain these so that their pupils can cope with a text which otherwise may not be too difficult for them.

Activity 3

1   Read this passage and then answer the questions below:

Timefrittoons   Most people have at least one timefrittoon. Many of us have several and some people acquire more as they get older. Erdgraben is a common timefrittoon, and it can be quite geldverlangend, though older people often have to make it ungeldverlangend. One elderly man devotes every single day to his timefrittoon. He doesn't mind that erdgraben can be a dirty timefrittoon. 'I don't find it very geldverlangend at all', he said recently, 'my cousin's timefrittoon is quite a bit more geldverlangend than mine and nowhere near as healthy.'

(a)   Give the names of three timefrittoons.
(b)   Which is likely to be the most geldverlangend?
(c)   Can erdgraben sometimes be a dirty timefrittoon?
(d)   Are all dogs healthy?
(e)   Write a short essay on 'Timefrittoons in the Twenty-first Century'.

2   What do you think the passage is about? How well did you answer the questions? You were probably able to answer some of them without even understanding the passage. For example, you could answer (a) in part, because the text tells you that erdgraben is a timefrittoon; the answer to (c) is also given in the passage, because erdgraben can be dirty; you could have answered (d) without even reading the passage, because it is quite clear that all dogs are not healthy (the mention of dogs is

a distracter, it has nothing to do with the passage) and you may have been able to waffle on in the essay in (e) with a bit of deft footwork. Answers to questions that appear on the surface to be 'correct' do not always guarantee understanding.

3   If you were a pupil, you would probably want your teacher to explain three unfamiliar terms to you – timefrittoon, erdgraben and geldverlangend/ungeldverlangend – so that you could understand the passage properly. So now read the text again, in the knowledge that:

timefrittoons are 'hobbies'
erdgraben is 'gardening'
geldverlangend/ungeldverlangend is 'expensive/inexpensive'.

4   Take a textbook or worksheet you are using with a group of pupils and identify any words or phrases that you think might cause them difficulties. Ask some of the pupils to tell you which terms they do not understand. Are your lists the same? Try explaining the terms to the pupils. Read some of the work on text readability (Harrison, 1996).

Coping strategies

Even well-informed teachers can be caught out by pupils' tricky questions. We have conducted a number of studies of teachers' own subject knowledge and the gaps in it. Even within a field like science there can be wide differences between teachers, depending on whether their major strengths lie in the physical or biological sciences. History teachers may have to cover thousands of years of history in many different lands and cultures, so they too will have gaps in their knowledge. Learning to cope with this, rather than becoming a bluffer, or turning into one of those teachers who covers ignorance by reprimanding the pupil for daring to ask the question, involves the development of coping strategies.

One of the most difficult problems is coping with unpredicted events or with pupils' spontaneous questions. When asked why an orange floats with its peel on, but sinks when peeled, or why most sand sinks, but some grains stay on the surface, teachers would be bereft if they did not have the necessary grasp of such concepts as 'density', 'surface tension' or 'Archimedes' Principle', all of which may be necessary for an explanation of certain kinds of the phenomena associated with floating and sinking.

Teachers use various strategies for coping with their own lack of knowledge, including frank admission (one primary teacher began a lesson on electrical circuits with, 'Look, I have to be honest with you. I know nothing about electricity. I can just about change a fuse'), occasionally evasion, sometimes an offer to find out, or an invitation to the pupils to investigate for themselves.

There are several reasons why teachers need to learn to devise strategies for when they are explaining unfamiliar subject matter. There could be a safety issue (gymnastics and contact sports like rugby, the use of tools, especially those that are electrically powered or that cut); teachers who appear to know too little about their subject will eventually lose respect and continued personal growth is an important part of teachers' professional development.

Lack of sound subject knowledge can also affect teaching strategies. For example, if you didn't know what a capacitor is, in a lesson about microelectronics, you would neither give a convincing explanation, nor be able to think up an appropriate analogy, like, 'A capacitor introduces a delay in the circuit, so when you switch on, the bulb won't light up immediately. There will be a short delay with a small capacitor and a longer delay with a big capacitor. It's a bit like a bucket filling up with water. A little bucket will soon fill up and then overflow, but a bigger bucket will take longer.'

Most of the teachers we have interviewed said they wanted *people* to help them if they were stuck. Some used another specialist, like their head of department (it was particularly embarrassing when heads of department had to consult younger and more recently qualified colleagues!). Others used some kind of centre, like a university or specialist library. Many people use the internet, though this can be hazardous, because there is not the same degree of control over what appears on the internet as there is over what is written in a book, so thousands of erroneous pieces of information appear on websites and this is a real pitfall for pupils as well as teachers. Some teachers preferred asking a friend, sometimes a spouse, or a school governor who happens to be an expert, especially about cultural and religious matters in multicultural schools. One teacher even used a parent who was a science graduate. Think of the following possibilities, in your own case, should you find yourself on unfamiliar ground:

- *People who can help* – a fellow teacher, a friend, someone on a 'help' line, a librarian, an adviser;
- *Books* – encyclopaedias, library sources, dictionaries, specialist texts;
- *Multimedia* – videos, tapes, pictures, interactive technology, the internet, broadcast radio and television.

Finally, reflect on these strategies and consider how you would react if they were to occur in your classroom.

- You could avoid the issue (not fair, if you can manage to help, you should);
- you might ask the pupil to find out for him- or herself (but help is needed: a suggestion of a book, dictionary or source of information like the library or a database);
- you could promise to find out for another day (but you need to honour this promise, otherwise children feel let down);
- you might ask a group of people to find out (but again, help is needed – who does what? and where?);
- you could try to find out jointly with the class ('I'll write to X, you write to Y').

Activity 4

1   Ask a class to write down questions about concepts, issues, skills, ideas in your subject that they find difficult or do not grasp.
2   Read the questions through privately and decide how you will explain them.
3   Ask yourself which are the easy and which are the hard questions and why?
4   How do you explain the hard questions? What strategies do you use?
5   What do you do if you are confronted with questions about which your own knowledge is not entirely secure?

References

Harrison, C. (1996) *The Teaching of Reading: What Teachers Need to Know*, Shepreth, United Kingdom Reading Association, UK.
Howe, M. J. A. (1999) *Genius Explained*, Cambridge University Press, Cambridge.

PART 3

CURRICULUM IN ACTION

Some of the research I have done, such as studying how teachers manage their classes, has been undertaken in a general rather than a specific context. Other enquiries have concentrated on particular subject matter such as observing how teachers explain the nature of insects to 8- and 9-year-old children. Analysing teaching and learning brings you into intimate contact with many aspects of the curriculum in school: the subject matter being taught; implementation (whether teachers do what the curriculum developers intended, for example); notions of 'effectiveness' such as whether method A appears to produce more learning than method B (a research minefield if ever there was one); the 'hidden curriculum', what children learn that may not be on the timetable such as to condemn, or join in, the tormenting of fellow pupils and wider issues such as the teaching role played by classroom assistants, parents or members of the community.

Styles of teaching and learning themselves are an important part of the curriculum, though they are often omitted from discussions of it. If children spent all their life being instructed, for example, they might not know how to learn independently when they are adults. Impossible to ignore is the origins of curriculum – the extent to which it is imposed from outside or fashioned from within. Concerns about the curriculum have always been a second or third tier of interest for me but nonetheless a significant one.

The three chapters in this section cover different kinds of research. Chapter 10 is the opening chapter of a book looking to the future. Society was transforming at a rapid rate during the last few years of the twentieth and the early twenty-first century, and I wrote *The Cubic Curriculum* to demonstrate the multifaceted nature of the schooling that would be necessary to help young people cope with their own and society's future.

Chapters 11 and 12 are a pair extracted from a large-scale study of literacy teaching in the late 1990s. They illustrate the 'big picture/little picture' style of enquiry that I used for some of my research projects. Chapter 11 reports a national survey of 1,395 schools giving the fullest available picture of literacy teaching in primary schools immediately before the introduction of the compulsory literacy hour in 1998. National surveys can sometimes appear cold and clinical so Chapter 12 provides the flesh and blood describing individual case studies of different children. I found the story of Jack and Eva described in it quite astonishing. In a sample of several hundred children observed and tested from all over the country, they were the biggest improver and the biggest 'sinker' on a test of reading administered at the beginning and end of the year. So did Eva have a brilliant teacher and Jack a lousy one? No. They had spent the year sitting a few feet away from each other in the same class. Truly remarkable.

CHAPTER 10

A CURRICULUM FOR THE FUTURE

Originally published as 'Life in the Future', in *The Cubic Curriculum*,
Routledge, 1997, pp. 8–22

To some extent education is a vision of the future, since children in school today may still be alive eight decades after leaving full-time education. The opening chapter of my 1997 book *The Cubic Curriculum* analysed what the future may hold for young citizens who will probably live through most, if not all, of the twenty-first century, and how this might affect the school curriculum.

Some of the children in school today may see the dawn of the twenty-second century. With improved medical treatments being devised every day, there is a strong likelihood that children born in the late twentieth and early twenty-first centuries will, in many cases, live to be 90, 100, or more. In these circumstances the term 'future' can mean a very long time indeed. If education is society's investment in its own posterity, then a long- rather than a short-term strategy is essential.

It is easy to argue that education must be based on a vision of the future, but not so simple to describe what that future might look like. There have been numerous predictions about life in the twenty-first century, some gloomy, others more hopeful. Indeed, the same data can be quoted to support either a pessimistic or optimistic vision of what is to come. Forecasts that job opportunities may diminish can be used to predict boredom and street riots, or to welcome the release of people from dangerous and demeaning employment.

Speculation about the future involves intelligent guesswork about present and past trends and where they might eventually lead, so that key messages about the twenty-first century can be elicited. Predictions can, of course, go disastrously astray, which is why they should be read with caution. It would be a mistake to base a whole education system entirely on a single conjecture, especially when it is hazardous enough predicting next year's events on the basis of what is happening this year. Small wonder that the great oracles have often spoken in ambiguous terms. I propose to deal here, therefore, with a range of possibilities that seem to be worth considering, and see what the implications would be were they to materialise, though none of the following messages is offered with any certainty.

Employment or unemployment?

While the jobs that people hold do not consume the whole of their life, they are an important part of it. In the first half of the twentieth century many men, if they lived long enough, worked for some fifty or so years before entering retirement, while women tended to work in paid employment for fewer years, or did not return to their previous career after giving birth to children. Speculations about the future often concentrate entirely on the nature of employment or the lack of it. What is clear is that changes in work patterns have been dramatic in the last third of the twentieth century. What is less clear is where these changes are leading.

During the nineteenth century a succession of industrial revolutions saw masses of people move out of the rural areas and into the cities, as they left agriculture to seek work in factories. Whereas in early Victorian Britain about a third of the population worked on the land, the figure in modern times is of about 2 per cent of the workforce employed in agriculture, a remarkable transformation in the landscape of working life. Equally significant changes took place during the last three decades of the twentieth century, but the eventual outcome of these post-industrial revolutions remains clouded. The massive disappearance of jobs in manufacturing industry has not led to a single type of employer emerging to absorb those displaced during the labour-shedding process.

During the 1970s in the United Kingdom, over a million jobs were lost in manufacturing industry alone. Another $1\frac{1}{2}$ million went in the first five years of the 1980s. The turmoil continued towards the end of the century, and in the first five years of the 1990s some 5 million people lost their job. What was notable about these huge losses of traditional forms of employment was first of all that the vast majority of posts that disappeared were unskilled, semi-skilled or barely skilled. It is true that graduate employment also suffered, but the biggest decline was in areas where machines were brought in to perform the numerous tasks that had previously been carried out by armies of worker ants. Firms that used to employ dozens of girl school-leavers to fill cardboard boxes with their products, and dozens of boy school-leavers to load them on to lorries, replaced the girls with automated packing machines and the boys with a couple of fork-lift truck operators. For those without skill the prospects became bleak.

Another aspect of higher unemployment was that it appeared to be endemic rather than cyclical. Recessions earlier in the century had been followed by boom times. The order books emptied, but then filled up again, as world or national trading prospects improved. Workers dropped to a 3-day week, or lost their jobs, only to regain exactly the same posts later, often with bonus and overtime payments, as the economy moved into a higher gear. When the cycle stopped it was partly because, in the new automated economy, no employer was going to get rid of two fork-lift trucks and two drivers in order to employ 20 people with large biceps.

There also appeared to be a paradox, in that, even in areas of high unemployment, there were vacancies. Unfortunately the vacancies did not always match the talents and skills of the jobless. It was of little consolation to the dispossessed coal miner or steel worker to see a job advert asking for someone to repair video recorders or computers. This meant that retraining became an important matter. Those who either had no skills to sell, or whose skills had become outmoded, needed to acquire fresh knowledge and skills in order to become employable again. There were sad examples of people who did retrain and then managed to obtain another post, only to experience redundancy in their newly found career. For some people serial retraining was in itself to become a significant feature of their lives.

Nor was retraining confined to the unskilled or those who worked in traditional craft trades in manufacturing industry. Secretaries had to acquire the skills of word processing and other forms of information technology. Surgeons had to learn transplant surgery, the use of immuno-suppressive drugs, laser technology. Head teachers were pressed to turn into financial, marketing and resource-management experts. Trade-union officials, previously regarded as wage negotiators, found themselves increasingly involved in advising their workmates about compensation for accidents, or the workings of an industrial tribunal for those who had lost their jobs. As well as the oral competence that had always been necessary to fulfil their duties, they needed higher reading competence in order to cope with the literature on health and safety at work, or employment protection. Some forms of knowledge and skill seemed to have a very short life before becoming obsolete. Few employees escaped the remorseless march of novelty and innovation.

In addition to these kinds of change there were new working patterns for the many still in work. The development of new technology meant that certain kinds of activity could be done at least as well, and sometimes at lower cost, in the home, or in a remote satellite location at a distance from the main centre of production. Publishing, journalism, garment manufacture, design work, telephone sales, consultancy and advice, many of these could, given the right equipment, be carried out as easily in someone's attic, as in a noisy and crowded office or factory. There was also a shift to much more part-time employment, and women in particular often took jobs that required part of the day, rather than the whole of it. Many people moved to part-time employment as an element of an early retirement package. Hutton (1995) estimated the number of British part-time workers in the late twentieth century to be in excess of five million, of whom 80 per cent were women.

At its best this meant that some degree of control over time was returned to the individual. Instead of having to leave home in the early morning to ensure arrival at the start of the working day, only to have to battle against traffic once more in the evening, those with flexible working arrangements could sometimes suit themselves. The shift to part-time working and phased retirement liberated parts of the day and week for recreation or leisure, or for more time with family and friends.

At its worst, however, part-timers and home workers were exploited, paid low wages, denied the same safety and employment protection rights as full-timers. Since some 70 per cent of all new part-time jobs were for 16 hours a week or less (Hutton, 1995), this meant that the holders of them had no right to appeal against unfair dismissal or to redundancy payments. Much time had to be expended, by those who would have preferred a full-time post, trying to stitch together several part-time jobs. There were numerous examples of families dropping to a lower standard of living, because the male adult had lost his full-time job and the female adult had only been able to obtain a part-time post.

As traditional jobs disappeared in the manufacturing sector, so new ones began to appear in service and support industries. Alongside smaller numbers of the big employers of labour, there sprang up numerous small- and medium-sized businesses. Unfortunately a number of these did not succeed, and bankruptcies increased as several small concerns ceased training. This added to the problems of those seeking work, as small firms closed and some failed entrepreneurs returned to being employees of someone else.

The messages about employment prospects in the twenty-first century from this rapidly changing environment are mixed, but some possibilities emerge that need to be considered by those working in education. They include the following, all of which might continue into the future along similar trend lines:

- The numbers of unskilled and semi-skilled jobs appear to be in considerable decline, therefore a *much higher level of knowledge and skill* will be necessary from those wishing to enter, or remain in employment.
- More jobs in service and support, leisure and recreation, rather than in factories, means that *social skills*, the ability to get on with others, may become more valued.

- People may have to retrain significantly several times in their adult lives, perhaps every five to seven years, so *flexibility* and *willingness to continue learning* are important.
- As more people take part-time jobs, or work from their own home or in a place remote from their employer's headquarters, qualities such as *independence, resourcefulness* and *adaptability* may be highly valued.
- People will need to know their rights and entitlements, as well as their obligations to others, if they are to play a full part in society and not be exploited by the unscrupulous.

Home and family life

It is not yet entirely clear whether a reduction in the time spent at work will in practice lead to more time being available for home and family life. This is partly because of a paradox. Although the number of unemployed has increased since the 1950s and 1960s, those who have full-time jobs often worked longer hours than they did in earlier times. Some people have too little to do, while others have too much.

The increase in working hours is explained by a number of factors. It is partly because of what Handy (1994) called the '$\frac{1}{2} \times 2 \times 3$' formula, from a company's point of view, productivity and profit could be increased if half the previous workforce were paid twice their salary to obtain three times as much output. Another explanation is the increased commuting time, as employees travel greater distances to seek work, without wanting to move house as well. A further reason is the tendency, during a recession, for people to take on additional evening or weekend jobs, or to pursue income-generating 'hobbies', like vegetable growing, collecting (buying and selling artefacts), decorating or car repair.

Uncertainties in the workplace can lead to insecurity in home and family life. Part-time workers, as well as those likely to lose or have to change their job, are less able to secure the sort of mortgage that will purchase a good-quality home. Those working long hours may have less time and energy left over for family and social life. Some factors appear to have combined to reduce the time spent on physical activity. The degree of strenuous exercise necessary to reduce the incidence of heart disease is thought to be three periods of 20 minutes per week in which the heart rate rises to more than 140 beats a minute. Relatively few adults reach this level, as do few children. The availability of considerable opportunities for spectator entertainment, such as watching multi-channel television or attending sports events, may prevent many adults from being more physically active.

Even in home and family life greater knowledge and skill appear to be necessary than in former times. Families may run into considerable debt if they are unable to manage their own finances. In desperation some may fall victim to 'loan sharks' and others who prey on the ill-educated, paying vast amounts of interest on small loans which leave them in thrall for years. The predators in society exploit those whose rudimentary levels of numeracy, literacy or oral competence mean they are unable to calculate percentages, read legalistic agreements, or argue with articulate and persuasive usurers. In our complex bureaucratic society those unable to compose a letter, attend and speak at a public meeting, or combine with others to lobby decision-makers, may find their child is unable to obtain the school place of their choice, or that a six-lane highway is to be driven through their back garden.

Recreation and leisure require knowledge and skill. It is quite true that those with little knowledge and skill can still enjoy their leisure, but their choices may be fewer. Under the 'minimal competency testing' programme run in several parts of the

United States, one paper on 'life skills' was partly based on the guide to Yosemite National Park. The minimal competency tests were an attempt to identify those who might quit their schooling with only rudimentary competence, ill-equipped to face life in the twenty-first century. Responses to this chapter on 'life skills' showed that some pupils were unable to read the guide well enough to understand what there was to be enjoyed.

Inability to read proficiently, understand map signs and conventions, calculate the time and cost of taking a family on an outing, do not prevent people from visiting Yosemite, but the less competent do have more limited opportunities than the competent, in recreation as in work. When the working week is reduced, some people fill it up again with 'leisure' activities that are not unlike what would be 'work' for others, hence the popularity of 'do-it-yourself' stores, as well as pastimes such as gardening, decorating, cookery and car maintenance. Many of these hobbies and pastimes require the same or similar knowledge and skills as would be needed for someone in paid employment, like understanding how electricity works, the ability to use a power tool, read instructions, or work harmoniously alongside others.

This last point is also an important one more generally, and relates to a number of messages for education for the future which emerge from looking at home and family life.

- In the twenty-first century, especially if the working week were to be reduced, or more people worked in their own house or flat, extra time would be available away from the workplace to be spent in the home or community; some would use these additional hours for work-like activities, others for leisure.
- There may be a trend towards less personal physical activity and more spectating, with possible consequences for individual health.
- In home and family life, the ability to get on well with one's fellows is an important quality, if breakdowns in relationships are to be avoided.
- Consideration of both working and social life in the future suggests that the needs for both domains may be similar, if not identical.
- Wide rather than rudimentary knowledge, a broad range of skills, the ability to relate well to others, personal qualities and traits, such as imagination, determination, flexibility, a willingness to learn throughout one's life are important prerequisites for all aspects of adult life.

The Four Ages

One of the most notable trends during the twentieth century was the changes in what are sometimes called the Four Ages. The First Age is the age of full-time education and training, the Second Age the period of working life, the Third Age the years of healthy retirement, and the Fourth Age represents the time of infirmity. Since the nineteenth century, when large numbers of people never even reached the later ages, the transformation has been dramatic. Children in school today, for example, may find that it is their Third, rather than their Second Age, which occupies the greatest number of years.

Furthermore, the Four Ages may become increasingly fluid and ill-defined, flowing and fusing into each other, as many people stay in education, while others enter work, or some retire early, while their contemporaries work on. In the twenty-first century one 45-year-old may wish to take up a new job and therefore commence a significant programme of retraining, possibly on a full-time basis, effectively returning to the state of dependency of the First Age. Another 45-year-old may be contemplating starting a lengthy period of part-time employment between the ages of 45 and 70, dropping first to a 4-day week, then to half-time, and eventually to one day a week, blurring the boundaries between the Second and Third Ages. A third 45-year-old may be finishing work entirely, entering the Third Age two or three decades ahead of other contemporaries. Yet another person of the same age may never have held a job at all, and therefore effectively have skipped from the First to the Third Age, without a Second Age in between.

Each of the Four Ages has transformed dramatically since the last century. The First Age has tended to become longer in recent times. For much of the nineteenth century children were not required to attend school at all, and in many cases commenced employment at the age of 10 or earlier. The twentieth century saw a significant lengthening of the First Age as, in the United Kingdom, the school-leaving age was fixed at 14 following the First World War, at 15 after the Second World War, and at 16 in the 1970s. Subsequently, the advent of higher unemployment produced a variety of youth training schemes, first of a few months and later lasting one and eventually two years. This effectively lengthened the First Age from less than a decade in the nineteenth century, to more like 18 years for the majority by the late twentieth century.

During this period there was another important change. Evidence from earlier in the nineteenth century shows that girls, on average, entered the age of menarche – that is, started their periods – at about the age of 17. By the late twentieth century the average age of menarche was down to about $12\frac{1}{2}$. Boys tend to start their adolescent growth spurt a year or eighteen months later than girls, so this meant that most children were reaching physical adulthood at around the age of 14 rather than at about 18.

Whereas in the nineteenth century children left the First Age physically immature and were still children for the first few years of their Second Age, when they commenced work, by the late twentieth century it was the exact opposite. They reached physical maturity, only to find that they had to spend at least four, and possibly up to ten more years in the First Age, unable to start in a job. Given that boys in particular often go through a period of aggression on reaching physical maturity, secondary schools found that they had to contain and educate potentially aggressive young adults who, 100 years previously, would have been well into their Second Age and off school premises. What had been an external social problem in Victorian times had now become an internal school problem. The school-leaving age cannot rise indefinitely, nor can the onset of adolescence fall continually, but a longer First Age looks likely to be a feature of the twenty-first century, when it might become 20 years or more for the majority.

As the First Age has lengthened, so the Second Age has shortened, and at both ends. Children entered work later, and adults began to leave it earlier. For many in Victorian times the Second Age was virtually their whole life, as killer diseases like typhoid and tuberculosis, the ravages of war, and deaths in childbirth robbed millions of their Third and Fourth Age. The age of retirement came down to 70 and later to 65, but then it moved lower still during the late twentieth century, as more and more opted for early or phased retirement, or simply lost their jobs and had to take enforced leave from paid employment. Fifty years and a gold watch gave way to 40 years or less, followed by a part-time post for the more fortunate. It is difficult to say what the Second Age will become in future for those currently in school, as it may be that improved health in later years might lead to its lengthening once more, if people choose and have opportunities to work into their seventies.

Present indications are that for many people it may not last more than thirty-five years.

In stark contrast, the Third Age, the period of healthy retirement that was non-existent for most in the nineteenth century, when a mere 6 or so per cent of the population was over 60, is becoming dramatically longer, as the 60-plus age group swells to a quarter or more of the population. Handy (1994) cites surveys showing that only a third of British adults over the age of 55 are still in paid employment, and in France and Italy the figures are 27 per cent and 11 per cent respectively. Many children currently in school may, therefore, experience 20, 30 or even 40 years in the Third Age. This particular social change has considerable implications for education, since children who are disenchanted with their schooling may be reluctant to take on fresh intellectual challenges in their Third Age.

The evidence suggests that older people are perfectly capable of learning new knowledge and skills. Although they may need a little more time and slightly longer intervals between 'lessons', they can often draw on a wider range of strategies than are available to younger people with more limited experience. Indeed the 'University of the Third Age' is an institution that caters for those who, in retirement, wish to use their knowledge and experience to teach one another. The Open University has thousands of students who go on to graduate in their seventies and eighties. Even during the Fourth Age, the time of infirmity, when the elderly may be confined indoors, most will be perfectly capable of continuing to learn something new, and continued mental activity in old age is often closely associated with better general health.

The story of centenarian Charles Warrell is interesting here. A retired teacher who lived to be 106, he became well known as the author of the *Big Chief I-spy* books and newspaper columns which sold over 40 million copies. At the age of 92 Charles bought an old oak chest. He tried to find out when it had been made, but without success initially, so he went to the library, sent away for furniture books, and eventually, after much assiduous research, managed to track down its origins. A year later, aged 93, he then wrote an article about the chest which was published in a national magazine. When he was 104 he was still telephoning friends to find out about recent developments in schools. It may be exceptional today for someone to develop and pursue with determination a fresh interest in his nineties, and to be still interested in his former profession after reaching the age of 100, but this may be a commonplace in the later twenty-first century for those currently in school. Already, according to 1990 census data, there are more than 36,000 centenarians living in the United States. Hence the importance for the highly significant Third Age, and the not insignificant Fourth Age, of effective groundwork, particularly during the First Age.

The messages for education from these massive changes in the Four Ages are clear:

- The longer First Age, with its more extended period of education, lays down foundations for what could be another seventy years or more of active learning; it is vital, therefore, that this first phase is well conceived and regarded as a positive experience.
- The Second Age, though shorter than in previous generations, is none the less a time when continued learning and the flexibility to adapt are likely to be extremely important, both in work and recreation.
- The Third Age may for many people be the longest of the Four Ages, a time when they may have the time to take on significant new interests, making it even more important to lay firm foundations on which to build during the First and Second Ages.

- Even those who are housebound in the Fourth Age will want to continue to be mentally active and this can be beneficial for a longer and healthier life.
- The boundaries between the Four Ages may well become much more diffuse, and individuals will enter and pass through them at different times, in different ways and at different speeds.

The knowledge explosion

It is several centuries since the 'Universal Man' was thought to be capable of grasping all the knowledge available to the world at the time, and it was dubious then whether anyone could really absorb all of what was known. In the eighteenth century writers like Goethe, who composed poetry, novels, plays, historical and philosophical works, and even a scientific treatise, were admired as complete scholars. Yet even at that time they only knew a fraction of what had been discovered.

Today the quest for universal knowledge would be an impossibility, as millions of books, articles, films, radio and television programmes, as well as ideas expressed in electronic media, are produced every year. Even with access to international data-bases containing millions of research findings in every field, it is inconceivable that anyone will personally know more than the tiniest portion of all knowledge available in their discipline or area of interest. It is both impossible and undesirable to halt the gathering of knowledge; it seems to be an activity which will, if anything, continue to quicken in future.

The consequences for education of this remorseless addition to the store of human knowledge are of several kinds. First of all, though we cannot know everything, we have to know something. Hence the interminable debates and discussions about the *content* of various subject curricula. In a vast field like health education, for example, what should children study at the age of 5, 8, 11 or 14? When can they best learn about dental care, the need for a healthy diet and exercise regime, or the effects on health of smoking, alcohol or drugs? What information, skills, attitudes and forms of behaviour might they need to acquire? When might be too late and when too soon to study a particular topic? These questions will be discussed in a later study, for they lie right at the heart of the first dimension of the cubic curriculum, the subjects being learned.

The second consequence of the knowledge explosion is that if we cannot learn everything in school, and have to settle for a small proportion of what exists, then we have to know how to *find out* for ourselves. The ability to track down vital information, abstract its essence, work out how to apply what we have learned, often without external help, is a key element of independence of mind and action. Most adults have to make numerous decisions on their own during the day, some trivial, like where to shop, others more profound, like what actions to take in their working or home life. This ability to explore, discover and then act, often with tenacity and imagination, is particularly crucial given the points made earlier about the length of adult life and the importance of the Third Age. It is also an important element of the second and third dimensions of the cubic curriculum, the cross-curricular themes and forms of teaching and learning, as people will need to acquire these crucial transferable skills at an early stage if they are to be autonomous in adult life.

The third major consequence of exponential growth in knowledge gathering is that if we can neither know nor find out everything, then we will probably need to *work with others*, in order to amplify and enhance our individual efforts. While it is true that a committee would not have painted the Mona Lisa, or composed

Beethoven's Fifth Symphony, it is also the case that no individual could have sent a manned spacecraft to the moon. The advantage of working in a team is that, if it is successful, its collective effort should exceed the sum of what its individual members might have achieved.

The United States government agency NASA (National Aeronautics and Space Administration) is able to employ some of the world's leading authorities on the calculation of rocket flight paths, the materials out of which spacecraft are made, rocket fuels, diet during space flights, the fabrics of astronauts' clothing, the psychology of being in space, medical aspects of space travel and a host of other topics. If a space mission has an accident and goes astray, it is rescued not by one heroic individual, but by a huge team of experts working in collaboration. In the twenty-first century major social, as well as technological and scientific problems are likely to be resolved by small or large teams.

The ability and willingness to make one's knowledge and skill available to others will be a major contribution to many successes in the future, and this has relevance for all three of the cubic curriculum dimensions. Developing a high level of expertise in a particular field is a prerequisite for being in a position to offer knowledge and skill in the first place, and the specialist field may become more and more narrow as more and more is discovered within its domain.

This is an issue of vital importance to the first dimension of the cubic curriculum. If expertise tends to narrow, then developing interests and understanding beyond the confines of one's specialism is also important, and this is germane to the second dimension, the cross-curricular. Nurturing the ability to collaborate with others is the next vital step, and this notion is central to the third dimension of the cubic curriculum, for the ways in which children learn and are taught may transmit significant messages about how they should conduct themselves in their adult life.

The messages being emitted from analysis of the continuing rapid growth of knowledge, therefore, are manifold, but they include the following:

- Since pupils cannot learn everything, thought must be given to what might best be learned at different stages of their development.
- Not being able to learn everything means that the ability and willingness to find out for oneself is an important prerequisite for lifelong autonomy.
- Major social, technological and scientific problems will be solved by smaller or larger teams of players, each member being highly knowledgeable and skilled, but also able and willing to make expertise available to others.
- As knowledge expands, fields of expertise may continue to narrow, and this has significance for each of the dimensions of the cubic curriculum.

New technology and learning

The development of any new form of technological aid in education is usually over-hyped by its developer. It will, the public is told, revolutionise teaching, allow all those who have failed by other means to reach genius level in a short time, and probably replace the need for having a teacher at all. The truth, alas, is often more mundane, as the latest miracle takes its place in history alongside all the other pieces of machinery that added to the learning opportunities available, but did not solve every problem.

The development of radio as a teaching tool in the 1920s, and the advent of slide projectors, film, television, tape recorders, teaching machines, all these were hailed as the ultimate solution to numerous problems: ending the shortages of qualified teachers, catering for the difficulties faced by children in remote areas, providing work exactly matched to the needs of the individual learner. Each did indeed perform a useful service and, sometimes in modified form, has found a niche in the repertoire of many teachers. Subsequent technological developments may pass through a similar cycle: over-hype by developers – adoption by enthusiasts – spread to a wider constituency of practitioners – assumption of a modest, or more significant place in the mainstream of teaching aids.

What characterised the forms of new technology developed in the last few years of the twentieth century was (1) huge memory, (2) the opportunities for interaction and (3) the use of several kinds of media – print, graphics, voice, music, animation, still and moving photographic pictures – alone or in combination. The micro-computer, CD-ROMs, adapted games machines, 'virtual reality' and the 'information superhighway' as it was sometimes called, all these offered more opportunities for interaction, for the learner to interrogate and probe, than did earlier, more passive forms of educational technology.

While studying a topic like 'the structure of the atom', people might watch a video, or listen to a tape, but when using interactive technology, they are able to ask questions, albeit often in limited form. Pupils using a video or sound tape about atomic structure have to be fairly passive, as the programme-maker has decided what information shall be transmitted and in what form. The same pupils using a CD-ROM, or other form of interactive technology, could look at a model of an atom, add to it or subtract from it, rotate it, and at the same time learn the consequences of what they have done. For example, the periodic table might be displayed on their screen and they might be told that what started off as a hydrogen atom has now become an atom of helium. It is as if they have their own set of coloured components and an individual teacher to tell them after every move what they have just done. Moreover, the memory power of the machine allows every key stroke to be recorded and profiles of progress to be assembled at the press of a button.

The history of some new technology is that it began its life principally as a leisure or games machine which then became used for educational purposes. The exceptionally powerful memories of certain games machines were especially suited to education, offering many opportunities to combine film, still picture, animation, sound and written text. 'Virtual reality', originally regarded in the popular mind as a games helmet, worn over the head by those who wanted to pretend they were up in space zapping invading aliens, soon became used to train surgeons or to explore environments that children might not be able to visit normally, like the rain forests or the moon.

The information superhighway, the fibre-optic communications network of finely spun, hair-like slivers of glass that could carry film, sound, music, graphics and text to every home and institution in the country, was also heralded as another great educational breakthrough that might one day remove the need for teachers. However, the presence, in multi-media form, of immense amounts of information, is no guarantee at all that learning will take place.

Information is not the same as knowledge. Information is 'out there'; knowledge is what is inside the brain, digested and understood. Indeed, children in particular, unable to chart a path through the dense mass, might despair if left to explore unaided. What is essential in this burgeoning expanse of information is people who can structure and track what is going on, in other words *annotators* who can help to unravel and explain what might otherwise be an enormous bewildering maze. Possible annotators include not only teachers, but also writers, publishers and broadcasters. In the future, as in the present, numerous sources of information will be available to pupils other than what their teachers choose to bring before them, and it will be important for them to develop the skill and resourcefulness not only to act on advice and help, but also to pursue their own pathways through what they are studying.

The messages about the use of current and as yet unimagined new technology include the following:

- People will be even more liberated than they are at present from dependence on a teacher as the single source of knowledge.
- Learning in remote locations, with or without others, will become easier, so the ability to learn autonomously will be important.
- The huge memory and the highly interactive nature of many of the newer forms of educational technology permit many different forms of teaching and learning.
- Information is not the same as knowledge, and so annotators, like teachers, writers and broadcasters, are important agents for ensuring that complex and diverse information is properly understood.

A curriculum for the future

Many of the speculations and guesses in this chapter are interlinked. If both work and home life really do become more complex and require more knowledge and skill, then citizens of the twenty-first century will require far more competence than the simple notion of 'basics' put forward by some politicians. The modest ability to 'read, write and add up', proposed by British Prime Minister John Major at his party conference in 1994, is far too rudimentary for the demands of the future. The disappearance of millions of unskilled jobs, and the pressures and stresses faced by many quite ordinary people in their daily lives, combine to increase substantially the entry fee into our society for young adults in the twenty-first century.

If many of the children now in school have to retrain several times during their working lives, and if most of them can look forward to many years of good health in their Third Age, then their appetite for learning must stretch way beyond the years of compulsory schooling. In order to flourish over what could be a very long lifetime, they will need a firm foundation of knowledge, skills, attitudes and forms of behaviour, alongside positive personal characteristics, such as determination, flexibility and imagination. They will also require the social intelligence and will to pool their strengths with those of their fellows, as well as the independence of mind to act autonomously. This strong combination of personal and intellectual qualities is particularly important, given the massive explosion of knowledge, which continues to gather pace. The many forms of new interactive technology available require vision and tenacity from those wishing to benefit from them, if they are to be used to their full potential.

In the circumstances, a single dimension view of the curriculum would be inadequate. It is simply not enough to conceive of a school or college curriculum as nothing more than a flat, unidimensional list of subjects or topics. In order to develop the range of talents needed for a prosperous future, children must learn over a wide range and in a variety of ways. That is why a multi-dimensional view of the curriculum makes good sense. The most significant and exciting challenge facing the whole of society, not just those who work professionally in education, is how to devise and provide a coherent programme for young people that recognises the many forces at work, anticipating successfully some of the needs of an uncertain future, synthesising the distilled wisdom of hundreds of generations, while at the same time sponsoring both autonomy and teamwork.

If this can be done successfully, then teachers can actually help their pupils to shape the future, rather than find themselves the unwitting and impotent victims of it. The role of driver can be much more attractive than that of passenger.

References

Handy, C. (1994). *The Empty Raincoat: Making Sense of the Future*. London: Hutchinson.
Hutton, W. (1995). *The State We're In*. London: Jonathan Cape.

_____

CHAPTER 11

IMPROVING LITERACY

Originally published as 'The National Survey', in *Improving Literacy in the Primary School*, by Wragg E. C., Wragg C. M., Haynes G. S. and Chamberlin R. P., Routledge, 1998, pp. 35–65

Shortly after we completed the Primary Improvement Project, a compulsory literacy hour was introduced. This chapter from our 1998 Routledge book *Improving Literacy in the Primary School* reports practices and beliefs about literacy in 1,205 primary schools. It was the last major study of teachers' own spontaneous practices before the government itself began to determine the structure of literacy classes.

The first part of our analysis of what schools do to improve literacy, was based on a national survey of a large sample of primary schools. The 'zoom' strategy we had adopted, whereby we planned to move from the large-scale national and regional perspective to the individual classroom teacher and pupil level, required a broader picture of practice to be assembled. We decided to send out a wide-ranging questionnaire to head teachers of primary schools to help construct this overall description of what schools said they were doing.

Drawing up a 'national' picture is not easy. With millions of children in thousands of different primary schools, there is bound to be considerable diversity. An 'average' or percentage, therefore, will conceal numerous individual differences. The use of questionnaires is common in these circumstances, as it allows researchers to gain a great deal of information from a large audience of respondents, many of whom are at a distance from the investigators and might not be easy to reach. It also permits respondents to reflect on their responses in private, without feeling the face-to-face pressure that an interview might engender. The disadvantages of mailed questionnaires are also well known. Amongst these are: that there may be a low response rate, 10 per cent being often the case, that the respondents might not be 'typical', that the investigator cannot verify easily what is written, and that the information is often in a form that is easily quantified and may, therefore, oversimplify the issues. Oppenheim (1992) has written a full account of the use and construction of questionnaires.

Nonetheless, we decided that it was worth trying to collect some national data, as these would form a useful background to the more fine-grained and longer-term scrutiny of local authorities and of individual teachers and pupils in other parts of this research.

The national questionnaire

A questionnaire was constructed which elicited reports from head teachers, or their designated respondent. Most replied themselves, though about 20 per cent delegated the task to their deputy head or language co-ordinator. The questionnaire was constructed from the interviews we had conducted with head teachers, in which elements thought to be important in the teaching of reading had been identified. It contained sections on 'organisation and language policy', 'the teaching of reading', 'assessment', 'LEA involvement' and 'constraints'. Many of the questions involved responding to a set of predetermined categories, but some invited free-hand responses. Analysis and statistical calculations were carried out using Statistical Product and Service Solutions (SPSS) for the quantitative data, and a consensus 'rate until agreement' principle for the qualitative data. This latter involved discussion between members of the research team on what meaning was being inferred from written free-hand statements until a particular interpretation was agreed.

Copies were sent to a random sample of 1 in 8 primary schools, producing 1,395 returns, a 53 per cent response rate, with some replies from every local authority in England. This is a good response for a mailed questionnaire. Nearly 59 per cent of the replies were from combined infant and junior schools, 26 per cent from infant and first schools, and 15 per cent from junior or middle schools. About half the schools were urban, while a quarter each said they were rural or 'mixed'.

We wrote to all Birmingham schools (excluding those previously included in head teacher interviews), since the city was a particular focus in the Project, and 151 responses were obtained. There were 1,244 responses from schools in the other English LEAs; hence the grand total of 1,395 schools. In order not to distort the 'national' picture by overweighting it with Birmingham schools, we assembled a special 'national sample' consisting of the 1,244 responses from English LEAs and twenty Birmingham schools chosen at random from the 151 respondents, so as to include roughly the same number of Birmingham schools pro rata as the rest of the sample. Thus the 'national sample' in this chapter consists of 1,264 schools.

One of the sections of the questionnaire asked schools about what their local authorities were doing in the field of literacy. The whole of the next chapter will be devoted to reporting what LEAs do, so at this stage we shall only report that, in their answers to the national questionnaire, 46 per cent of head teachers replied that they were aware of a local authority initiative concerned with the teaching of reading. In Birmingham the figure was a much larger 94 per cent.

Organisation and the role of the language co-ordinator

Most primary schools said they gave a high priority to literacy, as one would expect and that the language co-ordinator, a feature in virtually all schools, was a key person responsible for organising and supporting the efforts of others Some fascinating detail emerged from the survey about the role of language co-ordinator, including the following:

- Over 90 per cent of schools said that they had a language co-ordinator who took special responsibility for literacy.
- In 10 per cent of the schools it was the head or deputy who held the post.
- Only 3 per cent of schools said that nobody had special responsibility for language.
- About 40 per cent of post-holders are not paid any special allowance for their responsibilities.
- About 30 per cent of post-holders do not have any non-contact time to do the job.

• Amongst those that do give non-contact time to their language co-ordinator there is considerable variation – nearly 20 per cent of respondents have one period of time per week or better, and a quarter are given time for specific tasks, rather than on a regular basis.

These overall averages and totals conceal a wide variety of practice and the position is noticeably different in Birmingham, where 94 per cent or language co-ordinators are paid a special allowance and 86 per cent are given non-contact time.

The role of the language co-ordinator is generally regarded as crucial. Almost all schools said that a major responsibility was to ensure teachers knew the school's language policy, though not all the individual teachers we interviewed seemed fully knowledgeable about it. Beyond this assignment, the ten most common functions of the language co-ordinator, in descending order of importance, can be seen in Table 11.1. The need to monitor language teaching and give regular advice to other members of staff, mentioned by 84 per cent and 81 per cent of all schools, were regarded as being right at the top of schools' priorities.

Almost all schools said that they already had a written language policy (87 per cent) or were currently preparing one (12 per cent). Most of these policies were said to have involved a wide range of people. About 90 per cent of schools stated it was compiled mainly by the language co-ordinator and the class teachers, working with the head. Some three-quarters mentioned the special needs co-ordinator. The predominant influence on this policy was from the head and teaching staff, but about half cited the governors, and a quarter said they had involved the LEA and classroom assistants, though how profound or perfunctory this involvement was we are not able to say from the questionnaire responses.

Many of the written comments of heads were about the heavy workload of what were called variously 'English', literacy' and 'language' co-ordinators. They also mentioned the constraints under which they laboured. The head who suggested that English co-ordinators are unnecessary because all teachers are supposed to know about teaching English was overwhelmingly outnumbered by those who felt the job was too big for one person, especially for someone with a full-time teaching commitment. This theme was often accompanied by references

Table 11.1 Ten major responsibilities of language co-ordinators (1,264 schools)

Responsibility	Percentage of schools mentioning
1 Monitoring and evaluating teaching	84
2 Providing advice to staff on a regular basis	81
3 Advising on reading materials	68
4 Leading in-service training	66
5 Ordering resources	60
6 Organising the school library	42
7 Running meetings for parents	35
8 Devising language resources	35
9 Working with teachers in their classroom	35
10 Assessing children's reading problems	19

to funding, as these two comments reveal:

> Our deputy head is the language co-ordinator. She has several other areas of responsibility too. I am concerned about her work load and the pressure she is under. The severe financial constraints do not allow her non-contact time to fulfil her role as she would wish.

> Fulfilment of her role and of my post-holder's potential is hampered by our constant, perpetual, never-ending lack of money to support initiatives by freeing staff during the teaching day.

Heads of small schools frequently pointed out their particular problems:

> In a small school we all take on subject co-ordinator roles in two or three subjects.

> Often in a small school like ours the co-ordinator is not the specialist.

> In a small rural school, three full-time staff means that the head teacher is responsible for, or leads, all curriculum co-ordination.

Heads took the responsibility for literacy for other reasons also: because they did not have teaching commitments, because of its importance, and sometimes because of the difficulty of finding someone else to do the job to the head's satisfaction.

One way some schools attempt to overcome the problems of excessive workload is by sharing the responsibility, though for others this was not always feasible:

> The work of the language co-ordinator is of major importance since it impinges on the whole curriculum and is central to it. The role ... is really too great for one person to carry out and in an ideal world with a greater level of staffing available, a language team should be created to include the special needs co-ordinator and the school library organiser – each with language responsibility points.

Although most evaluative comments on the role of language co-ordinator were positive, some were negative. Problems mentioned were related to staff ability, knowledge and attitude:

> As a newly appointed head teacher I found that the subject co-ordinators had not got any job descriptions nor any real concept of the role of a co-ordinator.

> The language co-ordinator has reluctantly taken responsibility.

The teaching of reading

When it comes to books and teaching methods, most schools believe in the 'pick and mix' approach. Despite frequent press reports that teachers have abandoned the use of reading schemes, or indeed systematic and structured approaches in general, our survey showed a different picture. We asked for information about several aspects of teaching and learning that were of interest for different reasons, either because they figured in debate and speculation, or because they were commonly believed to be important elements of practice. The answers in the questionnaire provided both quantitative and qualitative data.

The areas addressed included the following:

1   the use of reading schemes;
2   the colour coding of books according to difficulty;

3   the use of approaches like 'phonics', 'real books' and 'look and say';
4   current initiatives in the school;
5   the teaching of children with reading difficulties;
6   the involvement of parents and others;
7   what respondents thought teachers could do to raise standards of reading.

Summaries of lesson observations by HMI (DES 1991, 1992) concluded that very few teachers used one exclusive approach to the teaching of reading, only 5 per cent of teachers being said to use exclusively the 'real books' approach, and only 3 per cent to employ a solely phonics-based strategy. Since the National Curriculum in English requires children to acquire 'phonic knowledge', to develop a sight vocabulary of words they can recognise instantly, as well as to read a range of fiction and non-fiction, it would be very difficult to justify using one sole strategy to the exclusion of others. A wide variety of findings emerged from this section, including the ones described here.

Reading schemes, books and teaching methods

•   Some 99 per cent of schools say they make use of reading schemes.
•   About 53 per cent of schools (infant stage, 54 per cent; junior stage, 52 per cent) say they use several schemes.
•   About a third of schools confine themselves to either one or two reading schemes for their classes (infant stage, 38 per cent; junior stage, 20 per cent).
•   One principal use of reading schemes for a minority of schools is as a 'safety net' for certain children (infant stage, 12 per cent; junior stage, 23 per cent).
•   Differences in practice within the school appear to be discouraged, as only 2 per cent of schools replied 'yes' to the item 'some teachers use reading schemes, others do not' (infant stage, 1 per cent; junior stage, 3 per cent).
•   Approximately half the schools (infant stage, 48 per cent; junior stage, 47 per cent) employ colour coding to identify the difficulty of books.
•   Some 97 per cent of schools say that they prefer 'a mixture of teaching methods'.
•   More schools mention the importance of 'phonics' (31 per cent) than 'look and say' (10 per cent) or 'real books' (8 per cent) when describing their 'main' or 'most favoured' approach.

This last finding may be either a true reflection of practice, or an 'expected' response, given the criticisms in the press about the supposed lack of structured methods in the teaching of reading. Phonics was used mainly in the infant school and where necessary for less able children in the junior phase. Many schools talked about 'structure' and 'progression' and timetabled phonics sessions seemed common:

> Written phonics policy with clear progression used throughout school – some commercial, some home-made resources. Part of, but not whole, approach to teaching reading.

> Children are assessed on arrival at school (junior school) on their phonic knowledge. From this assessment children follow a programme until they have *learned* sounds, blends etc. Children are withdrawn in groups of 4–6 for this.

> [Phonics] plays an integral part in our school. Each day at 10.20 the whole school work in sound workshops for 20 minutes. Each teacher runs a different workshop (progressive) and the children work at their own pace throughout the workshops.

In the popular press 'look and say' is often reported as a 1960s' progressive approach to reading which displaced phonics. The meaning that most lay people would naturally attach to the phrase is that children would look at a word and pronounce it, much as adults do. Developing a sight vocabulary of instantly recognisable words is not exactly a recent phenomenon. In an attempt to clarify possible confusions, Goodacre (1975) distinguished between 'look and say', where the teacher would often give children a word, speak it, and then ask them to repeat it, and the 'whole-word' approach, where flashcards might be put onto pictures, or taken home to be learned. 'Look and say' responses to our questionnaire revealed diversity in interpretation and practice. Many respondents tended to use the approach for building up early sight vocabulary. Some linked it to their reading schemes, while others were rethinking, feeling that words on their own might mean little:

> Children start with this [look and say] via the Ginn 360 scheme, taking flashcards home.

> We have just stopped the practice of sending home reading scheme words (decontextualised) in boxes. Now they still go home, but can make sentences.

'Real books' is also a confusing term for both lay and professional people. On the one hand it describes a methodology or, more precisely, a set of approaches to the teaching of reading, some of which involve using a range of fiction and non-fiction, graded according to their difficulty, instead of working through a reading scheme. The common meaning of the term in everyday speech, however, would embrace the actual books that one might find in any library or bookshop. Responses to this section of the questionnaire revealed a range of interpretations of the term. Some indicated that real books were used mainly by more 'competent' readers, while other schools talked of their use at the very earliest stage of reading. Others indicated that they had colour coded the real books and had integrated them into their core reading scheme:

> Whilst we recognise the need for good quality books and the need for a range of reading materials we do use the structure of a scheme. 'Real Books' are graded and colour coded to fit in alongside the scheme to give the child the breadth and balance they need.

Several respondents were vociferously opposed to the use of real books as the sole approach to the teaching of reading. Indeed, some said they had tried the approach earlier but discontinued it:

> [We are] totally opposed to this approach. Yet we believe in real books being used to support children whose reading is taking off.

> The children are surrounded by books throughout the school and are encouraged to 'use' them . . . but osmosis is out!

> We originally just used real books but found that some children learned very little from this and required some structure. We still have a lot of real books and prefer them for our more fluent readers, although we don't prevent the others taking them.

> [Real books] had been in place prior to my arrival. Not working – very poor results.

The phrase 'mixture of methods' has become a common feature of reports by HMI, such as those in 1991 and 1992 (DES 1991, 1992). It represents not just an eclectic but a pragmatic view of teaching. Few schools in our sample seemed to be committed to an exclusive approach, the overwhelming majority (97 per cent) preferring flexibility. The main reasons for this, seemed to be (1) the belief that children need as many tools as possible when learning to read, and (2) that there is a need to match strategies to a child's individual need. Some expressed their regret at extreme polarisation in discussions on the teaching of reading:

> Reading has to be a joint approach. No one method or scheme would enable a child to learn to read adequately.

> Word recognition and phonics run side by side. A fluent reader needs to have both in order to succeed and be able to tackle unknown texts.

> Our emphasis is on reading for *meaning*. Children are encouraged to use any clues available from context, pictures, sensible prediction etc. I emphasise diagnosis of individual need and provision of an approach to meet that need.

> It is unhelpful for different approaches to be presented as if it is an either/or issue. This has not served the reading debate well. Planned teaching of skills plus quality literature and skilful assessment are needed.

Current initiatives – involving parents

When it came to the question of whether schools are taking any special measures to improve reading, some 58 per cent of schools reported that they currently had a particular initiative. These are included in Table 11.2 in descending order of frequency.

Perhaps we should have included a definition of the term 'initiative', but we did not. As a result schools described a varied set of practices, many of which may have been new to the school concerned, but would have been regarded as commonplace in other schools. It is difficult to state, in reply to a questionnaire, that no initiatives are being taken, of course, as this might imply that the school is complacent or inert, so perhaps some heads felt the need to report something under this heading. The result is a substantial collection of comments on what

Table 11.2 Current reading initiatives reported (1,264 schools)

	Percentage of schools
Involving parents	20
Evaluating current policies	9
'Reading recovery' (or similar)	8
Paired reading	8
Getting additional adult support	7
Reviewing/updating reading schemes	7
Changing/reviewing assessment procedures	7
Group reading	7
Working on 'higher-order' reading skills	5
'Enrichment' activities	5
Improving library	5
Staff development	5

respondents report as a novelty in their own school, and the majority of these are about either specific new projects, or changes in policy or practice.

Initiatives involving parents were top of many schools' priority list and they fell into four major groups, with considerable overlap. These were:

1　Parents helping in school.
2　Parents helping at home.
3　Informing/educating parents about policy/child development/how best to help.
4　Improving parents' own literacy and language skills.

In the first group, the fact that parents were parents was almost incidental. They were in school as helpers:

> Early Years Reading Workshop. Teachers, ancillaries and parents work with small groups to develop a true understanding of the world of reading: discussion, comprehension, information gathering etc.

> Each day begins with a 30 minute reading session to which parents are invited.

Similarly in the second group, parents were convenient and important helpers whose ability to help at home was often taken for granted. Reading diaries were mentioned, but in some cases the taking of books home became more structured, with a period of intensive activity and/or systematic instruction:

> Shared reading project – 8 weeks annually. Intensive programme of home reading, checked daily in school.

> Reading project with Year 3 children. Parents are asked to hear their children read every day for 8 weeks. Many now think their children no longer need to be heard and are amazed at their improvement over the 8 weeks.

> Six weeks' training for parents of new children in the term before main school entrance (*after* training for all staff – teaching and non-teaching) covering the relationship between learning to speak and learning to read, approaches, choices, parents' views, making literacy games, sharing a book.

Some initiatives were targeted on particular groups of parents. Occasionally the focus was on fathers, but by far the most common targets were parents of nursery, Reception or pre-school children. There were also programmes aimed at those families where English was not the first language, or where levels of literacy might be low:

> We are currently talking to fathers about ways in which they can encourage and motivate their sons in literacy skills.

> We are spending much time with parents of nursery pupils encouraging them to become involved with 'early learning' activities. To help this we have produced a booklet and a pupil pack for children to work with at home. As this is a 'family stress' area, children don't have pencils, crayons etc at home.

> (We run courses in) English for Bengali speaking mothers.

> A family literacy project running, whereby a group of parents work with their own child with support of a teacher and adult tutor. The parents then work with the Adult Education Tutor to improve their own literacy skills and the children get time with the teacher in a small group situation.

Table 11.3 Percentages of adults other than class teacher involved in teaching reading (1,264 schools)

Adults involved	Frequently	Occasionally	Not at all
Classroom assistants	80	15	5
Parents/grandparents	69	23	8
Special needs teachers	61	25	14
Other volunteer adults	49	32	19
Head teacher	22	53	25
Student teachers	18	52	30

Table 11.4 Home/school links reported (1,264 schools)

Home/school link	Percentage of schools
Reading record sent home	92
Spellings sent home to learn	90
Key words sent home to learn	82
Meeting on reading for new parents (pre-school)	79
School bookshop	65
Booklet or video on reading for parents	50
Meetings on reading for current parents	50

Schools were asked whether various groups of adults, not just parents, were involved in the teaching of reading 'frequently', 'occasionally', or 'not at all'. Classroom assistants were the biggest category of adults, who were not the class's regular teacher, followed by parents and grandparents. The results shown in Table 11.3 do not signify that every class in a school had a classroom assistant, parental help, or whatever. Schools were simply asked if people other than class teachers helped at all.

Sending books home for children to read with parents is virtually universal, only two schools in the whole sample saying that they did not do it. Most schools say they send home spellings and key words, but the frequency varies considerably. About half the schools say they use a booklet or video for parents on how to teach reading, while two-thirds have a school bookshop. Half run meetings for parents. Table 11.4 shows some of the relevant figures.

Current initiatives – evaluating policy and changing organisation

Evaluation of policy and changes in organisation were the main or partial focus of a number of the initiatives that heads described. Some schools worked alone, developing staff expertise on projects such as:

> Reviewing phonic progression.
> Research into gender differences in reading achievement.
> Looking at book provision...how we plan and assess reading.
> Totally revising the English policy and scheme looking for ways to make it more efficient.

A two year School Effectiveness Project with the local university to focus on extending the more able readers by extending our current classroom practice and provision and knowledge of children's books.

Banding in ability groups.

Emphasis on literacy in Reception by 'sidelining' other areas of the national curriculum.

Reading Roundabout – where children are taught reading in a systematic way...organised in groups and there are 5 reading related activities every day. Each group visits one activity each day throughout the week on a rota basis.

Giving certificates for reading effort and achievement.

Rewards (given) for building a list of books read at home.

The introduction of new teaching methods was mentioned frequently by respondents. Many schools were trying some version of group reading, sometimes in mixed, sometimes in similar, ability groups. The substance of this activity varied from groups of children hearing each other read to groups with additional classroom support being taught 'strategies for reading, meaningful guesswork, phonic and picture cues...punctuation, writer's style and much more'. Paired reading, and its transatlantic relation 'Buddy reading', were also being introduced, sometimes between children and parents, but more frequently between children of different ages. Specific remediation programmes like 'Reading Recovery' and its offspring 'Our Way of Learning' (OWL), Kickstart and Freshstart, also received favourable comment:

> We now have individual support monitored by our ('Reading Recovery' trained) special needs co-ordinator, delivered by classroom assistants trained by her. We are thrilled by the results and received £2,500 from the LEA's initiative for raising reading standards. We are now finding that having dealt with the worst difficulties, those children have overtaken the group above. Most significantly, the trained classroom assistants are taking the skills learned with individuals into group and class situations.

> We currently have a Reading Recovery teacher based in the school – the most valuable resource any school should have.

> We are in our second year of using Reading Recovery.... This has influenced many teachers' understanding of the teaching and learning of reading.

> This programme (Project Read) started as a response to failing readers in American inner cities. It is highly structured and involves reading and writing skills. It is fun. It is small group oriented and can be used with 6–8 children at a time. It is therefore economical compared to Reading Recovery.

The events and procedures covered by the 5 per cent of schools that reported 'enrichment activities' included poetry workshops, authors in residence or attendance, dramatic performances, book weeks, a library club, competitions, bookshops, the 'production of school-published reading books based on our environment, using a grant from Birmingham's Year of Reading', and 'A story telling event with local schools. We aim to publish one story from each school in book form.'

References

DES (1991). *The Teaching and Learning of Reading in Primary Schools. 1990: A Report by HMI.* London: DES.

——(1992). *The Teaching and Learning of Reading in Primary Schools. 1991: A Report by HMI.* London: DES.

Goodacre, E. J. (1975). *Methods: Including an Annotated Reading List and Glossary of Terms.* Reading, MA: Centre for the Teaching of Reading, University of Reading.

Oppenheim, A. N. (1992). *Questionnaire Design, Interviewing and Attitude Measurement.* London: Pinter.

CHAPTER 12

LEARNING TO READ

Originally published as 'Pupil Case Studies', in *Improving Literacy in the Primary School*, by Wragg E. C., Wragg C. M., Haynes G. S. and Chamberlin R. P., Routledge, 1998, pp. 250–7

These case studies, from the same book as in Chapter 11, describe how individual children did, or did not, improve their reading. Some of the findings were astonishing, like the stories of Jack and Eva, two children who represented the extremes of improvement and its obverse in a national sample of several hundred children, yet who were in the same class at school.

[...]

Case studies

Case studies show the individual nature of learning to read. This chapter offers some interesting contrasts.

Charlotte, aged 4, Reception

Not all improvers received informed help at home, as the case of Charlotte shows. When she started Reception class a month before her fifth birthday she obtained one of the lowest scores in the sample on the LARR language test. She had little preparation for school. Her mother had had a poor academic record herself, frequently playing truant when she was a child: 'We never read to her before she started school. I missed a lot of school myself, like, when I was a girl.' Miss Williamson, a very experienced Reception class teacher whose classroom had a rich language environment, had selected her as an improver because she had taken to reading so quickly.

During the year Charlotte became excited at everything to do with language. 'This word says "cow", c–o–w, cow', she would volunteer in a non-stop torrent when observed. 'I can write my name'...'Do you know what this book says?' Her teacher set her and the class several pre-reading exercises and drew their attention to the large amount of print in their classroom and external environment. Charlotte created a number of simple self-made books and Miss Williamson steered her through a wide range of beginner fiction and non-fiction books.

By the end of the year she was the second-best reader in the class and obtained one of the highest scores on the LARR Test. Asked why she thought she had done so well, she herself attributed it to the help she had received from a fellow pupil: 'Because Daniel [the best reader in the class, who sat next to her] gives me all the words.' She smiled with pride at having signed up her own free private tutor.

Her mother, surprised at her progress, could not explain it. She had not particularly been helped at home. In interview she expressed astonishment that Charlotte had been interested in a crossword puzzle when she had seen her father doing one. She apologised all the time for not being able to help Charlotte, as she was not a particularly good reader herself. Indeed, Charlotte was often very persistent in her desire to learn to read and she had to be referred to her father when she met a word she did not recognise, as her mother often had no idea either.

By the end of the school year Charlotte was asking her mother to spell out words she did not know and actually showing her how to split difficult words into two. This was one of the few examples we encountered of a reverse of the norm – child shows parent how to attack a difficult word. Charlotte seemed to be a bright girl with a strong desire to learn to read, who only needed school and a skilful teacher to discover her talent in language and personal relationships. She will quite probably go far.

David, aged 9, Year 5

At the beginning of Year 5 David was adamant in our first interview: 'I absolutely hate reading. It's boring. I just don't like it.' Only his Liverpool Football Club comic was of any interest. This was an unusual response and his face distorted as he uttered the words. Interviewers will normally obtain a positive response to this question, as most children, when asked, will say that they like reading, almost as if this is expected. Some are indifferent and a few admit to disliking it, but David was one of the few to express strongly negative feelings, and almost the only pupil to use the word 'hate'.

Mrs Jackson selected him as an improver because his attitude to reading changed dramatically during the school year, as he went from being hostile to enthusiastic. As was the case with Charlotte, neither his mother nor his father ever read to him, even when he took books home. The school had a very positive attitude to parents and even before children commence school they are visited by one of the two Reception class teachers or by the head herself. During this home visit the teaching of reading is described specifically and each parent is handed a booklet written by the teachers which explains what the school does in the teaching of reading. Despite this preliminary visit and a programme of parents' evenings, David was still unaided by either parent.

When observed in class he was a seasoned procrastinator, able to turn finding a pencil into a five-minute task. Mrs Jackson ran an orderly classroom and the figures obtained from pupil on-task studies were amongst the highest we have ever recorded in classroom observation research. At the beginning of the year, less so at the end, David was often the one pupil not applying himself to his task. Mrs Jackson would often detach herself from a group momentarily to scan the class when pupils were working on their own or in groups. 'David, I'll be over in a minute', was a common public remark when she noticed him distracted from what he was supposed to be doing.

By the following June, however, he was transformed. 'Reading? I really like it', he said in his final interview. The interviewer reminded him of the beginning of the year when he had graphically described his intense dislike of everything other than his football comic. Asked why the change of heart, he was equally unambiguous:

It's Mrs Jackson. She's given me some really good books, adventures and that sort of stuff, and books that made me laugh.

Patrick Burson's *The Funfair of Evil* had been particularly enjoyed. Mrs Jackson's personalised approach increased both the time and effort David spent on reading. She described in interview how she had sought out books on sport, adventure and humour, knowing that these would interest him. Although his reading test score had only improved slightly, by 1 point, from 95 to 96, his attitude and the number and range of books he read had soared. For a boy who was, by the end of the research in July, within a year of starting secondary school, where a hatred of reading would be a severe handicap, this represents a different, though nonetheless very important, kind of 'improvement'. It makes the interesting point that attitude, while not a substitute for competence, can be a useful accompaniment to it. In David's case, given the lack of support at home, improving his attitude to reading would have to be an important precursor to improving his competence at it, though whether he would go on to become a better reader in secondary school was outside the scope of this enquiry.

A big sinker and an improver within the same class

Mr Martin walked into his new Year 3 class of thirty-two children on the first day of the new term with his usual enthusiasm both for teaching generally and for the teaching of literacy in particular. He did not know, nor could he, that within the group were two pupils whose progress would diverge considerably during the year. The class was new to him and new to the school, so he explained to the pupils how their literacy activities would be conducted over the year. His exposition included content and process: the difference between fiction and non-fiction books, when they would visit the school library, that they would have a story time together. Then he seated everyone on the carpet and a long session took place during which he introduced the class to the different books on offer. He later explained why he did this:

> The idea was to choose books all in one place. If you do one table at a time, there's always one group who have to go last (thereby getting less choice)....
> There's the opportunity to introduce lots of books, authors, pictures and fliers. It provides an opportunity for the teacher to show his enthusiasm. It's a non-threatening, gentle way to get into choosing a book. The children then looked through them naturally.

However, despite Mr Martin's enthusiastic approach, marked sense of fairness and willingness to offer opportunities for all, at the end of the school year his class housed a pupil who had made one of the largest gains on a reading test in the entire sample and another who had regressed the most.

Like all the teachers in the sample Mr Martin had been asked to choose pupils who represented high, medium and low ability at reading. He chose Eva as a high-ability girl stating that she was unusual and very unworldly and Jack as a high-ability boy saying that he was very able, but was the youngest in the class, having 'loads of talent', but often working very slowly. It was Eva who made a staggering leap forward in her reading score and Jack who seemed to fall behind during the school year. Both were tested using the Norman France Primary Reading Test twice, with Eva scoring 102 at the beginning of the year and 134 at the end and Jack, by contrast, scoring 125 at the beginning and 100 at the end. Mr Martin's class average standardised score had improved by over 5 points during the year, but the pattern showed an interesting split, with fourteen high risers (gained 8 or more points), but five big sinkers (lost 4 or more points).

Eva's potential was celebrated by Mr Martin right from the start of the new year. On the first day of school Eva brought in a substantial book she had made over the school holidays, full of pages of written work all carefully presented. One child asked if he could see it. The teacher, who had everyone seated on the carpet, said he was going to share it with the whole class. Mr Martin told everyone that he thought it was amazing and he was therefore going to give her a Year 3 certificate which would be presented to her by the head teacher. He went through the different pages with the class drawing attention to the different things she had done and praising her on her work: 'I think it's amazing, I don't think I have ever seen anything like this from someone your age. It shows what an amazing young lady you are. I think it's brilliant.'

Mr Martin commented after the lesson why he had reacted to her work in the way he had:

> It was a celebration of what she'd done and an acknowledgement of her qualities [and also] to provide an inspiration to others. Her sister...didn't get a certificate all the way through the school, so I wanted to celebrate. I hadn't planned it, it just happened. It was prompted by Sean who wanted to read it.

Lesson observation showed that Eva's and Jack's approach to work in class differed significantly. On each occasion when systematic observation of the six target pupils took place, Eva was always observed working assiduously. Jack, by contrast, only appeared to concentrate on his task sporadically. One day, when they were both working on the same written task, Eva wrote ten pages saying that it had not taken her very long because she had had all the ideas in her head. Her spelling was almost perfect, with one exception, and she used speech marks, question marks, apostrophes, abbreviations and exclamations without fault. She was able to read her own story with expression and explain why she had introduced irony into the text. She told the researcher that she always checked words she did not know. This piece of work was later marked by the teacher and given a star.

Jack was also observed working on the same task. He spent some of the time writing, but also sat and chatted with the boy next to him. When he had finished his conversation, instead of returning to work, he stared around the room whilst sucking his thumb. At the end of the lesson Jack has written one page and his story was selected by Mr Martin to read to the class. Although commenting that he had not finished, Mr Martin praised Jack for having made a good start.

On one observation visit, Eva again worked conscientiously throughout, whereas Jack was absent from school. In the last observation of the year, the pattern was similar to previous occasions. Eva worked assiduously on her task without losing concentration, whereas Jack was alternately on- and off-task, once again being observed sucking his thumb whilst staring around the room and fiddling with his pencil. He did, however, seem more on-task than off during this particular lesson and managed to complete about three-quartets of the task, using apostrophes and exclamation marks correctly.

The two pupils themselves seemed well aware of their own progress. In interview, Eva stated: 'I *love* reading. I *love* reading stories because it's exciting. Because I read lots of books and I'm older now, it's easier and you get on quicker.' Although Jack said that he *liked* reading because he too thought that books were exciting, he only thought that his progress had been 'all right'. Unlike Eva, who had no problems explaining any of the punctuation used in her book, Jack could not explain the difference between an apostrophe and a comma and had not mastered yet what speech marks were used for.

Mr Martin was a teacher whose on-task scores indicated that most of the time the pupils were highly involved in the tasks they were working on, with an average over the year of 82. His deviancy levels were, however, slightly higher than one would expect with this level of on-task involvement, averaging out at 5.3, above the average for this group of teachers of 3.5. This meant that 3 pupils might be misbehaving slightly, rather than this group's average of 1 or 2. Midway through the year Mr Martin was asked to reflect on the pupils he had chosen and rate them on scales of 1–6 for their abilities as a reader and behaviour such as social skills, determination and independence. He rated Eva consistently higher, marking her high to very high (points 5–6) on most of the attributes whereas Jack was more consistently placed in the medium to high categories (points 4–5 on the scale).

Eva's home background was one of encouragement. Her mother, in particular, took every opportunity to introduce her to new experiences and encourage her to progress in her school work. Over the summer holidays she had taken her to numerous events and attractions and encouraged her to write accounts of these in the copious book she had brought into class at the beginning of the year. Jack, by contrast, was less fortunate and the teacher had succinctly explained at the beginning of the year that he was 'going through a difficult time', as his home and family life disintegrated.

The difference in the two children's home backgrounds was evident by the comments Mr Martin made about the two children at the end of the year. Of Eva he said:

> She is a voracious learner. She loves stories and words. She's read unbelievably, had loads and loads of book experience. If you look at her reading diary, it's phenomenal. I guess it may be due to less pressure [on her].

Jack had not had the same chances that year:

> He hasn't had an easy year, his parents have separated. He's probably stood still in terms of progress. He lacks confidence, has missed quite a bit of school, and is a bit of a loner.

These two cases illustrate the differences in the personal fortunes of two pupils in the same class receiving, on the surface, a similar education. Eva's mother was exceptionally interested in Eva's development and the pressure she may have inadvertently brought to bear on earlier occasions may have hindered her progress. Once Eva became more successful this pressure seemed to be relaxed and her increasing maturity and ability were able to thrive. The 'book of summer experiences' may have been an important turning point. Jack seemed a troubled boy who probably needed the extra support at home to give him confidence, but may not have received it whilst his parents were trying to resolve their own problems. As he missed class, day-dreamed, sucked his thumb, lost concentration, his reading appeared to regress. Even within the same class pupils' fortunes can diverge and produce quite different outcomes. 'Improvement' is certainly not a uniform process, nor are the conditions and opportunities for it universally bestowed on children.

Different patterns of improvement

In terms of test scores taken at the beginning and end of the school year, all except one of the classes showed a gain. The movement of scores was not uniform, however. The case of Jack and Eva's hugely divergent achievement in Mr Martin's class is the extreme case in the present study of differing progress under ostensibly the same regime, but there was no case of all the pupils in the class improving their standardised score at the same or even at a similar rate.

Indeed, although this was a generally improving, rather than regressing, set of classes, there was still an interesting diversity. In order to describe how some of these salient differences might look, in more readily comprehensible form, the sample of pupils was first split into three equally sized groups: the lowest third were labelled 'sinkers' (their scores had fallen by 4 points or more), the highest third were called 'risers' (their test scores had risen by 8 points or more) and the middle third were called 'similar' (they showed a movement of between −3 and +7 points, compared with first test score). Each class was then inspected to see what type of 'improvement' could be discerned and three different overall patterns of improvement emerged:

1   *Improvement pattern A – little change*   Between a half and three-quarters of pupils stayed within a few points of their original standardised score, but a number of pupils improved by 8 points or more, while very few declined.
2   *Improvement pattern B – big riser*   Over 40 per cent of pupils showed significantly increased scores of 8 points or more, with a similar number staying about the same and very few declining.
3   *Improvement pattern C – even spread*   Over a third of scores rose by 8 points or more, roughly a quarter declined, and 40 per cent remained about the same.

'Improvement' is a portmanteau word which can in practice enclose many different forms inside itself, both in terms of the fluidity of movement within a whole class or group and the changes that occur in the accomplishments and fortunes of individual children. The analysis of whole-class patterns and the various pupil case studies in this chapter show some of the many kinds of improvement that can be witnessed in primary schools.

Accounting for the various causes and origins of changes for the better is no easy matter. Some seem to be explained by immense personal effort from the pupils themselves, often against the odds when children are unsupported at home, do not speak English, are teased for their bookishness, or acquire a reputation for poor behaviour. Others seem attributable to particular efforts by teachers or parents, reflecting some of the recurring themes in this research, such as matching books to interests, praise and encouragement, giving confidence, offering a path to autonomy as well as a degree of direction and structure. Most propitiously these conditions can act in powerful combination, though it is not uncommon for children's own personal qualities, like persistence and determination, sociability, concentration and independent-mindedness, to exert a forceful influence on their school achievement.

PART 4

EDUCATIONAL POLICY AND ITS IMPLEMENTATION

During the period covered by these writings the fashions in research changed several times. One notable feature was the extent to which, in many countries, there became a greater emphasis on research into policy itself and policy-related practice. The journal I have edited for many years, *Research Papers in Education*, specialises in publishing longer articles on policy and practice. It has become noticeable how more and more articles submitted describe investigations into practice deriving from the educational policies of different countries' governments, rather than from individual schools or teachers. Furthermore, research funding is often readily available for policy-related research, but not so easily obtained for 'pure' research.

The fashion of the 1960s and 1970s was for investigations of the relationships between personality and learning, or the influences of home background on school achievement. The 1990s and the twenty-first century saw a shift towards studies of the impact of policy A on population B. Although I have increasingly looked at policy and practice, my major focus has always remained inside the classroom and school. Indeed, I find many aspects of policy, and the chicanery that some politicians bring to its implementation and evaluation, extremely irksome. Hence the satirical strand of what I do, shown later in this book, in Part 5.

There are four chapters in this part, and I have always felt particularly proud of the first two. Chapter 13 was written in 1980. It described ten steps which any government which was so minded could take to ensure state control over the knowledge being taught. Only the first step was being taken at the time, but now all ten steps are in place. Chapter 14 was my attempt to predict the downside to the *1988 Education Act*, a centralising Bill which brought teaching and assessment under the direct control of the government. Virtually all the events and outcomes I predicted eventually happened.

Chapters 15 and 16 are from large-scale studies of teaching competence and incompetence. Chapter 15 reports a large-scale study of performance-related pay. Chapter 16 describes what was probably the largest study of allegedly incompetent teachers ever undertaken. For obvious reasons it is not easy to study incompetence. Indeed, such allegations usually have a searing effect on both accuser and accused, as the research showed.

This was a study in the round, as we were able to analyse several hundred cases, giving the perceptions and experiences of heads, teachers, pupils, parents and governors, as well as of union and local authority officers. It was the most difficult project I have ever carried out, but it needed to be done, as heads and teachers were eager to talk about their experiences, though a small number found it too harrowing to relive the horrors they had gone through. The comment by one head 'I went to hell and back' illustrated perfectly, albeit tragically, the anguish felt by almost all the people involved.

CHAPTER 13

STATE-APPROVED KNOWLEDGE?

Ten steps down the slippery slope

Originally published as 'State-approved Knowledge? Ten Steps Down the Slippery Slope', in M. J. Golby (ed.), *The Core Curriculum, Perspectives 2*, University of Exeter, 1980, pp. 11–20

A chapter from a collection of Exeter University 'Perspectives' series entiled *The Core Curriculum* written in 1980, which predicted ten steps any government could take (like introducing a compulsory curriculum, prescribing tests, teaching strategies, compiling league tables, sacking non-compliant teachers) if it wanted to control teaching. At that time (1980) only the first step existed, and this article was meant to be a dire warning. A senior civil servant of the time described it at a conference as 'unnecessarily alarmist', since no government, he assured everyone, would ever go beyond step three. Now all ten steps, and more, are in place. I still find it chilling to re-read it.

A frisson of anxiety was experienced by many when the DES paper *A Framework for the School Curriculum* tried to put some percentage figures into the debate about a core curriculum. I suspect the phrase that rippled the pool in the secret garden came in the first paragraph, when it said, 'there is an accumulation of evidence, reinforced by the replies to DES circular 14/77 . . . and by the two surveys of primary and secondary education carried out by H.M. Inspectors . . .'

The educational community, used to blandness on-the-one-hand and to no-offence-please pronouncements in HMI discussion papers on-the-other-hand, was not sure how to respond to threats enforced by research-type muscle developed from large-scale surveys and the Assessment of Performance Unit.

The question of central control over the curriculum is a contentious one. On a continuum ranging from, at the one extreme, the central control exercised in many Eastern bloc countries or western countries like France, to, at the other extreme, the anarchy of a laissez-faire adhocracy where every teacher does his own thing, we tend to place ourselves towards the liberal end.

What series of steps would be necessary for tighter state control to be brought about? I describe the following ten. They are not meant to be a watertight conceptualisation, as there are many different ways of looking at the matter. All the steps are not only possible, but, with twentieth-century magic such as computers, test item banks or behavioural objectives, also technically simple to implement. Indeed many of the procedures described are already in operation here or elsewhere, and are not in themselves sinister. What makes the later steps more ominous is that they represent an accumulation of central controls which, if unscrupulously applied, would result in only state-approved knowledge, skills, values and attitudes being peddled.

Step 1: centrally prescribed 'broad aims'

Examples can be found in statements from documents such as *Curriculum 11–16* or the Green Paper which say that schools should 'help pupils to use language and number effectively' or 'help pupils develop lively, enquiring minds'. They are so imprecise, permissive and generally laudable that only misanthropists or psychopaths would demur. Dry cleaned of threat, this is the language of many government reports and HMI discussion papers, which is as innocuous as saying that children may get wet when it rains, or that Tuesday tends to follow Monday.

Step 2: centrally prescribed 'time allocations'

This occurs in a rudimentary form in *A Framework for the School Curriculum*, with its suggestion that a minimum of 10 per cent of time be spent on maths, English, science and a foreign language. A much tighter control would be to prescribe more precise amounts of time for non-core subjects. It is still a distance away from those countries or regions where the whole timetable is more or less centrally determined, but it steers into state-approved line those schools who do not already follow what is fairly common practice. Shrewd Heads will be able to use such policies to advantage. After all, if someone insists on every child spending x per cent of his time on a certain subject, then teachers must be provided to fulfil the commitment.

Step 3: an 'agreed syllabus'

Such a syllabus is usually expressed in broad terms, and the emphasis is on 'agreed' rather than 'imposed', which would make it a later step. We are already used to the notion of an agreed syllabus in subjects like R.E., and indeed it can sometimes protect rather than inhibit teachers. For example, because an agreed syllabus in R.E. may include Marxism, the individual teacher will not fall foul of angry parents or pressure groups who accuse him of subversion. Being able to say that (a) everyone teaches it and (b) the bishop has blessed it, tends to pacify critics. On the other hand, choice is narrowed for most teachers as they are unlikely to be personally involved in negotiations, since union, professional or sectional representatives usually deliberate on and determine such matters.

Step 4: more 'precise objectives'

This is a distinct tightening of the noose, particularly if objectives are expressed in behavioural terms. There is a move towards this position in Appendix II of *A View of the Curriculum*. Largely non-behavioural objectives are listed for mathematics teaching at various age levels, for example, for 5–8 year olds: 'The understanding of whole numbers and their relationships with one another'. Some subject sections of *Curriculum 11–16* describe objectives in more behavioural terms.

Contrast this, however, with practice in the San Jose School district in California, where the Board of Education specifies mathematical competencies in distinctly behavioural terms, accompanied by what it calls 'performance indicators'. An example from a list of older high school children is given here:

Competency 1

The student can add, subtract, multiply, divide and find the percentage of a number using whole numbers, fractions and decimals.

Performance indicators

Of the performance indicators, there are thirteen for competency 1

1.1 The student can add up to 4 whole numbers, each of which has 4 or fewer digits
1.7 The student can multiply 2 decimal numbers, each of which has 3 or fewer digits
1.9 The student can add any 2 fractions (or mixed numbers less than 10) with denominators of 2, 3 or 4 and express the sum as a mixed number in simplest terms.

Many American teachers welcome the precision of these statements and feel they offer sensible goals; others lament the amount of time given over to the publicly approved objectives at the expense of other worthwhile activities.

Step 5: centrally prescribed objectives and 'teaching materials'

One major development in British education during the 1960s and 1970s has been the proliferation of teaching materials. Teachers can choose from over 100 published schemes for teaching, reading, and a visit to the National Textbook Library at the London University Institute of Education reveals what great variety is available for most age levels and subject areas. Furthermore, individual teachers or consortia have produced colossal numbers of booklets, worksheets or project files, so that Banda sniffing has probably ousted stress as the major health hazard in the profession. In some countries with central control, only one textbook is approved. In West Germany 3 or 4 years ago teachers in a number of the Länder were sent letters reminding them that they risked losing their job if they used books not on the official list. German teachers often complain that the panels which approve new additions to the permitted list contain the authors of successful brand leaders who are hardly likely to threaten their royalties by permitting too many newcomers. I find a system of centrally approved materials suffocating and it would certainly reduce the spontaneity of the more inventive teachers.

Step 6: centrally prescribed objectives, teaching materials and 'strategies'

Some *persuasion* about teaching strategies at local levels might be no bad thing. For example, most systematic studies of teaching report that the vast majority of teachers' questions are closed and require nothing more than data recall – 'right' answers, in many cases one word replies (Is Belgium in the Common Market? What is the colour of this liquid?). Questions requiring higher order thinking are more rare (e.g., evaluative thinking: 'Did the United Nations do a good job in Cyprus', or speculative thinking: 'What would have happened if the United Nations headquarters had been built in Moscow?'). It is one thing to work with teachers *at school level* to persuade them to look critically at the strategies they use, as we have in our own Teacher Education Project at Nottingham and Exeter, and quite another to pronounce on approved strategies from some central mausoleum. In some parts of West Germany, a few years ago, it was decreed that foreign languages should be taught by direct method, that is, that the foreign language should be used exclusively in the classroom. Many teachers were unable to sustain this form of teaching.

Although teaching strategies are not usually *prescribed* in Britain, in controversial areas they are sometimes *proscribed*. Two incidents, one where a teacher wrote swear words on the blackboard, and the other, where forms of birth control were the answers to crossword puzzle clues, received widespread publicity in the national press. Both teachers were teaching legitimate content matter from an approved syllabus, so attacks were deflected on to the strategies employed.

Step 7: centrally prescribed objectives, materials, strategies, tested with 'test items drawn from the APU test bank'

Once assessment is introduced into the story the pulse quickens. Given the existence of the Assessment of Performance Unit and the nature of the controversial Rasch model, assembling a bank of state-approved test items filed in a vault with a difficulty level tag attached is technically a simple process. Local authorities can then easily 'borrow' items for their own tests. Although this looks like local control, it is not. Few local authorities are currently equipped to undertake the considerable work involved on their own, and the notion of a central bank becomes an attractive alternative to expensive local outfits. It is unlikely that nationally banked test items can ever have a local flavour, nor are they likely to be controversial or adventurous. At its best the system offers information about progress which is of considerable professional interest. The national testing of educational progress in the United States of America has allowed the co-ordinators in Denver to produce profiles of what children of various ages know and can do. Amongst a mass of information about 17 year olds we learn that: most (over two-thirds) know the names of particles that make up the atom, which jobs usually involve union membership, and can infer social implications from newspaper cartoons; some (one-third to two-thirds) can multiply two negative integers, know of ways to fight poverty, and can use apparatus to demonstrate the daily and yearly cycles of the earth; and few (less than one-third) understand probability, can convert Fahrenheit to Centigrade from the formula, play a musical instrument, or read poems or plays outside school.

At its most sinister, however, there would be little freedom for teachers who would find themselves trapped into spending much of their time preparing children for orthodox, safe, short-back-and-sides, unchallenging-of-the-status-quo test items. At periods when national and local government were of the same political party, collusion about objectives and procedures would hand control even more firmly to the centre.

Step 8: centrally prescribed objectives, materials, strategies, test items and 'remedial programmes'

The development of computer-assisted instruction and the spread of microprocessors make this step relatively straightforward technically. It is very easy with machine-scored, multiple-choice items to programme the computer to direct the pupil to the appropriate next step. For example, pupil A follows the unit of instruction, takes the ten-item test at the end of it and scores full marks. The machine directs him to the next unit. Pupil B scores 8 out of 10, is given supplementary information about his 2 errors and directed to the next unit. Pupil C, however, only scores 1 out of 10 so he is routed to a remedial programme which takes him through the same material at a slower pace. To remove even the option for a teacher to use his wit with children who fail to learn, and prescribe state-determined remediation would constitute a most severe blow to the professional challenge which for many teachers is one of the most rewarding parts of their job.

Step 9: centrally prescribed objectives, materials, strategies, test items, remedial programmes and 'publication of results by school'

This could be a most powerful form of central control. In the quest for information about a school's effectiveness, quantified league-table data has a great appeal, hence the sporadic demand for schools to be rank-ordered on their GCE and CSE results. Again the widespread availability of computers facilitates printout by schools. Inevitably most teachers' time and energy would be spent on those aspects of the curriculum which were to be systematically tested and publicly rank-ordered, and HMI themselves commented on the hypnotic effect of public examinations on secondary school teaching in the secondary school survey. At its worst we would see a dreary return to the chanted 'right-answers' of Victorian times, such as can be seen in the splendidly confident and jingoist tomes on history and geography produced by the Rev. Dr. Brewer (about 1870):

Question: Who was Henry VIII?
Answer: Son of Henry VII.
Question: What was his character?
Answer: As a young man he was bluff, generous, right royal and very handsome.
Question: What is the climate of England?
Answer: Moist, but healthy.
Question: What is the character of the English people?
Answer: Brave, intelligent and very persevering.

In the United States the demand for accountability via published test scores gave rise to Performance Contracting whereby outside agencies guaranteed to improve reading or number skills and were to be paid according to their test results. The system fell largely into disrepute when many of the charlatans and fly-by-nights who set up in business were shown to be merely teaching children the test answers.

Step 10: 'dismissal of teachers' who fail to deliver

The final step, short of incarceration or liquidation, in any system of state control, is to fire those who fail to implement policies either through incompetence or unco-operativeness. It is extremely difficult to secure agreement on what constitutes effective teaching, and a number of reviews of the research literature have pointed out how frail are our criteria and procedures for measuring competence. If published test scores were available, however, it would not be difficult, in the absence of other hard-looking information, to argue that those teachers whose pupils, after allowing for differences in initial ability, fail to reach a prescribed standard, must be incompetent. At a time of falling rolls, when the teaching force is being reduced, and redundancies and early retirements are not unlikely, seeking out those who should be shown the door becomes an embarrassing priority.

An unscrupulous central authority might use the opportunity to weed out the ideologically opposed alongside the incompetent. It is not unknown for teachers to be dismissed for failing to teach a syllabus. In recent times wide publicity was given to the dismissal of a teacher who was said to have taught a literal interpretation of Genesis instead of the R.E.-agreed syllabus version.

The debate about control of the curriculum is confused and sometimes even bitter. Like any parent I was dismayed when my daughter did dinosaurs for the third time at her primary school and tried unsuccessfully to persuade myself it was a spiral curriculum. I strongly endorse the notion of freedom for individual teachers, but I can see the problem of having thousands of home-made courses each called 'Humanities', hundreds of different forms of CSE mode 3 ostensibly in the same subject, and over fifty different 'A' level maths syllabuses.

The alternative to such diversity, however is not heavy-handed central control, either through the DES or an over-dominant LEA, whose central palace may seem to the teachers and pupils of Alderman Harry Ramsbottom County Primary School to be as remote as London. Fine tuning of the system can be achieved through the existing partnership between the DES, LEA, school governors and teachers, which can easily be improved, certainly at local level when some of the Taylor Committee proposals are implemented.

I find nothing objectionable in the first two steps described earlier. Indeed an American friend, a very liberal Superintendent of Schools, welcomed *A Framework for the Curriculum* as introducing minimal sanity into what he sees as a healthily anarchic system, and was astonished that the NUT had gone into catatonic trance about it. Central *guidelines* at the third and even the fourth step on certain aspects of the curriculum, such as appear in *Curriculum 11–16*, can be equally valuable, but central *prescription* at these or later steps would represent a distinct change from our present system where much of importance is decided at school level under local surveillance. It would be a change that I personally would find highly undesirable.

CHAPTER 14

EDUCATION IN THE MARKET PLACE

Originally published as a pamphlet by the National Union of Teachers, 1988

This treatise was written for the National Union of Teachers while the 1988 Education Act was progressing through Parliament. It was meant to be another dire warning about what might happen in a free market. The outcome, sadly, was as predicted. Schools became factories, children were regarded as 'outputs', like cans of beans, and teachers turned into operatives.

The market philosophy

The Government's 1988 Education Act will undoubtedly be a radical reform of the education of all our young people from infant school to higher education. The preliminary papers and written words of the Bill itself, as well as the words spoken by Kenneth Baker, the Prime Minister and those who have presented it to Parliament and the people, propose far-reaching and potentially damaging changes in the present education system.

These drastic proposals are based on a set of assumptions which are closer in spirit to trading in goods and making profits than nurturing the many talents of Britain's children. The principal thrust is the proposition that what works for sellers of pots and pans must also be appropriate for, and therefore imposed on, those charged with one of society's most important assignments – educating the next generation.

This chapter looks at the ideology which underpins the Bill, in particular the principle of the free market in education, as well as the associated notions of competition, privatisation and efficiency. It also considers the possible intended and unintended consequences of each of the major set of changes being proposed.

Market forces

The buying and selling of goods may take place under many different conditions. At the one extreme there is the perfect monopoly, when a single seller can dictate the price of goods, provided people are able to pay it. At the other extreme lies the perfectly competitive market, where prices find their own level as a result of competition from several rival sellers. Most markets in real life lie somewhere in between these extremes.

There is no doubt that a certain level of competition can help the customer in the purchase of some kinds of commodity. If one retailer offers a washing machine at £300, another sells the identical model with the same manufacturer's guarantee at £275, and a third shop only asks £250, we should be tempted to buy at the lowest price. One hazard, of course, is that the third shop may have pitched its prices too low, subsequently declare itself bankrupt, and thereby deprive us of our proper after-sales service, but there is still, nevertheless, something to be gained from such competition and the customer can weigh up any risks involved.

There is equally no doubt that too powerful a monopoly may lead to indolence, poor standards of reliability and sloppy service. The conscientious monopolist will make sure none of these happens, but the ruthless monopolist will exploit the situation in the absence of any challenge from other providers of goods or services.

The Government believes that these same basic economic principles can be applied to the education service. It sees local authorities as holding a monopoly of provision, argues that more competition will increase choice for consumers (children and their parents), improve standards and lead to a more efficient use of resources. The competition it seeks to increase will, it envisages, come from the private and independent sector and from the Government itself. Hence the proposals in the 1988 Education Bill to establish new kinds of school like the City Technology Colleges and the opted-out Grant Maintained Schools.

It is one thing to defend free-market forces in the selling of six-inch nails but quite another to advocate it for education. Even amongst commodities there can be considerable variation in what is being bought and sold. Units of a certain model of a manufacturer's washing machine will be identical and it make no difference in whatever shop one purchases it, but there is no such singularity about something like 'wool' where the quality, colour and texture can vary enormously from shop to shop. Even less uniformity applies to the notion of 'child', when we have nine million young people, ranging in age from 2 or 3 up to 25 or older, being educated in 30,000 different nursery, primary, secondary schools, colleges, polytechnics and universities.

Hence the unease which many felt at the language associated with recent and current educational legislation. Words which fit easily into the transactions of commerce sound mechanical and insensitive when applied to education. Instead of children being 'taught', a curriculum is 'delivered', fine for the morning papers, milk or next week's groceries, but somewhat alien for the nurturing of human talent. Local authorities 'purchase' in-service for teachers in the most 'cost-effective' way. No one is opposed to the skilful use of scarce resources and the careful disbursing of money, but the language of these matters has become that of accountants and traders.

The language of the market sees education in term of 'products', measurable outputs during or at the end of the child manufacturing process. Hence the emphasis on testing in the Education Bill, with the education service being judged by its 'performance' on largely quantitative measures, in this case frequent tests of short-term memory recall.

Indeed, it was illustrative of the same point, that, in interviews after the draft of the 1988 Bill was published, when asked about a possible rough passage in the House of Lords, Kenneth Baker referred to his skill at soft talking the Lords on previous matters which had been contentious, in particular the privatisation of British Telecom. The Prime Minister has likened aspects of the Bill to the sale of council houses. There is no shortage of analogies with the buying and selling of inert objects when Government ministers talk about their education proposals.

Competition

At the heart of the Government's attempt to push education into the free market lies the notion of competition. The argument for competition appears on the surface seductive, not least because the argument against competition sounds at first untenable, an endorsement of sloth and smugness. What is critical here, however, is the nature and consequences of competition.

In the world of commerce few tears are shed if a small business goes bankrupt. The owners or shareholders have put their capital at risk. They knew what they were doing, the argument goes, they should have invested in something else or ensured that their business was more efficient, and the employees will simply have to find jobs elsewhere. Bankruptcy is the inevitable consequence of dog-eat-dog competition, it is said, and the inefficient or unlucky must perish so that the efficient can flourish.

This flinty-hearted view of life only has partial relevance to education. The consequences of, say, a village school closing are not merely disappointment for a few shareholders, who will in future place their funds more judiciously, nor for a number of jobless employees who must join the dole queue, retrain or obtain a post elsewhere. The outcome of a small rural school closing would be children as young as 5 having to walk miles or be bussed to a distant school, as well as the interruption at a critical stage of their education and anxiety for them and their parents. The analogy with the world of commerce would only hold up if someone's inefficiency were to blame, and then only partially so.

A further factor is the actual nature of competition, for it is not a single entity. There is the friendly competition such as exists in most amateur sport, where winners and losers shake hands and drink or eat together afterwards, grateful for the exercise and enjoyment. This idyllic version is not at all like the cut-throat competition of some professional sports or business which, at its worst, can result in sharp practice by those eager for success and extinction for the losers.

Equally there are competitions which are clean and where all participants have a fair chance, and others where the event is rigged, with especially favourable conditions for some competitors and the odds unfairly stacked against others. There are serious dangers in the Government's many increased powers and the escalation of its direct control which will result from the 1988 Education Act if the Bill goes through in its present form. One is that schools and therefore pupils will be rank-ordered and labelled as first, second or third division. Another danger is that the competition between local authority maintained schools and the new Government sponsored schools will be unfairly loaded. It will be akin to asking two athletes to compete in a race, one being given a fast sports car, the other having his legs tied together.

Privatisation

Implicit in a free market in education with increased competition is the provision of better opportunities for private enterprise to flourish. The privatisation of education has increased in recent years so there is nothing new about this move to enlarge and favour private provision. The Assisted Places Scheme introduced following the 1980 Education Act, whereby the Government paid the fees of thousands of pupils who wanted to go to independent schools, put millions of pounds of public money directly into the private sector.

At a more local level the severe shortages of books and equipment experienced by schools in recent years have led to parents being asked to contribute more and more to the running costs of the school. Her Majesty's Inspectors, in their annual reports on expenditure in schools, have reported that in half the primary schools they visited it is parents who are providing one-third of the school's disposable income.

Reports from the Education Publishers' Council show that, despite these increased contributions, private day and boarding schools still spend between twice and three times as much on books per pupil as Government maintained primary schools.

Professor Richard Pring, in a number of his surveys of and writings on privatisation, has pointed out that some schools now urge parents to covenant money on a regular basis, so much a part of normality has this become, with one Avon school, for example, raising £15,000 per year this way. There are different consequences when the funds are injected from industry. Whereas parents can afford to be altruistic in their financial support, industrial sponsorship tends to seek a *quid pro quo*. The *quid* from business is said to be in the millions by those responsible for the City Technology College Scheme. It is the *pro quo* that is the worry. Privatisation has already driven a thicker and deeper wedge between the well-heeled first division schools and the down-town third division schools.

Ideology and the Bill

There are several major proposals in the 1988 Education Bill. Kenneth Baker in his address to Parliament during the Second Reading of the Bill categorised them under three headings – standards, freedom and choice. To effect these aspirations radical reforms are envisaged in several fields.

The national curriculum and tests

There is a tension felt in all the major political parties about local control. Each party, in its 1987 Election manifesto, hankered after a degree of central control whilst endorsing the tradition of localism. The Government, however, made no secret of its wish to take to itself much greater powers in this respect.

Oddly enough there had been the makings of a consensus despite the considerable opposition to the Government's Bill from within the teaching profession, on the question of general central guidelines. There were differences of opinion over detail of the size and nature of any centrally recommended common core, but not especially great hostility about the basic idea.

What has aroused dismay is, first of all, that the initial proposals were extremely close in concept to the 1904 Regulations. Many teachers felt that what was needed was a forward look to the twenty-first century, not a nostalgic backward glance at the nineteenth. But of even greater concern was that it was not the needs of children and young adults in the future which would determine what was taught, but that regular testing would represent the source of influence on the school curriculum.

This notion is central to several aspects of the Government's ideology described earlier. Industrial and commercial efficiency is commonly estimated in terms that can easily be quantified: the amount of profit, the number of complaints, the failure rate during quality control checks. All these, it should be said, are perfectly acceptable ways of measuring industrial performance, if properly and sensibly undertaken. Indeed some of these precepts also have a limited application in education.

The essential difference when evaluating human endeavour, however, is the qualitative dimension. Music teachers as well as parents would probably be more interested in their children showing a lifelong interest in music, listening to different kinds of music alone or with their friends and family, playing an instrument, singing, going to concerts, rather than merely being able to answer snappy questions about the value of a crotchet. In other words it is not just the *quantity* but the *quality* of their musical experience which counts. Most pencil and paper tests as envisaged by the Government for children at 7, 11, 14 and 16, would tend to test short-term recall rather than lifelong enjoyment or competence. It is often the most easily measured aspects of learning which are tested, and care for others, team-work, imagination, persistence, thoughtfulness, aesthetic aspects or longer term development tend to slip the net.

The real political motivation underpinning the curriculum and testing proposals has emerged little by little, more in asides than in the fine sounding words of written papers and public speeches. In the debate on the Second Reading of the Bill Norman Tebbit said, 'I counsel him (Mr Baker) also to be absolutely firm on testing...Of course, resistance to testing comes not from pupils and parents but from teachers. It is a fear of quality control.' Earlier, Kenneth Baker had listed three reasons for the testing proposals, the third of these being 'to indicate through the results of assessment the achievement of schools and local authorities generally'.

Both these statements reveal a complete misunderstanding of the nature of testing generally and of teachers' anxieties in particular. The ideological assumption beneath these two speeches is straight from the economics of the market place. All manufacturers (schools) have equal opportunities to make quality goods (educate children), the argument goes, therefore if some produce more goods and make higher profits (obtain higher test scores) this is a proper measure of their efficiency.

If this were really the case in education, then those dedicated teachers who devote their lives to teaching children with some kind of mental handicap would have to be deemed perpetual failures, resistant to testing, according to Government ministers, because they have something to hide. Under this assumption doctors and nurses devoted to helping the terminally ill would appear equally shifty if they were hostile to 'fatalities' being the sole measure of their professional success or failure. If Liverpool Football Club were to beat the Little Piddlington Cubs XI by eight goals to nil, it would be a triumph for the 10 year olds rather than for the professional footballers. Teachers resist crude league tables of schools or class-rooms because they ignore the many different starting levels, not through fear of being rumbled.

Another piece of political ideology was revealed when it was announced that independent schools would not have to implement the national curriculum, and later that clever pupils in independent schools would be allowed to take the national tests a year early. This betrays one of the numerous logical flaws in the Government's political thinking. There is supposed to be healthy competition between the private and public sectors, yet the one can offer any curriculum it chooses in order to make itself attractive, the other must provide only what is laid down by the Government. Furthermore, the Government gives the impression that really clever children only go to private schools. It is another example of the rigged race between the runner given a Government sports car and the rival whose legs are tied together by the same Government.

It also reveals the same three-tier view of humanity implicit in much Government dogma. Rhodes Boyson said in a radio interview that children who performed poorly on national tests would have to make good in the summer vacation. This is a punitive view of children which sees those who do less well as 'slackers'. In a competitive ethic those in the third division are passengers. Indeed the Government's consultative papers on the Bill made only a single sentence reference to children with special educational needs.

It was as if, in the competitive climate endemic in the market view of education, they were an embarrassment. Whereas throughout much of this century teachers have sought to give dignity to children not endowed with as much natural talent as many of their fellows, the principle of survival of the fittest, central to the Government's view of curriculum and testing, renders them a shadow, is likely to restore the image of 'cripple' so firmly shaken off since the last century, makes them the hidden unmentionable relative.

This reveals a further flaw in the free-market ideology. Consumers of commercially produced goods and services may well be reassured to find that machines, wool, cars or wine have been publicly labelled with some indication of quality. Parents and children themselves are not going to be happy with public tags around their neck. Although the Government claims individual results of tests will not be published, there is no way, given massive press coverage of national tests, that gradings will be concealed. Relatives will be anxious to know scores, neighbours will enquire, children will discover from each other. It will be the worst kept secret in Britain.

Government supporters, like Oliver Letwin, former adviser to both Lord Joseph and the Prime Minister, argue that, if children are failures, they should know this as early as possible. Oliver Letwin dismissed the labelling argument, in a *Panorama* interview, as 'absolute rot'. If a wine is labelled third class, the actual label exerts no influence on the wine itself, whatever effect it may have on the producer. When 7-year-old children have a 'third class' label put around their neck, it becomes a self-fulfilling prophecy, and only the most determined will shake it off. It is yet another confusion in Government thinking between inert objects and human beings, and between those successful and robust people who may thrive on competition, and those lacking confidence who may be buried by it. Hundreds of thousands of talented adults once failed the eleven plus. Many carry to this day an unnecessary sense of intellectual inadequacy. The free-market plans in curriculum and testing will restore and extend the stigma of premature failure.

Opting out and the semi-private sector

Following the spirit of its free-market view of education the Government seeks to extend competition by establishing its own schools. These are of two kinds, the City Technology Colleges funded partly by the Government and partly by industry, and those schools which choose to opt out of local authority control, the Grant Maintained Schools, which would receive a grant directly from the Government. Such is the importance of this second type of school that forty-two clauses have been put into the Bill, representing one of the most complex pieces of educational legislation in recent times.

It is here that the market philosophy is at its most flawed. In theory the provision of two more kinds of school will spur on other schools to improve what they do, though there is no evidence that the mere existence of Eton or Manchester Grammar School has in itself achieved this in the past. The real motivation, however, was revealed in the pre-election and post-election disagreements between the Prime Minister and Kenneth Baker. At a press conference before the election she saw greater use of selection by ability, a return to the grammar school system, he did not and had to convene his own press conferences to dismiss this and any suggestion that fees would be charged. After the election in an interview with the *Independent* she clearly wanted most schools to opt out. He said few would, but then limited the damage of their disagreement by saying he was talking about the shorter term, she about the longer perspective.

On the surface this appears to be a straight advocacy of more choice and higher standards for all through competition. The reality is, in fact, much more sinister.

First of all this is a prime example of a rigged market. The Government-sponsored schools are semi-privatised and the likelihood is that, like fully private schools, they will, one way or another, have more money and resources than maintained schools. This is because the City Technology Colleges will receive money from industry (though it will be interesting to see how long sponsors will maintain support if their own financial position becomes gloomy), and because the first opted-out schools are more likely to be in better off locations rather than deprived city centres, so extra parental contributions will be more easily solicited.

It is also a rigged market because the Government itself, anxious to demonstrate the success of its scheme, will, and this is a common enough practice when competition is cut-throat rather than friendly, find ways of giving extra resources. Although Grant Maintained Schools are only supposed to receive the per capita allowance current in their locality, it would be easy for the Government to offer extra cash through a competitive specific grants scheme, analogous to that already offered to local authorities for in-service, special priorities or particular projects such as the Technical and Vocational Education Initiative (TVEI).

If the Prime Minister really does intend most schools to opt out, the process would be quite easily induced. Kenneth Baker is probably correct in his assumption that few schools will opt out in the first instance. The apparent success of the first well-funded and undoubtedly well-publicised opted-out schools may well induce others to join them, until the see-saw tips and most schools do indeed opt out when faced with an emaciated local authority stripped of many of its support services, personnel and cash. But the sting in all this is that the disproportionate favouring of the few will give way to a less benign treatment once most schools are in the steely grip of Government control. It will be the difference between the first 14 TVEI schemes in 1983 when schools were given extra teachers, buildings and thousands of pounds for equipment, and TVEI extension to the whole country four years later when the funding was at a much more modest level.

Since semi-privatised schools will also be judged not merely by the quality of their facilities or the number of books they own but also by test and public exam results, another form of rigging will take place. Whatever is said by Ministers or supporters these semi-privatised schools will seek to recruit the most able and socially privileged pupils. Given the Government's league table view of education it would not be in their interests to do otherwise. Social class is the highest predictor of examination success, often correlating at 0.7 or above. Any school with a high social class intake has more than a head start over one with a low socio-economic clientele. Even if these schools are required by the Secretary of State to take some pupils with special educational needs, the *general* trend will be to favour the more able, giving a final average IQ of nearer 110 than 100.

The outcome of the rigged market in a few years' time will thus show, to no one's surprise, that the test scores in the first semi-privatised schools, with their higher socio-economic intake, their enhanced income and their massive publicity from the Government's own well-oiled publicity machine, are indeed higher than those in local authority schools. It will be hailed as a triumph for the free market and the 1988 Act. It will in reality be nothing more than the victory of the athlete in the Government-provided sports car over the runner whose ankles have been tied to the starting gate.

Other proposals in the Bill

Several other proposals in the Bill are based on the same philosophy, rigged or unrigged version. The idea of Local Financial Management rests on the assumption that financial decisions are most effectively based on local autonomy. This is in keeping with the belief that small businesses can be efficient and benefit from freedom from bureaucratic interference.

In itself this view has much to commend it, and, were it to be implemented in a good spirit, would in general be welcomed, though many school governing bodies might be shocked to discover that the 30 to 40 per cent discounts common to a large local authority bulk purchase consortium, might be replaced by 10 per cent off for cash in the case of small purchases by a single school.

The real hazard, however, is that schools will be given little or no professional financial help, will be funded on the breadline, and will then either be told to raise extra cash if they are hard up, or find their head teachers and governors blamed for fecklessness and poor housekeeping. This would accord with the Government's belief that public expenditure must be reduced and self-help must replace what the Prime Minister calls the nanny state.

The effects of this ideology have already been experienced in Higher Education. Following the severe cuts in 1981 and since, universities, polytechnics and colleges have been pressed into raising more cash themselves rather than relying on Government funds. Ministers have regularly accused academics of being indolent when they have complained about shortage of cash or out-of-date equipment. They should go out and earn it, is the reponse. Yet many Arts and Social Science subjects have little opportunity to win external funds.

Some ingenious ways of raising or saving money have indeed been discovered, it must be said, but there has been a price to pay. One severe cost is the drain in time and energy of trying to wring money out of hard-pressed industrial concerns who barely have enough to cover their own operations. Another is the launch of pro- grammes designed principally to attract wealthy students from abroad. In a free- market system rich foreigners are more welcome than Third World students. Severe reductions in public contributions and pressure to earn support in the market rep- resent radical surgery. Sometimes that is what is needed to cure an ailing patient. In the case of education too much of it saps time and energy which would be better spent on teaching, and lowers morale. The gains are relatively slight, analogous to chopping off a man's leg and then rejoicing because he learned to hop.

The wider application of market principles to Higher Education is also embodied in the Bill. The two new Funding Councils responsible for universities, polytech- nics and colleges will each have between 6 and 9 of their 15 members appointed by the Government from industry, commerce and finance. It does seem odd that British Higher Education, which has long been admired throughout the world, should in future be directed by British Business which has not, but again the Government's belief is that the practices of the commercial market must be imposed in education.

Higher Education demonstrates another flaw in the Government's market philosophy. The assumption behind these views is that a free market benefits the customer. There is an interesting example of the wrong-headedness of this view in the field of in-service education for teachers. By changing the in-service financial arrangements and giving money to local authorities for national and local priori- ties, it was assumed that Higher Education institutions would compete to offer courses and undercut each other's fees to drum up business. Some simply reduced their in-service, however, because it was financially more advantageous to put their energies into recruiting overseas students paying fees of £3000 plus per annum than mount in-service courses at high cost for low fees. The market does not always work in favour of the customers for whom it is intended.

Another aspect of the Bill which exposes education to market forces is the notion of open enrolment. This is a variation of the more pure market form, the voucher scheme, which, in theory, would have allowed parents to cash in their education voucher entitlement at any school of their choice. Open enrolment appears to enhance consumer choice by allowing schools which are popular to expand up to, and indeed beyond their full capacity, provided they can still offer an efficient service.

This is another attempt to create a better system and a wider choice through competition. On the surface it seems sound enough: let the better schools expand and the less popular schools perish. In reality, however, choice may well be reduced for many parents, if enhanced for others. Those likely to suffer will be the poorer parents unable to drive their children longer distances or afford the cost of public transport on a regular basis.

Take a city with six secondary schools. Falling secondary numbers during the next few years already put one of these in jeopardy. Expanding the two most popular schools would probably eliminate another school if not two. Imposing a 1,000-pupil City Technology College would further upset the local ecological balance and probably eliminate one more school. Thus the original choice of 6 schools would have been reduced to 3, and whether parents would be happy with a choice of 2 very large local authority schools and 1 City Technology College, probably recruiting the more able, is by no means a certainty. Gambling on market forces offering extended choices may turn out to be a disastrous and irreversible folly.

The consequences of the ideology

The ideology underpinning the Bill is not especially sophisticated. It is not the work of a gifted thinker, nor does it manifest internal consistency or shrewd insights about the future. On the whole it is a flawed, self-contradicting philosophy based on intuition and improvisation. The intellectual basis is suspect, and in the early stages of debate, ministers tended to look poleaxed when asked, for example, whether tests would be diagnostic. A great deal was improvised on the hoof when spokespeople were quizzed by reporters and found themselves bereft of convincing answers or a solid rationale.

The internal contradictions are manifold: Kenneth Baker has talked about devolving power from the hub to the rim of the wheel, with the rim being individual schools. Yet these apparently liberated schools will have to teach his curriculum, give his tests, get their money from him and take numbers of pupils determined by him. Even members of the Conservative Party are dismayed at the degree of central control in the Bill. During the Second Reading of it Edward Heath said, 'The Secretary of State has taken more powers under the Bill than any other member of the Cabinet, more than my right hon. friends the Chancellor of the Exchequer, the Secretary of State for Defence and the Secretary of State for Social Services.' It gives the lie to the claim that power is being devolved.

The consequences of this cavalier application of market forces to education are plain to see. They include the following:

1   There will not be a true system of competition. Such monopoly position as local authorities hold (and since most allow their several hundred schools to make many of their decisions at local level it is difficult to see how this can be a true monopoly), will simply be taken over by the Government when most or all schools opt out. Lest it be argued that the Government will be more benign

it should be pointed out that this is not typically the case when education is tightly controlled at national rather than local level. The Burlescombe case illustrates this well. When Burlescombe village school decided they did not wish to take a redeployed teacher, Kenneth Baker overruled the local authority and decreed that they should not be compelled to. Were he responsible for 30,000 schools and colleges and 400,000 teachers he would not have been so benign with every village that objected. In ten years' time there will be a position of oligopoly, that is few providers, these being simply the Government itself and the private schools. Local authorities will have been obliterated.

2   Not only will competition not be genuine, it will be rigged. In a true competition all providers would have a fair opportunity to prove themselves. In the rigged competition which will follow the 1988 Act everything will be loaded in favour of City Technology Colleges and Grant Maintained Schools, intake, finances and publicity. Already expensive glossy brochures have been produced for City Technology Colleges. There are no such Government financed publicity puffs for jobbing local authority schools. Indeed the Government's propaganda machine has worked consistently against them, and they, their teachers and their achievements have been consistently belittled or ignored, and the failures in the system emphasised and exaggerated.

3   The competition will also be dirty. There is now a well established tradition of Government spokespeople attacking critics as being either left-wing or representing vested interests. Thus the BBC is castigated for being left-wing and has been frightened into being less trenchant in its reporting than it used to be, and doctors, nurses, teachers or others working in education who criticise financial cuts are accused of defending the status quo, being reactionaries generally, or simply speaking up for their personal interests – Yet most spend their lives working in medicine or education to help their patients or pupils. Edward Heath during the Second Reading of the Bill said, 'We all know what happens today to people who hold differing views from those held in Government circles...They are afraid that they will lose their jobs.' If reforms work the Government will take any credit, if they fail then teachers will again be blamed.

4   There will simply be too much testing. Even in industry there are limits on the time and money spent on quality control. Schools with 14 and 16 year olds will have to give national tests at both 14 and 16 and run mock as well as actual GCSE examinations. Before long teachers, parents and pupils will be heartily sick of the plethora of practice test papers and National Tests they are expected to undergo. As the league table philosophy begins to predominate, the less able will increasingly be seen as cripples, people whose low performance brings down the overall batting average. It will be unpleasant, inhumane and contrary to what many have striven for. Furthermore the process will reinforce and self-fulfil the three-tier view of humanity, with three different levels of school, the fully independent, the semi-privatised and the proletarian schools. The labelling will be even more pronounced than it is in our present society.

5   Imagination and initiative, supposedly at the very heart of British enterprise and inventiveness, will be stifled. Part of the reason for British success in inventing and imagining, though not always in implementing, is explained by an education system which encouraged teachers and pupils to experiment and explore outside the tight shackles of central Government control. *Statethink* was unknown in this country until the 1988 Bill. It will be the norm in future. Already Mode 3 examinations are being squeezed out of the GCSE, and the

craft skills of curriculum development many teachers regard as central to their professional competence are in danger of withering away, as happened in the Chinese Cultural Revolution.

6   Money and the language of accountancy will dominate educational discussions. Just as students who hear about the vast salaries of yuppies feel drawn to jobs in the City, or a faint sense of guilt and failure if they do not obtain a highly paid post after graduating, so too the market philosophy will create a new kind of accolade. Appointing Committees for headships will quiz applicants about their ability to raise money. Bank managers and accountants will be recruited willy-nilly on to governing bodies. Time normally spent on teaching will be sucked away into fund-raising, with an adverse effect on pupils' learning. It will introduce a note of dreary materialism, and, in poorer areas, futility, to what used to be a source of some excitement and enthusiasm.

In his speech to Parliament during the Second Reading of the Bill, Edward Heath made several mentions of the philosophy of Disraeli, Balfour and Butler. The divisive philosophy and ideology, such as it is, underpinning the Bill will foment competition at the expense of collaboration, success for few but failure and ignominy for many and represents a backward-looking, reactionary rather than a progressive view of education.

Instead of looking ahead to the twenty-first century it looks backwards in our history to the many failures which were rejected at the time in favour of reforms which united rather than divided, fostered individualism as well as teamwork. Butler and others before and after him tried to put right the inadequacies of earlier education systems by strengthening local authority provision, abolishing fee paying, ending separation and stigma at an early age. Unravelling these reforms will recreate the unfair society which the free market of the nineteenth century brought about. The 1988 Education Bill does not have the consent of the people that Butler and Chuter Ede secured for the 1944 Act. It will take another such Act to unscramble it, if its market-mad dogma has not ruined schools beyond redemption in the meantime.

CHAPTER 15

PERFORMANCE-RELATED PAY

Originally published as 'Paying for Performance', in *Performance Pay for Teachers*, by Wragg E. C., Haynes G. S., Wragg C. M. and Chamberlin R. P., RoutledgeFalmer, 2004, pp. 171–83

Eight years after a major study of appraisal, we reported our three-year research into performance-related pay. This is the summary chapter (Chapter 9) of our 2004 book *Performance Pay for Teachers*, describing the views of over 1,100 headteachers and several hundred teachers on the implementation of the government's performance-related pay policies.

It is unusual for a whole country the size of England to witness the imposition of a performance-related pay scheme within a short period of time, such as happened from 2000 onwards. This research project was able to scrutinise closely and document the programme as experienced by participants at every level: classroom, school, regional and national. Although the scheme was meant to be introduced uniformly across 24,000 primary and secondary schools, its actual implementation was as irregular and varied as schools, heads and teachers themselves.

There are two sets of issues, one generic, the other specific, to be explored in the light of this research. The first is the nature and impact of the particular version of performance-related pay introduced in England, which we studied during the first three years of its implementation. The second is the general matter of paying teachers extra according to their performance.

The performance-related pay scheme in England

The framework – a command structure for uniformity

The introduction of performance-related pay in England in 2000 came at a time when the nature of national and local organisation and control of education had changed dramatically, compared with a decade or so earlier. The pattern of local control, which had predominated throughout most of the twentieth century, had given way to much greater central direction by the end of the 1980s.

Until the mid-1980s this strong tradition of *localism*, whereby schools devised their own curricula, under the somewhat variable supervision of local education authorities, was relatively unchallenged. The introduction of a national curriculum and testing programme, by a Conservative government in the 1988 Education Reform Act, changed the whole system to one where central government exercised much tighter direction of policy and practice that had previously been determined locally. The Labour governments of 1997 and 2001 strengthened this direct control through a series of measures, including the imposition of daily literacy and numeracy hours in primary schools, in which the general content of every few minutes of time was prescribed.

The national pattern of education had thus become dominated by a triangular command structure. At the very top of the triangle was a small but powerful unit, run directly by the prime minister. From this Number 10 Downing Street policy unit a series of initiatives ebbed down to school level. The route flowed through ministers and civil servants directly into schools, sometimes via private agencies. Local education authorities were largely bypassed. Teacher unions became less influential than in earlier times, able to nibble at the edges of a policy, but not influence it as substantially as they might have done formerly.

The introduction of performance-related pay was a prime example of this determined and direct triangular command structure. The scheme was devised and imposed nationally. Private companies were employed to carry out the training of headteachers, while teachers themselves were given no induction, other than what they received from their unions and what trickled down from their headteachers.

Uniformity was intended to be imposed via the training of heads, vital links in the chain of command. This research showed, however, that headteachers, especially the more experienced, were not always willing to implement policies blindly. Many challenged them, even when the pressure to comply was considerable. The route from prime minister to classroom is not an untrammelled one. It may progress smoothly in the first stages, from the capital city to the gates of 24,000 primary and secondary schools, but thereafter a significant filtering process awaits.

In order to reduce the likelihood of individual variation, the private companies charged with organising and running the induction courses gave all the trainers exactly the same set of overhead projector transparencies to use in their induction sessions. The timing of each of these was prescribed by the minute. One head-teacher interviewed during the research said, 'I'm not exaggerating. The man suddenly looked at his watch and said, "Oh my God, it's ten past eleven and I'm only on 10:45".' This style of induction was seen by headteachers as a ludicrous one for professional people and roundly condemned. Questioning the trainers was not encouraged. The very fact that headteachers were expected to be unquestioning, in itself reveals the essentially command style governing the whole operation. Compliance was more important than debate.

Shifting ground rules

When there is strong central direction of an educational initiative, as there was in this case, individual professional judgements become displaced, or reduced in scope, since overarching decisions are made by people outside, rather than inside the profession. A system of performance-related pay is inevitably influenced by the number of people awarded such a bonus.

A *proportion principle* applies here. Different proportions of successful and unsuccessful applicants produce different effects: the greater the percentage of overall successes, the more acute the humiliation suffered by those who fail. If only a few are successful, then good or even excellent performers 'fail' and the reward system fails too in its aim to motivate the workers. A system is only motivational if those subject to it feel they have a good chance of being rewarded. The sense of envy and injustice, however, is shared by the majority, so the collective sense of disappointment can mitigate the impact on individuals. By contrast, when large numbers are successful, the small proportion who fail to obtain an award feel much more isolated, stigmatised and humiliated.

The performance-related pay scheme introduced in England is a good example of this proportion principle at work. In theory, five standards of teaching had to be met if teachers were to progress through the pay threshold and on to the upper pay scale. In practice, the number who actually met these standards was determined by the government, which then passed the message down to schools via the private companies involved in training headteachers.

Headteachers described the confusion that arose when the information they were given about likely success rates changed during their training. Originally about half of all teachers applying were expected to meet the standards. This was then modified: almost everyone would meet them. In the event 97 per cent of applicants were actually successful. The teachers we studied reflected these changes in their own attitudes. There was much less use of the term 'divisive' by them once they knew they had been successful. Those who failed to meet the criteria became extremely bitter, some leaving their school, or indeed the profession.

One consequence of the shifting ground rules governing the criteria for deciding whether or not teachers were meritorious, was that the standards, far from being seen as firmly based or absolute, were regarded as pieces of elastic, stretchable by political rather than professional judgements. A system designed to reward the especially meritorious had suddenly been transformed into a general pay rise, with a small number of exclusions. Hence the condemnations of teachers and heads about the amount of bureaucracy involved. Many saw this mass award more as a right, than as a bonus for outstanding performance, and so resented having to apply for it in such detail.

There is, of course, an argument that teachers should have been grateful for a pay rise they would never have gained had it not been seen as subject to performance assessment. Other public-sector workers filing for a salary increase at a similar level could be told that only those teachers with high performance had been rewarded. These are political, rather than professional matters, however, which do not always strike a chord with teachers themselves. Most of the ones in this sample, successful or unsuccessful, saw it as a mass pay rise and did not like the idea of filling in forms for what they regarded as their due.

Social relations among teachers

There are certain aspects of the predominant social climate to be found among teachers in many schools in England that are germane to this research. First of all, they tend to value *collegiality* more than *competition*. In interview teachers were quick to point out that they did not want to work competitively against their colleagues in order to compete for a merit award, because they saw themselves as a team, hence the extensive use of the word 'divisive' in the early stages, before it became clear that the vast majority would be successful. In some schools this belief is especially strong.

In a study of Inland Revenue staff by Marsden and French (1998), nearly two-thirds of staff had become less willing to assist their colleagues when put in competition with them for performance-related rewards. There was no sign of that rejection of collegiality in our research and often the reverse was the case. When collegiality was threatened, people would soften, rather than harden. The case study of Mr Adams shows how his team leader, the deputy head, dropped his demand for a particular target to be set, when he thought about the link between objectives and pay, not wishing to jeopardise the prospects of his fellow teacher.

A second aspect is the tradition of support for staff that many headteachers claimed was already in place when performance management was introduced. A number felt that their existing forms of professional development were superior to what they were being asked to implement. This was often verified by the teachers in the school, but on other occasions there was a mismatch between heads' and teachers' perceptions. Some heads, for example, claimed that regular observation and appraisal of teachers already took place, but their version of current practice was not endorsed by the teachers interviewed.

A further feature is the preference among many heads and teachers for independence of mind, so they show no inhibition about criticising initiatives with which they disagree. Some teachers felt so hostile to the very idea of performance assessment that they became *principled objectors* to the scheme and refused even to apply. This could be seen as a defence against possible failure by those who suspected they would be unsuccessful, except that 49 out of the sample we studied of 50 principled objectors who swallowed their dissent and applied in the second round, were subsequently successful.

Another relevant point is the *high stakes* nature of headship in a culture where accountability had increased considerably. The head of a primary or secondary school often had to take the blame if something had gone amiss. At the time when performance-related pay was introduced, many heads had resigned before reaching the age of retirement as a result of a poor inspection report, criticism of other kinds, or stating that they were weary of office.

As a consequence headteachers who were new to a school were under strong pressure, sometimes from school governors, parents and the community, to secure rapid improvements. In a previous study conducted of several hundred teachers alleged to be incompetent (Wragg *et al.*, 2000), it was notable that a change of headteacher could provoke allegations of incompetency, usually contested, at which point the teachers concerned would allege that the previous head had been satisfied with their work.

There were certain *new headteacher* effects noted in this research. Newcomers were significantly more enthusiastic about performance-related pay than very experienced heads and were more likely to have teachers on their staff who were thought to be unsuccessful at meeting their objectives. [...] Whether a policy succeeds or fails to win the support of the staff can be influenced strongly by the perceptions, attitudes, values and behaviour of a new leader.

General issues in performance-related pay

A considerable amount of what has been distilled in the research described earlier applies to performance-related pay generally. Although the details and the style of implementation may differ, the underlying principles and outcomes of remunerating some teachers more generously, if they are thought to be especially competent, are often similar, despite different settings.

Changing teachers' behaviour

One prime objective of performance-related pay is to improve the quality of teaching. Since nobody is perfect, every teacher needs to change judiciously in order to become more effective, however that elusive notion is defined. It is not easy to change the habits that teachers have acquired over many years, especially when the profession consists largely of middle-aged and older practitioners with decades of classroom experience.

If teachers engage in, on average, a thousand or so interpersonal exchanges in a single day, with as little as one second or less in between them (Wragg, 1999), then this means millions of rapid transactions spread over a professional lifetime. Since becoming more proficient by following exactly the same patterns of behaviour is a logical impossibility, unpicking deep internal structures laid down over decades becomes a central matter. Yet the sheer intensity of verbal traffic during a lesson means that there is little spare time available to teachers to reflect on, and modify their teaching, while actually doing it.

The options open to those seeking to improve teaching include the following, which can be used separately, or in combination:

- *teaming* – two or more teachers working together on their skills;
- *sponsored autonomy* – encouraging teachers to decide their own improvement strategy;
- *persuasion* – offering advice that is accepted;
- *shaming* – humiliating and embarrassing someone;
- *coercion* – the use of power to compel;
- *rewarding* – offering promotion, cash payments, praise, privileges.

Performance-related pay is one form of the last of these, usually offered in combination with others, like *teaming* or *persuasion*. How it is implemented will reflect the management style of those in positions of leadership.

The performance management element of the scheme did seem to raise teachers' awareness of what they were doing and gave them welcome opportunities to discuss what professional development they needed. The evidence from this research, however, is that *cash payments* themselves appear not to be influential on people's actual teaching behaviour. Most heads and teachers themselves reported that there was little change. The main differences attributable to actual pay seem to be in personal mood and morale, depending on the individual teacher's success or failure in progressing to higher pay scales.

This is not unimportant, because improvement can be closely related to emotional state, but one of the few changes attributed by teachers themselves to the whole scheme was that they kept more detailed records of their pupils' progress as a result of its introduction, so they would have the information to hand when needed. There were very few instances of teachers being able to identify strategic changes in the way they taught, other than merely setting themselves overall pupil attainment targets. Indeed, a number could not even remember, when asked, what their objectives for improvement were, as other priorities had consumed their attention since they had been set.

This strong focus on outcome, in the form of pupil attainment targets, or management objectives, rather than on actual processes in the classroom, was reinforced by the humble place lesson observation and analysis occupied in the scheme. Only one classroom observation session was required for the performance management element of the programme, and even that was not universally carried out, though many schools used classroom observation more regularly as part of their own procedures within the school. External assessors, to the satisfaction of the teacher unions, were effectively excluded from watching lessons. Their decisions had to be based on a scrutiny of paperwork.

If teachers are to change how they teach, it is difficult to see how this can be achieved without closer scrutiny of the thousands of transactions that take place in lessons every single week. The principle that this should be undertaken in collaboration with others was, on the surface, built into this particular manifestation of performance-related pay, with its pairing of teacher and team leader. In practice, however, the main thrust was more bureaucratic than strategic, as many teachers strove to meet targets and supply paper proof, rather than modify how they taught on the basis of sustained self-analysis.

During the period of its introduction a number of national pupil test scores did in fact improve, but the examination results of 16 and 18 year olds had gone up steadily for many years beforehand. The scores of 11 year olds actually plateaued, but again, so far as our research is concerned, this cannot be attributed to the effects of the pay policy. Many teachers stated in interview that what they had done in response to the demands of the scheme, they would have done anyway. This included tactics which they were expected to use because of the pressures produced by published league tables of school test scores, such as 'borderlining', which involves working especially with those pupils whose projected results lie at the boundaries between critical points in the grading scale, in order to push them into a higher band.

Decisions about whether teachers have 'improved', by changing their teaching strategies for the better, depend on the criteria used to determine what constitutes 'improvement', and test scores are but one such measure. There is no supporting evidence for or against the effectiveness of performance-related pay in improving the quality of teaching to be drawn from national outcome measures, as this was not a controlled experiment, so the factors influencing any annual fluctuations cannot readily be identified.

Power relationships and patronage

Power in education in England ebbed and flowed from one source to another during the 1980s and 1990s. Successive legislation, under both Conservative and Labour governments, redistributed power. More control over national policies and the detail of their implementation accrued to the government, as local education authorities found their role diminished. Certain forms of patronage passed to headteachers and school governors, both in terms of control over their own budgets and the appointment of teachers. Local authorities played no formal part in the introduction of performance-related pay, though some voluntarily offered advice and training to headteachers.

The overall control of performance-related pay lay substantially in the hands of the government, which determined the form of it, the numbers of teachers likely to be successful, the nature of the standards to be met and the form of external assessment that had to be employed for monitoring. While the individuals to be rewarded were identified locally, decisions had to be made strictly within the rules and conventions that had been laid down nationally. The levels of the five standards that teachers had to satisfy may have appeared to be decided locally, but the crucial determinant was, in practice, the government's switch from expecting half of teachers to meet them, to almost all teachers being successful. This message was passed down to headteachers through the private companies charged with providing their training.

The relationship between and among the key players and agencies was a complex one. As some headteachers pointed out in interview, they were empowered to make decisions about giving sizeable payments to teachers as an inducement to come and teach in their school, or in recognition of extra duties, but they were subject to external scrutiny over these financial decisions related to competence. In practice, however, there was only an infinitesimal level of disagreement between external assessors and heads, each party being anxious not to provoke conflict with the other.

At school level the implementation of performance-related pay closely mirrored the management style operative in the school. Headteachers who were very direc-tive tended to be equally forceful in the way the scheme was administered. This was revealed by the closeness of fit between the teachers' objectives and their own, or the degree of congruence with the school's development plan. One of the case studies showed how Mrs Smith, a secondary teacher in a school with a generally *laissez-faire* management style, experienced the same lack of structure and purpose when performance-related pay was introduced.

Within schools power relationships hardly seemed to change. Although the role of team leader was designed to introduce an element of collegiality, rather than direct patronage by the head, team leaders were still subject to the predominant style of management that existed already. The intricacy of such relationships inside a school is neatly illustrated by the case study of Mr Adams. As a head of depart-ment in a secondary school he was in a fairly senior position and so had power over how the department functioned. The deputy head who acted as his team leader was, in a hierarchical sense, more potent, since he was not only Mr Adams' team leader, but also his direct line manager. Yet he was also a member of his department, so in that respect he was a subordinate.

The elaborate counterpoint, during which the deputy head tries to persuade Mr Adams to make greater use of information technology in the subject area, as one of his management objectives, shows the complexity of such relationships, as power flows from one to the other during the dialogue. There is a significantly diffuse boundary between the *de jure* power of the deputy head and the *de facto* potency of Mr Adams, who withdraws from the conversation and subsequently manages to neutralise the objective he dislikes. The deputy head, mindful of the sensitivity of his position as a patron, since he is effectively able to determine his colleague's salary, quietly accedes.

In those schools where there was firm direction, performance management was introduced briskly, with the head taking a strong lead, often opting for the shorter 9-month, rather than the longer 18-month cycle. Such schools were sometimes into their third cycle before the less driven schools had completed their first. Changes in the balance of power were most likely to occur under a new head, depending on whether the newcomer sought to acquire it, or distribute it.

Headteachers themselves often stated that they desired more direct power of patronage over merit pay decisions. Teacher unions, on the other hand, were anx-ious to minimise patronage, hence their favouring of external assessors to monitor heads' decisions. Ultimately, however, it was the government that held the real power over performance-related pay. Once the decision had been made that almost every teacher would be successful, other matters, like the determination of the actual levels of the five standards, fell into place.

Belief and actuality

One problem with soliciting the views and experiences of major players, like heads and teachers, is that there can be a mismatch between the perceptions of different participants. Some headteachers, for example, stated in interview that there was already extensive classroom observation in their school, but certain of their colleagues reported that this was not the case in their experience. It is not easy, especially when there is a strong emotional overlay, to describe a process with great confidence if individual informants' perceptions do not concur.

Various forms of triangulation were used in this research to help overcome these obstacles. *Data triangulation* involved collecting information at different times and from different people, like heads, teachers and team leaders. *Methodological triangulation* was achieved by using interviews, questionnaires and observation and through both quantitative and qualitative approaches. *Investigator triangulation* required all four members of the research team to cross-check interpretations with each other throughout the research, from the time initial interviews were undertaken right up to the writing of the final account. *Theory triangulation* was brought about by adopting no single set of beliefs about the events being studied, but rather grounding interpretations in the light of what was actually witnessed.

Even with these precautions there was still bound to be uncertainty. The beliefs and values of heads and teachers exert a strong conditioning effect on the way they perceive people and processes. Teachers opposed to performance-related pay wanted to believe that it was a waste of time, but even sceptics were sometimes able to point to benefits. Many of those principled objectors who refused even to apply, in the first round, to pass through the threshold to the upper pay scale because of their dislike of the whole procedure, changed their minds and applied in the second round, almost always with success. Some said that they hated doing so, but most persuaded themselves that a pay rise was their just due. It was a time of torment and uncertainty and minds were not always clear when people were asked about what was happening.

Unsuccessful teachers often stated that the headteacher, or the external assessor, or both, had been culpable in some way. This may have been true in certain cases, especially the unusual instance of several teachers in the same school failing to progress, contrary to what happened elsewhere. Obversely, some headteachers complained that unsuccessful teachers in their school had not taken the trouble to give a proper account of themselves. The extremely high level of agreement between heads and external assessors does not offer comfort here, because there were strong social pressures for the two groups to agree.

Researchers cannot make a personal judgement about the rights and wrongs of questionnaire responses from people they have not met, but the intensive case studies conducted over nearly three years revealed that there were indeed examples of people reporting different and sometimes conflicting accounts of what were, in theory, the same events. Belief and actuality can be exceedingly difficult to disentangle in events relating to pay, status and the complex nexus of relationships that are engendered when decisions are made about rewarding teachers for their performance.

Purposes and outcomes

The prime purposes of performance-related pay are often stated to be the recruitment, retention and motivation of the workforce, based on the assumption that the best quality employees are attracted to organisations where their ability will be suitably recognised and rewarded. The message to the existing workforce is that good performers are valued, while poor performers are not. Money is assumed to be a prime incentive to work harder. A second major purpose of performance-related pay is said to be the achievement of a closer fit between the goals of employees and the organisation, the skills and behaviour rewarded highlighting what their employer considers to be important.

It is not always possible to link purpose and outcome with any certainty in this research, because so many other factors are at work. In the case of *recruitment*, for example, economic factors can override salary and incentive issues. When the graduate employment market is buoyant it is harder to attract teachers, while during an economic recession recruitment is much easier. The study by Wragg and Wragg (2002) showed that trainee teachers at the end of their course regarded conditions of service and excessive bureaucracy as more important factors than salary. On the other hand, *retention* may have been helped by the scheme, because a number of teachers, including some of the most hostile, mentioned in interview that they were conscious of the need to augment their pension by securing the highest possible terminal salary.

Kessler and Purcell (1991) identified five purposes (1–5 below), and three further ones (6–8 below) are mentioned in a study of performance-related pay in the public sector by the Organisation for Economic Co-operation and Development (1993). Some of these can be commented on in the light of this research:

1   *Weakening the power of the unions by making individual rather than collective contracts*   This was not an overt issue, as unions had already been weakened by 1980s legislation. Teacher and headteacher unions were consulted, and the National Union of Teachers took the government to court in the early stages, but the processes accompanying the policy could not be seen as a deliberate means of curbing them, more a reflection of a state that already existed.

2   *Making managers responsible for taking decisions*   Certainly the introduction of performance management was intended to make all schools conscious of the need to appraise what teachers were doing. The principal decision-making on the format of this process, however, was in the hands of the government, while the senior management only had control over local detail.

3   *Giving better value for money*   It is not possible to say whether this occurred. Self-scrutiny is time-consuming and it is open to argument whether the time invested was well spent.

4   *Advertising the organisation's core values*   This occurred among insiders, though not to the general public, in those schools that made the effort to link teachers' individual objectives with the school's development plan. In other schools there was no deliberate connection of individual and organisational aspirations.

5   *Changing the culture of the organisation*   New headteachers were the group most likely to fasten on to this particular purpose. In most other cases the process mirrored the existing culture. A number of schools, however, did introduce a system of performance management where little had existed previously.

6   *Encouraging greater accountability*   In the preceding years there had been a shift in education from a high trust/low accountability climate to the polar opposite: low trust and high accountability. Heads and teachers already complained about the large amount of bureaucracy with which they had to contend, so most saw this as an unnecessary addition to their load.

7   *Saving money by reducing automatic increments*   Performance management involved an annual review of what had previously been almost automatic: progression up the *basic* incremental scale. It was possible, therefore, to block someone's advance to the next incremental point, but we do not have the evidence about how often this occurred.

8   *Enhancing job satisfaction*   The general issue of motivation is an important one. Vroom (1964) postulated an Expectancy Theory, which stated that prospective rewards will motivate employees only if they believe that (a) they can improve their performance by working harder, (b) if they do work harder

there is a high probability they will be rewarded, and (c) if the thought of having more money appeals to them. Some teachers in this study stated that they welcomed the interest in them and their professional development, and that they were pleased to have been paid an additional sum of money. Most believed they were working as hard as they could, however, so they saw the money as a right and were muted about its effect on their motivation.

The future of performance-related pay

Irrespective of what happens in any country or region that tries out a performance-related pay experiment the general issues will not go away. As we pointed out at the beginning, the scheme studied in this research was introduced by a Labour government in England at the very time when a Labour administration in Australia was terminating its programme. Attempts to reward teachers differentially according to their perceived competence will continue to be made.

It was argued by Odden and Kelley (1997) that a successful scheme needs the involvement of all the key parties, adequate funding, training, no quotas and persistence. There was mixed success on these criteria in the programme we studied. Some key parties were involved, but universal commitment was not secured, as a persistent 60 per cent of headteachers in both our national samples, taken at a two-year interval, were opposed to the policy. Local authorities had to carve out a role, as none had been envisaged for them.

Among the other factors for success identified, *funding* became an issue as time passed. With two-thirds of teachers aged over forty and a 97 per cent success rate, there was a huge bunching at the higher points, with a consequent strain on school budgets. Many schools, faced with other demands on their funds, reached a financial crisis. *Training* was a problem because most heads saw their own induction as mechanical and demeaning and teachers received nothing other than what trickled down to them from their headteacher. *Quotas* were not directly imposed, in terms of a given figure, but the signal was that almost all would succeed, though this generosity began to wane as more and more teachers passed through to higher incremental points. *Persistence* endured for the period we studied, but financial strains began to exert an increasingly negative effect. The government moved from funding all the pay award at the beginning of the process to only paying 30 per cent of the cost three years later. Cordes (1983) discovered that 17 per cent of US school districts which eventually dropped their merit pay plans did so, wholly or partially, for financial reasons.

Some of the teacher unions, when we interviewed their representatives, wanted the programme to be terminated. The National Union of Teachers (NUT) and the Professional Association of Teachers believed that the process should be abolished. The NUT acknowledged there was one 'silver lining' in that teachers were more aware of what they did. The whole process, however, was described as a 'dog's dinner' which had failed to motivate or retain teachers, was over-bureaucratic and expensive, and it was said that the £125–130 m spent on the process would have been better applied in schools or put into teachers' pay packets. The Association of Teachers and Lecturers was content for the procedures and standards to remain the same for the time being, but felt there should be a rigorous evaluation to find good practice and areas where change was required. All the unions were concerned about what they saw as unfairness for non-standard teachers, like part-timers, supply teachers and home tutors.

For the heads, the National Association of Head Teachers was concerned that teachers were being demotivated. The Secondary Heads' Association wanted to see the process of assessment and the standards simplified. They were particularly critical of the one about pupil progress. They also wanted to see a reduction in the bureaucracy.

The research described shows the reality of implementing performance-related pay in all its complexity. Process at classroom and school level can bear little resemblance to the neat orthodoxy of policy flow charts and diagrams. Despite attempts to impose uniformity through training, there was considerable variation in what we saw, varying from enthusiastic adoption to adamant rejection, from carefully sculptured and detailed management of the process to near indifference, with minimal compliance.

The major success of the scheme was in bestowing a significant pay rise on the vast majority of teachers and, in those schools that particularly needed it, introducing a more carefully considered means of clarifying what the school was trying to achieve and whether it was fulfilling its aims. Moreover, the *performance management* element of performance-related pay needs to be considered as an element separate from it. Performance management did seem to make many teachers more aware of what they were doing and how it fitted in with their school's ambitions. Furthermore a number of teachers were able to secure opportunities for dialogue and professional development that might not otherwise have been available.

The most significant failures of the policy may be the limited effect that the offer of additional pay seems to have had on actual classroom practice and teaching strategies, and the lack of success in winning support from the majority of teachers and heads. A related negative factor is the amount of paperwork involved, which was seen by participants to be an unwelcome additional chore, rather than a means to improve practice.

If change for the better is to be brought about, then a fuller and more sophisticated understanding is needed of how teachers lay down, over many years, the deep structures that determine their teaching styles and strategies. One of the significant findings of this research is that the offer of more money alone appears to be insufficient. Interpersonal and social relationships are much more crucial. Even brilliant teachers can improve, but features like mutual respect between teacher and mentor are required if people are to unscramble the habits of a lifetime and redesign significantly the way they teach.

References

Cordes, C. (1983). 'Research Finds Little Merit in Merit Pay', *American Psychological Assocation Monitor*, 14, 9: 10.

Kessler, I. and Purcell, J. (1991). *Performance-related Pay: Theory and Practice*. Paper presented at the Tenth Colloquium for European Group of Organisation Studies, Vienna, July 1991. Oxford, Templeton College: the Oxford Centre for Management Studies.

Marsden, D. and French, S. (1998). *What a Performance: Performance Pay in the Public Sector*. London: Centre for Economic Performance, London School of Economics.

Odden, A. and Kelley, C. (1997). *Paying Teachers for What They Know and Do*. Thousand Oaks, CA: Corwin Press.

Organisation for Economic Co-operation and Development (OECD) (1993). *Private Pay for Public Work: Performance Related Pay for Public Sector Managers*. Paris: OECD.

Vroom, V. (1964). *Work and Motivation*. New York: Wiley.

Wragg, C. M. and Wragg, E. C. (2002). *Staying Power. Managing Schools Today*. October: 32–35.

Wragg, E. C., Haynes, G. S., Wragg, C. M. and Chamberlin, R. P. (2000). *Failing Teachers?* London: Routledge.

CHAPTER 16

THE PROBLEMS OF INCOMPETENCE

Orginally published as 'Implications and Consequences', in *Failing Teachers?* by Wragg E. C., Haynes G. S., Wragg C. M. and Chamberlin R. P., Routledge, 2000, pp. 207–30

I had always wanted to study 'incompetence', as it was a neglected area of research and most of my research was into 'competence', rather than its obverse. But how do you knock on someone's door and say, 'I'm doing a study of incompetence and the head has given me your name as someone who appears to have a great deal first-hand information on this interesting topic'? In the end we didn't do it that way, but we did carry out the biggest analysis of allegedly incompetent teachers ever undertaken. This is from Chapter 11 in our 2000 book *Failing Teachers?*, in which 685 headteachers described cases of incompetence they had dealt with and several hundred teachers accused of incompetence told their own story, as did children, parents, governors, local authority officers and teacher union officials. It was a searing experience for most and in many ways a harrowing project to carry out, because of the stress and distress many of our informants had experienced.

The absence of detailed research findings in a field can be both a blessing and a curse. During the Teaching Competence Project we carried out the largest systematic study of its kind ever undertaken in the United Kingdom into allegations of incompetence in the teaching profession, with hundreds of responses from head teachers, teachers, governors, parents, pupils, teacher union and local authority officers. The advantage of working in a field where there has been little research is that one can try to establish some fresh baseline information, which may be limited, but can be illuminating. The disadvantage is that there is little else with which to compare the data, or on which to hang the findings, and fundamental first-time research projects often contain more flaws than replications or research which investigates a field where there are numerous previous studies on which to build.

There are many ways of interpreting what we found during the research. Sometimes informants contradicted each other in what they described, though there was often corroboration from different constituencies of several of the main observations. Personal views colour the extent to which people will view the findings as good news (for example, many teachers were thought to have improved), or bad news (many of the heads and teachers involved became severely stressed). Pessimists will feel that those who lack competence have simply blighted the education of the children they failed to teach effectively. Optimists would say that, since the overwhelming majority of teachers are regarded as competent when inspected, the problem is over a small minority of incompetents.

Few would argue that there is no problem when incompetence has been alleged, even if one is only talking about a single case. Every professional practitioner ought to be competent, so it is grievous if even one is thought not to be effective, especially when judgements about cases are contested. Discussion needs to focus on the nature of any perceived problem, whether or not it is a serious problem, the origins of the allegation, the impact it has made, what can be done in the circumstances, how similar difficulties might be avoided in future.

In this chapter some of the main findings will be brought together, to see how they reinforce or contradict each other. There will be an analysis of a number of the theoretical issues and practical implications of what has been found. We also report a small number of interviews with school inspectors and subject specialists, undertaken after the main data collection had been completed, to elucidate some of the issues. As often happens, this research partially answers some questions, while posing yet more.

Significant findings

There are numerous conclusions of one kind or another, some tentative, others more firmly supported, that have been described in various works. There is no point in merely visiting them. It is worth considering, however, some of the main ones that can be derived from the national survey of head teachers and the hundreds of inter-views and questionnaires completed with heads, teachers, governors, officers of teacher unions and LEAs, parents and pupils. Caution must, of course, be exercised, as not all of these works were drawn from stratified random samples, though several of the major studies were. Here are 20 overall, if tentative conclusions that emerged from different sources.

1. *Most cases of alleged incompetence originated from complaints*   Head teachers reported that complaints from fellow teachers were their most common first sources of information, followed by their own formal or informal monitoring and complaints from parents and pupils. Parents said they were most likely to complain about work not being matched to their child's ability, poor classroom discipline, or some aspect of relationships between teacher and pupil or between pupils, as in the case of bullying.

2. *The most commonly identified problems concerned clusters of the same set of features*   Teachers' expectation of their pupils (usually too low, but sometimes too high), inadequate preparation and planning, lack of pupil progress, classroom discipline (usually too lax, but occasionally too strict), and negative relationships with others were commonly cited by several groups as the most likely features of cases they had experienced. The great majority of cases involved a combination of several characteristics, rather than just a single one.

3. *There was a high degree of emotional stress for those involved*   Many head teachers, teachers alleged to be incompetent, and those fellow teachers working alongside them, stated that the events had caused them great stress. Heads were torn between their duty to children, which came first, and their responsibilities as the senior manager of someone not performing well. Teachers alleged to be incom-petent saw their lives blighted by the accusation and often felt their health and personal problems had not been understood. The different parties described the impact on themselves and their family in almost identical terms, using words like 'hell' and 'isolation'.

4. Perceptions of events could differ with different groups and individuals
Some teachers, seen as 'lazy' or 'incompetent' by their heads or colleagues, regarded themselves as misjudged or misused victims, bullied by those in authority, or as dissenting from the head's ideology, especially when the head was new to the school. Head teachers sometimes expressed frustration that teachers thought to be incompetent by colleagues, pupils and parents, tried to deny there was a problem. In other cases, however, there was general agreement about poor performance between the various people concerned, including the teacher alleged to be incompetent.

5. Most of the teachers alleged to be incompetent were in mid or late career
About three-quarters, in some samples more, of all the cases in the various samples were teachers over the age of 40 with fifteen or more years of experience. There were very few cases of young or newly qualified teachers. Many were experiencing some of the problems often associated with middle age, such as ill health, stress in work and home, broken marriages and relationships, elderly relatives, or difficult adolescent children. Considerable caution needs to be exercised here, however, since about two-thirds of the teaching profession was in any case over the age of 40 during the period when the research was carried out.

6. Willingness to face up to the problems was a key requirement for success
Head teachers, union and LEA officers were among groups which believed that denial of the existence of a problem was the biggest single obstacle to improvement. Some teachers alleged to be incompetent stated that they were not in denial, but rather that their particular problems, or their philosophy and practice, were not fully understood or supported by those in authority.

7. Support was critical if teachers were to succeed   Some teachers alleged to be incompetent felt they had no chance of keeping their job because the head or their colleagues wanted them to fail. Union officers believed that if the school wanted teachers to succeed there was a high likelihood that they would. Head teachers, when asked to explain why some teachers did improve, pointed to in-house support: assigning a mentor, sending the teacher on a course, encouraging lesson observation of fellow practitioners thought to be competent, in the same or another school. These approaches were not always successful, however.

8. About a quarter of teachers improved   Head teachers reported that about a quarter of cases improved, while three-quarters did not. Union officers and local authority advisers believed that, with appropriate support and early identification, about half of the teachers were likely to improve what they did. Having a positive attitude and responding to advice and support were seen as key elements.

9. Each case was unique   While there were, on the surface, certain common features, each of the hundreds of cases studied was unique. Some teachers might, for example, appear to have a shared or generic problem, such as 'failure to adapt to change', but one could be a secondary teacher resisting the philosophy of a new head, another a primary teacher lacking the relevant subject knowledge in a field like science or technology, while a third person might simply have become overwhelmed by the detail of a rapidly changing curriculum, alongside other personal problems.

10. The context was important   One teacher studied was regarded as a failure in her first school, but as a success when she moved to another school. Heads in schools with few social problems felt that some teachers might have great difficulties in schools in which it was more difficult to teach. There were teachers in primary schools who were competent in certain subjects, but regarded as incompetent in one particular key subject, like mathematics.

11. Heads used a wide variety of coping strategies   'Damage limitation' was one of several coping strategies used by head teachers, such as reducing the teacher's programme, removing some of the more difficult pupils, assigning the teacher to different classes. Others included: confront the teacher with each allegation from parents, pupils or colleagues (some heads used the term 'break' the teacher); bring in an external authority, such as a LEA adviser; assign a mentor from among the staff; involve other senior managers, such as the deputy head (there was a particular problem, as happened in some schools, when the teacher alleged to be incompetent was the deputy head or another senior person).

12. Agreed procedures were not always followed   About 1 in 6 head teachers said they did not follow an agreed procedure. This was a cause of dismay to local authority officers. Accused teachers and union officers felt especially aggrieved when this happened and unions usually insisted that the whole process should start again.

13. Earlier action, before escalation, was often advocated   Many heads, when looking back on events, said they wished they had taken action earlier. Union officers and LEA respondents believed that early intervention was a key element of success. Teachers alleged to be incompetent often said they only realised at a late stage how serious their predicament was, because they had not been given a clear indication there was something wrong. The transition between the informal and formal stages of the process often proved the most difficult to manage.

14. Lay people often had some apprehensions about making or dealing with complaints   Only a third of parents interviewed had made a complaint about their child's schooling, mostly in an informal manner, but a number were reluctant to complain, often because their children had urged them not to make a fuss. Children sometimes stated that teachers would probably show professional solidarity with each other, so they talked instead to parents or friends. Parents felt they lacked the professional expertise to put their view across and, when their complaints had not been addressed, few were willing to take the matter further, unless it was an issue like bullying. Some governors also felt excluded, though others said they were well informed, or did not wish to become more involved.

15. Most allegations led to the teacher leaving the school   Over three-quarters of teachers alleged to be incompetent left their post, mostly taking early retirement if they were in their fifties (an option which was virtually eliminated in March 1997), retiring through ill-health, or simply leaving their post or the profession. Only a few took a teaching post elsewhere, but when they did, this often caused concern or resentment from heads, fellow teachers and LEA officers, the last of whom felt powerless to stop something over which they had once had control. On the other hand, some teachers said they had got a post elsewhere and done so well they had been given senior posts in their new school.

16. Few teachers were dismissed   Only about 3 per cent of teachers were actually dismissed from their post and another 3 per cent made redundant. Persuasion to retire or leave was a much more likely policy from both head teachers and union officers. An 'exit with dignity' was the phrase often used by different groups to describe what they sought when there was sympathy for the teacher concerned.

17. The role of union officers and fellow teachers was not always as is commonly assumed   There is a popular assumption in the public mind, often reinforced by press accounts, that union officers and fellow teachers band together to protect the incompetent. This was not in evidence in this research. Indeed, although many teachers expressed gratitude for their union's help and for that of their colleagues, some teachers accused their colleagues and their union of not defending them strongly enough against allegations, of colluding with head teachers. A few actually went instead to other organisations that take on advocacy of a teacher's case. Union officers often said that their first duty was to the children and did admit to brokering deals in some cases, making their own personal judgement that the teacher was indeed not performing well. Fellow teachers were often more critical of colleagues said to be incompetent than were other groups studied.

18. *There was a shared belief that cases had taken too long*   Head teachers reported that about half the cases had taken between one and three years and most felt this was too long, only 1 per cent saying it was too short. The likelihood of the teacher concerned going on sick leave was often stated as one of the reasons for the prolonged nature of the process. Even teachers alleged to be incompetent believed, in many cases, that events appeared to have dragged on and a shorter time scale would have caused them less distress, though their main concern was that proper procedures should be followed, or about the injustice, as they saw it, of the original allegations, which needed time to refute.

19. *Many wanted a shorter process but were concerned about 'fast-track' proposals*   Some period between one and two terms was felt by many groups to be better than a more long drawn out process. Head teachers, governors, LEA and teacher union officers were all worried about any 'fast-track' dismissal procedure of four weeks that left them looking vulnerable in the eyes of an industrial tribunal. They were aware that to seek dismissal in a very short time would make it appear that the school had not acted soon enough.

20. *A change of head teacher was often critical, yet few had been trained to recognise and deal with incompetence*   Many cases were said to have arisen when there was a change of head teacher. New heads spoke of 'inheriting' a problem, while accused teachers felt aggrieved that they did not satisfy the new head, when the previous head had not complained. Only one-third of head teachers said they had had any training in identifying and dealing with professional incompetence. The overwhelming majority of the rest said they wanted training.

Reflections on the processes observed

A study of this kind inevitably raises several consequent issues: about human competence, power and authority in society and in institutions, the nature of teaching as a job, the rights of pupils and teachers. These can be both practical and theoretical in nature. For example, the use or misuse of power and authority raises theoretical issues, in that one can analyse the concepts involved, or speculate about meanings, manifestations and effects, but it is also an intensely practical matter when one considers how power and authority are actually used in schools and classrooms, or what practices might need to change.

Human competence

One of the reasons why there was often a substantial emotional overlay to the cases of alleged incompetence studied during this research is because any attack on professional competence is seen as an attack on the person. Accountability became a key term in discussions about public services during the last two decades of the twentieth century. There are many forms of accountability that can be deployed, and in the United Kingdom what might be termed a 'low trust, high accountability' model was in operation. Close scrutiny of education by press and politicians in particular led to an extension of the bureaucracy associated with teaching, the more frequent imposition of models and procedures from the centre.

The curriculum, national tests, financial formulae, even the forms of school reports and records of attendance, or the shape of a literacy hour, were all determined by the government and passed down to schools. Many teachers, despite the rapidity and frequency of change, coped well, but others were unable to accommodate what was happening so successfully. Numerous informants in this research cited the changing style of governance in education and the greater demands as possible reasons for some teachers becoming incompetent.

'Competence' is a notion capable of several interpretations. 'Functional competence' involves being able to operate at a level judged by society, employers or peers as appropriate to the demands of the job. But functional competence, like 'literacy', is not a stable concept, for it depends very much on circumstances. In the nineteenth century, for example, it was not thought to be important if a primary teacher knew little science and technology. Nowadays these are regarded as two key subjects in the curriculum and those lacking the knowledge, or the necessary skills to teach them, are seen as incompetent. As in other fields, like medicine, the entry fee to the profession has gone up.

Employment is also an important part of people's lives. The nature of work may well have changed, but it is difficult to separate the person from the job: an allegedly incompetent teacher becomes an incompetent person. Most people, especially in the middle years of life, have significant financial and personal commitments to members of their family and community, so any threat to their livelihood is seen as an attack on their own well-being and that of the members of their family. For this reason many heads commented on the torment they felt when pressing a teacher to leave a post, realising the likely economic and personal consequences, even though they knew they had to put the welfare of children first.

Power and authority

In theory, many elements of power and authority in English education have been devolved to local level. The introduction of a competitive business type of model in the 1988 Education Act meant that school governors effectively became teachers' employers, the head teacher being responsible for the daily running of the school and for giving them professional advice, acting as their chief executive. This theoretical model of power, however, does not always withstand scrutiny. All these parties must act within the conditions and terms of employment law. If they dismiss an employee for incompetence, they must face the consequences, should the teacher sue for unfair dismissal. That is why head teachers, governors and LEA officers were so concerned about the up-to-date accuracy of their knowledge, and indeed about their own position, should they fall foul of the law. Many head teachers felt shrouded in a web of legislation, highly accountable to their governors and to the wider society, apprehensive about teacher unions, unable to act as quickly or as freely as they would like, so they expressed a sense of impotence rather than potency.

By contrast, many accused teachers saw themselves, and sometimes their union, as lacking power, seeing the outcome of their case as a foregone conclusion. It was one of many ironies in this research that heads in turn frequently saw unions as powerful forces against whom they had to be wary. For accused teachers the perspective was often quite different: head teachers were in authority, able to make decisions over their lives, so they felt resigned to their fate, believing there was nothing that an individual teacher could do. This had the effect of paralysing some and galvanising others. Consequently power could shift, depending on the determination with which a particular teacher was prepared to pursue the case and the degree of support available. Some heads said they were aware that a teacher might marshall the rest of the staff against them, if they pressed the case too hard.

Power is, therefore, much more fluid and elusive than it may appear. Some governors felt they lacked it, or did not want it, but governors as a group were seen by some teachers as society's uncritical endorsement of the head teacher's authority over them. Yet head teachers sometimes felt they had so little direct power that one head teacher union officer expressed envy of heads in independent schools who could dismiss teachers much more readily. Parents and pupils often saw themselves as impotent, but several heads and teachers regarded them as a powerful source of complaint which exerted pressure on the school.

Power relationships, in this context, therefore, sometimes appear to be diffuse. One party or another may seize control over events to advantage, only in turn to see it wrested away on another occasion. Sometimes it is only in retrospect that one can make a judgement about where true power over outcomes lay, or who appeared to be controlling what happened at any particular point. The participants themselves, their judgement frequently coloured by their own experiences and role, are not always in the best state or place to see the position clearly.

Expediency and pragmatism

Even where there are carefully worked out procedures and conventions, pragmatic considerations sometimes take over. Head teachers have to run a school and teachers and pupils have to work in one. Difficult decisions must be made setting the impact of one kind of decision against that of another. Most frequently, when head teachers decided to pursue the case, despite some of the difficulties, they found there were critical events along the way that caused them to rethink: the teacher's performance improving; the union becoming involved; the teacher being away ill; further complaints from parents, pupils or fellow teachers. The process is not a simple linear one with a clearly defined path.

Instead events are more like a branching program, a series of successive options to take one route or another, so that progress is erratic at times, especially when the unexpected occurs. In such circumstances each decision makes an impact, the consequences of which cannot always be clear. For example, if the head teacher has made an error at any stage of the proceedings, like failing to give a written warning, the union is likely to insist that the process loops back on itself to an earlier stage, possibly even to the beginning, so that the correct process can be followed. Similarly, if a teacher appears to be making progress, then the formal proceedings may be relaxed or terminated; but if there is a further decline they may be reinstated, and if the teacher then goes off on sick leave, the whole process may lapse once more into uncertainty.

Written procedures often assume that events will follow a clear linear path – informal advice, then oral warning, followed by written warning, next a final chance to improve with structured support, followed by threat of dismissal, assessment and actual dismissal. Analysis of hundreds of cases in this research shows that the process may appear to be following the written procedures, but not so smoothly as is assumed. More usually it takes unique pathways, via a succession of small feedback loops, each influencing what happens next.

Consequently the parties concerned have to accommodate each other for the sake of expediency. This may lead to compromise, where people agree to waive some of their demands or expectations in order to reach a solution thought to minimise harm or disruption. An example of this occurs when a union brokers a retirement deal, to the satisfaction, or sometimes to the wrath of the member. The assumption is that excessive time and costly litigation can be avoided by compromise and negotiation. Another example is when a teacher's duties are reduced, which minimises the negative effect on classes and allows the teacher time for retraining or observing other teachers. Head teachers are often key players in these cases of trade-off and accommodation, deciding almost on a daily basis when to concede and when to insist.

The vocabulary of the process is difficult here. 'Compromise' is a word that can be seen as an honourable and intelligent appraisal of what is best, or as a feeble collapse of principle. It is difficult to dry-clean such words as 'compromise', 'expediency' and 'pragmatic' of their various connotations. In the end it is the individual circumstances that determine whether an assessment of the events that took place should be positive or negative. A sensible negotiated settlement in one context will be a more acceptable 'compromise' than an abandonment of scruples or judgement in another.

The rights and responsibilities of pupils and teachers

One of the most tormenting issues that all participants faced during incompetence procedures was the clash of rights and responsibilities of the different groups concerned. There was no ambiguity among any of the groups studied about the rights of children to receive a decent education. Heads said it was their first duty, as did union officers. Teachers accused of incompetence, aware of their responsibility to do their job effectively, often said that they felt guilty if their classes' education was disrupted in any way, though a few blamed the pupils for indiscipline in lessons or for their failure to learn.

What was more problematic, even given the overwhelming consensus about the primacy of pupils' rights, was that teachers have rights which may, in some cases, clash with those of pupils. For example, natural justice decrees that anyone accused of incompetence must be given a clear indication of their shortcomings and a chance to improve. But in order to improve they must be given the opportunity to carry on teaching, albeit under more controlled conditions, which means that, if the allegation of incompetence is correct and they then fail to improve, more children will be in receipt of substandard education.

Head teachers, in particular, felt torn. They all stated that children's interests came first, but they then had a legal responsibility, acting for the employer, to ensure that failing teachers were given every chance to succeed. It was not an easy balance to strike. Even when heads had given teachers support, several talked in interview of their sense of personal failure if the teacher failed to improve. It was a dilemma that caused many of them considerable inner turmoil and stress, especially when they were not able to discuss the case with anyone.

[...]

Failing or succeeding?

Although the research we conducted provided a great deal of information and suggested numerous possibilities for improving practice, we never expected that it would answer all the possible questions that could be put. There are many reasons for this, not the least of which remains the difficulty of picking out objective 'truth' through a miasma of emotion.

Objectivity in an emotionally charged climate

One factor became very clear from many different groups and individuals during the research. Such was the emotional strength of people's reactions, not just accused teachers, but fellow practitioners and heads, that a degree of objectivity was desperately sought. Teachers wanted a neutral 'friend in residence' who did not take sides, but just offered honest counsel and support. Heads sought an external evaluator who could pronounce more coolly on the evidence and give intelligent, but objective advice to all the parties involved. In the case of heads who were facing an incompetence allegation for the first time, what they wanted was an expert mentor who could offer advice and help on the basis of first-hand personal experience. Such people were often not available outside the head teacher unions.

There is a distinct lack of people with the relevant professional, legal and counselling expertise. In many cases both heads and teachers felt a sense of isolation which a number expressed graphically. It was as if they were entangled in a lethal web of stress, intense emotion, conflict, often ignorance and loneliness. Without objective guidance the combined pressures often became intolerable, threatening the mental and physical health of those involved, whether accuser or accused. The provision of a mentor support scheme does seem to be a priority, especially if it prevented minor problems from escalating into major ones.

Failing teachers?

It is not easy to confront possible failure. The very word is often taboo in education, for it can condition events, especially where self-confidence is low. Most of our previous research has been into teachers in primary and secondary schools who are regarded as competent in their work, and in some cases we have studied teachers who were regarded as experts, so this research into the minority that are alleged to be incompetent has been different.

There is no doubt that some of the teachers studied were failing to reach the standards which society rightly expects. Many agreed themselves with the judgements of those who felt they were falling short of what was required. A number of these wanted to do something about it, others simply wished to quit the profession with a dignified exit. The consequences of incompetence were often dire: ineffective teaching and class control, complaints, strained relationships, manoeuvres of one kind or another, ill health, the termination of a career. The price of failure could be high for all concerned, not least for the teacher, but also for the pupils, the head, the teacher's colleagues and the whole community, especially in a small primary school.

There is also little doubt that some teachers were being failed through inaccurate judgements, lack of support, even open hostility. These may well have been in a minority, but there was sometimes ambiguity, differences of opinion about a person's proficiency, lack of advice and support. There were teachers who did badly in one context, but better in another, or who felt that their desperate personal circumstances or illness were not understood. Equally there were heads who felt that nothing they tried was working, or that the teacher was determined to resist any attempt to modify practices for the better, merely blaming children, circumstances, changes, or external forces. The best news is that a quarter of teachers were thought to have improved, but the depressing finding was that many did not and eventually left the profession.

So to some extent the story told in this research may be seen as an account of failure, sometimes by individual teachers, sometimes by those around them. But this has to be set in the overall context in which teaching and learning take place. The story we have tried to tell is located in settings in which most teachers are far more successful than many of those we have described here. In any profession there will be some people judged to be failing. One can either ignore this or try to analyse it so that future practice can be improved.

Despite the contested nature of some of the allegations, many messages from these research findings are clear. Teachers need to be selected with great care, both at the initial training stage and when appointed to vacant posts in school. They should be supported in their work, but also monitored so that possible problems are identified early, rather than at a point when it is too late to improve. Most early warnings came from complaints, often emanating from colleagues as well as from children and parents, so the informal stage of the process must be handled skillfully, as must any transition from informality to formality, since this was shown to be a difficult phase. Training is important here, for few heads and even fewer teachers said they had received any proper preparation for what was involved. The context of teaching is especially important, so this will need to be scrutinised to see what might be done, not just to make teaching easier, as this can simply throw more responsibility on to fellow teachers, but to assist teachers struggling with changes, unusually difficult classes, or negative personal relationships, to manage their teaching more effectively.

In the intensely subjective and sometimes highly charged emotional atmosphere in which allegations may be made or denied there is also a desperate need for objectivity, for people who are detached from the immediate issues, but aware of the circumstances and able to offer expert and effective advice: mentors for teachers and heads, external appraisers, advisers or counsellors. It does not require all of these, as too many disinterested people may actually confuse matters, but perhaps one or two key players who can lubricate the process, help to improve what the teacher is doing, even heal the wounds. That is why it is also important that procedures are well known and are followed, since many of the people we interviewed said they had not been. Failure to follow agreed procedures, or indeed ignorance of them, can lead to frustration, aggravation and possibly litigation. There are dozens of other important conclusions that can be drawn from the many findings in this research, depending on people's own particular role or circumstances, for the issues are very much ones that need to be dealt with sensitively at an individual level.

PART 5

COMMUNICATING WITH PROFESSIONAL AND LAY PEOPLE

In Chapter 12 I described how I once interviewed a 9-year-old boy as part of a study into how schools taught literacy. 'Do you like reading?', I asked. Most children reply 'Yes' to this question, though some merely offer an unenthusiastic 'It's OK'. David answered, 'I absolutely hate reading. It's boring. I just don't like it'. The only piece of reading that brought him pleasure was his Liverpool football club comic. As a researcher one simply writes these words down, probes beyond them, faithfully recording the responses, remaining professional, keeping a straight face. As a human being, however, you die inside at the thought of somebody so early in life detesting the very activity that might get him out of the relative poverty in which he lived.

There are two major reasons, therefore, why this somewhat unusual Part 5 is included. The first is that I have always regarded it as part of my duty to communicate directly not just with fellow researchers, but also with teachers and lay people, like parents and taxpayers generally, so I do a lot of radio and television broadcasts and write in some of the newspapers and magazines that members of the public read. The second is that, inevitably, I see events, phenomena, trends in classrooms and schools that are related, but not necessarily central, to the particular enquiry I am undertaking. For example, no one visiting schools to look at lessons and study children in England in the 1990s and twenty-first century could fail to notice the massive amount of personal and corporate accountability, box ticking and form filling, that had become predominant.

In research tomes and articles language usually has to be muted – 'on the one hand this, on the other hand that' – neutral, precise sounding, focused on specifics. In newspaper articles the constraints can fall away. This part includes two chapters. The first contains articles written in newspapers to inform teachers and the general public about findings or implications of research I have conducted. The second contains satirical articles. I would not go so far as to call satire a research genre, though it arguably is one, it is rather a parallel means of reporting aspects of the educational process that do not always lend themselves to conventional analysis and narration. It is often the sustained harrumph, rather than the ashen-faced treatise. What is more, it is immense fun, good therapy and quite effective communication.

In Chapter 17 there are pieces from national newspapers and magazines, like the *Guardian* and the *New Statesmen*, and some from the papers that teachers read, the *Times Educational Supplement* and the *Times Higher Education Supplement*. There is also an internet forum piece, eliciting responses about the nature of research. Chapter 18 includes a number of back page satirical articles from the *Times Educational Supplement*, especially those satirising ministers and their sillier policies, of which there has been an abundance. People inside the ministries have sometimes told me that these satirical pieces have been very influential. I doubt whether this is entirely true, but it would itself be a piece of satire if an 800-word lampoon, written in about an hour and a half, could exert more influence than a 100,000-word book describing three years of research. In any case, I have to say that it is damn good therapy to pound out frustrations on the keyboard, and it certainly allows you to say wicked things that are not usually possible in the sober milieu of research reports.

CHAPTER 17

COMMUNICATING WITH TEACHERS AND THE PUBLIC

Not many academics communicate directly with the profession or the public, preferring to write in books and research articles. This collection of articles from the national newspapers shows how I have conveyed my own research and enquiry to a wide professional and lay audience, sometimes syndicated on all over the world. The first two articles were written in the *Guardian* in 1978, an attempt to summarise what was happening in education for a lay audience. 'Don's Diary' told of my research trip to the USA, a formative experience in 1978, while 'Why don't your teachers riot?' explained to *New Statesman* readers what awaited British academics trying in vain to explain some of our government's madder policies to foreigners. The next two pieces translate research findings into prose for the interested teacher: class-management research and a study of boys' under-achievement in literacy, the results of which were reported all over the world. The next piece is an internet polemic about why practical intelligence is unappreciated and the final article tells the inside story of being a researcher.

FUNNY THINGS HAPPEN ON THE WAY TO THE CLASSROOM
(Originally published in *The Guardian*, 2.1.1979)

I once went to a large multi-site school and met one of the deputy heads (timetabling and blackboard cleaning) in the playground. He told me there were 86 staff at the school. Two minutes later I bumped into another of the deputy heads (caning and paper ordering). 'I didn't realise you had 86 staff', I said. 'We haven't', he replied, 'there are 93, I counted them myself only last week'.

After striding over the bodies of several more deputy heads, I eventually penetrated the innermost sanctum and found the Führer himself who, fortunately, was a good friend. I could not resist teasing him. 'There seems to be some uncertainty about staffing here. One deputy tells me that there are 86, another that you have 93 teachers'. Unperplexed he stepped quietly down from his throne, glanced casually in one of his four ceiling-to-floor mirrors, and said, 'There's no uncertainty at all. I made my returns yesterday and we have 84'.

The story is 90 per cent true, give or take a bit of minor exaggeration here and there. It always raises a hollow laugh from teachers who now find themselves in a larger unit than ten years ago, for the process has been, in almost every case, for schools to get bigger and more complex. With the exception of certain inner-city and other areas where population was moving away, five teacher primary schools and 700-pupil grammar became eight teacher schools, 400-strong secondary modern schools merged to become units of 1,000, 1,500, or 2,000, often on two or three different sites.

The inevitable consequence of this growth in size and complexity was an increasing bureaucratisation of life in school. People who for years had communicated face to face began sending each other memos.

Indeed training courses for heads nowadays commonly make use of the in-basket technique, whereby the poor devil under scrutiny has to go through an imaginary Monday morning in-tray full of shirty notes from Blandly-Smiling, the music teacher, objecting to the caretaker locking the music-room at dinner time, and others from Ramsbottom the caretaker (who had never written memos in his life, but is now a dab hand at it) claiming that Blandly-Smiling has been rude to him. Such are the strains of headship nowadays it is probably as well that caretakers still run the school.

A second feature of increased bureaucratisation is the higher incidence of meetings. Many decisions in the past were taken over coffee, in the corridor, or during bridge. In large units, decision-making has to be ritualised.

The process usually begins with an organisation chart containing so many boxes it looks like the back of a Tesco warehouse. These boxes are linked by multi-coloured arrows, transforming the picture to one of the Battle of Agincourt or a horde of escaping convicts, seen from behind. The really cunning head puts his own box in the middle and links all the rest with a circle of arrows, so that the unwitting junior member of staff trying to reach him feels like a foreigner cruising round and round Marble Arch unable to get out because all the exit roads look alike.

The second stage of bureaucratisation is a meeting structure for deputy heads, year group tutors, house tutors, teaching departments, or for the whole staff. Inevitably this involves people in more meetings than used to be the case, with a concomitant drain on teaching time or nervous energy. Large group dynamics being what they are, a degree of frustration can result as most members remain silent. When acrimony is generated, it becomes fuelled by the publicness of the arena, scapegoating takes place, special interest groups intrigue behind the scenes.

Hence the many attempts in schools to reduce the size of subunits to something approaching the order of previously existing smaller schools, within which pupils and staff could know each other well, or at least by sight.

It was interesting to see what became known in the late 1960s as the 'schools within schools' movement in the United States. Typically a large high school of 3,000 students would split into four smaller units of 750 pupils, each self-contained and with its own head, but sharing certain campus facilities and some teachers of scarce subjects.

'How big is the ideal school?' 'What form would perfect school organisation take?' are amongst a series of recurring questions to which there is no single answer. The 'small is beautiful' movement was reinforced a few years ago when Barker and Gump in their book, *Big School, Small School*, tried to argue that schools of 400 or 500 pupils seemed able to provide a varied curriculum and also allow great intimacy of personal relations. Yet many teachers and pupils are now quite used to larger units, and do not regard them as being impersonal places in which to work.

No teacher in this country finds himself in the same mesh or organisational complexity as his counterpart in highly bureaucratic states elsewhere or in the gigantic American high schools. A few years ago I visited a friend who was principal of a high school in Brooklyn. The school was built for 2,500 pupils but had to house 7,000. We went into the timetabling room where twelve men sweated full-time over computerised timetables produced by an ecstatically humming IBM, which they claimed stood for 'It's Better Manually'.

The day's print-out revealed the horrific state of play: there were 1,100 truants, 650 pupils who spoke little or no English, and on the first day of the school year a further 600 pupils had appeared unexpectedly. There was no possibility of the 400 part-time and full-time staff ever meeting as a group, pupils on the early shift which began at 7 a.m. never saw students on the afternoon shift which ended at 5.30 p.m. Even so, the principal managed to engineer a great deal of curriculum reform, and often watched and guided young teachers in their classrooms.

One major source of discontent amongst teachers in recent times has been that posts of higher responsibility appear to go to those who best sustain the bureaucracy, such as head of year groups or house tutors, rather than to skilled classroom teachers. This may or may not be the case, and it is certainly easier to argue who has been given a particular task, than to determine who is the most skilful teacher.

In spite of team teaching and open plan schools, teaching is still an isolated box classroom job for most people. If merit payments were introduced for the 'best' classroom teachers, there would be a great deal of unease about any attempt to send in evaluators to choose the master teachers who should receive such awards.

Another effect of more complex organisation which sometimes causes concern is when certain areas of face-to-face human relations become bureaucratised. Perhaps the most striking examples of this are pastoral care and classroom discipline. In the United States most large schools have a sizeable counselling department. The head of this enterprise often wields great control over decisions about careers, subject choices, rewards and punishments, to the chagrin of other teachers. British counsellors are far fewer in number and tend to prefer working alongside rather than separately from their colleagues.

Classroom discipline can be equally problematic. It is certainly the case that class control has become more difficult in recent years, and that those teachers unable to maintain friendly and orderly relationships with their groups are under great stress. The stress is not always relieved when pupils have to be dispatched elsewhere to heads of year, house tutors, or deputy heads, clutching their 'on report' slips. It seems to underline to the other children that the individual teacher cannot or is not being allowed to cope. Hence the nostalgic yearning for smaller, more intimate units where interpersonal relations seemed to be natural rather than sculptured.

Unfortunately this quest for smaller units may be resolved in a most tragic fashion unless skilfully handled over the next few years. Between 1964 and 1976 the birth rate dropped by a third, and low age cohorts are already reaching primary schools with even lower ones to come.

Falling rolls will be more devastating for secondary schools in the mid-1980s because of the specialist nature of secondary teaching. Many schools will find they have about three quarters of their current population. In areas of population drainage, the fall will be bigger; in new towns or near new estates, the drop will be much less. The process is inevitable and irreversible until larger birth cohorts come along.

No one has yet worked out the effect of reduction from, say, 1,500 to 1,000, or from 5-form intake to 3-form entry on curricula, personal relationships, staff morale, promotion prospects, and resources. Even if the nation is awash with North Sea oil, and even if staff–pupil ratios are allowed to become very favourable, there will still be some overall reductions.

There are dozens of consequences. Many young teachers have obtained good promotions to posts of responsibility early in their career. In future there will be greater delay before promotion is obtained. The teaching unions have already begun what is likely to be their most important fight for many a year.

SUPERTEACH AND THE DINOSAURS
(Orginally published in *The Guardian*, 16.1.1979)

A hundred years ago teacher training institutions in Europe and North America were often known as 'Normal' schools, on the grounds that there was a single accepted way of teaching, the 'norm', to which each generation of novices must be introduced. Today there are myriads of teaching strategies, text books, packages, schemes, and notions, each with its adherents. Someone familiar with every aspect of old and new curricula, if he existed, would have earned his blue skin-tight suit and cloak with the prominent red letter 'S' on his chest – Britain's first Superteach.

There was a time when the textbook world was ruled by a series of nationally known 'brand leaders', such as the Beacon readers, Whitmarsh French, School Certificate Chemistry. It was rumoured, falsely perhaps, that the fortunate authors had retired at the age of 45 to luxury in the Bahamas.

Occasionally the books were revised, a process known to old hands as 'son of Whitmarsh' or 'Ridout rides again', and publishers told gleefully of their letters from 'Disgruntled of Wigan' protesting at the removal of the photographs of German policemen in spiked helmets from their German textbooks, even though such headgear had not been worn for thirty years.

Young teachers coming into the profession found that most other members of staff had used familiar text books for years and could readily advise on every known wrinkle. From 1960 onwards, all this changed quite dramatically.

First, several rivals of the brand leaders began to appear, often similar in style but more attractive and modern in presentation. Second, well-funded Nuffield and Schools Council projects sometimes produced radically different curriculum packages, often multi-media in nature, so that the teacher sporting his shiny new sack of tapes, flash cards, film strips, loops, booklets, kits, and overhead projector transparencies, festooned these on his classes like a happy Santa, only going into hiding when his head received the bill.

This was largely because, anxious to 'go Nuffield', he had, when asked the price, quoted the cost of Stage 1A, which at £40 seemed not unreasonable. Unfortunately Stage 1B cost another £40, and by the time Stage V was reached a further £200 would have to be shelled out for a full-sized inflatable plastic elephant. They gave you a free National Health Service truss with every pack.

The position today is that no individual can possibly know all the curriculum materials available in the field. Whenever I browse through collections in the National Textbook Library in London I am astonished at the range of books available. Choose any area, primary school maths, reading schemes, secondary school science, English, foreign languages, backward readers, and there are shelves full of single and multi-volume courses. Go to a collection of specialist materials at a place like the Centre for Information on Language Teaching (CILT) and you can see rooms full of textbook and audio-visual courses.

A further development has been the rapid growth in home-made courses. Many teachers, sometimes because of a switch to mixed-ability teaching, occasionally from dissatisfaction with existing courses, often because they seek a local context which no nationally produced course can provide, have produced their own booklets, film strips and work packs. These can be of a very high standard, and some booklets are of a quality of graphics and layout rivalling professional products, having had enormous amounts of care and time invested in them. Be careful next time you pass a glassy-eyed teacher, by the way, he may be high on the Banda fluid. Worksheet sniffing will shortly oust stress as the major health hazard in the profession.

There are considerable implications for classroom teaching because of a wide range of choice available. First, changing to a new set of materials can be a time-consuming business. Surveying the field, discussing the change, planning implementation, all take up a great deal of time.

Second, there is the problem of innovation without change. Teaching consists of a well developed set of verbal and non-verbal habits, some of it engineered in the subconscious. Much of daily life is in the same category. Few of us eat breakfast in an original way each day, by lobbing the bacon in the air and catching it behind our left ear. Nor do we, for a change, hop backwards across the road, except after a trying day, perhaps. Yet some new curricula demand a radical change of well grooved habits.

Take the Stenhouse Humanities materials which required the teacher to play neutral chairman during discussions on the family, relations between the sexes, or education. For some teachers this was an easy transition, in that they already preferred this style in classroom discussion. For others it involved a switch from talking perhaps 80 per cent of the lesson to only 10 per cent of it.

Most other new curricula, if faithfully implemented, require a similarly radical change of teaching tactics. New maths and science packages suggest the teacher should develop skill in leading children on to make discoveries, recent foreign language courses require considerable use of the foreign language during lessons, home-made courses involve the teacher in a great deal of progress monitoring and skilful record keeping. My daughter, when once given the same maths workcard for the third time, completed it again because she thought it was easier than waiting in the queue to explain it to the teacher.

Indeed the question of assessment, either in its ritualised public form or more private record keeping, becomes highlighted when curricula change. Part of the public concern over accountability, usually manifested in demands for national tests or public debate about standards, reflect unease about methods of teaching said 'not yet to have proved themselves'. It is, of course, difficult for any new form of teaching to prove itself, as the teacher's aspirations are often different from his former ones.

For example, there may be more emphasis on oral work in languages or science, maths teachers may require a greater intuitive understanding of concepts rather than solely the ability to calculate mechanically and without comprehension. Thus we can test children today to see if they can do 'old maths' as well as pupils who did similar tests twenty-five years ago, but we cannot go back in time to test whether those children of the 1950s could have understood the concepts of new mathematics.

The technology of testing has developed considerably during the last few years. A much wider range of assessment procedures is now available: multiple choice tests, oral examining, project work, as well as the more traditional formal tests. There is also great interest in what is often called criterion-referenced testing. Most tests spread the candidates over a normal distribution with pupils in the middle scoring 50 per cent and the rest scattered over a range from 20 per cent up to 80 per cent or beyond. A criterion-referenced test is a pass/fail situation, like the driving test.

There is a great deal of interest in such tests in modern languages, for example, where pupils passing at level 1 might be able to understand simple French, at level 2 sustain conversation on everyday topics, at level 3 translate for a friend, and so on. Pupils can try the appropriate level until they pass. The approach is said to be highly motivating, particularly for the less able and disaffected, and could be applied to a greater or lesser degree in all subject areas.

Changes in curricula and assessment procedures are not always fully understood by those who have to implement them. The intentions of the curriculum developers are not always made clear to teachers who, in some cases, do the exact opposite of what is recommended, either from ignorance or because they have a valid alternative. One investigator looked at the way different teachers taught the unit on photosynthesis in the American BSCS biology course. He found many different interpretations and little of the inquiry method supposedly built into the unit.

There is thus a necessity for teachers to learn to analyse and evaluate their own teaching when curriculum changes take place. In the United States and in Britain, courses aimed at developing teaching skills such as questioning and explaining have been amongst the most popular kind of pre-service and in-service training. At Nottingham they are developing training materials and ideas for use with student teachers as part of a four-year DES funded Teacher Education Project. Students are videotaped at work and learn to analyse and improve their own teaching strategies during teaching practice.

Finally it is most important in a rapidly changing educational system that change should not be overdone. Schools where nothing changes are as unhealthy at those where nothing is ever the same. Dinosaurs had no adaptive routines and so became extinct, chameleons are able to blend in with their background. On the other hand dinosaurs are so attractive my daughter has now studied them three times, and chameleons have never seriously challenged tadpoles and sticky buds as a project topic. In any case even chameleons must welcome a rest once in a while.

DON'S DIARY
(Orginally published in *Times Higher Education Supplement,* 29.9.1978)

Synergised

Spending 17 days in the United States looking at teacher education developments and research into teaching at the Universities of Stanford, Los Angeles, Houston, Austin and Teacher's College, New York, was both an exciting and frustrating experience. It was exhilarating to meet and discuss matters of common interest with researchers I knew well through correspondence, but frustrating to be able to spend so little time with them.

The Pan Am jumbo jet to San Francisco had wall-to-wall stewardesses with wall-to-wall teeth. Try to sleep during the 13-hour flight and an ever-attendant hostess hits you with drinks, food or an inflight movie. It was a relief to arrive and have a rest.

I spent three days in the San Francisco area. My first visit was to the Far West Laboratory situated in a fine building with a Mexican museum on the ground floor. There is a very interesting beginning teacher evaluation study, not unlike the teacher education project at my own university. In an attempt to elicit why some pupils learn better than others, they have turned their attention to academic learning time, that is time spent on the task. American investigators are currently interested in this aspect of learning. It is of critical importance, especially in informal classrooms.

A Far West publication catches my eye. The publicity blurb for Woody Clark's *Violence in Schools* describes it as 'an integrated perspective incorporating Blumer's symbolic interactionism, Marxist conceptualisation of praxis and Steward's multi-linear levels of socio-cultural development, in which Dr Clark has synergised a massive databank'. Keep synergising, Woody baby, and keep your book.

Smalltalk

'We gave the world micro-teaching and then pulled out', said Nate Gage, director of the Centre of Research on Teaching at Stanford University when I visited him. Astonishingly the teacher training effort at Stanford is now slender, and he is embarrassed when visitors expect to see the extensive micro-teaching of ten years ago. There are only about forty trainees on roll and, like many other universities, Stanford has switched its emphasis away from initial training and towards research and advanced courses.

Nate Gate is engaged in some very interesting research. Taking the results of correlational studies where certain kinds of teacher behaviour were shown to be correlated with pupil learning, he has translated these into a series of experiments. Teachers follow a checklist of those acts of behaviour more regularly associated with pupils' learning (called 'Teacher should...') and the effect on pupils is studied. The results seem encouraging, but I explain that we are less prescriptive and that my own faith in the current reliability of any so-called science of teaching is less than theirs. We have an absorbing discussion about this.

I could not leave Palo Alto without calling in at the Xerox Research Centre and seeing some astonishing work with computers. They are attempting to produce a portable computer with a screen roughly the size of a student's file, called a 'Dynabook'. It will soon be achieved, I suspect, but no one can say as it is surrounded by government-protected secrecy.

A larger version is being piloted in schools. It is the most creative approach to computing I have yet seen, using a language called 'Smalltalk' and inviting pupils to interact with the machine to create artwork, music and solve problems, a glimpse of the twenty-first century when such things may be commonplace.

Each morning I ran through San Francisco, up and down the steep hills. No one gave me a second look. What is one more nut in this freaky place where weirds are the norm? Wear a grey suit if you want to turn heads. On my last morning I ran across the Golden Gate bridge. The view over the Pacific was magnificent. In the other direction lay Alcatraz, which looked surprisingly like the school of education back home. I wonder what you had to do to get sent to the meeting room.

Obliterated

Everything about Texas is big. Even the cows seem to have been persuaded to produce T-bone steaks in the shape of the state.

I went there to visit Houston University, said to have the most innovative programme of teacher education in the United States of America, and the University of Texas at Austin, which has one of the largest centres for research into teaching. The visits turned out to be extremely fruitful.

Houston University has 20 items where British universities possess 1. I saw one room equipped with a class set of sixteen electric pianos. The CCTV provision is lavish, at least twenty cases containing portable televisions were lying in a store waiting to be signed out. One member of staff who had just received a one-million-dollar research grant wondered if two secretaries would be enough. The resources centre is as big as one floor of our own university library, and there is a satellite section in the floor below.

A team of very inventive and hard-working teacher educators have put together a most impressive set of self-instructional materials. There are numerous boxes containing videotapes, tape-slides, sound tapes, films, etc., probably about 600 in all. I decided to test the system.

First attempt a sound tape of Charles Galloway on non-verbal behaviour. I put on my headset and sit back. Nothing. I wind on. Nothing. Perhaps he is manifesting non-verbal behaviour rather than talking about it. Eventually his voice breaks in, 'Teachers are the only group of people who...'. Silence.

I fill in the computerised evaluation form. Sound quality? – Difficult to say, the ten seconds extant sounded pretty good. Anything missing? – Yes, all of it. Any problems? – Yes, some idiot has erased it. Any suggestions for improvements? – Yes, for Christ's sake, with all the money available why not fly Galloway back down to re-record it?

The woman at the desk receives my evaluation form with indifference. 'Put it in the box'. 'But it's been obliterated'. 'Yeah, OK put it in the box'. 'But I'm an English academic with years of ethnographic observation and an international reputation for astute critical comment on things like obliterated cassettes'. 'Yeah, OK, put it in the box'. 'Is there a human being in the house?'

Prizewinners

Actually this is unfair. The place is marvellous. Everything else I viewed was in excellent condition, and people went out of their way to be hospitable. The dean, Bob Howsam, has put tremendous energy into planning a remarkable operation. The building itself is unique. It is entirely open plan, and partitions are used to separate areas, though there are some enclosed rooms. The message is a clear one of openness in the widest sense of the word, and flexibility.

Bob Houston, another member of the faculty, has done some very good in-service work among the most innovative I have seen. He has just been awarded the 'Texas Teacher Educator of the Year' prize. Perhaps we could have one in Britain, a sort of Oscar ceremony, with Racquel Welch reading the nomination, 'And the winner, for his contribution to educational controversy...Dr Rogue Bison'. Thunderous applause, and 'I owe it all to Norman Singeing Grievous' speech.

The space programme is everywhere in evidence in Houston, and conversation at the next table over breakfast goes, 'But I didn't realise just how irregular the surface of the moon was, and plotting a straight line was a nightmare'. Perhaps they are all charlatans. If I had someone to talk to I might join in and try 'As I said to Neil Armstrong...', but you can get your databanks synergised for things like that.

Tooition

Pictures of the United States linger in my memory. There is the buoyant confidence in places like Stanford, UCLA, Houston and Austin where substantial research is under way, that some of the correlates of pupil learning are being substantiated so regularly in experiments, that one can, with some certainty, enter a more prescriptive mode of teacher education.

By way of contrast with the zest and exuberance of researchers and curriculum developers I cannot forget the squalor of New York, permanently on the verge of bankruptcy, its city leaders improvising from one week to the next, cutting services till they barely exist; nor the lurking violence which has led to a policeman being stationed by city law inside every high school; nor the intensive course on each of several major drugs.

Not for New York a quick chat and a short film, pupils die of the stuff. The best teachers were excellent, the poorer ones had their classes sitting and spectating in resigned bewilderment, making grade D PGCE students back home look like Socrates. In this context the inventive work on pupils' task involvement I saw at nearby Teachers' College seemed a sad irrelevance.

My enduring memory of the USA is of sitting next to two burly Texans at the Astrodome one evening, watching incredibly athletic floodlit baseball which made cricket look crude. Between innings (and there are nine) they downed pints of beer and shouted abuse at the pitcher ('You daawg, Niekro, get back to the Cubs').

Eventually the more uncouth shaggy bearded one brought me a beer. 'Oh, that's very kind of you' I said in my unmistakable Yorkshire voice. 'You English?' 'Yes'. 'How much are the tooition fees at Oxford?' he asked. 'I wanna study over there next fall . I love them.

'WHY DON'T YOUR TEACHERS RIOT?'
(Originally published in *New Statesman*, 2.10.2000)

It was a dark and stormy night on the San Francisco waterfront as the intrepid band of travellers huddled together in the candle-lit gloom. 'A flagon of your finest ale, landlord', one of them called, amid clamour for him to recount more incredible tales from his strange homeland far away.

'Come closer, me hearties', he whispered, 'and I'll tell 'ee stories that will turn yer blood to water and curdle the very innards'.

Well, it wasn't quite like that at my evening with fellow academics in the lush kitsch of Fisherman's Wharf during the American Educational Research Association conference, but any Brit who attends an international education meeting nowadays is besieged by foreigners wanting to know if the mad stories they have heard about us are true.

'You English?'

'Yes, I am. actually.'

'Say, is it true that your government tells the teachers what to do every 15 minutes?'

'Er, I think you might mean the literacy hour, and it could be every ten minutes – 15, 15, 20, 10 – that's the prescribed pattern for each hour.'

'For every class, every day?'

'Correct, and two-thirds of the hour must be whole-class teaching, with not more than two ability groups permitted during the other 20 minutes.'

'Well I'll be darned. Do they tell you when you can scratch your ass?'

For 10 or 15 years, the global education community has regarded us with a mixture of astonishment, amusement, pity and horror. They used to say that New York's today was the rest of the world's tomorrow. Now people tremble in case their own government is tempted to follow Britain, for there seems to be a planet-wide trading of loony wheezes from one country to another.

In the late 1980s, Kenneth Baker took central political control of education, launching ten fat folders which spelled out every tiny sliver of the statutory curriculum. Postmen delivering to schools got a free NHS truss, as they herniated themselves carting government missives by the ton. When a committee under Ron Dearing began planning the first of several revamps of this monster curriculum in 1995, smart schools sold shelves of Baker memorabilia as waste paper for £50 a skip, or recycled them as *papier mâché* nodding dogs.

There were seventeen different branches of science and 4,000 years of history for 7- to 11-year-olds. In addition to all the invaders and settlers from King Ug to the last busload of Japanese tourists, these junior Einsteins were supposed to master such topics as 'The history of transport before and after the wheel', a touch over the top, I always felt. Sneeze and you missed the Spanish Armada.

'You must be mad', a Swedish academic said to me at a Council of Europe meeting. 'We're going in the opposite direction; ours is down to about 15 pages.' While the rest of Europe, especially old eastern bloc countries, thinned out government influence, we passed them in the opposite direction, piling on more, ignoring the wise advice in R. A. Butler's speech on the Education Bill 1944 to avoid politicians' whims.

I met a group of MPs from a former Soviet republic, visiting London to look at developments in education.

'We used to have that style of control in my country, but then it all changed', said their leader.

'What, you mean when the Berlin Wall came down?'

'No, when Stalin died.'

What puzzles foreigners most is the cowed resignation with which this country accepts crazy-horse ideas. J. K. Galbraith said that the Thatcher experiment could only have been tried in long-suffering Britain. Anywhere else, it would have provoked a revolution.

A group of French visitors asked why our teachers never riot. 'In France, the children would take to the streets, never mind the teachers', said one, amazed at the absence of manure at the entrance to the Department for Education and Employment. It is yet another difference between the English and the French: *nous ne riotons pas en Angleterre*. In France, the crap is deposited at the front door of the ministry by angry protesters: in Britain, it is delivered to schools every second day in official envelopes.

'You put your schools into league tables, according to their examination results?' a German head teacher asked me in Munich.

'Yes. that's right.'

'But don't you realise that the schools with the poorest children will be at the bottom of the league and the selective schools will always be at the top?'

'Yes. yes. everybody knows that.'

'So why, then...?'

It is pointless trying to answer. They omit the words 'you poor simpleton' because they are too polite, but the look of disbelief says it all: why don't you spineless bastards riot? *Aber wir rioten nicht* in England.

Now, more streetwise, I always precede any lecture I give abroad on the English education system by making it clear that I shall describe current educational developments, which I do not necessarily endorse, although I like some of them. In order to avoid the 'poor sap' label, I once asked the translator at a Spanish conference to explain that I had been quite critical of some ministers, calling Kenneth Baker, for example, 'Mr Bun'.

He looked perplexed.

'I am afraid this joke will not translate.'

'Oh really?'

'You see, there is a word *"buñuelo"*, but a Spanish *buñuelo* is not quite the same as an English bun.'

'Why's that?'

'A Spanish *buñuelo* looks very nice from the outside, but is hollow in the middle.'

'Spot on, squire.' So Señor Buñuelo it was.

Nowhere is the triumph of style over substance more apparent than in some of the pronouncements emanating from the Office for Standards in Education, or rather, from the chief inspector.

'This Mr Woodenhead', an Austrian inspector once asked, with unconscious bathos, 'why does he always attack your teachers? Does he not realise that people will act on criticism only if they are respected?'

They've heard all about Ofsted in other lands, from Montana to the Australian outback. 'Could it happen here?' they wonder. Their unions have frightened them with Grimm's tales of inspectors trained for five days in the Hotel Eldorado, Clacton, before being turned loose with clipboard and checklist. Generations ago, our ancestors told similar lurid stories, but of wolves roaming the forest and ghoulish creatures of the night.

Now I shall have to explain to foreigners William Hague's vision of the future. Hague wants 400,000 teachers to negotiate individual contracts. ('But won't that bury your head teachers?' 'Yes, I know.' 'So why, then ...')

The commonest perception of Labour abroad is that it embraced the policies of the previous government too enthusiastically. That is only partly true. At least Labour cares about all children, not just an elite, and millions are going into books, equipment and buildings, sadly neglected by Hague's predecessors.

Hague also wants yet more coshing of schools, with parents able to call an inspection at any time and Ofsted going in completely unannounced. That should do wonders for our teacher recruitment crisis, as Wee Willie runs through the town in his nightgown, rapping at the windows, crying through the locks: 'Ofsted are coming today, pal, at nine o'clock.'

'I really admire your teachers', a Spanish primary head teacher told me last year. 'They are so professional. I first visited English infant schools in the 1970s and I thought they were the most innovative and exciting schools I have ever seen. Why do your newspapers attack them so much?'

'Innovative' – now there's a watchword for the future. Many teachers are terrified of trying anything unusual, for fear of retribution. Sticking to the recipe is safe, and indeed demanded. It is not exactly the breeding ground for an Escoffier.

And if there is really only one government solution in teaching, what is the single solution for poverty, crime, cancer, conflict?

I shall return to San Francisco the next time 12,000 educational researchers from all over the world assemble. 'Gather round, me hearties', I shall say. 'Reason has returned to education in my homeland far away; no more *Loony Tunes* schemes from politicians.'

'Tell us more of the new ways in your land', they will cry eagerly, 'of the pigs that fly and the fairies that dance at the bottom of your garden.'

A FIVE-DAY WEEK IN THE LIONS' DEN
(Originally published in *Times Higher Education Supplement*, 28.5.1993)

'I can't cope with two of them, so I don't know how that woman manages with 30.' The speaker was a mother that I interviewed some years ago. Her children, aged

6 and 8, led her a merry dance at home and she could not understand how a teacher coped.

The Leverhulme Primary Project, which we conducted at Exeter University, was one of the largest studies of primary teaching ever undertaken in this country. My own part of the investigation was into different aspects of teachers' class management, which is much more complex than is commonly realised. In a busy day teachers have to manage several different tasks, their own and those undertaken by their pupils, as well as pupil behaviour, resources, the use of time and space, the application of rewards and punishments, relationships, tensions, conflicts and their own repertoire of teaching strategies.

Class management is often seen as something unidimensional. In the popular mind it is perceived as 'discipline' and little else. Yet the control of pupils' behaviour and dealing with disruption when it occurs, though time and energy consuming in classrooms where there is severe misbehaviour, is only a small part of management in many classes. Much more energy is spent on classroom routines, resource management, looking after the task in hand, deciding which strategy to use in each situation, or monitoring progress.

In the Leverhulme project we studied teachers at the beginning of the school year, meeting their new classes for the first time, and saw the skill with which first encounters were managed. In most classes, rules became clear quickly and were fairly and consistently enforced. In those classes where this was not the case, relationships soon broke down and behaviour deteriorated, as children 'tested the limits' to see what was and what was not permitted. 'Firm but fair' was how most teachers saw themselves in these first few days.

Our studies of classroom behaviour revealed that most misdemeanours are noisy talk and illicit movement; there was very little of the mayhem portrayed in the popular press. Visiting Martians would describe the average primary class as orderly, but might comment on the amount of chatter not relevant to the task in some classrooms. They would be more likely to hear children being lippy to the teacher in city, rather than country, schools. When pupils were told off, arguments with the teacher occurred in about 12 percent of classes in London schools, compared with 2 or 3 percent elsewhere.

We interviewed more than 400 children to see what they thought about pupil behaviour. Most were aware of what would get them into bother. One 6-year-old showed a clear understanding of the tolerance for mock fights but not for the real thing. 'I just plays on my own with my cousin and some of my friends. We plays a little fight, it's not a real fight, it's a play fight. You just pretend to punch like that (demonstrates mock blow)... You won't get told off... You stand near the wall when you're naughty. I don't stand near the wall. I don't be naughty outside.' I suppose the National Curriculum Council will now be cross with our researcher for not leaping in and teaching him how to conjugate a verb in the present tense.

In one particularly interesting exercise we showed photographs of disruption to both teachers and pupils. According to pupils, teachers would shout a lot in response, but teachers' own replies were much more guarded, and not one used the word 'shout', though most did yell when exasperated. 'I shout at children' is not a phrase that most of us can get through our lips, and you can probably be locked up for it under the Children Act.

I found our studies of questioning and explaining particularly fascinating. Some questions are incomprehensible out of context: 'Have you hidden your tongues?' (to a class that failed to answer a question). 'Did I say go and do a quick scribble?' (to a child whose work was unsatisfactory). About 57 per cent of questions we analysed were to do with management. Only 8 per cent were the sort of higher-order questions that required more than just the recall of information, and I found this a bit disturbing. Though there is no ideal ratio of one type of question to another, my own objective judgement of both the primary and secondary lessons I have analysed is that there is a place for more questions that invite speculation, analysis, grouping and labelling, or a leap of the imagination.

Explaining is the skill most admired and respected by children, and we looked at successful and unsuccessful explanations of topics like 'insects' and 'electricity'. Effective explanations had clear central ideas expressed in appropriate language, examples were usually elicited from pupils rather than given all the time, and the teacher's voice was clear and well modulated. Some ineffective explanations were factually wrong, as teachers struggled to explain scientific principles they did not fully understand themselves, especially in answer to unexpected questions.

Successful explanations were a pleasure to behold. I saw one teacher in a small market town whose pupils all scored virtually full marks in a test given after his lesson on insects. 'Is a bird an insect?' was his starting point, and he built skilfully on the responses to this opening teaser, a 'not' analogy. When I suggested he should write about his teaching, especially as he had so many good ideas, he was overcome by modesty and the fear that his four colleagues might think he was showing off. Imagine surgeons being bashful about their new techniques.

It is a pity that so much debate about primary teaching is stereotyped around crude opposites, like 'traditional' and 'progressive'. Anyone who looks closely at classrooms, would see that a much more subtle and fine grain analysis is needed.

OH BOY
(Originally published in *Times Educational Supplement*, 16.5.1997)

It seems to have been a long time coming, but the twenty-first century is almost here. With more effective medical treatments available, children who are now pupils in schools may live through most of the next 100 years.

As we enter the next millennium it is the under-achievement of boys that has become one of the biggest challenges facing society and schools. Improving their performance should be given the highest priority by the new Government, but not at the expense of girls, whose achievements have improved significantly and should continue to do so.

Alvin Toffler, the American futurologist, said that all education was a vision of the future, and that failure to have a vision was a betrayal of the nation's youth. It is easy to argue this, but not so simple to describe what that future might be. One pressing concern in education today is the need, in a rapidly moving and changing society, to prepare children for work, family and social life. All of these are becoming more demanding and complex.

We live in what is sometimes called a 'credential society'. Jobs that a few years ago required no formal qualifications now ask for GCSEs. Those that wanted A-levels now recruit graduates. Home and family life are tougher to sustain, as loan sharks and other predators hover round the unwary and unschooled. So far as young people are concerned, the entrance fee to society has gone up substantially.

If twenty-first century life is ultra dynamic, then personal qualities like flexibility, imagination, drive, the ability to be a positive member of a team, become vital. This extract from the recruitment literature of a major national employer is typical: 'We'll be looking for people who can be described as "flexible"...You'll actively seek out new experiences...You'll be open-minded and not afraid to challenge the way things are done. Independence is important because in this fast-changing organisation, you may not always have clear paths and procedures to follow.'

It is essential that children leave school well equipped to face an uncertain future. Our national curriculum is about to be revised, with the new version starting in the year 2000. In my book *The Cubic Curriculum*, I argue that in order to prepare children for uncertainty, the school curriculum must be seen in several dimensions, including the subjects being taught, the methods of teaching and learning, and those qualities and characteristics that make us human, like language, aesthetic, personal and social development. Boys, in particular, are failing to achieve their potential in each of these fields.

During the 1970s in the United Kingdom, more than a million jobs were lost in manufacturing industry alone. Another million went in the first five years of the 1980s. The turmoil continued towards the end of the century, and in the first five years of the 1990s, some five million people lost their jobs.

What was notable about these huge losses of traditional forms of employment was that the vast majority of posts that disappeared were unskilled, semi-skilled or barely-skilled. It is true that graduate employment also suffered, but the biggest decline was in areas where machines were brought in to perform the numerous tasks that had previously been carried out by armies of worker ants. Firms that used to employ dozens of boys to load goods on to lorries, replaced them with a couple of fork-lift truck operators. For those with little knowledge or interpersonal skills the prospects became bleak.

Another aspect of higher unemployment was that it appeared to be endemic rather than cyclical. Recessions earlier in the century had been followed by boom times. The order books emptied, but then filled up again, as world or national trading prospects improved. Workers dropped to a 3-day week, or lost their jobs, only to regain exactly the same posts later, often with bonus and overtime payments, as the economy moved into a higher gear. When the cycle stopped it was partly because, in the new automated economy, no employer was going to get rid of two fork-lift trucks and two drivers in order to employ 20 people with large biceps.

If we want to improve significantly the overall national level of achievement for the twenty-first century, then it is the massive under-achievement of boys that must be tackled vigorously. It is causing a major headache to those who educate them, and the evidence of their relatively low performance is now overwhelming at all stages of education.

Consider just some of the evidence. In the 1970s there was justifiable concern about the under-achievement of girls. Many were leaving school at 16 with a portfolio of good O-levels, perfectly able to take A-levels, but not pursuing them. Though predominant in fields like modern languages and literature courses, girls were heavily outnumbered by boys in applications to many other subjects in higher education. They were even denied the opportunity, in some schools, to study technology, or take science to a high level. Quite rightly, sex discrimination legislation outlawed such practices, and teachers gradually became aware of the need to give girls a fair chance.

Now the position has changed dramatically, and girls are outperforming boys on a significant scale. The most recent figures available show the following dire statistics:

- In 1983–84 there was less than a 1 per cent gap in the number of boys (26.3 per cent) and girls (27.2 per cent) who obtained five high grade GCSEs A to C. By 1995–96 the gap had become a gulf, with boys on 39.8 per cent and girls on 49.3 per cent.

- In English at GCSE the difference is huge, with nearly two-thirds of girls (64.4 per cent) achieving a high grade, compared with fewer than half of the boys (46.9 per cent).
- Even in a traditionally 'male' area like design and technology, about half the girls (48.6 per cent) get a high grade, compared with a third of the boys (33.1 per cent).
- At A-level, girls overtook boys in the later 1980s. In 1983–84, there were 11.1 per cent of boys obtaining three or more A-levels, but only 9.5 per cent of girls. By 1994–95 the figures were 20.5 per cent for boys and 24.2 per cent for girls.
- Although until recently universities used to have far more male than female students, the position has now been reversed. In 1995–96 there were 453,600 male students enrolled in full-time undergraduate courses, compared with 470,500 females.

The situation is also bad among lower achievers who do not go on to further and higher education. Recently I spoke to employers in a city with high youth unemployment. A number had made special efforts to find work for 16-year-old boys, but discovered too many were virtually unemployable, lacking interest, drive, enthusiasm, or the social skills increasingly necessary in fields where personal relationships are important. The city has a successful football team and some adolescent boys see themselves as achieving status and success through association with that, rather than from their jobs or academic achievements.

The problem has really started much earlier than adolescence, however. As part of the Leverhulme Primary Improvement Project at Exeter University, we have been studying the progress of several hundred children around the country aged 5 to 11. On NFER reading tests, where 100 is the score of the average child, we found that boys began the school year between 4 and 5 points behind the girls. At the end of the year the figure had hardly changed.

What was worse, the youngest boys we tested, who were six at the beginning of Year 2, were already several points behind the girls in their classes. They never caught up. In each age group we tested from Year 2 to Year 6, the boys began and ended the year at roughly the same distance behind the girls. They start down, and they remain down.

Trying to explain this sustained disadvantage is not easy. It may be a case of later maturation, as girls in primary schools have traditionally done better than boys in language. Recent research, in which brain activity is scanned during language activities, suggests that the female brain is active in both halves, the male brain predominantly in one. Equally it can be said that lower motivation leads to less time being spent on the task in hand, so less learning takes place.

We studied a target group of 6 children in each of several classes. There were 3 boys and 3 girls, covering high, medium and low ability. Teachers rated the boys significantly lower than the girls on attitude to reading, ability to concentrate, determination when facing difficulties, productivity in class, and social skills. They also estimated the help they received at home to be lower, something the boys themselves confirmed.

Language lies at the heart of learning. Yet in the early years, boys find it hard make a good start on reading. From their point of view, it is a more female than male activity. Almost all infant teachers are women, and in the Leverhulme project we found that mothers were much more likely than fathers to read with children at home. Some of the early books they read do not engage the boys, and we discovered that teachers who produced big improvements in reading performance were more likely to match the reading to the pupil, selecting sports or adventure books for those boys who liked such topics.

Behaviour can also be a problem. Boys will sometimes be more disruptive in class than girls. Indeed, they may lose more classroom time because they are sent out the room or even sent home.

Five times as many boys as girls are permanently excluded from school. In secondary schools, 7,191 boys were excluded in 1994–95 compared with 1,663 girls. The pattern begins even in primary schools, where 1,177 boys were excluded compared with 91 girls.

Even if they can get a job, many of the boys now in school will have to retrain several times during their working lives and most of them can look forward to many years of good health in their Third Age, so their appetite for learning must stretch way beyond the years of compulsory schooling.

In order to flourish over what could be a very long lifetime, they will need a firm foundation of knowledge, skills, attitudes and forms of behaviour, alongside positive personal characteristics, such as determination, flexibility, imagination. They will also require the social intelligence and ability to pool their strengths with those of their fellows, as well as the independence of mind to act autonomously. This strong combination of personal and intellectual qualities is particularly important, given the massive explosion of knowledge which continues to gather pace.

If boys are to improve enough to be able to face the next century with confidence we need a massive and co-ordinated attack on their under achievement. There are many areas in which action can be taken and I am proposing a ten-point plan.

The education of all our children to their full potential is said to be our top priority. I repeat that we should not neglect the education for girls when addressing the problems I have identified. However unless we improve significantly the achievement of boys in our society we are storing up immense problems for the whole of the twenty-first century.

A ten-point plan

1 Start early   Boys should be encouraged to attend nurseries, so they make an early start on language activities in particular, and learn to behave well in class.

2 Help at home   More fathers should help at home, especially with reading and writing, so language is not seen as a purely 'female' activity.

3 Early intervention   There should be skilled individual specialist help for the many boys in infant schools who make a slow start to reading. There have been many success stories of 6-year-old boys whose reading improved in the Reading Recovery Programme.

4 Appeal to boys' interests   Humour, adventure and sport are among the topics that appeal to young boys, so these should be incorporated into what they read wherever possible.

5 Improve boys' behaviour   Some boys are easily distracted and then, in turn, distract others. Their behaviour in class needs to improve so they spend more time on task.

6 Raise teacher awareness   When teachers became more aware of girls' under-achievement, results improved. Awareness about boys' poor performance must be raised, not the least amongst boys themselves and their parents, so that trying hard at school is not seen to be 'swottish', but normal.

7 Use new technology   Many young boys like using new technology, such as CD-Roms and virtual reality, and they often concentrate more when they use it.

8 Involve boys in their own learning   Today's pupils are tomorrow's citizens. They need to be directly involved in improving their own performance, so they can set themselves targets, maintain focus, ask questions of themselves, pick out important information, improve relationships, and know when to ask for help.

9 Identify 'at risk' pupils   Early intervention in the primary school for those falling behind is essential, but there should be another safety net in secondary school, so that boys aged 13, likely to be 'at risk' when they leave, are identified and helped.

10 Redesign key stage 4   We need a co-ordinated programme for 14 to 18 year olds for the twenty-first century, in which pupils can choose from a set of what are sometimes called 'academic' and 'vocational' modules, so that programmes can be tailored to individual needs and interests.

WHY RON LEFT THE WENDY HOUSE FOR THE TOILET
(Originally published in *Times Educational Supplement*, 11.6.2004)

According to some research handbooks, nothing goes wrong. Every study has neatly balanced samples, no pupil is ever awkward, or, for that matter, absent. Teachers obediently follow instructions. Statistical tests provide brilliantly clear conclusions.

The writers of these clinically clean, paragon tomes must never have ventured into a real classroom, dragged muttered responses syllable by syllable out of the adolescent acne brigade, been distracted by gruesome tales of a dead rabbit from some 5-year-old with a very runny nose and a livid scab, or witnessed the terrifying sight of data disappearing for ever from a computer screen.

I've been conducting educational research for more than thirty years. Does long service confer immunity from pitfalls and hazards? Does it hell. It just makes you better prepared and fills your head with first-hand tips for the unwary. That said, I think all teachers should carry out research into their own school, class, or the teaching and learning in which they are involved. If keen GPs can monitor diabetics, investigate young patients with glandular fever, or systematically test new treatments, why can't equally curious teachers study their immediate world?

Research is a fundamental human and professional activity, despite the potential pratfalls. Anyway, we expect our pupils to do it as part of their lessons or coursework.

The insider story is fascinating. Sara Delamont of Cardiff University once told how she had to wear white gloves and carry a handbag while she was researching a fee-paying girls' school in Scotland, otherwise she would never have got past the ferocious headmistress.

My Exeter colleague Ron King was known as 'The man in the Wendy house' when he carried out his seminal study of infant schools. As a strictly non-participant classroom observer, Ron had to escape the curious eyes of young children by hiding in the Wendy house, so he could scribble up his notes. If children were playing in it, he retreated to the gents' toilet instead. The staff thought he had a weak bladder.

I once supervised a teacher who said he wanted to do 800 interviews, as that was the number on roll in his school. What is more they would be 'in depth'. No one ever does shallow interviews, of course; all interviews claim to be 'in depth'. The first rule of bog-up avoidance is: pilot what you are going to do first. Even one 'in depth' interview, administered, transcribed and analysed, would reveal how many lifetimes were needed to do 800. Only masochists sign up to the undeliverable.

Another huge error is to use leading questions, as these automatically discredit the answers. A few years ago, one pressure group came up with a blinder. 'Is there too much sex and violence on television and what are you going to do about it?' Er, yes indeed. Not much doubt where you're coming from, sunshine.

Experimental research is notoriously hazardous in education. Most experiments work, because they are conducted by enthusiasts for the programme being tested, who unwittingly or intentionally manipulate the conditions. When psychology PhD students testing out behaviourist learning theory used to run rats through mazes, some of the more unscrupulous were observed giving them a prod: 'Turn left, you little bastard – my thesis is at stake.'

Carrying out a true experiment involves controlling the conditions under which the experimental and control groups operate. Some researchers have tried scripted lessons (you can write questions for teachers to ask but, sadly, not prescribe the answers), or have produced what they claim are 'teacher-proof' materials. Some of these are about as teacher-proof as kerosene is fire-proof.

One experiment, where children filled in specially written story booklets designed to make them think more imaginatively, failed ignominiously. The teacher administering the supposedly teacher-proof programme was Mr Dreary, who constantly told the class how bored they looked. The control group was given to Mr Fizzbang, who had just been on a creative drama course, to do what he liked with. When the post-tests were given, the control group won hands down.

The biggest minefield can be interviewing the family Frankenstein at home. Poisonous snacks, scalding or freezing tea, long-winded interviewees, are the minor problems. Ferocious or – even worse – amorous dogs; unruly toddlers smearing half-chewed lollies over you; grand-dads smoking what smells like, and probably is, shredded horse manure, are a much greater health hazard. 'Yes, we do read with our child at home – when we're not actually killing each other.'

Finally there is writer's block. The data analysed, the computer screen clear. No more wretched hourglass and meaningless triangular warnings about memory, illegal acts and insufficient flobbabytes. Now you just have to write up the results.

Hmmmmm. One more cup of coffee?

One more game of solitaire?

Bugger it. I'll do it tomorrow.

THEORY GOOD, PRACTICE BAD
(Taylor & Francis Education Arena, Discussion Forum, 2003)

A few years ago the Vice Chancellor of a technological university wanted to invite a distinguished engineer to be an honorary professor in his university. He argued his case: the man had masterminded one of the most significant developments in the modern world, involving the delivery of a particular service to millions of homes (I won't say what this was, as it would reveal the person concerned); it was a phenomenal piece of mass engineering by someone who was arguably a modern Brunel.

The university Senate demurred, 'Where were his academic papers? Never mind whether he was a Brunel lookalike, what had he published? Tut tut. Can't have any old Tom, Dick or Michelangelo being called a professor, might bring the university into disrepute.'

Why is intelligent action so despised in academic society? The Research Assessment Exercise would probably give more stars to the person who counted up all the quavers in Mozart's musical works than to Wolfgang Amadeus himself. Build a phenomenal bridge, compose a wonderful symphony, solve the problems of crime or poverty, and you may get an honorary degree from a university. If you want a substantive one you will have to write a thesis about them instead. Writing is simply more valued than doing.

In educational research you are probably better off, in terms of peer esteem, if you pen an article in a journal read only by theoreticians than if you mount an action research project that influences thousands. Work written by subject tutors who work on initial training courses was said to be amongst the weakest submitted for the last Research Assessment Exercise in 2001. Why? Was it really weak? Or was it more practically than theoretically orientated? If the former, then fair enough. If the latter, then shame on us for not valuing intelligent thought and action.

Wittgenstein was one of many outstanding academics who wrote relatively little during his life, but led one of the foremost schools of philosophy of the century. Socrates is highly esteemed, but not as a writer, for his beliefs, practices and arguments were written up by others. Neither would earn a star rating in today's research assessment. Jobbing plodders who churn out routine articles would gain more brownie points for their university.

Yet in educational research many of the great problems and challenges will not be resolved by theoreticians, not yet at any rate. Problem solving in education is more like a wind tunnel than a theoretical model. Suck it and see. Test out some intelligent piece of action, see how it works, refine it, try it again. Eventually it may provide a solution which can then be analysed retrospectively. Solutions often elude the rational a priori approach.

Here is a little problem to solve. Hire the world's finest mathematicians, ballistics experts, climatologists, physicists. Give them an inflated spherical object of a certain weight and challenge them to discover exactly how much force, at what angle and in which direction will be needed to deliver it accurately to an object moving at 20 mph some 50 m away. How long will be needed (a) to complete the calculation, (b) to construct a machine that will successfully complete the assignment? A day? A week? A year?

Next, give David Beckham a football and five seconds later it will be nestling precisely at its intended target. No written calculations, reports, analyses, a split second to decide. Ah, but surely that is mere rudimentary animal cunning, not cerebral at all (hard to see how you would do it without a brain).

I am not, for one moment, arguing that there is no place for theory in educational research, far from it. My argument is more that intelligent action is not at all esteemed. Indeed the very word 'action' seems to disqualify the descriptor 'intelligent'. If you actually do it, how can it rank alongside the more ethereal?

The nice thing about theory, of course, is that it does not have to be very good, or even be demonstrably accurate. Many theories in education are either completely untested, merely paraded, or they are pure casuistry: this is a theory because one can quote an example of it in practice. Schools fail because they educate children solely for work, the bell at the end of the lesson being like the factory hooter (Marxist interpretation). Schools fail because they do not prepare children properly for the world of work (capitalist interpretation).

Intelligent action is not often seen as being founded on rigorous enquiry, though it might have been, nor is it regarded as being the application of profound scholarship, when again this might be the case. Consequently it goes down in history as something ephemeral, transient, insubstantial, driven by the groin rather than the brain. Try writing a school textbook and the curled sneers will soon dilute the pleasure.

Programmed learning was one of the most carefully and systematically researched forms of teaching in the history of schooling. It appeared, on the surface at any rate, to meet all its own criteria: self-pacing, immediate reinforcement and confirmation, small steps at a time, with remedial loops and subroutines for those who fell off the conveyor belt. Yet the products of it were so brain-corrodingly tedious, and the reaction of learners so negative, that it lapsed as a serious mode of teaching.

I would like to see a much more serious exploration of the intuitive, mercurial, action-oriented than we have seen so far. Rational a priori approaches to enquiry have stood us in good stead, particularly in the sciences. But in human affairs there may be some time to wait before all is explained. Teacher effectiveness research, for example, is like gene mapping: it would take millions in cash and labour even to scratch the surface of what constitutes effective teaching, because of the near infinite variety of micro- and macro-contexts in which it takes place.

In the meantime pragmatists are left with trial and error learning, simply because action-oriented research, and indeed intelligent action itself, are seen as (a) problematic and (b) beneath the salt in terms of their prestige and intellectual standing. It would take a massive change in belief to reverse the situation, but it is a direction that should be explored.

CHAPTER 18

EDUCATION, SATIRE AND POLEMIC

I suppose my use of satire is unconventional for an academic. Every fortnight, for nearly a quarter of a century, I have written satirical articles on the back page of the *Times Educational Supplement*. Sometimes the driver is an off-shoot of my own research and investigation, so it is an unusual, possibly unique genre. It is a healthy outlet for pent-up emotions, not easily releasable in more conventional writing. There are teachers who think I spend all my time writing satire, perhaps because I have also written scripts for the satirical impressionist Rory Bremner, or even that there are two of us – E. C. Wragg, the straight academic who writes sober books, and his reprobate brother, Ted Wragg. The pieces reproduced here cover about twenty years. Most fun is satirising politicians – Sir Keith Joseph, Kenneth Baker, Kenneth Clarke, Tony Blair – but there are countless other easy targets. I think I had more letters about the 1990 article 'Who put the ass in assessment?', lampooning the testing arrangements for 7 year olds, than anything I have ever written.

SIR KEITH: EPILOGUE
(Originally published in *Times Educational Supplement*, 30.5.1986)

There is a phase in life known as pre-retirement. It is those twilight years of a working career when some people prematurely hang up their boots and spend their time crossing days off the calendar or throwing darts at photographs of the boss.

There are other kinds of pre-retirement phenomena. One common state is that demob happiness when nothing can be taken seriously. A delirious head once told me: 'I'll sign anything at the moment, because six weeks from now I'm fireproof'. Her corridor was jammed with smiling teachers clutching scraps of paper and order forms.

Sir Keith Joseph manifested a third type of pre-retirement behaviour, that of the epitaph writer, for it is not unknown for distinguished people in positions of leadership to spend the last few years of their career imagining their eventual obituary. It was especially vital for Sir Keith to quit on a winning brief when he arrived at the DES in September 1981, because the press had labelled him as the dotty minister who, in his previous incarnations, had not only endorsed high-rise flats, but also rescued lame ducks in industry after preaching the need for government abstinence. He arrived eager to *do* something.

Back in 1981 the bookmakers, had they taken bets on these unpredictable matters, might well have offered evens on Sir Keith's chances of winning the Epitaph Stakes. After all, he succeeded a string of ministers whose impact on education had been about as potent as a speck of dust landing on the Pacific.

Fred Mulley infuriated his officials by protesting that the only power he had was to close temporary buildings in school playgrounds; Shirley Williams was loveable, talked a good game, but failed to deliver; and Mark Carlisle never got beyond tens and units. Only a pulled hamstring, it seemed, could prevent Sir Keith cantering up the home straight and collecting his winner's sash and pension book, before being driven off to a well-earned timeless graze in the House of Lords.

Evaluating Sir Keith's achievements these past four-and-half years is like filling in a profile on a student who gets marks of A or E with little in between. After Fred Carlisle and Mark Prentice, or was it Reg Mulley?, the memory plays cruel tricks with these non-entities – a reforming minister was quite a change, and reform he did, with the vigour of a thinking zealot. Even if one did not endorse his every move, he must deserve grade as for his courage in grasping the nettle of 16-plus examination reform, expressing more than concern for the bottom 40 per cent, rescuing technical education when it was in danger of slipping off the curriculum, trying to improve the quality of teaching and teacher education, strengthening parents' rights, ending the politicians' stranglehold on governing bodies, and securing a better financial base for in-service training.

In addition, he deserves a grade A for not being afraid of offending his own party (but then he was not afraid of offending anybody else, so why should his party be exempt?), for his considerable industry, because anyone who reads every HMI report is either an incorrigible masochist or first in line for the next George Cross, and for his flexibility, as evidenced by his rejection of a parents' majority on governing bodies, or the linking of teachers' pay and assessment, in the light of negative reactions.

The debit side of his profile records how he failed monumentally on something he himself always valued highly, the ability to manage his fellow human beings. Many heads, administrators and teachers are sad that he allowed that precious commodity, goodwill, to evaporate. Goodwill in schools is a little bit like the helium in a balloon, invisible and taken for granted. It is only when it is removed that you realize what he did. For demolishing it, something even the most cretinous and ham-fisted of his predecessors had failed to do, Sir Keith must be given E quintuple minus.

The weakness of his less competent twin brother, Sir Monty Python, was of two kinds. The first was a psychological inability to utter soothing words about teachers. I have no idea why this should be. Perhaps he was unkindly treated by teachers in his youth. Was he, one wonders, given a detention for putting tin tacks on the teacher's chair, running a book on the Derby, or smoking behind the bike shed? Hardly, I imagine him as the bright, industrious pupil picking up high grades and eschewing the sort of behaviour that would have brought him up before the beak.

During a radio programme, in which I had chided him for not recognizing the countless good things that teachers accomplished, he said he would like to give more praise, but, if he did so, large numbers of parents would say: 'That man's talking rubbish'. After the recording I promised to send him some examples of good practice which he could use. A few months later I wrote to him giving him details of the notable achievements of teachers, pupils, and indeed parents, in the 12,300 schools that had surveyed the United Kingdom as part of the BBC Domesday Project. I pointed out that it was the most impressive collaborative project by such a partnership anywhere in the world, and he could safely mention it in a speech as a plus for the education system. He never did.

The second kind of ineptitude showed in the many bizarre Crazy Horse stories about his regular eccentricities. Most of them stemmed from his essentially alien status as KJ the benign extra-terrestrial mega-genius, a million light years away from the proletariat in particular. Hence the substantially true stories of conversations with bemused LEA officials ('Are your primary schools really rigorous?'), low-achieving fifth years ('What do you think of integrated humanities?'), or, it is said, with his boiled egg during breakfast. Actually it was probably not a boiled egg at all, but rather his leader Zarg.

Yet each time I met him I liked him more, and it is a pity that most teachers never saw him relaxed and good-humoured. On television he was a nightmare, unhappy, tense, his craggy features etched deeper by the minute with angst. With radio he was more comfortable, though still not entirely at ease. I did four Radio 4 interviews with him in his enormous throne room at the DES. 'Why are parents having to pay so much money towards the basics of education like books, Sir Keith?' Deep dismay. Sir Keith sighs, sinks his head deep into his hands and lapses into a 30-second coma. 'You see ... the Government ... the Government ... just a minute, I'm going to get my syntax wrong ... are we still rolling? ...' Another 20 seconds of anguished silence, BBC sound recordist and producer go quietly crazy. It was not his fault, thoughtful man that he is, that the wretched mass medium required a convincing over-simplification of the complex in less than a minute.

Another face that was never seen publicly was the liberal politician defending schools against the intemperate right wing. He once came to address a Saturday meeting of his political supporters in our own lecture theatre. My colleague Professor Richard Pring and I were due to meet him afterwards. As the room filled up with a mixture of solid citizens and the kind of ferocious retired brigadiers who send nervous citizens like me scuttling for cover, Richard and I debated how we might eavesdrop on this momentous event without actually donning false beards and dark glasses.

We decided to tiptoe up the back stairs and hide in the projection room, somewhat undignified for two university professors, but, if rumbled, we could always pretend to be cleaners, or argue that Sir Keith's cuts had forced us to use the attic as our study. The event was marvellous to behold. As one beetroot-faced critic after another sprang up to ask what he proposed to do about all the left-wing teachers fomenting revolution in South-West schools ('Where on earth were they?' we asked ourselves), Sir Keith urged them to produce evidence, not hot air, and defended schools in a way not often witnessed publicly.

I shall want to remember him as a bright, likeable and compassionate man who had the best of intentions. His tendency to invent policy on the hoof could be alarming, but at least he cared a great deal and worked hard at his brief and that must count for something in a world where politicians frequently appear to the public to be indolent and indifferent.

Teachers are the easiest people in the world to work with, and unfortunately it is here that Sir Keith irrevocably and comprehensively blew it. I suspect his successor, Mr Bun the Baker of the smiling spectacles, will reap credit for the angular Sir Keith's groundwork, but I hope history accords Sir Keith some decent measure of recognition too.

He reminds me of the man in the restaurant seen weeping profusely by embarrassed fellow diners. Eventually one plucks up enough courage to ask him why he is so upset.

The man stops sobbing briefly and replies: 'I don't know why, but nobody likes me, fish-face'. If only he could have brought himself to love teachers just a little.

THE FARCE OF THE FLASHLIGHT BRIGADE
(Originally published in *Times Educational Supplement*, 4.11.1988)

There was a distinct sense of gloom among the conference of primary heads I was addressing. They had just heard on the radio that Mr Bun, fresh from his trans-Siberian tour of photo opportunities, had announced in his speech to the Conservative Party conference that he was going to restore traditional teaching to primary schools, whatever that might have meant.

Most seemed afraid that he might be knocking on their school door the next morning, accompanied by his usual posse of photographers, cracking a horsewhip and shouting, 'Chant your tables, you swine'.

I tried to reassure them that, if you want to be Prime Minister, you don't harangue your party conference about the virtues of progressive primary education. Tell them you will restore capital punishment for teachers who don't set daily spelling tests and a standing ovation is assured. Party conference time is a game with its own set of rules and conventions. The primary heads were still inconsolable.

It set me thinking about what a daft and over-simplified debate it had all become. The very word 'traditional' immediately secures knee-jerk reactions. Mutter it to one group and a round of drinks will follow to toast solid British virtues such as industry, determination and thoroughness. Utter it in different company and the jeers will ring in your ears as people assume you are out of date, backward looking and embarrassed to the tips of your sensible shoes.

I reflected on a class of 7 year olds I had been teaching. Had I been traditional or progressive, or, for that matter, did anyone give a hang? I had told them things, which sounds trad enough, but we had done a fair bit of group work, so perhaps I am progressive. On the other hand, I had told some of the groups what to do, so I must be a traditional progressive, apart from when they are allowed to discuss the task I have set them with fellow pupils, because at these times I am a progressive traditional.

What the primary heads feared was that Mr Bun would try to import the styles of teaching he had seen in between posing for snapshots in the Soviet Union. It would not be so strange if Comrade Bunski had been over-impressed by the sort of primary school we used to have, in the nineteenth century, since therein lie the roots of his Education Act.

Just in case too much nostalgia for those awful days overwhelms us, perhaps we should recall some of their less happy features. Much of the time young children chanted by heart, slogans and epithets they ill-understood, like the capes and bays from Blackpool to Hong Kong when they knew neither what a cape nor a bay was. It made the 'ere we go', 'ere we go' equivalents of modern football crowds sound positively cerebral.

While he was in Russia Mr Bun did, of course, give his own exceptionally traditional lesson, which one journalist told me would have secured E-minus on any teacher appraisal. It was shown on national television news when he was seen declaiming 'The Charge of the Light Brigade' to an utterly poleaxed group of Russian teenagers.

My journalist friend tells me it was one of the rummest events he has seen in his cynical life. Apparently Bunski rushed into this room full of bewildered Russian students and produced, as if by magic, a class set of *Bun's Bumper Funbook of English Verse* which he just happened to have with him.

A hapless DES menial had lugged them across Siberia waiting for the right photo opportunity. He is probably now in hospital suffering from a double hernia. It was as if Gorbachev had descended on some unsuspecting GCSE class at Little Piddlington Comprehensive, put on a record of *Gorby's Greatest Hits* and proceeded to do a Cossack dance for the assembled press.

Suddenly this crazy stranger with the manic smile and glinting glasses was ranting on about a battle at which 600 rode into the valley of death. Here was the embarrassing situation of a son of the nation which, during the Crimean War, sent the Light Cavalry Brigade on one of the most futile charges in military history, reading a poem about it to the descendants of those who had slaughtered them. It had all the ingredients of the bad trad lesson, the oblivious preaching to the uncomprehending.

So why had Bun suddenly gone a bundle on resurrecting what was condemned as a failure by successive nineteenth-century critics? Listen carefully to the words of his poem and all becomes clear. Canon to the left of him, Canon to the right of him. There were also a few Nikons, Leicas and Sony television cameras back and front.

WHO PUT THE ASS IN ASSESSMENT?

(Originally published in *Times Educational Supplement*, 16 2 1990)

There has been a great deal of public and press concern that the new ailment which has been found in cattle could be caught by humans. The symptoms are unsteady gait and uncontrolled lassitude. A related form of the illness has now been detected in teachers.

I refer, of course, to Mad Curriculum Disease, the symptoms of which are unsteady gait and uncontrolled laughter.

I first realized I had caught Mad Curriculum Disease when I noticed people giving me strange looks as I lurched around unsteadily while laughing uproariously at my latest mailing from the School Examinations and Assessment Council. If you have not already received your *Guide to Teacher Assessment* packs A, B and C, then get hold of these three gems quickly.

They don't actually cure Mad Curriculum Disease, but they do confirm whether or not you have got it.

Take the first of the three exceedingly glossy brochures in your right hand, open it at the first page where Philip Halsey, chairman and chief executive, has his cheery 'welcome aboard' statement and progress through at a steady pace, deciding at the bottom of each page whether to laugh or cry. I decided to laugh, Phil, that's why I am currently in the Mad Curriculum Disease isolation ward.

The doctors tell me that, when they first brought me in here, I was not sure whether I had been reading about measuring children or measuring curtains. The first rib-ticklers were the various checklists. Honestly, Phil, I couldn't keep a straight face. From the moment you defined the word 'recently' for me, just in case its meaning had eluded me over the years, I was doubled up. The problem was that I couldn't think of any serious answers to the checklist questions. For example, in reply to the item, 'Was the child puzzled, worried?' I wrote, 'No, but I was'.

Next, as instructed, I turned to Chapter 2 on 'Test anxiety'. When I read your question, 'Which tasks might make it necessary for a teacher to disguise the intention to assess children?' it cracked me up again. Do you have any cute tips on actual disguises, Phil? Would it fool them if I dressed up as Santa Claus and went in saying, 'Ho, ho, ho, everybody, look what Father Christmas has brought you to celebrate the middle of February, a sack full of standard assessment tasks'?

I was, by the way Phil, immensely grateful for the section headed 'problems'. I am glad you pointed out for me 'Children do not progress at the same rate', as

I would never have spotted this. Similarly, there was the helpful bit which said that 'the children may "run away" with or prematurely complete the activity'. Mine just ran away with it, Phil, muttering, 'Why do we have to do all this, we're only seven?' or 'Bugger this for a game of soldiers', and haven't been seen since.

When I reached the section that asks whether children were frequently absent, I had to report that mine were now permanently absent, so I turned, as instructed, to Chapter 7 and the tips on how to deal with absentees. I must admit, Phil, I was a bit confused here, because your advice says, 'The safest course with such children may be to increase the frequency of assessment rather than take short-cuts in curriculum delivery'.

I don't want to appear churlish, but my problem is this: they're not actually here, Phil, so it is not easy to test them more frequently.

I'm afraid the Mad Curriculum Disease struck me again and I was left pounding the floor helplessly with mirth.

In any case, you know me. Would I take a short-cut delivering the curriculum? What with the one-way system round here nowadays and the van reluctant to start on these cold mornings, it's bad enough delivering the milk, let alone the curriculum.

In the same section you will recall, you ask whether 'children became obsessed with your record book'. Mine did, Phil, I'm afraid. Several followed me around all day trying to grab it, and one actually ate it. That solved the problem you raise under 'Clipboards and checklists', when you ask if it is possible to 'minimize the intrusiveness of the device'.

Incidentally, Phil, I am very worried about all the reporting and recording of this caper. You know where you say 'Teachers do not need reminding that planning is essential. But they may need reminding that it requires time' – well thanks again for the reminder, you're a pal. However, I did feel a teensy bit overwhelmed by all the pages of coding you suggest, such as: '10 MA 4a – understand and use language associated with angle', '16 SC 3b – be able to measure time with a sundial'. The second of these is quite handy, because we can't afford a clock, but does it have to be so complicated with all these elaborate codes?

Have you any idea how long it is going to take for teachers to fill all this garbage in, Phil, even if they haven't got Mad Curriculum Disease? I gather that your outfit, SEAC, was keen to publish everything by attainment target, but that Ministers wanted something simpler. Good old Ministers, is all I can say.

We have 17 attainment targets in science, 14 in maths, between 5 and 8 in other subjects. Eventually there will be at least 70 of these. Can you tell me, Phil, what would be the point of giving any child, let alone a 7-year-old, a string of 70 digits? And what about those who get 70 grades, all at level 1?

Do you realize that in 1992, when test scores are published, the term 'level 1' will become the new form of playground abuse, replacing 'thickie' and 'spasmo' of yesteryear?

Finally, Phil, thanks for the mnemonic you made up to help me remember everything in your three packs, you know – INFORM, where each letter is the beginning of a telling phrase. The Mad Curriculum Disease has really got a hold on me now, so I'm not sure I've remembered it all perfectly, but I think it went like this:

Is this monumental bullshit really necessary?
No one who applies it to the letter will remain sane.
For goodness' sake throw it in the bin and start again.
Only 25 hours a day will be needed.
Radically reduce the bureaucracy.
More teachers will quit the profession if you don't.

DESCARTES THINKS BUT CLARKE DISNEY
(Originally published in *Times Educational Supplement*, 7.2.1992)

The news that several teachers had applied for jobs with Euro-Disney in France was depressing, especially when some said they did not care what job they took so long as they could escape, but it did not surprise me. It was probably the best chance they would ever get to present Mickey Mouse with a Kenneth Clarke watch – no hands, just two fingers pointing at the nearest school. Imagine arriving in Paris and finding that Clarkie and Michael Fallon had landed the plum jobs as Donald Duck and Goofy.

I nearly joined them myself when I read that Kenneth Clarke had been described by a colleague as 'one of the party's deeper thinkers'. *One of the party's deeper thinkers?* We are talking huge national emergencies here. Dial 999 immediately. Ask for the whole lot – police, ambulance, fire brigade, 7th Tank Regiment. If Clarkie is the party's Plato, then please, Euro-Disney, hire me immediately as a chipmunk, Snow White, anything, before I meet the party's Pluto.

Take the National Curriculum, for example, what is desperately needed here is partly better thinking, partly better management. Anyone with more than 10 brain cells, Plato or Pluto, can see that it has become exactly what was predicted: a nightmare of 10 discrete, overly prescriptive, separately conceived subjects, rather than an intelligent framework for an organic whole curriculum. A real thinker and manager would find a way of making the enterprise simpler, clearer, challenging, but feasible.

Back in late July 1987, when Kenneth Baker began a lengthy consultation process that was to last well into the following week, some 11,790 people wrote in to offer their comments on the proposed National Curriculum. Many were in favour of a central core, but, according to Julian Haviland, who read all the replies and then summarised them in his book *Take Care, Mr Baker!*, precisely 11,790 out of 11,790 were against what was being proposed. This must still be the British, Commonwealth, European, World and Inter-galactic record for fore-warning.

Unfortunately Kenneth Baker, star of the Hollywood blockbuster *jungle Macho Guy* ('Me future leader [pounds chest], me plough on to end of furrow, me no deviate under any circumstances from crappy plan') ignored all the unambiguous advice about the folly of locking 10 different groups of subject enthusiasts in 10 different rooms for several weeks. Everyone else knew that what they collectively produced would not cohere and would probably add up to at least 200 per cent of the week.

In theory there was a way out, as the National Curriculum Council would later make sense of disparate and possibly self-contradictory proposals. Had John MacGregor, the only real ministerial thinker and manager in recent years, stayed at the DES, this two-tier strategy would have worked. Unfortunately the next Hollywood blockbuster saw the screen debut of Kenneth Clarke in *Jungle Macho Guy* 2 ('Me future leader [tries to pound chest, has difficulty finding it, eventually swings fist, but misses], me plough on to end of six-pack, me deep-thinking Greek philosopher Pluto'), and the whole Silly Symphony then became political, more about power and control than sense.

The problem is that the first sifting of National Curriculum documents was usually done by right-wing pressure groups, whose pronouncements were given more prominence in the press, and taken much more seriously by ministers, than the original reports. So English was supposed to have no grammar or structure, history no facts, and music was all reggae and no Mozart. The truth of the matter is that Brian Cox, chairman of the English working party, has had to write his own book to put the record straight (*Cox on Cox*, a very good, if disturbing, read), and the history syllabus is dripping with knowledge spread over five millennia. Many of our best classical musicians wrote to John Major saying they *liked* the music report and did not want children spending half their time learning how to spell Beethoven, instead of composing and performing.

Were Kenneth Clarke really a good thinker and manager, he would now get the National Curriculum reduced to a single pamphlet, as in most other countries, introduce some flexibility and imagination, and abandon the empty rhetoric about teachers being trendy progressives who do not believe that children should know anything. Instead he neither thinks nor manages. His 'thinking' is confined to stating the blindingly obvious, like saying that trainee teachers should be able to control a class, as if no one had ever thought of it before. Not exactly Immanuel Kant.

His 'management' consists of flooding schools with more and more changes, and then having the cheek to berate teachers, in a television interview, for being unwilling to face up to change, as if there were only one or two minor amendments to cope with.

It is customary to say that people with Clarkie's penchant for management could not manage a whelk stall. But have you ever wondered what would happen if he really did apply the management philosophy he employs with teachers and the National Curriculum to the proverbial whelk stall?

Just imagine you are working behind the counter of the great thinker's whelk stall, ''Arry Stottle's Mucho Macho Whelk Emporium'. The first thing he would do is deliver 20 tons of whelks. Before you had time to unpack them, 50 tons of mussels, 60 tons of periwinkles and 70 tons of cockles would arrive. By now up to your ears in marine gastropods, you would just be able to see 100 pantechnicons pulling in to drop off loads of cabbages, lettuce and tomatoes.

As you disappear from view, smothered, unable to find a single bloody whelk, let alone sell anybody one, consoled only by the thought that, with Baker and Clarke in charge, there will be no need to order oil and vinegar for the salad dressing, you are dimly aware of the great philosopher telling the press the usual Kant: it is all your fault and you will have to stop being a trendy whelk-seller. If Euro-Disney is looking for a really deep thinker to play the part of Dopey, then Kenneth Clarke, the Ludwig Wittgenstein of Westminster, must be their man.

ON THE WARPATH WITH SPIFFY
(Originally published in *Times Educational Supplement*, 19.2.1999)

Why does education use so many military metaphors? It must be nostalgia for the 1940s. You would think that World War III had broken out to read some newspaper stories about education. Schools are 'beleaguered'. Superheads are 'parachuted in' to rescue failure. Teachers are the 'troops', heads 'run a tight ship'. It is complete tosh.

Any normal professional debate about a commonplace educational issue soon becomes a 'battleground' with two opposing factions 'lined up' against each other, before someone 'fires the first round'. Everyone tries to 'capture the middle ground', while 'taking no prisoners' of course, until one side emerges 'victorious' and goes on to 'claim the spoils'. Bang bang, I'm king of the castle.

How on earth, for example, does 'parachuting in' actually work? I suspect that, in reality, someone merely says, 'Let's get old George in, he'll soon sort them out', whereupon old George downs his gin and tonic, removes his cardigan, puts on his least threadbare St Michael suit and swans off to ratchet Gasworks Comprehensive up the league tables.

To read the military account of events, however, you would think there was some secret airbase where superheads are trained in readiness for action. Probably in a camouflaged hangar in deepest Norfolk, at this very moment the crack Superhead Squadron is gearing up for action after their basic training, just as in those 1950s war films with Richard Attenborough and Kenneth More.

So let's go the whole hog, mix up the metaphors, clear the decks, splice the main-brace, chocks away, look for the hun in the sun, prang the beggars, give Jerry a thrashing, back to blighty, damned good show all round, angels one five, fancy a snifter, mine's a double, tickety boo old bean, roger and out. Norfolk, here we come.

'Right chaps, pay attention.This is it. We're going in.'

'Sir, have we got time to ring our loved ones?'

'Sorry Spiffy. Hun's on the warpath, I'm afraid.Time to scramble. Now some of us may not come back, so let's just pause to think briefly of the folks back home, and then it's time to get airborne.'

'What about kit, sir?'

'It's standard issue on this mission. Make sure you've got your two key documents: Charles Atlas's *You Too Can Have a Body Like Mine* and your *Bluffer's Guide to the National Curriculum*. Then you should have your list of sound bites.'

'The sound bites are a bit dicky, sir. Any chance of some new ones?'

'No can do, Fortescue, you'll have to make do with the old ones. Stick to your top three sound bites, if possible, that's: "Tough targets will be set", "Firm action will be taken" and "No stone will be left unturned in our quest for higher standards and expectations". Keep using the word "tough" in every sentence.'

'What do the sound bites mean, sir?'

'Mean, Simkins? We're about to parachute in and you talk about meaning? Damn it, man, we're here to rescue failing schools, not ponce about doing a bally philosophy degree. Now if you look at the map, you'll see where we're going. Jenkins, you and Taffy take out Swinesville School and Community College.'

'Is that both of them, sir, or just the one?'

'Both. The Community College bit is just a temporary hut with a half-sized snooker table and a juke box. If your chute doesn't open and one of you roman candles straight into the bike shed, the other one scrapes him off and buries him under a bush. Kipper, you take command of Scumbag Primary. Have you got your spelling tests?'

'Roger, sir.'

'Once you land, chute packed tight and hidden behind the dustbins. Hush Puppies on and straight into the staffroom. As soon as you open the door, lob number one sound bite "Tough action will be taken" and then suspend the first three pupils you meet in the corridor, for dumb insolence. Any questions before we scramble?'

'Just one, sir, If I don't come back, could you...I mean, supposing by tomorrow I've, well, bought it, would you mind awfully taking this parcel round to Felicity? It's got great sentimental value.'

'Of course, Spiffy, What is it?'

'It's my £70,000 a year salary cheque.'

DIGGING HOLES IN MATHS TESTS
(Originally published in *Times Educational Supplement,* 18.2.2000)

The maths test set by the Teacher Training Agency (TTA) for student teachers brought a tear to my eye. Good old TTA. All those 'realistic' sums based on the mathematics that teachers are supposed to know, like working out scores on tests, reminded me of sums in my childhood.

'If it takes two men four hours to dig a hole six feet square and three feet deep, how long will it take nine men to fill a bath?' Well, it was something like that. The memory plays cruel tricks after a few years.

My whole childhood seemed to be full of men digging holes and people filling up baths. I loved it. 'Realistic maths', that's what it was all about.

Indeed, you may have been wondering why every town, city and country area in the whole land has been dug up during the last year or two. Don't believe anything you read in the press about laying cable for the white-hot communications revolution. It is all lies. Not one inch of cable has even been laid.

In fact, it is people of my generation, digging all those holes we practised so long for in our childhood. After years of withdrawal symptoms we finally broke out and decided to apply our hard-won 'realistic' maths. Me and my mates will be popping round to fill your bath some time next week.

But the interesting thing about all this 'realistic' maths was that it was only realistic on the planet Neptune. If one man can dig a hole in four hours, how long will it take two men? Two hours? No, only in maths tests. In real life it would not be so simple.

Think about it. Two men would chat to each other, swap a few jokes to while away the time, find snags, get in each other's way. They would take at least four hours, exactly the same as one man on his own. Four men would require even longer: probably write a forward plan, fill in a docket, hold a safety meeting, elect a union rep. I would say ten hours at a conservative guess.

The TTA will have to be very careful before asserting that its maths test assesses the sort of competence teachers need in their daily job. If you are an experienced teacher you are actually able to operate a kind of maths that even Einstein could never fathom, for it has its own logic and rules.

So I offer the TTA my own set of 'realistic' maths questions.

Question: If it takes a child two minutes to write one sentence, how long will it take to write ten sentences?
Answer: An hour.
Reason: That's how long the lesson lasts. All written work expands to fill the total time available.

Question: If a class of children can walk a mile in twenty minutes, how long will it take to walk the half mile from the city baths back to school?
Answer: Thirty minutes.
Reason: Darren Rowbottom will have lost his wallet and everyone will have to go back and search for it.

Question: A teacher starts marking a set of thirty books at 6 p.m. If each book takes three minutes to mark, at what time will all the books have been completed?
Answer: 7:45 next morning.
Reason: Mark ten books, watch *Eastenders;* mark four more, kids want their supper; mark another couple, kids falling out; mark five more, one little sod refuses to clean his teeth; bugger it, it's now 10 o'clock, I'm knackered; tell you what, I'll get up early and do the rest tomorrow.

Question: Sally Farnes-Barnes takes a school test where the maximum score obtainable is fifty marks. She gets ten marks in section A of the test and two marks in section B. What is her final mark?

Answer: 87 per cent.

Reason: Her dad is chairman of governors and decisions about performance-related pay are being made next week.

Only seasoned pros will get all these sums right. Nobel Prize-winning mathematicians don't stand an earthly.

TELL SID: BEWARE OF FLOBBABYTES
(Originally published in *Times Educational Supplement*, 17.3.2000)

There is a bloke called Sid Cyberspace who is ruining my life. I suspect he is also giving a hard time to everyone else working in education.

Sid is an obsessive twenty-four-hour-a-day workaholic who never sleeps. I don't know what he looks like, where he lives, or what he eats for breakfast. I only know what he does, or rather what he probably does, since I have never met him.

'Did you get my e-mail?'
'What e-mail?'
'Don't say the e-mail is down again. We've been having problems all day.'

That is just one typical example of Sid Cyberspace at work. He spends much of his time tampering with the Internet and e-mails.

Before anyone is awake he is busy typing neat little screen notes with yellow exclamation marks, saying 'connection to server has been severed', 'host not known', and 'all proxies are down'. They are as informative as an Albanian thesaurus to most of us, farcical even, but that is Sid's style.

He used to work for the railways, writing those smeared felt-tip messages on whiteboards: 'Trains to Little Piddlington will be delayed because of operating difficulties in the Greater Piddlington area.' 'Operating difficulties' meant that some poor passenger, driven to desperation by Sid's little japes, had hurled himself off a bridge.

The moment you log on to your computer, Sid Cyberspace will slip in one of his bits of gibberish. As a result you can never be certain that your e-mails have been received, so you send them again, just to make sure. That is why e-mails, like buses, often arrive in pairs.

In offices, schools, universities, I see person after person sitting in front of a screen, staring vacantly. What did people working in education do before computers started to dominate their lives, for goodness' sake? Talk to someone? Read books? Teach?

Why, in former simpler times, did we waste our time on these trivial pastimes? We could have been gazing longingly at our monitor, waiting for Sid's wretched hourglass to go away.

Just when you've had enough and want to close your computer down, escape at long last from the cyberworld and re-enter the real one, blinking uncertainly in the light, rubbing your eyes, wondering who these people with legs and a head are, what does Sid do? He flashes up his bloody hourglass.

So you sit there, open mouthed, hopelessly hooked to the end of time, in my case screaming, 'Come on, shut down, you evil bastard.' When, in sheer desperation, you simply pull the plug, just to get rid of the irritating little icon, Sid waits until the next time you switch on to get his revenge.

'Your computer was shut down prematurely.' Yes, Sid, I know it was. I pulped it with a sledge hammer, so I could get some sleep. It is no good protesting. He will make you run Scandisc, or Rumpelstiltskin or something, before you can play again.

Then you bump into one of Sid's human-form pals, not realising they are his agents. Their job is to tell you that you need an even bigger, faster hard disc and yet more RAM. You've probably got 64 trillion megabytes of junk already, but Sid's mates will talk you into buying another truck load.

The correct scientific term for this phenomenon is 'Sid's Law of Halves'. According to Sid's Law you always have exactly half of what you actually need. You've got 32 flobbabytes? What a pity, Sid's chums will gleefully pronounce. You should have at least 64. Only for a while that is, because once you've got 64, you will need 128.

Unfortunately you cannot outrun him. He is insatiable. He gulps down bowls full of ROM and RAM like cornflakes. In the end you actually phone people to check if your e-mail has arrived. The tinkling noise from your computer is Sid laughing hysterically at the irony of it.

I now know what we in education must do. Each of us should buy a million flobbabytes of everything and ram it all into our computer in a tangled heap. That will show him. If Sid Cyberspace is in there, I hope the spiteful little bugger suffocates.

TAKE TONY ZOFFIS' BULLETS AWAY
(Originally published in *Times Educational Supplement*, 22.9.2000)

Apparently the armed services are so short of money they cannot afford to pay for ammunition, so somebody has to shout 'bang!' instead.

> 'What do you do in the army then?'
> 'Er, I'm the bloke who shouts "bang!"'

I have been baffled for some time about a man whose job it is to shout 'bang!' at those working in education. I kept hearing his name – Tony Zoffis – over and over again.

> 'Where's that funny idea come from?'
> 'Tony Zoffis.'

According to journalists this Tony Zoffis firmly believes that attacking teachers pushes you up the opinion polls, sad if true. But what was the origin of the name Zoffis? Italian, maybe?

Then it dawned on me. There should be a glottal stop, if you'll pardon the expression, after the 'z' sound – Tonyz (glottal stop) Offis. At last it made sense. It was *Tony's Office*, the Prime Minister's hidden coterie.

The latest 'bang!' from Signor Zoffis to strafe the teaching profession, billed in the press as an 'attack', was Tony Blair's speech about comprehensive schools having too much mixed-ability teaching and not coping with able pupils. It seemed contrary to such facts as exist.

> *Point 1*   The attack is odd, coming immediately after the record numbers of GCSE and A-level successes, including those obtaining top A grades.

Point 2 Some comprehensive schools may be poor, but as a genre they have been a success. One in ten pupils went to university in the 1960s, when they were introduced, and about 80 per cent of school leavers had absolutely nothing to show for their secondary schooling. Now only 7 per cent of pupils leave with no certificate, nearly half the population gets five high-grade GCSEs, a third go to university.

Point 3 A survey of 1,560 comprehensive schools showed mixed-ability teaching operates mainly in the first year. In the second year 83 per cent of schools use ability setting, and by the third year over 93 per cent do so.

(Caroline Benn and Clyde Chitty, *Thirty Years On*,
David Fulton Publishers, 1996)

Another oddity was the criticism of what the prime minister called the comprehensive schools' 'one-size-fits-all mentality'. This seemed both unfair and inconsistent. Diversity is important, I agree, so why does the government lay down the same national curriculum for all schools?

Why do we have the highly prescriptive 'one-size-fits-all' literacy hour, where the government has spelled out an identical 15–15–20–10-minute pattern for every primary class, young or old, every single day?

Let us be clear what I am saying. I agree with specialist schools, education action zones, much of what the government is doing. I have seen some superb examples. I welcome the emphasis on helping all children and not just a few, and the significant sums of money for books, equipment, school buildings. I like the literacy and numeracy initiatives, but not the detailed prescription.

Nor is there anything wrong with the Prime Minister asking for a review of comprehensive schools, or of being critical when necessary. He seems a decent family man, genuinely interested in education.

I just don't think the Tony Zoffis approach to schools and teachers is right, with its language of 'zero tolerance' (fine for criminals, not for professionals), 'tough' this and 'tough' that.

One Thursday, last October, the new college for head teachers was opened. It was an excellent move, but on the previous Sunday a story was planted in a national newspaper saying that the Prime Minister would be putting the boot into teachers at the opening.

Why does Tony Zoffis spin against teachers in this way? It might win a few votes, but it is cheapskate, no way to enthuse teachers, a bit like saying, 'Join our crusade, you clueless bastards.'

I have agonised while writing this piece – walking round the room, sharpening three more pencils (funny this, I use a word processor) – since I would be mortified if Hague and his loony right-wing pals got back. But teachers deserve better than Tony Zoffis firing verbal bullets at them and it would be dishonest not to say so.

Bang! Put him in a cupboard for a few months. He won't be missed.

INDEX